Implementing Information Security in Healthcare

Building a Security Program

Edited by

Terrell W. Herzig, MSHI, CISSP
Tom Walsh, CISSP
Lisa A. Gallagher, BSEE, CISM, CPHIMS

Routledge
Taylor & Francis Group

LONDON AND NEW YORK

First published 2013 by HIMSS

Published 2018 by Routledge
2 Park Square, Milton Park, Abingdon, Oxon, OX14 4RN
52 Vanderbilt Avenue, New York, NY 10017

Routledge is an imprint of the Taylor & Francis Group, an informa business

ISBN 13: 978-1-938904-34-9 (pbk)

About the Editors

Terrell W. Herzig, MSHI, CISSP, was Information Security Officer of the University of Alabama at Birmingham (UAB) Health System, the UAB HIPAA Security Officer, and an adjunct professor of Health Informatics at the UAB. Mr. Herzig taught graduate courses in Information Engineering, Programming, Computer Networks, and Information Security in the UAB School of Health Professions. During his tenure at UAB, he served as director of Information Technology for the Civitan International Research Center and Director of Informatics for the Pittman General Clinical Research Center. Mr. Herzig also consulted on numerous informatics projects with external groups, including Southern Nuclear and the U.S. Army Medical Command. He is the author of *Information Security in Healthcare: Managing Risk*, which was published by HIMSS in 2010. Mr. Herzig died on July 7, 2012.

Tom Walsh, CISSP, has partnered with Brian Evans, CISSP, CISM, CISA, CGEIT, to assist healthcare organizations throughout the country with building regulatory compliant information security programs. Mr. Walsh is a nationally recognized speaker and a co-author of three other books. Prior to starting his own healthcare consulting business in 2003, Mr. Walsh's experience included being the first information security manager for a large, multi-hospital healthcare system in Kansas City. He has more than 21 years of information security experience.

Lisa A. Gallagher, BSEE, CISM, CPHIMS, serves as HIMSS Vice President, Technology Solutions. In this role, she is responsible for all of the privacy and security programs and provides privacy and security content support for HIMSS' federal and state government relations/advocacy work. Ms. Gallagher currently serves on the ONC Standards Committee's Privacy and Security Work Group and the Patient Matching Power Team. Ms. Gallagher has a Bachelor of Science degree in Electrical Engineering, was a certified trust technology evaluator (NSA), and is a Certified Information Security Manager (CISM) (ISACA). She is also a Certified Professional in Healthcare Information and Management Systems (CPHIMS).

About the Contributors

Michelle Bigelow is Senior Director of Technical Services for the University of Minnesota Physicians and has been in health IT for 21 years. In her role, Ms. Bigelow has been instrumental in bringing IT process management and continual process improvement to healthcare. Ms. Bigelow is practitioner-level certified in ITIL v.3 service level management and has implemented the IT infrastructure library methodology across IT.

Mary Anne S. Canant, MBA, CISA, CISSP, CHFP, is a Senior Information Systems Auditor at the University of Alabama at Birmingham (UAB), for which she provides audit and advisory services for the academic, clinical, and research enterprise. Her focus includes information technology, security, and data risk, control, and governance. Ms. Canant was a contributor to the book *Information Security in Healthcare: Managing Risk*, which was published by HIMSS in 2010. In 2011 and 2012, as a guest speaker for the UAB Health Informatics masters course Security and Privacy in Healthcare, she presented and led discussions on topics of IT, security, and data governance; effective information security programs; and the foundations of information assurance.

Jennifer L. Cole, MSHI, is an Information Services Consultant for the Information Services department of UAB Health System (HSIS). She has more than 17 years of healthcare experience, 13 of which have been in the project management domain. She is a 15-year employee of UAB, having started in HSIS by working on the Y2K Project. Ms. Cole currently manages the American Recovery and Reinvestment Act (ARRA) Meaningful Use project for the Health System while continuing to assist with the Health Insurance Portability and Accountability Act (HIPAA) project, focusing on privacy and security. As one of the HIPAA project leaders, Ms. Cole has been involved in security risk assessments, audits, and incident investigation, resolution, and education. She also oversees the Joint Commission Information Management Chapter for UAB Hospital, where she is responsible for the information management plan and implementation of the standards associated with the chapter. Ms. Cole has served as a liaison between HSIS and the Health Information Management Department for the past few years, specifically assisting with the shift from paper to electronic documentation. Ms. Cole has a Master of Science degree in Health Informatics, as well as an undergraduate degree in Mathematics from Bethel College.

Joseph Dalton specializes in cyber security, business intelligence, database architecture and development. He is currently the Technology Director at Clinical-Security, and Course Director at Full Sail University where he teaches databases and information security. He holds a Masters Degree in Modeling and Simulation from the University of Central Florida, with an emphasis in mathematical modeling.

Darren D. Dannen, CISSP, has extensive work experience in enterprises as an information architect, technical engineer, project manager, security specialist, and consultant. Additionally, he has extensive training through the United States Navy in Information Assurance and has an MS in Network Security from Capitol College and an MBA from University of Mary. He is aggressive in pursuing the strategic use of technology to improve the role of information security.

Mark W. Dill is the Director of Information Security at Cleveland Clinic. Mr. Dill is responsible for the deployment of information security and disaster recovery best practices and compliance with HIPAA, PCI, and Internal Control Effectiveness/SOX regulations and standards. With more than 25 years of IT and technical management experience, Mr. Dill's focus is on implementing strategic and tactical security initiatives.

Brian Evans, CISSP, CISM, CISA, CGEIT, has partnered with Tom Walsh, CISSP, to assist healthcare organizations throughout the country with building regulatory compliant information security programs. With more than 20 years of combined experience in health IT management, consulting and information security, Mr. Evans previously served as the Information Security Officer at The Ohio State University Health System. He also led the Computer Incident Response and Forensic Investigations teams for Nationwide Insurance, and was Vice President, IT Risk Management, at KeyBank and JPMorgan Chase. Mr. Evans held IT management positions at the Ohio Department of Health and started his career as a medic in the US Air Force. He has earned a Master's in Public Administration from the University of Cincinnati and a BS in Business Management from the University of Maryland.

Susan Gatehouse is a tenured expert in health information management with more than 25 years' experience in revenue cycle–related matters to include the management and protection of healthcare data. Ms. Gatehouse is a nationally recognized speaker regarding health information management and the revenue cycle. Ms. Gatehouse has also served as editorial advisor and technical editor for The Coding Institute publications, authored a coding manual for medical device manufacturer Medtronic Sofamor Danek, and acted as a lead consultant in a national Medicare fraud and abuse investigation. Ms. Gatehouse was a contributing consultant in the development of "A Purchasers Guide to Clinical Preventive Services, Moving Science to Coverage" for the Centers for Disease Control and Prevention (CDC), Preventative Health Services Division. Ms. Gatehouse has developed and implemented numerous coder training programs for inpatient, outpatient, and physician services, as well as delivered educational seminars and produced operational assessments for a range of nationwide healthcare facilities. She has facilitated ICD-10 introduction, training, assessments, and APC readiness programs for hospitals ranging from 100 to 900 beds. Most recently, Ms. Gatehouse implemented clinical documentation improvement programs for community and teaching acute-care medical centers. Additionally, she has implemented a hospital and physician coding compliance program for one of the top 10 largest health systems in the nation. As remote coding has become commonplace in the HIM industry, Ms. Gatehouse has assisted facilities in implementing remote coding programs as well as establishing the framework for supporting and sustaining virtual coding management. A member of the Certified Coding Specialist (CCS) Construction Committee and the Coding Roundtable Committee for Georgia, Ms. Gatehouse is Past President and Legislative Chairperson of the Greater Atlanta Health Information Management Association. She is an active member of the American Health Information Management Association, and American Academy of Procedural Coders. She is the recipient of the 2007 Professional Achievement Award, presented by Georgia Health Information Management Association. Ms. Gatehouse is a Certified ICD-10 Coding Trainer.

Buddy Gilbert, CCNA, is the Network Architect for UAB Health System. He is involved in all aspects of design and implementation of the data network and services, connecting close to 30,000 Ethernet ports. His team is also responsible for network security firewalls, VPN connectivity, server load balancing, DNS/DHCP, URL filtering, more than 3.5 million square feet of wireless network, and managing a team of 10 people. Mr. Gilbert has worked for UAB Hospital for more than 24 years and has witnessed first-hand the exponential growth and change the industry experienced in the last quarter century.

Dennis Henderson is a Security Professional with 26 years' industry experience. He is a 12-year Air Force military veteran and possessed a top secret clearance. He was also the Director of Security for Major Midwest Bank for nine years. Mr. Henderson is a Certified Information Security Manager with and is the lead consultant for a Midwestern security consulting practice specializing HIPAA security compliance.

Ander Hoaglund is a digital forensic analyst and incident responder. He received his Masters in Digital Forensics from the University of Central Florida in Orlando, where he works for a corporate security team. When he is not chasing hackers he is advising clients on how to best implement security solutions to prevent future breaches.

Judi Hofman, CAP, CHP, CHSS, is a Privacy and Information Security Officer for a four-hospital health system in central Oregon. Ms. Hofman has been co-chair for American Health Information Management Association's (AHIMA) national Privacy and Security Practice Council, is a contributing author, and presents nationally on HIPAA privacy and security. She is the current Director of Education for Oregon's Health Information Management Association state chapter of AHIMA. Ms. Hofman has her Bachelor of Science, certificate in Health Services Administration, and is working on her Master's degree in Biomedical Informatics. Ms. Hofman is a Certified HIPAA Professional (CHP), Certified HIPAA Security Specialist (CHSS), Certified Administrative Professional (CAP), and Certified in Healthcare Privacy and Security (CHPS).

Michele T. Kruse, MBA, RHIA, CHPS, has more than 30 years of experience in health information management and information systems specializing in EHR system implementation and support in a multiple hospital/large physician clinic setting, policy and procedure development, privacy/security concepts and standards, and regulatory compliance. She is an active member of AHIMA serving as a member of the Privacy and Security Practice Council.

Susan Lucci, RHIT, CHPS, CMT, AHDI-F, served as a privacy officer for nationally based organizations for nearly 10 years before launching her own HIPAA consulting business. She has written numerous articles for the *Journal of AHIMA*, *Advance* and *For the Record*. Ms. Lucci is the 2013 Co-Chair for the Privacy and Security Practice Council for AHIMA. She is a graduate of St. Petersburg College and the University of Cincinnati.

Margaret Marchak, Esq., is a shareholder in the Troy, Mich., office of Hall, Render, Killian, Heath & Lyman. Ms. Marchak primarily represents healthcare providers with technology procurement and agreements; hospital-physician transactions; HIPAA privacy and security issues; governance in nonprofit/tax-exempt organizations; and corporate compliance programs. She has a particular interest in health information technology law, including electronic medical records, software licensing, technology agreements, outsourcing, privacy and security issues, and HIPAA compliance. As part of her practice, Ms. Marchak works on various state of Michigan initiatives to facilitate health information exchange (HIE) in the state by serving as Co-Chair for the Legal Workgroup for the State of Michigan's Health Information Network (MiHIN). She also chaired another legal workgroup to identify state law barriers to, and opportunities for, HIE in Michigan for a HISPC project. Ms. Marchak has developed a RHIO Toolkit of forms for the Michigan Resource Center, which provides resources for regional health information organizations in Michigan. She also served on a HISPC Multi-State Steering Committee on 42 CFR Part 2 to develop approaches to facilitate HIE with respect to highly protected substance abuse/mental health records. Ms. Marchak has lectured nationally and locally on healthcare and information technology issues, including the HITECH Act's opportunities for HIE and its impact on HIPAA at the Annual HIMSS Conference & Exhibition, the HIT Summit, the HIPAA Summit, and other venues. Ms. Marchak is a Fellow of the Health Law Section of the State Bar of Michigan and a member of the American Health Lawyers Association, HIMSS, and the National Association of College and University Attorneys.

Melissa Markey, Esq., is a shareholder with Hall, Render, Killian, Heath & Lyman, one of the nation's top health law firms, and is licensed to practice as an attorney in Texas and Michigan. Her practice focuses on technology and life sciences issues, especially electronic medical records, data privacy and security, mobile medical applications, e-Discovery, health information exchange, innovations in health technology, and software licensing. She leads the Life Sciences team at Hall Render and has a particular interest in legal issues at the developing edge of technology. Ms. Markey is a paramedic, is on the Board of Directors of the American Health Lawyers Association, is a member of HIMSS and the Michigan chapter of HIMSS, and the computer law sections of the American Bar Association as well as the State Bars of Texas and Michigan. She is a nationally recognized author and presenter on electronic medical records, data privacy and security, clinical research and human-subject protection, the clinical-technology interface, research misconduct, and emergency preparedness and response law.

Joseph W. Popinski III, PhD, CISSP, CPP, CISM, CFE, is the acting Information Security Officer for University of Alabama at Birmingham's Office of the Vice President for Information Technology and adjunct assistant Professor at the University of Alabama in Huntsville (2005-2011) where he taught graduate courses in a Master's program in information security. He is responsible for information security at UAB, including security architecture, strategic planning, DR, compliance, cyber security investigations, risk management, security technical monitoring, forensics, and other security related functions. Dr. Popinski has a wealth of information security experience spanning a more than 40-year career, including serving in multiple information security positions at BellSouth Corporation, Internet Security Systems, KPMG, Dynetics, and NASA. He has a BS and MS in Electrical Engineering, an MBA, and a PhD in Information Assurance. He maintains several professional certifications, is a lifetime member of the IEEE, a senior member of the ISSA, is an (ISC)^2 test supervisor, and actively participates in multiple professional societies.

Kim E. Sassaman, CISSP, has more than 20 years of information technology security experience across multiple business verticals. His focus was primarily on the financial services sector having worked for Charles Schwab, Ameriprise Financial, and American Express. Mr. Sassaman has focused on healthcare the past four years. Mr. Sassaman is the Chief Information Security Officer for Presbyterian Healthcare services. Presbyterian is an integrated delivery system that is comprised of eight hospitals, 40 clinics, a physician group, and a health plan. Presbyterian is a pioneer ACO, has innovated home health and telemedicine, and is in the midst of deploying EPIC. Mr. Sassaman has a CISSP, is an ISO 27001 auditor, and graduated from Capella University with a BS in information security. He is a member of the HIMSS Privacy and Security Committee and is active in ISACA.

Shelia T. Searson, CIPP, moved to the position of Privacy Officer for the University of Alabama at Birmingham (UAB) Health System in October 2011. The Privacy Officer oversees all ongoing activities related to the development, implementation, maintenance, and compliance of the UABHS policies and procedures covering the privacy of and access to patient health information in compliance with federal and state laws and the UABHS information privacy practices. Prior to transitioning to Privacy Officer, Ms. Searson served as Program Director in UAB's HIPAA Office where she was a member of a UAB/UABHS HIPAA Team responsible for communicating and initiating activities needed to comply with the HIPAA Privacy Rule and Security Regulations and related to all UAB, as well as the UAB Health System HIPAA covered entities. Ms. Searson holds a baccalaureate degree in Speech Communications from Shorter College in Rome, Ga. Her professional affiliations include the International Association of Privacy Professionals, through which she is a certified information privacy professional, and the American Health Information Management Association.

Linda Wilson, MSHI, RHIA, is the Manager of the Record Center for the University of Alabama at Birmingham (UAB) Health System, an Instructor in the School of Health Sciences at Colorado Technical University, the President of the Birmingham Regional Health Information Management Association, and the Secretary for the Birmingham Chapter of the American Records Management Association. Mrs. Wilson teaches courses in health data management, healthcare organization, electronic health record and ethical/regulatory issues in healthcare. She has also taught in the Health Information Management program at UAB. Mrs. Wilson continues to demonstrate dedication to the HIM world by mentoring students and participating in the Action Community for Excellence program (ACE). She is a Registered Health Information Administrator through the American Health Information Management Association (AHIMA) and utilizes this credential in the offices that she has held on the Board of Directors, House of Delegates to the National Association, Community Education Coordinator, Advocacy, and Workgroup Delegate.

Table of Contents

Acknowledgments

Sincere gratitude is offered to those who made this book possible:

- To the Herzig family for their courage and loving kindness; our hearts are with you.
- To Matt Schlossberg of HIMSS for his patience and perseverance in making this book a reality; for deciding to continue the project in Terrell's absence; and for deciding to keep Terrell's name on the book as an editor and author.
- To Terrell's colleagues at the University of Alabama Birmingham and UAB Health System for their contributions in writing several chapters of the book.
- To Brian Evans for volunteering to write two chapters and co-author a third at the last minute.
- To Lisa Gallagher for her leadership and guidance.
- To Valerie, my wife, for her understanding of my long hours and for all of her help.
- To Jeff Brandt for his work with the mHIMSS Mobile Task Force and his ideas on mobile device security.
- To Jeremy Higgins for the cover artwork and design.

Thank you all for your help and dedication to this project.

Respectfully,
Tom Walsh, CISSP

A Tribute to Terrell W. Herzig

This book is dedicated to Terrell W. Herzig. His life was cut short while doing one of the things he loved best, riding his motorcycle home from work. He was a devoted husband and the loving father of three children and godfather to a fourth. Terrell was always enthusiastic about computer technology, and in information security he'd found the field he enjoyed best. He was excited to be working on this, his second book on the subject. He would have been proud to see the end result.

—Cindi Herzig

Terrell Herzig was a great person and a wonderful friend. It was a privilege knowing him. I believe the best way I can attest to this is by sharing a couple of short stories.

A few months after my son Matthew was killed, I received a call from Terrell. He told me he was dedicating the first HIMSS book he was working on to my son. I remember his call and the way it made me feel. Most authors dedicate a book to their own family or to someone they admire. Terrell never met Matthew, yet he decided that this is what he wanted to do. My family was very appreciative of that gesture and Terrell's legacy became incorporated into his name. At the Walsh household he is known as, "Terrell, the guy that dedicated the book to Matthew."

My second story deals with Terrell's friendship. Regardless of the time that had passed, every time Terrell and I spoke or met, our conversation would take off as if we

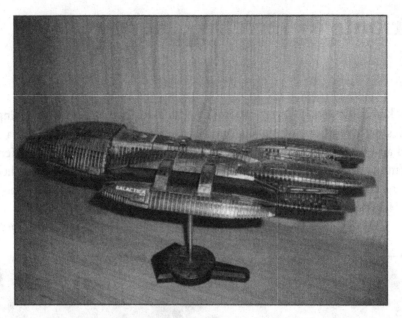

had just spoken the day before. I remember on one of my business trips to Birmingham, Terrell and I used some free time to get caught up on family and on one of our favorite TV series at that time, *Battlestar Galactica.*

About a year later during my next visit to Birmingham, Terrell surprised me with a gift. He had built and hand-painted a model of the *Battlestar Galactica.* It was very impressive. I asked him how long it took and in Terrell's typical, nonchalant Southern style said, "Oh, 12 or 15 hours." I could not believe it! He gave up that much of his time to do something like that for me. I asked him, "Why?" And he replied, "Because I knew you would appreciate it."

I did appreciate the model and proudly displayed it on a bookshelf in my office where it sits today. When family members saw it, they each had the same reaction and essentially the same discussion took place.

"Wow! Where did you get that?"

"My friend Terrell made it for me."

"The guy that dedicated the book to Matthew?"

"Yep, the guy that dedicated the book to Matthew."

Terrell will never be forgotten. "So say we all."

—Tom Walsh, CISSP

Although we knew each only for a few months, Terrell and I developed a great friendship and mutual respect for each other's abilities, skills, and accomplishments. We met every two weeks for coffee at Dunkin Donuts on the UAB campus to discuss how we could work together to improve the information security posture of both the UAB Health System and the UAB campus environments. Terrell "offered" me the opportunity to contribute to this book; little did I know at the time that by accepting this opportunity it would turn into his legacy. Terrell, I owe you a large measure of gratitude and thanks.

—Joseph W. Popinski III, PhD, CISSP, CPP, CISM, CFE

Terrell Herzig will forever be the optimist and a humble, endearing educator. He had a love of learning and a willingness to transfer knowledge that cannot be surpassed. He has placed his mark on an industry while translating complicated subject matter into simple terms. The mark of a true genius.

—*Susan Gatehouse*

Terrell was a man of integrity, devoted to his family, committed to his profession. He maintained a broad spectrum of interests and mastered more subjects and skills than most dare to explore. Terrell was generous. He shared his knowledge, friendship, and laughter. Those of us who knew him well loved him for these reasons and miss him dearly.

—*Mary Anne S. Canant, MBA, CISA, CISSP, CHFP*

Words cannot begin to describe Terrell Herzig, who was no ordinary man. I came to know Terrell as one of my professors while attending graduate school where he taught information security and database classes. He was always able to explain even the most complex computer or information security concept in language anyone could understand. He was impressive with his vast amount of knowledge and understanding; however, I came to really appreciate Terrell when I began working with him at UAB. Terrell became a trusted co-worker and, most importantly, a friend. He is missed greatly, especially his laugh; he will always be remembered.

—*Jennifer L. Cole, MSHI*

Where do I start, which perspective do I take, or even which decade do I reference as I write my tribute to Terrell Herzig? Terrell was my first computer lab designer/technician, my network class instructor, my project advisor for a statistics project in graduate school, my partner on a nuclear power consulting project, my lecturer on information security for whatever professional organization committee I was serving, my co-instructor for the privacy and information security class for 10 years, my constant unknown advisor for information security questions, my Information Security Officer, and one of the best friends a CIO could ever have. From this long list of "my's," it is obvious how long and how closely Terrell and I worked together and, therefore, very difficult to express just how much, in so many ways, I miss him. Terrell was a man of many qualities and varied interests who had a tremendous influence on my life. Most of all, when Terrell was here, no matter the information security crisis and how panicked I might become, I was always confident that Terrell would get us through the crisis, and he always did. I miss him desperately.

—*Joan Hicks, MSHI, RHIA, CIO for UAB Health System*

Terrell Herzig was dedicated to his family, friends, and work. He was brilliant. His knowledge, experience, and wisdom surpassed his 48 years—whether the topic of discussion was computers, car repair, photography, or general trivia—just name the topic! He laughed easily and often—taking his work seriously, but never himself. Terrell was my colleague at UAB for more than 20 years. But, most importantly, he was my friend. He is sorely missed and definitely remembered.

—*Shelia T. Searson, CIPP*

Terrell Herzig was an instructor, mentor, and friend to me. He paved the path for resolution to security issues and taught health informatics students more than just a thing or two about privacy and security. He was an encourager to each learner and a proud father, too. He always was willing to listen but was also ready to talk about his family. He loved his family, continuously sharing stories about his wife Cindi, and his children Jenna, Christopher, and Cassie. He was just as attentive about his teaching career, job, and hobbies. He treasured working diligently on his airplane models. He remained passionate about each interest. Terrell was a good friend and a great mentor to many.

—*Linda Wilson, MSHI, RHIA*

CHAPTER 1

The Importance of Information Security in Healthcare

By Terrell W. Herzig, MSHI, CISSP

Today, computers and the Internet are pervasive. We work with computers as a matter of our employment; we attend classes online; we use them for research, entertainment, shopping, banking, and social interactions. We carry laptops, tablets, and smartphones everywhere we travel. There is hardly anything we do today that does not involve interaction with a computing device.

While this technology enables us to be more productive—accessing a mass of information with a mere click of the mouse—it brings with it a host of security concerns. If the information on these systems is accessed inappropriately, lost, stolen, or is rendered inaccessible, the consequences could be disastrous. We may discover that our bank accounts have been depleted or our identities have been stolen. Our employers could lose millions of dollars, face prosecution, incur regulatory fines, and lose customer loyalty.

Technology continues to change at a rapid rate, with consumer devices leading the way on an almost-daily basis. Security typically takes a back seat during such drives of innovation and our ability to secure ourselves progresses slowly. This has resulted in a rapid rise in the number of reported incidents and breaches.

Information security is a concept that has never been more important to healthcare than it is today. The advent of more powerful computer technology and increased mobility means we can leverage this rise in technology to treat patients faster, more consistently, and with better outcomes, all while reducing cost. As healthcare moves from traditional brick-and-mortar infrastructures to health information exchanges, home healthcare, and accountable care organizations, mobility and access to information assets will be key to delivering patient care. Securing confidential information will not only be of importance to our patient populations, but to the success of your healthcare organization.

Information security is about protecting our assets. What kinds of assets need protecting? The answer is: a very broad range. While this would obviously include physical items with inherent value and value to the business, it will also include things such as intellectual property and intangible assets such as data, software, and source code. In today's information-rich environment, we find many of our logical assets at least as valuable as our physical assets. Finally, no discussion of assets would be complete without mentioning our most important organizational asset—people. We can't conduct business or treat patients without them.

While we can certainly secure systems, information security must always balance security with the value of the asset and usability of a system. For example, surrounding a hospital with rows of razor wire, attack dogs, and armed guards might contribute to the security of the hospital, but it certainly would not be inviting to patients seeking treatment.

So when do we achieve that ideal balance of security and risk management to cost and usability? First and foremost, security should never overvalue the cost of the assets we are trying to protect. This means we must consider the intangible value of assets, the cost of replacing the asset if it is lost, and establish reasonable levels of protection for the value of the asset.

In healthcare finding this balance point can be particularly challenging. We could look at the threats to our assets and ask ourselves questions. For example:

- Can others scan our systems from the Internet?
- Do we authenticate with passwords?
- Do we keep our systems up-to-date?
- Do we understand how our systems can be exploited?
- Do we monitor our systems for attacks?
- Do we provide a safe work environment for our employees?
- Do we provide a safe environment in which to treat our patients?

If we attempt to answer these questions in turn, we will no doubt discover a gap between our *current* state of security and our *desired* state of security. Once we are able to identify areas that can cause us to be unsecure, we can take the necessary steps to mitigate this risk. In fact, such a process is one of the key components of establishing a security program. Many of you will note the above process hints at a critical component in information security—the risk assessment.

In reality, there is no such thing as a completely secure system. This doesn't mean we can't take steps to reduce risk and move toward a secure environment. In fact, some bodies of law and regulation do make an attempt to define what is considered "secure" for particular industries. Certainly, healthcare is one such environment with many regulatory requirements in the area of information security.

HIPAA, the HITECH Act, and the Payment Card Industry Data Security Standard (PCI DSS) are but a few of the regulatory requirements that impact healthcare. Not only do each of these acts define security requirements, they also include requirements to address the failure of certain controls and the requirements for notification of patients in the event of such failures.

With the passage of the HITECH Act and mandatory breach reporting, the healthcare industry became the first industry required to report a security breach at the federal level. Since the establishment of breach notification, healthcare organizations have reported the loss of protected healthcare information on more than 21 million individuals.[1] The breaches have occurred all across the healthcare continuum, from small private practices to large multisite facilities. If you visit the Department of Health & Human Services (HHS) website for breach reporting, you can download the report data. At the time of this writing, a quick review of the data reveals the following information:

TABLE 1-1: Summary of Breach Data by Device Type—September 2009 to December 31, 2012.

Device Type	Number of Incidents	% of Total Incidents	Number of Patients	% of Patients
Laptop	123	23.4%	2,240,259	10%
Portable Devices	73	13.9%	1,540,070	7%
Desktop Computer	74	14.1%	2,323,094	11%
Hard Drives	1	0.2%	1,023,209	5%
Paper Records	124	23.6%	718,622	3%
Network Servers	59	11.2%	2,480,378	12%
E-mail	11	2.1%	242,684	1%
Electronic Medical Record	8	1.5%	1,826,057	9%
Backup Tapes/CDs	7	1.3%	6,291,655	29%
Mailings/Postcards	1	0.2%	3,400	0%
Other	44	8.4%	2,722,077	13%

Source: HHS Breach Statistics website.

Table 1-1 indicates the current classification of data breaches and the number of impacted patients. The incident types have been normalized to produce a much simpler chart as the incident type is inconsistently worded in the raw data.

In Table 1-2 and Figure 1-1, you can see the two key types of incidents are "Loss" and "Theft." These two categories alone account for the majority of the data breaches to date.

The data from HHS also contains information regarding the media involved in each breach case, allowing us to further detail the incident type into their respective media components.

Careful review of such metrics when conducting a routine assessment of risk can quickly reveal the low-hanging fruit for risk reduction and mitigation.

This is but one example of why it is important to establish a sound security program. Many security frameworks exist that would provide and guide sound security strategy. Healthcare organizations must adopt such frameworks and use layered control sets to properly protect information assets.

TABLE 1-2: Reasons for a Breach—Reported to HHS.

Reasons for Breach	Number of Incidents	% of Total Incidents	Number of Patients	% of Patients
Theft	292	56%	8,471,840	40%
Loss	61	12%	7,288,272	34%
Unauthorized Access	92	18%	1,093,196	5%
Improper Disposal	27	5%	160,513	1%
Hacking	40	7%	1,809,851	8%
Other/Unknown	13	2%	2,587,833	12%

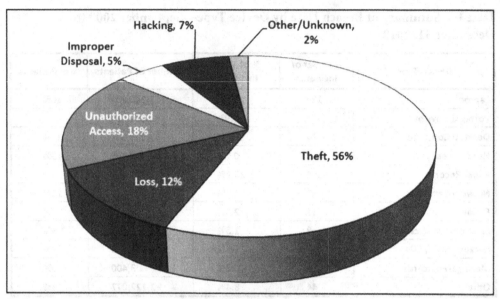

FIGURE 1-1: Reasons for Breach—December 31, 2012.

THE IMPORTANCE OF CONFIDENTIALITY, INTEGRITY, AND AVAILABILITY

Three common concepts of information security are confidentiality, integrity, and availability. If you have read books or articles on information security, you will often see these referred to as the confidentiality, integrity, and availability (CIA) triad. The triad gives us a model to frame and discuss security concepts, as depicted in Figure 1-2.

Confidentiality

When most people consider security they tend to think more about confidentiality than the other two components—probably because confidentiality is a concept similar to, but not the same as, privacy. Confidentiality is a necessary component of privacy and relates to our ability to protect data from individuals without permission to view it. Confidentiality can be compromised through a variety of different methods. Such methods include (but are not limited to):

- The loss of a device containing confidential information.
- Lost or stolen backup tapes.
- E-mail sent to the wrong individual.
- A fax sent to the wrong individual.
- Sharing or compromise of a password.
- A malware infection harvesting passwords or confidential information.
- A hacker penetrating a system that contains confidential information.
- Confidential information left exposed in a public area.

Note how the above list aligns with recorded breaches from the HHS website. I particularly want to point this out as we look at examples of where the failure of controls in security lead to a breach of privacy.

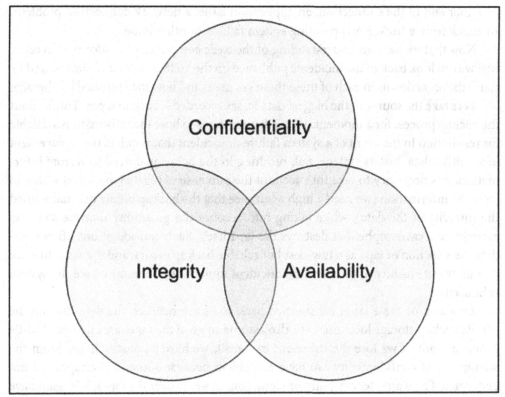

FIGURE 1-2: The CIA Triad.

Integrity

Integrity refers to the ability to prevent data from being modified or changed in an unauthorized or undesirable manner. This could be an unauthorized change or deletion of our data or it could be authorized, but undesirable—such as the malfunction of legitimate software that results in an unintended change or overwrite. Maintaining integrity requires controls that not only prevent unauthorized changes to our data but also provide the ability to reverse authorized changes that need to be recovered.

A good example of a modern control to enforce integrity includes transaction tracking systems found in most high-end relational database systems. Such systems contain the ability to "back-out" incomplete transactions or roll-back data updates in the event of an error. Such systems also contain extensive logging to aid in identifying issues related to the management of data and the users entrusted with the operation of the system.

Integrity is critical in our discussions where data provides the foundation for decisions; after all, isn't that the reason for collecting data to begin with? In healthcare, failure of data integrity can lead to loss of life, poor outcomes, and substantial financial impacts.

Availability

Availability refers to the ability to access data when it is needed. Access to data could become unavailable any time there is a break in the complex chain of systems interconnected to provide access. This could result from something as simple as a power failure on either end of the connection, an application issue, a network connection problem, an attack from a hacker, an operating system failure, or other issue.

Now that we have an understanding of the basic components of information security, we can look back to the incidents published on the HHS website and start to understand the breakdowns in each of these three key areas and how they resulted in a breach.

Let's take the source of the biggest data losses recorded—backup tapes. Think about the backup process for a moment. We back up systems to have the information available for restoration in the event of a system failure or incident that requires the replacement of sensitive data. Just as systems fail, resulting in the occasional need to restore information, it is necessary to take into account the purchase of reliable media on which to copy the information (we need a high assurance that the backup media has maintained the integrity of the data), while taking into account the possibility that the site may experience a catastrophe that destroys the tape itself. Such considerations often mandate the selection of tape as a low-cost but reliable backup media, and the need to store it at an off site facility in the event the incident impacts the location where the system is housed.

Let's assume these tapes are shuttled back and forth between the data site and the off site backup storage location. Let's also assume some of the tapes are encrypted while others are not. If we lose the shipment in transit, we have a security issue. From the standpoint of confidentiality, we have a problem because some of the tapes are not encrypted. From an integrity point of view, assume we recover the tapes. We again have an issue due to the lack of encryption on some of the tapes. The unencrypted files may have been altered and written back to the tape. In this event, we would not be aware the data have been altered. Finally, if the tapes are not recovered, we have an availability issue if we encounter the need to restore the data. To adequately maintain security we must enforce these three principles. Something worth noting in this particular scenario—the individual that obtained the unauthorized access to the backup tapes would need the proper equipment and software to alter the data and then restore it, which is unlikely. However, we cannot assume that is true unless we have conducted an investigation and a risk analysis to make that determination. This was an example for the purpose of illustrating the interrelationship of confidentiality, integrity, and availability.

REFERENCE

1.   U.S. Department of Health & Human Services. [website] Breaches Affecting 500 or More Individuals. Available at: www.hhs.gov/ocr/privacy/hipaa/administrative/breachnotificationrule/breachtool.html.

CHAPTER 2

Information Security Frameworks

By Joseph W. Popinski III, PhD, CISSP, CPP, CISM, CFE

Successful implementation of information security in a healthcare environment, or for that matter, in any corporate environment, requires an organized and referenced process. Many international and domestic standards organizations offer information security framework (ISF) to assist an organization's information security officer (ISO) in establishing a process to provide protection of confidential information on a repeatable and sustainable basis. This chapter will focus on and discuss several topics related to ISFs. Specifically, we will define an ISF, offer several industry best practices structures defining such frameworks, discuss the business case for an ISF, review the implementation approaches available from several standards-based frameworks, provide guidelines on how to select a framework, look at compliance issues related to and supported by a framework, and provide a "next steps" primer.

WHAT IS AN INFORMATION SECURITY FRAMEWORK?

Many definitions of an ISF exist. In the context of this chapter and the healthcare environment, an ISF is a business process involving all entity organizations, operational sections, and relevant participants to information security—all related to an ongoing process which, when fully developed, will position the organization to address the right security issues so that the business fulfills its mission.[1] Considering that today's information security threats are changing so fast and the threat surface is becoming increasingly more complex, providing the right security at the right time is a major challenge.

Frameworks are defined as basic conceptual and organizational structures that allow identification and categorization of process steps that make up complex tasks producing an acceptable and specific result. Applying this to information security gives us an orderly process to define, develop, implement, and operate an environment in a safe and secure manner with ordered security management controls. Combining these two ideas into a modern-day healthcare or corporate structure will offer a baseline of processes, controls, and guidelines from which an effective information security program can be executed.

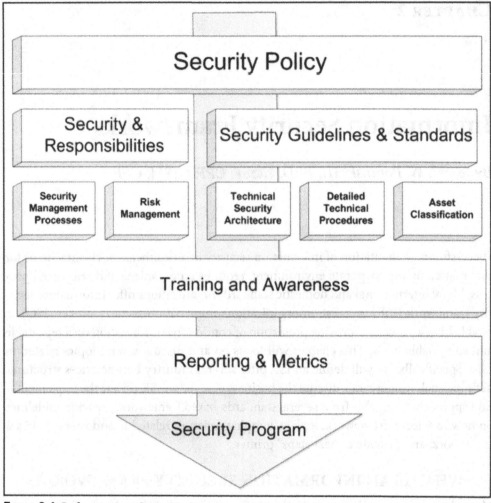

FIGURE 2-1: Information Security Framework Example.

As an example of an information security framework, Figure 2-1 shows the basic constituent elements. The two defining elements of the Information Security Policy are (1) Security & Responsibilities; and (2) Security Guidelines & Standards. Each has several sub-tending processes: security management, risk management, technical security architecture, detailed procedures, and asset classification. Together with the Training and Awareness and Reporting and Metrics tiers which, when taken as a whole, define an overarching Security Program.

All information security programs or processes have the same purpose in a business environment: namely, to reduce risks to acceptable levels. Each of these elements is extensive and requires effective tactical strategies for implementation. Volumes have been written on each item.

THE NIST FRAMEWORK

The National Institute of Standards and Technology (NIST) offers a Risk Management Framework as the structure to implement an information security program.[2]

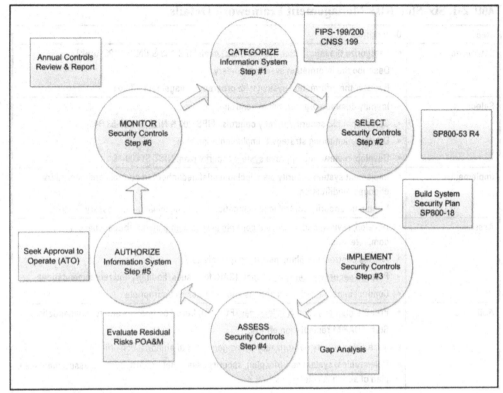

FIGURE 2-2: NIST Risk Management Framework.

This Risk Management Framework is designed to complement information security management from several perspectives. First, it integrates the underlying principles of a multitiered risk-reduction process to include both the Systems Development Lifecycle (SDLC) concepts and information security into one coherent process; and second, it provides a six-step management process to control and manage an entire program, ensuring that both frameworks support the organization's objectives with orderly controls, assessments, reviews, gap analyses, corrective action programs, and management authorizations. This six-step process is depicted in Figure 2-2, NIST Risk Management Framework. Each of the steps demonstrates how an organization can easily classify a system, select security controls, evaluate their effectiveness, perform a "gap analysis" resulting in a program to address the gaps, seek management approval for the system, and finally, review the process on an annual basis. This cyclical process integrates risk management and information security management into one coherent lifecycle approach.

One of the most challenging, if not *the* most challenging, activities that is a prerequisite to the NIST Risk Management Framework implementation is the definition of system boundaries for the process, system, organization, applications, etc., under consideration for framework control. Deciding where the boundaries lie is a paramount first step which, if properly done, sets the stage for an effective risk/information security management process implementation.

To provide more depth to understanding this six-step process, Table 2-1 gives additional details on the effort required. Organizations wishing to follow federal guidelines

TABLE 2-1: Six-Step Risk Management Framework Details.

Step	Description
Categorize	• Categorize the information system (Risk Level) FIPS-199 & CNSS 1199 (draft). • Describe the information system boundary. • Register the information system with program/management offices.
Select	• Identify common organizational controls. • Select specific security/privacy controls; FIPS-200 & NIST SP800-53 R4. • Develop monitoring strategy & implementation plan. • Develop, review, and approve system security plan; NIST-SP800-18.
Implement	• Implement system security plan, including defined/inherited controls and necessary changes/modifications. • Document security control implementation, including minimum necessary controls.
Assess	• Develop, review, and approve a controls assessment plan for effectiveness & completeness. • Assess controls per plan; perform gap analysis. • Prepare security assessment report (SAR) for issues, findings, and recommendations. • Conduct initial remediation actions and reassess as appropriate.
Authorize	• Prepare plan of action & milestones (POA&M) based on findings and recommendations. • Start POA&M remediation efforts. • Assemble security authorization package/submit to authorization official. • Deliverables: system security plan, security assessment report, controls assessment plan, plan of action & milestones.
Monitor	• Determine change impact to system (change control & authorization). • Assess technical, managerial and/or operational controls. • Conduct remediation actions: ongoing activities, risk changes risk, outstanding POA&M items. • Update SSP, SAR, and POA&M. • Conduct annual controls review per 800-53.

must (i.e., are required to) perform this cyclical process if federal funding is involved. A significant portion of healthcare research is federally funded and involves PHI/PII (protected health information/personally identifiable information) data, and therefore must follow this process. The E-Government Act of 2002, Public Law 107-247, establishes these requirements; Title III of the act identifies the required information security controls. Title III is commonly called the Federal Information Security Management Act of 2002 (FISMA).

Four formal deliverables (i.e., organizational or institutional authorized and approved documents) are the minimum required to fulfill the NIST Risk Management Framework process. Each requires a level of effort commensurate with the organization's risk appetite; the significance placed on compliance; the governance, risk, and compliance (GRC) oversight process; and management's general concern relative to due diligence. Each of these deliverables is defined by the NIST Special Publication shown in Table 2-2. Special attention is advised when using the NIST guidelines as a template, as the Risk Management Framework is complex and is not a "fill in the blanks" exercise. Realizing that in most organizations, tens of millions of dollars are involved and at risk, managing the risk process as part of an overall GRC effort is

TABLE 2-2: Risk Framework Deliverables.

Deliverable Title	Description
System Risk Categorization	• Performed per guidelines contained in "Standards for Security Categorization of Federal Information and Information Systems"; FIPS-199, Feb 2004.
System Security Plan	• Prepared in accordance with "Guide for Developing Security Plans for Federal Information Systems"; NIST-SP800-18 rev 1, July 2008.
Controls Assessment	• Prepared from information based on "DRAFT Security and Privacy Controls for Federal Information Systems and Organizations (Initial Public Draft)"; NIST SP-800-53 R4, Feb 2012.
Security Assessment Report	• Prepared from information based on "DRAFT Security and Privacy Controls for Federal Information Systems and Organizations (Initial Public Draft)"; NIST SP-800-53 R4, Feb 2012.
Plan of Action & Milestones	• Sample template available from csrc.nist.gov/groups/SMA/fasp/documents/c&a/POAM_template_01052007.xls.

not trivial. Adequate resources, both people and dollars, must be allocated to planning, designing, implementing, and operating a healthcare organization or corporate business in conformance with an acceptable GRC program. Compliance with myriad local, state, and federal regulations and law is not optional. In smaller healthcare organizations, functions related to compliance, information security, risk management and other related functions typically are handled by a small staff and sometimes by one individual. Compliance with the countless laws and regulations is challenging, and achieving reasonable degrees of conformance is possible by enlisting peer assistance, small group help, task forces, and other collaborative techniques to leverage limited resources. Demonstrating progress toward meeting NIST guidelines, HIPAA regulations, etc., is a key consideration.

BEST PRACTICES CONCEPTS AND DIFFERING VIEWPOINTS

Business and healthcare have evolved over time, refining implementation philosophies, techniques, and methodologies in the information security discipline to remain current with advances in computer systems and capabilities, clinical and research currency, patient privacy concerns, and necessary business functions. This evolution of business procedures is referred to as "best practices." Although the term best practices is not defined by *Webster's Dictionary*[7] per se, each term, when combined provides an understanding of the concepts involved:

Best (adjective)	Superlative of good: exceeding all others.
Practices (noun)	Actual performance or application; ready to carry out in *practice* what they advocated in principle.

The term is further defined in Wikipedia[8] as "...a method or technique that has consistently shown results superior to those achieved with other means, and that is used as a benchmark." Applying this construct to information security framework concepts can result in a risk reduction approach that excels in principle and performance.

An accepted practice by healthcare executives is the peer comparison process; i.e., reviewing current organizational performance to that of other organizations of similar parameters in terms of size, finances, number of beds, employees, geography, etc. This often leads to a chasing-the-numbers type of implementation of information security rather than a risk-based process. This is prevalent in a geographically diverse organization of multiple business units; vis-à-vis, a healthcare holding company with many operating units (hospitals, clinic, etc.). Comparing information security parameters on an aggregated basis may give a less accurate sense of information security for each component organization. Best practices tend to indicate that performance needs to be driven by specific local needs and requirements, not on an aggregated basis.

Considering local needs and requirements may be the optimal way to determine the "best" information security controls and processes to implement. This can be an extension of commonly used business continuity[9] (BC) principles which have proven themselves over many years and are taught in most business school Master of Business Administration (MBA) and Management Information Systems (MIS) programs. The first step in BC planning is to perform a risk assessment of the environment to methodically determine the risks facing the business, in this case the healthcare community, in achieving its vision and goals. Hundreds of books have been authored on risk assessment, and all are focused toward achieving the same goals. Once the risks have been identified and agreed to by senior management, the process of implementing controls to mitigate these risks can be initiated; this is the beginning of an information security framework.

Some individuals believe that applying technical controls to a healthcare environment per HIPAA regulations will be sufficient. This often is a temporary fix to the problem of improving security; however, delving in to the HIPAA regulations in depth reveals the need to address issues from a business perspective, including risk assessments and analyses. Attention should also be given to other areas outside of the ePHI arena such as credit card processing (Payment Card Industry Data Security Standard [PCI DSS]),[10] personally identifiable information (PII), unlicensed software on desktops/servers (aka, pirated software), and other areas of the information security continuum.

IMPORTANCE OF AN INFORMATION SECURITY FRAMEWORK

Many organizations attempt to implement information security using an "address the current issue" approach. This often results in a less than optimal, unsustainable solution to the broader information security problem of protecting sensitive data from unauthorized access and use. Considering the CIA triad (confidentiality, integrity, and availability) as basic tenants of a minimal information security program, addressing the issue du jour will not prove viable in the long term. A more sustainable and accepted approach is to adopt a strategy of implementing a vetted, best practices approach to an enterprise-wide process, which will address multifaceted information security issues. Use of well-known and industry-accepted guidance has proved to be most reliable and beneficial.

Mattord and Whitman's book[11] posits the McCumber Cube[12] (see Figure 2-3) as a model to implement information security based upon sound principles and research by the United States government. In following this model, an organization should implement an enterprise process covering all of the facets of the McCumber Cube: confidentiality, integrity and availability control characteristics; transmission, storage, and

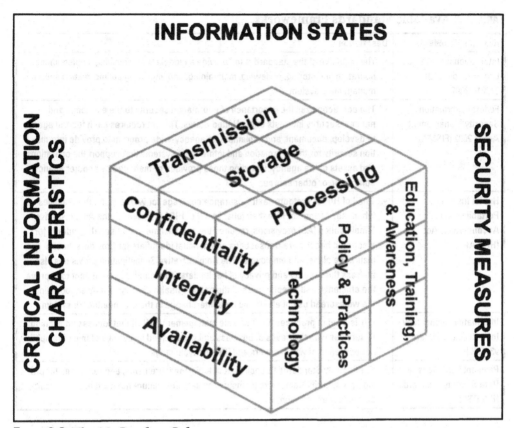

FIGURE 2-3: The McCumber Cube.

processing for data; and education, training, and awareness, policy and practices, and technology for metrics. Implementation following these 27 nodes or intersections is not trivial by any means and requires well thought-out, enterprise-wide workflows, full executive support, and strong centralized controls.

Implementation of any process in any organization must be based upon sound business principles, as the majority of healthcare entities are operated as going concerns (i.e., as for-profit or not-for-profit structures). As such, fiduciary responsibilities dictate that financial decisions must be based on detailed analysis and industry-accepted practices. Adopting and implementing an information security framework requires adequate resources, both monetary and people. Using a sound business case to present the business objectives to be achieved, the resources needed, the expected benefits and the implementation time frame allows healthcare executives to make appropriate business decisions. Once made, the selection of which set of standards to follow as guidelines becomes part of the implementation process.

Several guidelines or standards are available to implement an information security framework. Table 2-3 shows several of the most common standards in use today with their basic descriptions. Choosing one to follow is an executive decision based upon the healthcare entity's management philosophy with respect to risk tolerance, degree of process controls, centralized control structure, compliance conformance posture, centralization of IT functions, and other business principles. It should not be taken lightly;

TABLE 2-3: Available Standards Frameworks.

Available Standards	Description
International Standards Organization (ISO) 27001/27002	• The objective of the standard is to "provide a model for establishing, implementing, operating, monitoring, reviewing, maintaining, and improving an information security management system.
Federal Information Security Management Act of 2002 (FISMA)	• The act recognizes the importance of information security to the economic and national security interests of the United States. The act requires each federal agency to develop, document, and implement an agency-wide program to provide information security for the information and information systems that support the operations and assets of the agency, including those provided or managed by another agency, contractor, or other source.
Health Insurance Portability and Accountability Act (HIPAA)	• Title I of HIPAA protects health insurance coverage for workers and their families when they change or lose their jobs. Title II of HIPAA, known as the Administrative Simplification (AS) provisions, requires the establishment of national standards for electronic health care transactions and national identifiers for providers, health insurance plans, and employers. The Administrative Simplification provisions also address the security and privacy of health data. The standards are meant to improve the efficiency and effectiveness of the nation's health care system by encouraging the widespread use of electronic data interchange in the U.S. healthcare system.
Information Technology Infrastructure Library v3 (ITIL)	• ITIL is a set of practices for IT service management (ITSM) that focuses on aligning IT services with the needs of business and is published in a series of five core publications, each of which covers an ITSM lifecycle stage.
Payment Card Industry Data Security Standards (PCI DSS)	• PCI Security Standards Council's set of tools, measurements, and resources for providing a security framework to ensure the safe and secure handling of credit/debit cardholder information.

once a philosophy is chosen, changing between them is somewhat difficult and costly and conformance to selected elements in the other realms will be necessary. For example, regardless of the selected philosophy, FISMA controls will be necessary if federal grant/contract dollars are awarded to the healthcare entity.

There are several other frameworks available throughout the industry both domestic and international. Those identified here are some of the most common being implemented today.

COMPLIANCE CONSIDERATIONS

Many regulations and laws require compliance by healthcare organizations relative to the various terms and conditions. As such, compliance is a major factor in a well-designed information security framework. Of course the HIPAA regulations have been in effect for many years and compliance requirements with its many provisions is well known. The 2009 Health Information Technology for Economic and Clinical Health (HITECH) Act's incentive to implement an electronic health record process coupled with the American Recovery and Reinvestment Act (ARRA) provisions increase the emphasis on compliance and its companion, reporting. However, aside from the "daily operations" aspects of healthcare institutions, the associated research community compliance process is growing significantly each year.

A significant portion of this healthcare-related research is funded by U.S. government agencies, such as National Institutes of Health (NIH), Federal Drug Administration (FDA), and others. Title III of the E-Government Act of 2002 requires all federally funded agencies to conform to its provisions and report to the Office of Management and Budget (OMB), which in turn reports to Congress, on conformance to the Act's provisions. Title III is commonly called the Federal Information Security Management Act or FISMA. FISMA's controls are derived from the NIST standards/guidelines and are specifically referenced in the Act (SP 800-53, SP 800-37, and others).

Since NIST Special Publications have become the *de facto* standards of the majority of the compliance requirements (reference Special Publication 800-53 R4, Draft Security and Privacy Controls for Federal Information Systems and Organizations) where the required controls and specific reporting elements are clearly delineated, reporting compliance has quickly become a major effort. With the recent emphasis on continuous improvement from OMB, NIST, and other U.S. government agencies, implementing an effective compliance program across an entire entity is a major business process. Recently, many if not all research grants and contracts from the U.S. government contain FISMA compliance language. In many cases, this language is almost an exact duplicate of the wording in the FISMA law itself.

Compliance has increasingly become a necessity in today's healthcare industry. In fact, the healthcare industry is not alone in the arena, as any U.S. government-funded endeavor from Department of Defense contracts to Department of Education contracts to NIH-funded efforts and others all have a FISMA language clause. Figure 2-2, presented earlier, shows the NIST-based Risk Management Framework (a nontrivial implementation effort) which, when coupled with the entire funding process from OMB, requires each healthcare entity to fully address their compliance conformance and reporting. Volumes have been written on this topic in the past decade, and hundreds (if not thousands) of consultants can provide advice on compliance, reporting, implementation, etc. Introducing the concept of continuous monitoring adds another dimension to the rubrics cube approach to meeting the laws and regulations in the United States.

FINAL THOUGHTS

Based on research and the many standards organizations' recommendations, it is clear that following a structured, well-documented, executive-level supported information security framework is appropriate in today's IT environment. Both international and domestic standards bodies have fully documented the necessary guidelines to implement an ISF. NIST is the predominate organization whose guidelines are mandatory for federally funded programs, research, clinical studies and others, whereas ISO's and ITIL's guidelines are generally accepted on an international basis. Although the PCI DSS compliance program is not formally sponsored by a nation-state (e.g., a country or governmental body) it has become a *de facto* international standard as most healthcare organizations accept/process credit and debit cards as payment for healthcare services. PCI DSS conformance is driven by financial considerations.

Compliance is here to stay. Congress enacted several public laws and several government agencies promulgated regulations (carrying the weight of law) requiring all organizations that benefit from federal dollars to report their degrees of compliance to the appropriate agency. Many organizations have not fully complied with these laws and regulations for several years; however, there is a growing realization that compliance is a necessary and mandatory process to continue to receive federal dollars. For example, the HIPAA regulations that were effective in early 2000 have nearly become the norm by the public. Conformance to this particular regulation is part of the health-care fabric. Other compliance laws/regulations are slowly moving in that direction, vis-à-vis the FISMA initiatives. Therefore, it is imperative that compliance be considered a core program across our industry.

In the past few years, the philosophy of NIST guideline compliance has changed. Earlier, the entire compliance process was based on demonstrating conformance to the NIST Special Publication guidelines on a three-year cycle, or a point-in-time demonstration approach with all its subtending paperwork. Today, the compliance approach is toward a "Continuous Monitoring" process to ensure that on a day-to-day basis, organizations are maintaining and making progress toward 100 percent compliance. This is a somewhat radical departure from the past decade of point-in-time compliance demonstration. However, this approach will benefit our society as a whole, as it is designed to raise compliance on a more global basis.

Implementing a well thought out ISF based on NIST guidelines requires careful planning, implementation, and above all, appropriate executive-level support. Conformance to NIST requires an almost complete business process reengineering approach which, by its nature, will change how information security is implemented in the healthcare discipline. Many C-level forums, research organizations, etc., continually advise moving toward an IT environment that is agile, responsive and cost effective in meeting the organization's goals. Implementing a vetted information security framework, including effective compliance controls, is a major step in this direction.

REFERENCES

1. INNOVA. Information security management framework implementation. Available at: www.innova-sa.eu/security/information-security-management-isms.html. Accessed May 6, 2012.

2. National Institute of Standards and Technology. *Guide for Applying the Risk Management Framework to Federal Information Systems.* SP 800-37 Revision 1. Accessed May 2010.

3. National Institute of Standards and Technology. *Standards for Security Categorization of Federal Information and Information Systems.* FIPS-199. Accessed February 2004.

4. National Institute of Standards and Technology. *Guide for Developing Security Plans for Federal Information Systems.* SP800-18 Revision 1. Accessed July 2008.

5. National Institute of Standards and Technology. *DRAFT Security and Privacy Controls for Federal Information Systems and Organizations* (Initial Public Draft). SP 800-53 Revision 4. Accessed February 2012.

6. Plan of Action & Milestones template. Available at: www.csrc.nist.gov/groups/SMA/fasp/documents/c&a/POAM_template_01052007.xls. Accessed May 24, 2012.

7. Merriam-Webster Dictionary. Available at: www.merriam-webster.com. Accessed June 27, 2012.

8. Wikipedia. Definition of "best practices." Available at: http://en.wikipedia.org/wiki. Accessed May 26, 2012.

9. Whitman & Mattord. Principles of Incident Response and Disaster Recovery, Course Technology. 2006.

10. PCI SSC. Data Security Standards Overview. Available at: https://pcisecuritystandards.org/security_standards. Accessed October 30, 2012.

11. Whitman & Mattord. Principles of Information Security, 4th Ed., Course Technology. 2012.

12. Assessing and Managing Security Risk in IT Systems: A Technology-independent Approach. Available at: https://buildsecurityin.us-cert.gov/swa/downloads/McCumber.pdf. Accessed June 21. 2012.

CHAPTER 3

Information Security Planning

By Kim E. Sassaman, CISSP

This chapter's approach assumes that you are setting up your program for the first time. If you already have a program in place however, you will find good nuggets to reinforce your efforts.

Various frameworks that can be chosen to build your security program were covered in the previous chapter. In this chapter, we will discuss how to go about creating the security program, the operating plan and, ultimately, the security strategy based on the ISO 27001 framework. You might already be aware that there is a whole family of standards in the 27000 series. The 27001 standard, the management framework standard, is a close cousin to ISO 9001 quality management. The general principal of ISO 27001 is to take an approach of Plan, Do, Check, Act to risk management. ISO 27002 is a control workbook, which includes the minimal controls that an organization should consider when developing their security program; although the controls are not comprehensive, they are a general guideline. Should you decide to move toward ISO 27001 certification, you will have to go through each control objective in ISO 27002 and attest to why or why not a control is implemented, as well as meet the general requirements of ISO 27001. Frameworks can drive the planning process by defining the objectives of the plan, providing a process-based approach and removing the clouds of doubt and confusion that can easily creep in when addressing the security plan, by providing guiding principles and a standardized approach. While programs can be built without utilizing such frameworks, the frameworks provide for clarity by presenting agreed upon definitions and approaches.

It is of foremost importance that your strategic planning take a proactive approach. If you're consistently adjusting your security program's priorities, roadmaps, and deployment schedules, then more than likely you are in reactive mode. For example, had you suffered a breach due to an unencrypted laptop or mobile device, your new number one priority will become addressing those vulnerabilities. While such events can drive prioritization, they should not be the only source of truth for succinctly addressing risk in the environment. Being proactive in your planning will ensure that you look upward at organizational strategies—marketing that leverages social media, the IT organization's policies for employees bringing their own devices to work, the most recent risk analysis—and construct a holistic plan that aligns to those strategies and manages the risks accordingly.

Your strategy should at a minimum be reviewed on an annual basis or whenever the threat environment has changed. Is your organization visible or involved in research or potentially controversial activities that would draw the attention of hackers? Or are you wealthy and a possible target of financially motivated individuals? These various outsider motives can quickly change your risk environment should their related threats exploit your vulnerabilities.

LEVERAGING A FRAMEWORK TO DEVELOP THE PROGRAM

The proactive approach begins by choosing a framework. For our purposes here, we will leverage ISO 27001 as our framework. Perhaps you are wondering why we are using this standard. ISO 27001 is a management system standard, similar to ISO 9001—a quality management standard. ISO 27001 is the quality management standard for information security that was created by a group that included 120+ countries. The standard sets forth the requirements of what a management system shall contain, what an organization has to consider when developing an Information Security Management System (ISMS), and the requirements to maintain it. The ISMS approach is also consistent with the Information Technology Infrastructure Library (ITIL) v3, the National Institute of Standards and Technology (NIST) Special Publications 800-100 *Information Security Handbook: A Guide for Managers* and maps easily to HIPAA/HITECH, and PCI DSS to ensure that you have defensibility when confronted by the Office for Civil Rights (OCR), Office of the Inspector General (OIG), or any of the "big four" auditing firms when answering their questions regarding why, when, or how you are managing risk.

In developing your program, the first key area of focus should be on the relationships that you have to forge within the organization. Of course the most direct approach is to establish your relationships within the IT department, ensure you are the "Yes, if" security leader and not the "No!" leader. This way you always leave open the possibilities when the business or IT department wishes to pursue new technologies. An example of being a "Yes, if" leader can be tied to a personal experience. Our organization wanted to embrace a bring your own device (BYOD) approach. Any rational security professional would opine heavily on the bogeymen, hackers, and other workings of evil that could befall the organization should they do such a thing. Unfortunately, that approach would liken you to the many leaders who are not taken seriously. Therefore, I took the approach of "absolutely, let's do this," and "here are a few things we need to do to ensure we can pull this off":

1. Define a BYOD strategy that includes security.
2. Define BYOD principles for behavioral and technical expectations that include security.
3. Define a BYOD policy that includes security.
4. Define controls that include security.

This approach led to the organization not making BYOD a security endeavor, but rather a strategic initiative which *included* security. The approach is to blend security into initiatives rather than having security stand as a separate initiative. You not only accomplish the goal of increasing the security posture of your organization, but you also "build in" security into efforts, thus achieving a win-win situation. The most crucial relationships will be with your compliance, legal, and audit departments. Contrary to popular belief, these departments will greatly assist you in defining requirements—what you *have* to do vs. what you *want* to do. Internal audits also can provide you with great intelligence as to where current gaps are, what processes exist to evaluate controls and what, if any, risk assessment processes already exist. Making auditors and lawyers close confidants will provide you with strategic friendships that will help your program go. Involving them in policy creation, approval, and implementation also will ensure that they are the groups that are vetting regulation, identifying what you "have to do," and keeping you from being perceived as a lone ranger.

Once relationships have been established, the creation of a governance team to address information risk should be considered. Some of the members of this governance committee should be from Human Resources, Legal, Compliance, Clinical Informatics, Information Technology, Privacy, Health Information Management, and Revenue Cycle (also known as Finance). This broad representation will ensure that all facets of the business are represented. As risk to information assets (which are owned by the business) makes managing those risks a business process, members should be directors or higher to ensure that accountability is driven from the top down. This group will consist of primary captains of the security ship who review risks, audits, and findings and will also be charged with approving the security program and roadmaps, as well as providing updates on efforts and major risks.

Ensuring that information security occupies the spotlight more than any other priority is an undertaking that a security leader should not take alone. It is crucial to have management buy in, not just from the financial aspect or the staffing aspect, but buy in realized as a consistent tone present through vehicles such as monthly newsletters, reminders to staff about compliance and security initiatives, as an aspect of the steering committee, and always in every place ensuring that efforts consider the security implications that could arise from any decision that is made.

Once you have your relationships and governance team in place and are ensured of a consistently strong tone at the top, you have completed pouring the foundation of the security program. Now the real work begins. One of the first actions required of you is to establish context. To do so, you will want to create a security dictionary of terms. What is a *service*? What is a *risk*? What is a *control*? This is important because, as many can attest, establishing your context and definitions will be crucial to establishing understanding and removing confusion from the formula. Secondly, setting context for the program is to also define the services the program provides. For example, the information security program at Presbyterian (where the author works) provides the following services:

1. Vulnerability Management
   a. Risk diagnosis
   b. Risk treatment
2. Event Management
   a. Event detection
   b. Incident response
3. Personnel Management
   a. Identity administration
   b. Information security education
4. Conformance Management
   a. Information Security Management System (ISMS) administration
   b. ISMS evaluation
5. Operations Oversight
   a. Asset administration
   b. Infrastructure administration

Defining these key services provides clarity and an understanding of the span of control of the security program, rather than a departmental view, and defines exactly the functions of the program and its general objectives. It is a good idea to visualize your program as a graphic, as depicted in Figure 3-1.

As Figure 3-1 indicates, there are also processes tied to each service—how else would a service be delivered? These baseline processes provide for the execution of the services. Later, in Chapter 8 of this book, we will provide the controls that ensure the services are being adequately delivered. Once the services and processes are defined, the next crucial step in the formulation of your security program begins: defining the metrics. While many in history have been quoted as saying "You can't manage what you can't measure," a more common saying is "You cannot improve that which isn't measured." In other words, in order to drive quality, you need goals and current-state metrics. For example, if you're struggling with encryption of devices, a simple metric can be total assets encrypted divided by total assets, if you have 90 out of 100 assets encrypted you are 90 percent conformant to your encryption policy. Establishing metrics also allows you to set weekly, monthly, quarterly, or annual goals. For example, your governance team might agree with you that your encryption target is 95 percent of all assets, and therefore, you would report on this measure during your monthly governance meeting. Providing action plans to achieve this goal, or action plans when the goal suffers, is key to the execution of your strategy to achieve encryption.

A good source of metrics that make business sense—because honestly sharing that your firewall has millions of hits on it in a month might open eyes, but really tells no story of the effectiveness of your program—is Andrew Jaquith's *Security Metrics: Replacing Fear, Uncertainty, and Doubt* (FUD). FUD is now considered part of Security 1.0, or old school, as the kids would say. In the current era of Security 2.0, however, we have to show what features and added benefits will be provided by new policies, standards, specifications, processes, or controls.

Once metrics are in place, you are ready to start rolling the Plan, Do, Check, Act (PDCA) wheel of improvement up the hill, as depicted in Figure 3-2.

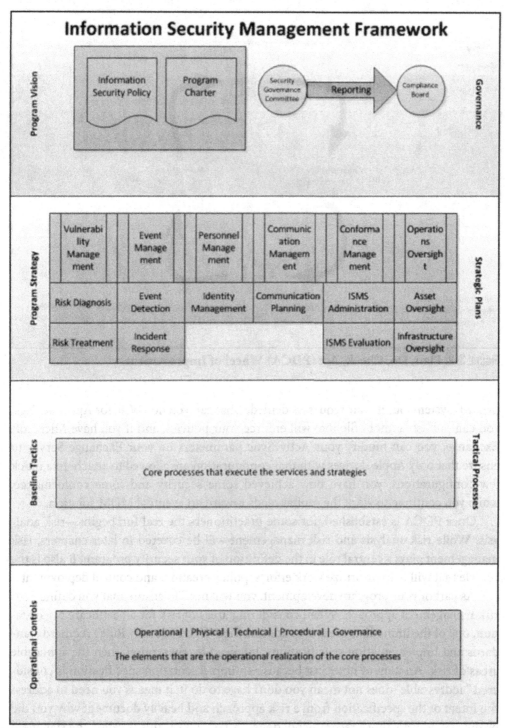

FIGURE 3-1: Example of an Information Security Management System.

Security professionals struggle with the concept of perfection and idealism. A saying we use extensively at Presbyterian is "Do not let perfection get in the way of good," that is, you don't always need the perfect solution to start mitigating risk. For example, in the mobile device world, you might want to procure a Mobile Device Management

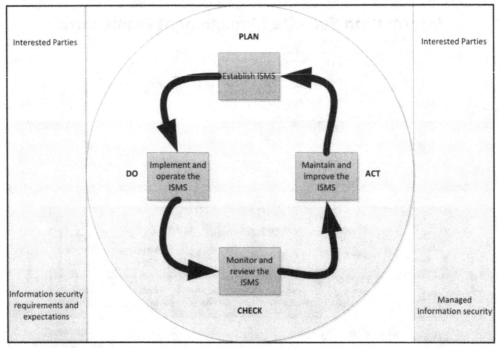

Figure 3-2: Plan, Do, Check, Act (PDCA) Wheel of Improvement.

(MDM) system, but if your request is denied, what can you do? Well, for Apple devices, you can publish a .mobi file that will enforce your policies, and if you have Microsoft Exchange, you can modify your ActiveSync parameters on your Exchange Server to ensure that only Apple devices with that configuration are allowed to attach. In a quick few configurations, you have now achieved some security and some conformance, while you continue to work the capital roads toward an eventual MDM solution.

Once PDCA is established, for some practitioners the real fun begins—risk analysis. While risk analysis and risk management will be covered in later chapters, risk management plays a central role in the definition of your security program. It also is the vehicle that will help prioritize work efforts, policy creation, and control deployment.

As part of your program development, you will need to ensure that you define your risk management approach. When considering areas of risk for a healthcare organization, one of the immediate areas is to address the HIPAA Security Rule's required standards and implementation specifications, followed by encryption, then the applicable areas of risk. An item of note: just because an implementation specification is considered "addressable" does not mean you don't have to do it; it means you need to address the intent of the specification from a risk approach and heavily document why you did or did not address those recommendations. In ISO 27001, this is called the statement of applicability. It is a document that defines the rationale on why controls were or were not deployed. Within the HIPAA Audit Program Protocol[1], for any of the 22 addressable implementation specifications, it states:

If the covered entity has chosen not to fully implement this specification, the entity must have documentation on where they have chosen not to fully implement this specification and their rationale for doing so.

Oversight of the risk management approach should lay with the Information Security Governance Team. A risk treatment and risk acceptance process should be clearly defined and documented, and the Governance Team should regularly review these plans and acceptances to ensure that the security posture of the organization is constantly improving.

CONCLUSION

To summarize, we provided guidance on leveraging a framework to define your program, define your services, create governance, ensure metrics are in place and poured the foundation for the development of the processes and controls necessary to adequately manage risk. One thing to remember: creating your security strategy should not be a single occurrence but an annual effort, to review and refine your strategy as the threat environment continues to evolve.

REFERENCE

1.   U.S. Department of Health & Human Services. Audit Program Protocol. Available at: www.hhs.gov/ocr/privacy/hipaa/enforcement/audit/protocol.html.

CHAPTER 4

Risk Analysis

By Susan Lucci, RHIT, CHPS, CMT, AHDI-F, and Tom Walsh, CISSP

People frequently conduct a risk analysis in everyday life without even realizing that they are doing so. For example, you are driving in your car and approaching an intersection when the traffic light turns yellow. What do you do? Well, that depends on a number of factors: road conditions, other traffic already entering the intersection, traffic immediately behind you, time of day, your sense of urgency to get to your destination, and the presence of law enforcement. These factors could be categorized as "threats." If you factor in the likelihood of the threat occurring and the possible impacts if the threat is realized, you've done a mini risk analysis.

Risk analysis is an important requirement of the HIPAA Security Rule that is challenging many covered entities (CE) and business associates (BA). Whether you are a single eligible provider (EP), an eligible hospital (EH), critical-access hospital (CAH), or part of a massive health system, this requirement must be completed, documented, and signed off by executive management. It is a living document that must be reviewed and updated periodically to reflect changes in systems, technology, and newly identified threats and vulnerabilities and at scheduled intervals. Risk analysis is also a required criterion for the attestation process for Meaningful Use Stage 1 and Stage 2.

Meaningful Use and HIPAA

These two rules intersect in more than a few places and the completion of the risk analysis is one of the key requirements in both rules now—a significant factor to keep in mind as we have entered the era of compliance audits conducted by the Office for Civil Rights (OCR) or their contractor. These audits serve to validate HIPAA Security Rule and Meaningful Use compliance. Now that certified electronic health record (EHR) adoption incentive money is paid out, be forewarned that OCR auditors will be looking for many documents for their inspection, including the risk analysis. Organizations that accepted incentive monies and do not have a documented risk analysis could expect the Department of Health & Human Services (HHS) to fine them or ask that incentive dollars are returned.

While there seems to be no shortage of information available on the web and through other research processes in finding examples, templates, and other guidelines for a risk analysis, it still remains one required process that if not done correctly can lead to fines and other remedies.[1]

Completing your organization's risk analysis can seem like an overwhelmingly detailed endeavor. This chapter is provided to help guide you step by step through risk analysis with some tips for your consideration. This chapter is based upon the original NIST SP 800-30, *Risk Management Guide for Information Technology Systems*. The National Institute of Standards and Technology (NIST) is a federal agency that develops standards and guidelines. In particular, the Computer Security Division is responsible for the creation of the Special Publications (SP) in the 800 series, publications that provide guidance on information security. Within the preamble of the HIPAA Security Rule[2] there is a reference to the NIST SP 800-30. This publication is used because it was referenced in the HIPAA Security Rule as well as the white papers and reports released by the Centers for Medicare & Medicaid Services (CMS).

In September 2012, NIST retired the original SP 800-30, replacing it with the NIST Special Publication 800-30, Revision 1, *Guide for Conducting Risk Assessments*. In March 2011, NIST released the final version of a companion document, NIST Special Publication 800-39, *Managing Information Security Risk*. These two documents provide a more detailed approach for assessing, analyzing, and managing risks.

However, the target audience for these documents, as well as the other special publications in the 800 series, are federal agencies of the United States. Healthcare organizations can use these documents as references, but should understand that the threats and risks associated with a federal agency may be different from those of a clinic, a community-based hospital, a clearinghouse, or a health insurance company.

GETTING STARTED

What is Risk?

Risk is present with any business operation. Risk analysis is not about the *elimination* of risks, because in some cases that is impossible. Instead, risk analysis is about determining what the risks are and communicating it to executive management so that they can make an informed business decision. That is why risk management is so closely related to risk analysis. Once risks are identified they have to be managed appropriately.

The amount of risk that an organization can accept and manage is a question that is unique to that facility. However, it is essential to understand the various risks that exist to manage them in the best possible way. The challenge for information security professionals is to balance the needs of the business with the need for securing business assets as a part of an overall risk management strategy. There is a balance point of providing reasonable security to the operation balanced with business and operational needs and the costs involved with securing data that will drive sound decision-making.

There's a saying, "In God we trust… all others must document." And so it goes for all of us in information security space. Although documentation may not be where our expertise lies, in this case and for all of healthcare, if it isn't written down, it didn't happen. Appropriate management of risks requires creating a documented assessment of information assets, considering the potential threats, existing controls, and remaining vulnerabilities. Next you must consider the probability of the threat circumventing existing controls to exploit the vulnerabilities and the potential impact if the threat actually occurred. This is the basic process in a nutshell.

It is important to explain terminology before proceeding. There is a difference between risk "assessment" and "analysis" although many people mistakenly interchange the two. Listed below are the definitions:

> Assessment: A judgment about something based on an understanding of the situation; a method of evaluating performance.

> Analysis: The close examination of something in detail in order to understand it better or draw conclusions from it; the separation of something into its constituents in order to find out what it contains, to examine individual parts, or to study the structure of the whole.

> *Source: Encarta Dictionary.*

Here is an example of how the two terms are different. Let's say you are driving in your car and you notice that it is shifting hard. You take it to a mechanic and he tells you, "Looks like it might be your transmission." That is an assessment. You then take your car to a shop that specializes in transmission repair. The mechanic at this shop pulls the transmission and provides you with a detailed description of the problem, what is needed to repair the transmission, what it will cost, how long your car will be in the shop, the likelihood of failure, and what the impact might be if you decide not to fix it. That is an analysis.

Therefore, risk analysis is a systematic and ongoing process of identifying threats, controls, vulnerabilities, likelihood, impact, and an overall rating of risk. Risk analysis sometimes is not a precise science. Assessing risks requires much "what if" thinking; it is an attempt to predict the possibility of a future occurrence that one does not want to happen. Frequently, when reviewing threats and vulnerabilities even the most logical information security professional is required to make their best guess and speculate the possibilities when determining the likelihood of an event taking place as well as the potential impact.

THE NINE STEP RISK PROCESS

Figure 4-1 is a graphic example of a risk analysis flow chart that outlines each suggested step.

Step 1: System Characterization

The first recommended step is to conduct an inventory of applications and systems that process and/or store electronic protected health information (PHI). To assess your risks, you must first determine what needs protecting. As you begin to log your organization's information assets, you may also want to include other applications and systems that require protecting either because of their criticality to the business and/or because of the sensitivity of the information that is processed and stored on the system. Continue on with logging all information systems (clinical as well as business operational systems) into an inventory.

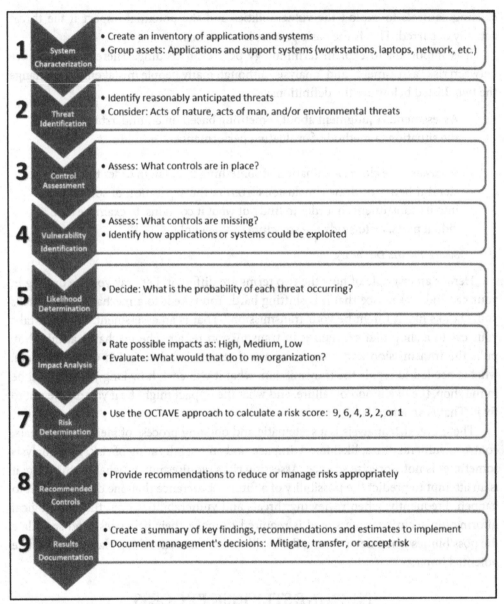

Figure 4-1: Risk Analysis Flow Diagram. *From Susan Lucci and Tom Walsh Consulting, LLC. Used with permission.*

System characterization is the process of classifying and grouping "like things" together to simplify the task of identifying the threats, controls, vulnerabilities, and assess overall risks. Listed below are examples of how some hardware devices could be characterized:

- Servers
- Networking components (routers, switches, firewalls)
- Computer workstations (stationary computers used in office and work areas)
- Mobile devices (laptops, tablets, hand-held computing devices, smartphones, etc.)

The threats to these devices will most likely be different. For example, the theft of a mobile device is more likely than the theft of a server or an entire rack of equipment. Another example would be the failure of a hardware device. The failure of a single computer workstation probably will have little impact to the organization as a whole, as compared to the failure of any key network component for which there is no failover or backup device. In this example, the workstation failure only impacts one person while the network failure could potentially impact everyone with network access. System characterization allows grouping of similar information assets to make it easier to determine their risk profile.

Step 2: Threat Identification

When you have completed the inventory of applications and systems, then it is time to consider what threats could be encountered. To keep things simple, threats generally fall into three basic categories: acts of nature, acts of man, and environmental. To further describe these: acts of nature refer to situations, issues, and disasters that are often beyond our control. Acts of man, on the other hand, are either intentional or accidental actions committed by people and some of these can be addressed or controlled. Environmental issues are events that could be prevented, or at least minimized by a planned response.

When it comes to identifying threats, apply a practical approach to your thinking. Going overboard with threat identification can derail your progress if you try to consider *everything* that could possibly happen. The term "reasonably anticipated" is used three times within the HIPAA Security Rule (twice in the Preamble and once in the actual rule) as it pertains to threats or hazards. Therefore, if you are concerned about listing space debris falling on the server room as a threat, it probably would not stand up to the litmus test of being "reasonably anticipated." As you go through Step 2, keep in mind such things as your organization's geographical location, past experiences, or the type of information asset as explained in the example in the previous section.

Step 3: Control Assessment

In this step you will identify and document existing security safeguards and controls to make the call as to whether or not they are adequate in either preventing or detecting a threat. In the case of issues like an earthquake or a tornado, the control analysis determines if systems can be adequately recovered and restored to their original functionality. Assurance testing or validation is another process that may also be used to determine if the existing controls are adequate.

Assessing controls and vulnerabilities is normally accomplished through the use of some type of checklist or by a survey of questions. Once a threat has been identified, there are usually at least three to five safeguards or controls that could be implemented to either prevent, detect, assure against, and/or recover from a particular threat. The absence of a safeguard or control would represent a vulnerability (Step 4). Keep in mind that policy in itself is a safeguard but not an effective control unless there is some other means (physical or technical) to monitor, measure and enforce the policy. For example, you have probably witnessed people blatantly violating a posted speed limit along a stretch of highway unless there is a state trooper present to enforce the speed limit.

Sometimes a single control can address multiple threats. For example, while assessing the controls for an application, you ask the following question: "Does the application lock out a user or set an alarm after a predetermined number of consecutive, unsuccessful logon attempts (such as five attempts)?" If the answer is "yes," then this is a control that would address two similar but different threats: (1) a hacker (an outsider trying to break into the application) and (2) an internal person attempting to gain unauthorized access by repeatedly trying to guess another person's password.

Step 4: Vulnerability Identification

Vulnerabilities are typically identified as the lack of a safeguard or control and may have been identified during the control analysis. Vulnerabilities may also be determined through some type of technical evaluation of controls. For example, a network vulnerability scan or penetration test may reveal other security weakness. Chapter 18 covers some of the possible ways to test technical controls and identify vulnerabilities.

Step 5: Likelihood Determination

Now that you have identified the threats, controls, and vulnerabilities for your information assets, the next step is to determine the likelihood or probability of a potential threat being successful in exploiting the vulnerabilities. Likelihood can be rated as high, medium, or low. To maintain consistency your organization should include some definitions of those ratings.

Likelihood should always take into consideration the existing controls. For example, if network perimeter controls would not be considered a priority, then the likelihood of a hacker gaining unauthorized access to your systems would always be "high." In general, the more controls that are in place to address a particular threat, the lower the likelihood of the threat being realized.

Step 6: Impact Analysis

The impact analysis is where you have to really consider the big picture and be brutally honest, thinking downstream into all areas of your operation. Table 4-1 lists some categories of impacts along with some examples.

It can be difficult to precisely quantify the impacts if a threat is realized. For example, would you know how to assign a financial impact to an organization and the resulting blemished image in the community as the result of a data breach? Therefore, it is suggested again that you assign impact ratings as high, medium, or low. It is recommended that the organization create definitions for the impact ratings in order to maintain consistency.

Impacts, regardless of the source, should take your organization's resiliency into consideration—how quickly you could recover from an incident once a threat is realized. This is one of the key reasons why it is extremely critical to have your incident response team identified, clear on steps that must be taken (including communication)

TABLE 4-1: Categories of Impacts and Examples.

Confidentiality
Disclosure of protected health information (PHI)
Access to credit card data used for committing financial fraud
Access to Social Security numbers used for identity theft
Disclosure of sensitive or proprietary research information
Integrity
Data entry errors
Data alteration (intentional or unintentional)
Data synchronization errors
Availability
Business interruption
Denial of service
Loss of productive time and operational delays
Replacement of lost information
Opportunity (financial)
Loss of business
Loss of competitive advantage or research grant
Equipment repair or replacement
Increase in cyber insurance premiums
Reputation
Loss of patient confidence
Decreased employee morale
Loss of physician confidence
Litigation
Criminal or civil case
Regulatory fines or criminal punishment for noncompliance

Reprinted by permission of Tom Walsh Consulting, LLC

and the priority of these steps. Remember: It's all about the management of risks, not the complete elimination of risks.

Step 7: Risk Determination

Assigning a risk score may on the surface appear to be a simple step, but this is more important as you categorize the long list of assets and is not a step that you want to ignore. The risk score is determined by likelihood and impact. Assigning a risk score provides the foundation for prioritizing limited resources allocated for information security. One of the ways risks can be scored is through the OCTAVE[SM] Approach, as illustrated in Figure 4-2. The higher risk scores of 9 or 6 indicate the areas where additional security safeguards and controls are needed. Risk scores 4 or 3 mean that additional controls may be beneficial. Finally, risk scores of 2 or 1 imply that risks are being handled appropriately and that no further action is required at this time.

Step 8: Recommended Controls

Control recommendations are made by examining the vulnerabilities. When there is a lack of control or a weak safeguard, the control recommendation must be strength-

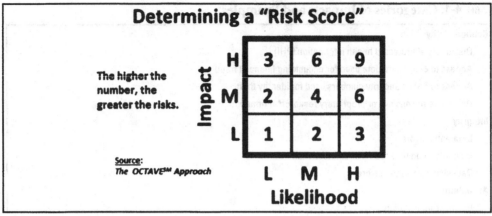

FIGURE 4-2: The OCTAVE^SM Approach.

ened. For example, Table 4-2 below lists some samples of how a stated vulnerability can be translated to a control recommendation. Essentially, a suggested control should be made for each corresponding vulnerability. However, this is not always possible because occasionally a vulnerability will exist for which there is no control.

Step 9: Results Documentation

Three primary documents which are created as a result of the risk analysis are:

- Risk profiles.
- Risk analysis report.
- Risk remediation plan.

Risk profiles are created to document the reasonably anticipated threats, existing security controls, vulnerabilities and the associated risks. The risk profiles document Steps 2 through 8 in a nine-step process. The profile contains the details of the risk analysis. Figure 4-3 is an example of a risk profile. The word "profile" implies an outline or a silhouette. It is a rough picture of your risks. Consider it to be like a connect-the-dots picture. While it will never be artwork that will hang in a museum, it's probably good enough to hang on the refrigerator door.

Future risk analysis reviews can be streamlined by updating the current risk profiles with any changes rather than always starting from scratch.

TABLE 4-2: Samples of Vulnerabilities and Corresponding Control Recommendations.

Vulnerability	Control Recommendation
Audit logs are not regularly reviewed and are primarily used for problem solving	Create procedures to randomly audit users; formalize log review responsibilities and procedures
User's account is not disabled after a predetermined number of unsuccessful logon attempts	Consider locking out a user's account after five consecutive unsuccessful logon attempts
Disaster recovery plan has not been created; a formal business impact analysis has not been conducted	Conduct a formal business impact analysis (BIA); create a disaster recovery plan that outlines a systematic approach to recovery based upon the needs of the business as documented in a BIA

Clinic·EMR →	(SAMPLE)	→			Risk·Profile¶			

Threats	Current Controls	Vulnerability	Impact or Loss	Like	Impt	Risk	Suggested Controls
1. Authorized user misusing their access privileges, tampering, or improper use	• Users assigned their own unique User-ID; there are no generic user-IDs¶ • A user account is disabled after three unsuccessful logon attempts¶ • Audit trails capture sufficient information to determine what events occurred and by whom¶	• Employees have been caught looking up other employees' medical records in violation of policy¶ • Audit logs are not regularly reviewed and are primarily used for problem-solving¶	Confidentiality¶ Integrity	Mx	Mo	4x	• Send employees awareness reminders regarding their access to patient records and the patient's right to an access report (who has been viewing their record)¶ • Formalize audit log review process and responsibilities¶
2. Unauthorized user or inappropriate access (Internal)	• Users assigned their own unique User-ID; there are no generic user-IDs¶ • Auto-logoff activates after 20 minutes of inactivity¶ • A user account is disabled after three unsuccessful logon attempts¶ • Audit trails capture sufficient information to determine what events occurred and by whom¶	• IT assigns users their password and it never changes; minimum password length is set at three characters and complexity rules are not enforced¶ • Audit logs are not regularly reviewed and are primarily used for problem-solving¶	Confidentiality¶ Integrity¶ Availability	Mx	Mx	4x	• Require users to change their initial password the first time they log into the EMR; set users' passwords to a minimum length of six or more characters and if possible, enforce complexity rules¶ • Formalize audit log review process and responsibilities¶
3. Accidental disclosure of PHI	• Unknown¶	• Users are not required to receive training in order to receive EMR access (their user-ID and password)¶ • Backup media is not encrypted¶	Confidentiality¶ Integrity	Lx	Ho	3x	• Consider requiring users to attend training prior to granting access to the application; training should include privacy and security requirements¶ • Work with the EMR vendor to determine if backup media can be encrypted¶
4. Program error, application bug, and/or operating system errors	• Daily backups are created¶ • Changes or upgrades are primarily provided by the vendor¶ • There are contingency plans or downtime procedures for planned or unplanned downtimes of the EMR¶ • The EMR server is located in a locked server room with adequate environmental controls including a UPS¶	• A copy of the backup media is not stored securely in an off-site location¶ • Vendor could potentially make changes to the application in the production environment¶ • There is no formal disaster recovery plan for the EMR¶	Integrity¶ Availability	Lx	Hx	3x	• Store at least one copy of the EMR backup media in a secure location¶ • Establish formal security requirements for vendor remote access; determine if an addendum to the existing BAA will need to be created for security to comply with ARRA (HITECH)¶ • Create a disaster recovery plan

[Organization name]—Confidential Risk Management Document → (Date) → Page 1 of 2¶

FIGURE 4-3: An Example of a Risk Profile.

The *risk analysis report* is instrumental for making executive management aware of the *residual risks*—the ones that remain despite all controls and safeguards currently in place. The residual risks, key findings, and the control recommendations for reducing risks are documented in the final risk analysis report. To keep the report from being too detailed, the executive summary should focus only on the vulnerabilities and control recommendations where the overall risk score exceeds the organization's level of acceptable risk. For most organizations, risk scores of 1 or 2 are acceptable which means there is no added value in investing additional resources to reduce the risks. Risk scores of 3 or 4 are marginal and usually need some level of remediation to manage the risks appropriately, depending on the system's criticality of the sensitivity of the data. Risk scores of 6 or 9 represent unacceptable risks that exceed the organization's risk tolerance and they must be remediated immediately. Table 4-3 is an example of how the

TABLE 4-3: An Example of Risk Rating Dashboard.

Likelihood	Impact	Risk Score	Color Rating
H	H	9	
H	M	6	Red
M	H	6	
M	M	4	
H	L	3	Yellow
L	H	3	
M	L	2	
L	M	2	Green
L	L	1	

risks are rated using a green, yellow, and red dashboard approach. Some recommendations might be considered "low-hanging fruit"—they are those that will not require significant resources (budget, staff, time, etc.) to implement and should be considered because they make good business sense.

The risk analysis report also documents executive management's decision regarding the recommendations for additional safeguards and controls. Essentially there are choices for each of the recommendations:

- **Implement** the recommendation to mitigate or reduce risks to an acceptable level;
- **Transfer** the risk (e.g., outsourcing) or purchase insurance to offset the potential impact of the risk (this option is not always available); or
- **Accept** the risks associated with operating the information system in its current configuration and do not implement the recommendation.

It is also helpful to identify the estimated resources in order to implement the recommendations. For example, will a recommended control cost $500 or $500,000 to implement? Resource estimates should include capital expenditures, ongoing expense, and the number of hours to implement. Management may be hesitant to make a decision unless they understand the estimated resources necessary. Whatever the decision, it needs to be indicated in the risk analysis report. Management's signature on the report is their acknowledgement of the corrective action and/or acceptance of residual risks. The documented risk analysis becomes the evidence that an organization took a systematic business approach to applying security controls. As vital as this last step is, it is often forgotten. Remember, "If it's important, get it in writing." Table 4-4 illustrates how the recommended controls could be documented in a report. You should note that if the risk cannot be transferred, that option should be grayed out to prevent an executive from checking or initialing the box.

Any of the recommendations that will be implemented should be documented into a *risk remediation plan* that tracks who is responsible for implementing the suggested safeguard or control and the start and end dates (actual and/or projected or both). The results documentation step is now complete.

TABLE 4-4: An Example of Recommendations in a Report.

Findings (Yellow = 4 or 3) *(listed in order of priority)*

The following findings rated risk scores of 4 and should be given serious consideration for remediation:

1. IT assigns users their password and it does not change; minimum password length is set at three characters and complexity rules are not enforced
2. No auto logoff after a predetermined period of inactivity
3. Notification from HR when an employee leaves is not consistent; HR may not always provide notification when an employee changes jobs, is on medical disability, or is placed on disciplinary suspension
4. Managers are not periodically provided a listing of their employees and their access privileges to review and verify that their access is appropriate
5. Inactive user accounts (Ex: More than 30 days since last use) are not disabled
6. Users can have concurrent logons under the same user ID
7. Audit logs are not regularly reviewed and are primarily used for problem solving

Recommendations

The following recommendations *(listed in order of priority)* should be considered to help reduce risks:

Suggested Controls	Estimated Resources (Capital, Expense, and Hours)	Information/System Owner – Decisions		
		Mitigate risks *(Approve the control)*	Transfer or insure against risks	Accept risks *(Deny the control)*
1. Set users' passwords to a minimum length of six or more characters and if possible, enforce complexity and initial and periodic expiration	30 hrs to implement password rule changes and notify users			
2. Consider establishing an auto logoff after 10 minutes of inactivity or activating computer workstation screen savers (in patient care areas) to trigger within five minutes to prevent incidental disclosure of PHI	5 hrs to investigate auto logoff capabilities 5 hrs to obtain buy-in 2 hrs to implement			
3. Establish a process so that HR quickly notifies IT when an employee terminates, changes jobs, is on medical leave, or is placed on disciplinary suspension	3 hrs to review termination notification process			
4. Work with managers on periodically reviewing user access privileges and roles to determine if access is appropriate	10 hrs every 6 months to review user access rights			
5. Create a process to automatically disable user accounts that have been inactive for long periods of time (Ex: 30+ days)	5 hrs annually to review manually; ___hrs to automate			
6. Eliminate concurrent logon capability	2 hrs to assess the feasibility; 1 hr to implement			
7. Formalize audit log review process and responsibilities	3 hrs to formalize log review process; 4 hrs/week to review			

Reprinted by permission of Tom Walsh Consulting, LLC

TIPS FOR SUCCESS

Now that you have the fundamental components, here are a few tips that will help you get started and see the project through.

Divide and conquer. As you begin to work on creating your organization's risk analysis, it will seem less daunting if you break it down into smaller steps. It makes sense to break up the risk analysis process initially into two high-level categories: (1) major applications, and (2) general support systems. Table 4-5 defines and illustrates some examples of each.

Think of the system characterization step as pieces of a puzzle. Each category of general support systems is one piece of the puzzle; each major application is also a piece of the puzzle. When you place all of the pieces together, you have the "big picture" of risk analysis. By dividing them up, it makes it easier and quicker to assess controls and vulnerabilities. Also, there will be a team of people responsible for "their piece" of the puzzle. Therefore, risk analysis profiles and reports are written for each application or system so that the responsible team can better understand their risks and what they need to do. You may also want to collectively gather all the high risks from each application or system and present the overall findings in a report to executive management.

The diagram in Figure 4-4 illustrates how there is overlap between the various applications and the general support systems. For example, if systems are hosted in a data center (also called a computer room or server room), then the system would more than likely share all of the same physical and environmental threats, controls, and vulnerabilities as all of the other systems in the room. Therefore, it is easier to do one risk analysis of the data center rather than repeat that portion of the assessment each time a risk analysis is conducted on another major application. Likewise, most systems share the same internal network. A single assessment of the network eliminates the need for repeating a network assessment as part of each application's risk analysis. By using this approach, the risk analysis for a major application would be focused on the security controls implemented within the application and the controls used to protect the data.

Make an educated guess. Determining what are reasonably anticipated threats as well as the likelihood and impact are, for the most part, educated guesses. That is because there is no accurate source for determining likelihood and impact. Sure, there are some computer crime surveys and news stories about organizations that have suffered breaches, but how accurate is the information? What is the likelihood that the circumstances are identical? For every computer crime or breach that makes the news, how many do not? Most executives want to keep these types of events from making the news.

Because of the breach notification rule that became effective in September 2009, breaches affecting 500 patients or more are listed on the HHS website in what is often referred to as the "wall of shame" as the name of the covered entity also appears on the website. This information can be useful in determining the likelihood of a particular threat being realized. For example, the authors of this chapter have been running quarterly reports ever since this data has been available to the public. The trend we have seen over the years of the reported breaches at the time of this writing (and these may vary over time) is as follows:

- Sixty-eight percent are caused by lost or stolen devices (laptops, tablets, smartphones, etc.) or media (USB thumb drives, backup tapes, CDs, etc.)—mainly because these devices and media are not encrypted.
- Twenty percent are caused by unauthorized access—mainly by authorized users misusing their access privileges to "snoop" at medical records of patients.
- Twenty percent are caused by business associates or their subcontractors; keep in mind that your cyber insurance policy (if you have one for your organization) does not cover your business associates.

Source: www.hhs.gov/ocr/privacy/hipaa/administrative/breachnotificationrule/breachtool.html.

TABLE 4-5: Major Applications and General Support Systems.

General Support Systems*	Description
Computer workstations	Hosts on your networks that staff members use to conduct business.
Mobile computing devices	Devices such as laptops, notebooks, tablets, other hand-held computing devices, and smartphones such as a BlackBerry or iPhone (whether company-owned or personally-owned) primarily used to access information from almost any location.
Network	Equipment used to support network connectivity (e.g., routers and switches, firewalls, etc.)
Wireless LAN	The internal wireless network(s).
Remote access	Systems that allow staff members to remotely access information via your organization's networks which could include a web portal.
E-mail	Includes the various servers supporting e-mail, the e-mail application—both the server and client, and systems used to protect e-mail.
Data Center or Server Room	Facilities that host your information technology infrastructure and that have physical and environmental controls for protecting information assets.
Operational practices	While not an information system, operational practices deals with people and processes such as policies, procedures, responsibilities, and training which apply to all major applications and need to be assessed.
Others	Any other type of information system that could be part of your threat scenarios, but does not fall into one of the above classes such as the Active Directory or an LDAP system.

Based upon: Managing Information Security Risks, The OCTAVE^SM Approach

** General Support System—Interconnected information resources under the same direct management control (usually the Information Technology Department) that share common functionality with other applications.
Source: NIST SP 800 Series*

Major Applications*	Description
EHR	Electronic health record—this is the primary clinical application that supports a hospital.
EMR	Electronic medical record—this is the primary clinical application that supports outpatient clinics.
Claims processing / Member management system	An integrated system used by health plans for their members managing enrollment, eligibility, claims processing, provider and plan information, utilization management, case management, etc.
Laboratory information systems (LIS)	Application used by labs to track orders, tests, and test results.
Human Resources / Payroll	System used to track employees, their job titles, salary, insurance information, timekeeping, etc. (While this system will not contain PHI, it does contain other confidential information that requires protection.)

* Major Applications—A Major Application is an application that requires special attention to security due to the risk and magnitude of the harm resulting from the loss, misuse, or unauthorized access to, or modification of, the information in the application. A breach in a major application might comprise many individual application programs and hardware, software, and telecommunications components. Major applications can be either a major software application or a combination of hardware/software where the only purpose of the system is to support a specific mission-related function.

Source: NIST SP 800 Series

Major App 1	Major App 2	A hierarchical
Data	Data	approach to
Application	Application	assessing controls and risks
Network	Network	Risk Profile
Hardware & Operating System	Hardware & Operating System	Risk Profile
Physical/ Environment	Physical/ Environment	Risk Profile
Operational Practices	Operational Practices	Risk Profile

FIGURE 4-4: Layered Approach for General Support Systems. *From Tom Walsh Consulting, LLC, used with permission.*

Using trend data like this can help rationalize a risk score. It also helps you identify common weaknesses in protected health information and can help frame your risk assessment questions. Although using the breach notification statistics can be helpful, each organization will have a different probability or likelihood of a breach based upon several factors including the types of controls they have implemented and geographical location, just to name two. Certain government agencies in Washington, DC are more likely to be targeted for political reasons than would a rural community-based hospital.

Your own history may help. If your data center is located in the basement of a hospital and the basement has flooded in the past, unless something drastic has been done to prevent it, there is a good chance it might flood again. Your organization's past experiences are key to conducting your risk analysis and may help in determining the types of threats that need to be addressed and their likelihood of occurring based upon reported incidents.

Incident reporting is required under HIPAA's Security Rule (§164.308(a)(6)(i) and (ii)) and is also useful when determining the probability and potential impacts of events. The downside? Information technology people are notorious for lacking documentation. Many incidents go unreported, but if they are reported they often lack enough detail to be helpful.

Snapshot in time. Threats change, systems and applications are constantly being updated, and new vulnerabilities are discovered daily. That is why a risk analysis needs to be performed periodically. The good news is that once a risk analysis has been conducted, updating the risk profiles and reports are much easier than the first time the risk analysis was conducted. Keep the original risk analysis documentation and save the file by a new name. We suggest using the date as part of the file name to make each document unique and to preserve the original documents. Remember that you will want to keep all your documentation that serves as proof of a risk analysis for a minimum of six years as required by HIPAA.

It is recommended that risk profiles be reviewed at least once every three years, or when significant changes occur to the computing environment, or when there are newly discovered threats or vulnerabilities. Significant changes include but are not limited to:

- Security incidents.
- Significant changes to the organizational or technical infrastructure.
- Newly discovered threats or vulnerabilities.

Keep it simple. Assessing controls is normally done through the use of some type of checklist or by a survey of questions. There are plenty of sources on the Internet for assessment questions. However, ask too many questions and no one has the time to complete the checklist or survey. If you do not ask enough questions, are you sure that you were thorough enough in your assessment? Finding the right balance is important. Remember the goal is to improve your practices and processes to safeguard your information assets. Identify your threats first, then formulate three to five questions around the controls that could be used to deal with that threat. Some questions will require follow-up questions. For example, if you ask the question, "Do you back up your data?" If the person responds "Yes," then here are some follow up questions to ask:

- **How often?** ("Daily" would be a control; if the answer is "Whenever I remember" that may be a vulnerability instead of a control, depending on the data and its criticality to the organization's mission.)
- **Where are the backups kept?** ("At a secure long term storage facility" would be a control. Answers like "On top of the server that is getting backed up," or "In my garage at home," probably represent a vulnerability.)
- **Is the backup media encrypted?** ("Yes" is a control; "No" is a vulnerability.)
- **Have you ever tested or restored files from the backup media?** ("Yes" is a control; "No" is a vulnerability.)

It is worth noting, there is no reason to ask any follow-up questions if the person initially responded "No," to the question "Do you back up your data?"

Tie remediation plans to business objectives. Wherever possible, an information security professional should link each planned security control to a business initiative. This requires a careful review of both the organization's strategic plan, as well as the IT strategic plan. For example, a single sign-on based on strong authentication could be linked to the organization's strategic objective to "improve physician satisfaction" and an IT objective to "increase physician use of computer systems." Physicians that practice at multiple hospitals or healthcare facilities may have several user IDs and passwords. The single sign-on could reduce the number of user IDs and passwords within an organization to one, thus making it easier for them to use the various computer systems.

Along with aligning with business objectives, security controls should also be linked to regulatory requirements. The list of regulatory requirements keeps growing.

Keep it confidential. Because the risk analysis report and the risk profiles document the vulnerabilities within an information system, these documents are considered confidential information. Consider either password protecting the documents or storing them on a network folder with restricted access rights.

Risk analysis—not a one-time event. Security controls must be validated and risks must be evaluated. Initially, controls can be assessed through an interview process. However, at some point an evaluation needs to be conducted to validate that the controls are in place. Sometimes an interviewee may state what they believe is a control setting, but an evaluation may prove that it is incorrect. For example, say the answer given by a system administrator in an interview to the question "What is the automatic logoff setting for application XYZ?" was "15 minutes" and that was noted in the risk profile. Later during the evaluation, the system administrator logs onto the application to validate it, only to discover that the setting is actually 30 minutes. This doesn't imply that the system administrator was uninformed, it simply means that he believed that was the actual setting. Perhaps at one time the setting was at 15 minutes but was later changed by another system administrator after numerous complaints from clinical staff. You can see the inherent risk in failing to update the documentation of system controls and communicating changes.

This is why HIPAA's Security Rule also requires:

> **§164.308(a)(8) Evaluation (Required)** Perform a periodic technical and nontechnical evaluation, based initially upon the standards and implemented under this rule and subsequently, in response to environmental or operational changes affecting the security of electronic protected health information, that establishes the extent to which an entity's security policies and procedures meet the requirements of this subpart.

Look for islands of data. Many departments create their own documents, spreadsheets, or even databases that contain confidential information including patient data or protected health information (PHI), Social Security numbers, credit card data or cardholder information, and other sensitive or proprietary information such as financial or personnel information. Each department may independently create and manage their confidential information often with little understanding of the risks or security process used to govern IT. This can be thought of as "islands of confidential data" with little or no protection of the shoreline.

Because of its simplicity, a user can create his own access database without IT involvement. Often, the database starts out as a small project or as a job aid. Later, it grows and user dependency increases. Before long, the simple database becomes a critical application for the department. If the database contains confidential information, then it begs the question, "What security controls have been implemented to protect the data stored within the database?" Access controls? Audit trails? Encryption? Chances are that few, if any, of these controls have been implemented meaning the database may violate regulatory requirements.

Confidential information may sometimes be extracted from larger, organization-wide applications or systems and then placed into Excel spreadsheets making it easier for users to work with the data. Again, what security controls are in place and does management understand the residual risks? How is data integrity preserved? This is especially important if the data from the spreadsheet is used to make key business decisions. Have you ever accidentally sorted a column on an Excel spreadsheet only to discover that you totally messed up the data because it is no longer properly associated with the correct row? What happens if the spreadsheet is the only source for aligning something vital back to a particular patient? Initially, the risk analysis should be conducted for all of the major applications used in the organization that have the highest potential for organizational risk. Later, you'll need to drill down deeper to find these isolated uses of data that could also place the organization at risk.

Make risk analysis a priority. When the final HIPAA Security Rule was released in February 2003, the standards and implementation specifications were listed in an order that the rule's authors felt were the order of importance. Therefore, it is worth noting that the first two implementation specifications in the Administrative category are:

> **§164.308(a)(1)(ii)(A) Risk analysis (Required)** Conduct an accurate and thorough assessment of the potential risks and vulnerabilities to the confidentiality, integrity, and availability of electronic protected health information held by the covered entity.

> **§164.308(a)(1)(ii)(B) Risk management (Required)** Implement security measures sufficient to reduce risks and vulnerabilities to a reasonable and appropriate level to comply with §164.306(a).

In addition, risk analysis is required in Meaningful Use:

> Conduct or review a security risk analysis per 45 CFR 164.308 (a)(1) and implement security updates as necessary and correct identified security deficiencies as part of its risk management process.

The deadline for compliance with the HIPAA Security Rule was April 20, 2005. Yet, the risk analysis is still cited as being one of the most common audit findings by the OCR.[3] New with the final rule for Meaningful Use Stage 2:

> Conduct or review a security risk analysis in accordance with the requirements under 45 CFR 164.308(a)(1), including addressing the encryption/security of data stored in CEHRT in accordance with requirements under 45 CFR 164.312 (a)(2)(iv) and 45 CFR 164.306(d)(3), and implement security updates as necessary and correct identified security deficiencies as part of the provider's risk management process.

CONCLUSION

Now that OCR has started auditing for compliance with security requirements under HIPAA, there is a sense of urgency to get this done, combined with an intensified effort to do it well. Meaningful Use incentive payments have begun and this incentive money was part of the overall goal of adoption of certified EHR technology. Attestations of a completed risk analysis were part of the requirement to qualify for the incentive and this has been identified as a document for review during audits.

The executive leadership of the healthcare organization has an inherent responsibility in ensuring this task is done and documented with recommendations as outlined in this chapter. The managers and directors then have the assignment of completing the task with a common sense, practical approach so that it is reasonable within budgetary guidelines for that organization. It is not possible to eliminate all risk.

REFERENCES

1.   U.S. Department of Health & Human Services (April 17, 2012). Available at: www.hhs.gov/news/press/2012pres/04/20120417a.html. Accessed June 30, 2012.

2.   HIPAA Security Rule (February 20, 2003). Available at: www.hhs.gov/ocr/privacy/hipaa/administrative/securityrule/securityrulepdf.pdf.

3.   Sanches L. 2012 HIPAA Privacy and Security Audits. [presentation] OCR Senior Advisor, Health Information Privacy Lead, HIPAA Compliance Audits (June 2012).

CHAPTER 5

Senior Management Oversight and Involvement

By Mary Anne S. Canant, MBA, CISA, CISSP, CHFP

Management has countless responsibilities. Among them is oversight and direct involvement in the organization's information security program. This chapter focuses on 10 security activities requiring management's and, in some cases, senior management's involvement. These activities were identified by searching for references to management actions in The Security Rule,[1] the Office for Civil Rights (OCR) HIPAA Audit Program Protocol[2] and summary results of the Centers for Medicare & Medicaid Services (CMS) HIPAA Compliance Reviews conducted in 2008[3] and 2009.[4] The Audit Program Protocol was developed in response to the HITECH Act requirement for periodic audits to ensure covered entities and business associates are complying with the HIPAA Privacy and Security Rules and Breach Notification standards.

Management activities featured in this chapter include assigning security responsibilities; reviewing policies and procedures; reviewing, revising, and completing security awareness and training courses; approving risk assessments; verifying staff experience and qualifications; authorizing user access; verifying the qualifications of those with emergency access to electronic protected health information (ePHI); identifying audit tools; retaining details of security incidents; and verifying the disposal of ePHI. Activities are introduced with at least one reference to relevant language in the Final Security Rule, HIPAA Audit Program Protocol, or from the summary reports of CMS HIPAA Compliance Reviews in 2008 and 2009. Weaknesses identified in the compliance reviews are presented with recommendations for corrective action. Additional guidance presented in this chapter was derived from the key activities and procedures described in the audit program protocol.

SENIOR MANAGEMENT ASSIGNS SECURITY RESPONSIBILITY

Performance Criteria: Standard §164.308(a)(2) Assigned Security Responsibility— "Identify the security official who is responsible for the development and implementation of the policies and procedures required by Subpart C—Security Standards for the Protection of Electronic Protected Health Information—of the Security Rule."

Security Rule Preamble: "Responsibilities would include the management and supervision of (1) the use of security measures to protect data, and (2) the conduct of personnel in relation to the protection of data."

Key Activities for Senior Management
- Select a security official to be assigned final responsibility for HIPAA security.
- Clearly define the Security Officer's roles and responsibilities in a complete job description.
- Communicate this assigned role to the entire organization.

Key Capabilities and Responsibilities of the Security Officer
The Security Officer should be capable of assessing effective security and serving as the point of contact for security policy, implementation, and monitoring. The Security Officer should be held responsible for the following activities:
- Overseeing the development, implementation, monitoring, and communication of security policies and procedures.
- Managing and supervising the use of security measures to protect data.
- Managing and supervising the conduct of personnel in relation to the protection of data.
- Conducting risk assessments and analysis.
- Handling the results of periodic security evaluations and continuous monitoring.
- Directing information technology (IT) security purchasing and investment.
- Ensuring security concerns have been addressed in system implementation.
- Accepting risk from information systems on behalf of the organization.

MANAGEMENT REVIEWS POLICIES AND PROCEDURES

Performance Criteria: Standard §164.308(a)(8) Evaluation: "Perform a periodic technical and nontechnical evaluation, based initially upon the standards implemented under this rule and subsequently, in response to environmental or operational changes affecting the security of electronic protected health information that established the extent to which an entity's security policies and procedures meet the requirements of the subpart."

Performance Criteria: Standard §164.316(a) Policies and Procedures: "Implement reasonable and appropriate policies and procedures to comply with the standards, implementation specifications, or other requirements of this subpart, taking into account those factors specified in §164.316(b)(2)(i),(ii),(iii), and (iv) [the Security Standards: General Rules, Flexibility of Approach]."

Performance Criteria: Standard §164.316(b)(1) Documentation: "(i) Maintain the policies and procedures implemented to comply with this subpart in written (which may be electronic) form; and (ii) If an action, activity or assessment is required by this subpart to be documented, maintain a written (which may be electronic) record of the action, activity, or assessment. The documentation standard has the following required implementation specifications."

- §164.316(b)(2)(i) Time Limit: "Retain the documentation required by paragraph (b)(1) of this section for 6 years from the date of its creation or the date when it last was in effect, whichever is later."
- §164.316(b)(2)(ii) Availability: "Make documentation available to those persons responsible for implementing the procedures to which the documentation pertains."
- §164.316(b)(2)(iii) Updates: "Review documentation periodically, and update as needed, in response to environmental or operational changes affecting the security of the electronic protected health information."

Analysis of results from the HIPAA Security Reviews conducted by CMS in both 2008 and 2009 revealed deficiencies in documented policies. Specifically, CMS observed the following conditions:

- Policies and procedures were few and inadequate.
- Policies and procedures did not fully address the HIPAA Security Standards and implementation specifications.
- Documented procedures were inconsistent with personnel practices.
- Controls were implemented although undocumented in the procedures.
- Policies and procedures were not reviewed and updated timely.
- Processes for developing and reviewing procedures were unstructured and unorganized.
- Policy and procedures were created but not implemented properly or as documented.
- Members of the review panels were unfamiliar with the HIPAA Security Rule and its implications for policy and procedure development.

In response to these conditions, CMS offered guidance to strengthen policies, procedures, and documentation. Guidance is outlined in Table 5-1.

Management Reviews, Revises, and Completes Security Awareness and Training Courses and 'Should be Held Liable for Failure to Train the Workforce'

Performance Criteria: Standard §164.308(a)(5) Security Awareness and Training—"Implement a security awareness and training program for all members of the workforce (including management)."

During its HIPAA Compliance Reviews in 2008 and 2009, CMS identified similar issues regarding Security Awareness and Training and recommended the following solutions to increase compliance with the Security Rule.

- Formally document policies for the development, administration and monitoring of initial and annual security awareness training courses. Include the following requirements:
  - All newly hired employees complete initial security awareness training prior to gaining access to ePHI. This requirement should include employees, temporary workers, contractors and vendors (if not previously arranged through a Business Associate agreement).
  - Individuals with access to ePHI complete security awareness refresher training at least annually.

TABLE 5-1: Key Activity—Verify the Review of Policies and Procedures.

Action Steps	✓
Verify the development and formal documentation of a policy requiring management's periodic review of policies and procedures.	
Ensure policies include the following specifications:	
An outline of the maximum time frame between reviews	
A requirement of management to review policy and procedures when there is a significant change to systems or the environment. Significant changes include, but are not limited to, the following events.	
Introduction of new systems	
Significant upgrades to existing systems	
Retirement or disposal of systems	
Physical relocation of IT assets	
Introduction of new lines of business	
Reorganization of the entity's management or business structure	
Develop and formally document a procedure for management to conduct periodic reviews of all policies and procedures.	
Design this procedure to allow management to conduct reviews timely and compliant with the entities' documented policy for frequency of this type of review.	
Outline the following steps for management.	
Identify policies and procedures for which management is responsible for reviewing.	
Gather the most recent versions of these policies and procedures.	
Assess the currency of each documented policy and procedure against the organization's operational and regulatory environment.	
Implement updates to the policy or procedure as necessary.	
Document evidence of management review and approval.	
Disseminate the updated policy and procedure throughout the organization.	
Evaluate the process for disseminating and adopting updated policies and procedures to determine if employees are aware of updates.	
Communicate updates to organization-wide policies and procedures to all employees	
Include updates in refresher security awareness training	
If possible, deploy tools to centrally manage and distribute policies and procedures. (Ideally, tools allow individuals to register for automated notifications when management updates policies or procedures.)	

>   ▫ Management reviews and revises both the initial and refresher security awareness training courses at least annually to ensure currency with the organization's environment.
>   ▫ As new risks are identified through the risk assessment process, incorporate potential threats into the training program to further awareness.
> • Develop and formally document a procedure for initial and refresher security awareness training:
>   ▫ Coordinate this procedure with the account provisioning/management process.
>   ▫ Require verification that new users have completed initial security awareness training prior to granting them access to ePHI and require security awareness training on an annual basis thereafter.

TABLE 5-2: Key Activity—Verify Implementation of the Security Awareness and Training Program.

Key Activities	✓
Verify development and approval of the training strategy and plan.	
Verify results of the training needs assessment.	
Maintain appropriate awareness of training content, materials, and methods	
Verify implement of the training.	
Monitor and evaluate the training plan.	
Verify implementation of security reminders.	

- ▫ Design, document and put in place a process to monitor compliance using tools to support the process.
- Develop and formally document procedures to:
- ▫ Monitor course completion, and
- ▫ Escalate issues involving users who have not completed their annual security awareness training timely by applying predetermined sanctions to those who are not in compliance with this requirement. Sanctions may include:
  - – Notification of the user's direct report when initial deadlines pass without completion.
  - – Revocation of the user's access when final deadlines pass without completion.
- Use role-based training to ensure workforce members with remote access to ePHI recognize the enhanced risk of accessing and manipulating ePHI from a remote location.

Key activities for verifying implementation of the security awareness and training program are listed in Table 5-2.

MANAGEMENT APPROVES RISK ASSESSMENTS

Performance Criteria: Standard §164.308(a)(1)(ii)(A) Risk Analysis—"Conduct an accurate and thorough assessment of the potential risks and vulnerabilities to the confidentiality, integrity, and availability of electronic protected health information held by the covered entity."

Although the Security Rule requires covered entities to conduct risk assessments, the standard does not provide guidance on how (or how often) to perform assessments.[5] Based on the results of the HIPAA Security Compliance Reviews in 2008 and 2009, CMS recommended risk assessments results be approved by management, and the approver should not be the individual responsible for completing the risk assessment or an individual involved with the day-to-day operation of the assessed system. CMS released the following observations made in its 2009 reviews, noting that areas of noncompliance were identical to those observed in its 2008 reviews:

- Covered entities did not perform a risk assessment.
- Entities did not have a formalized, documented risk assessment process. Many entities had performed risk assessments, but did not have a policy requiring the creation or periodic update of these assessments.

TABLE 5-3: Key Activity—Require and Verify Risk Assessments.

Management Action Steps	✓
Verify that a formally documented policy requires completion of a periodic risk assessment covering all systems and applications storing, processing, or transmitting ePHI.	
Verify the policy includes a requirement for existing risk assessments to be reviewed at least annually to ensure risks previously identified had been remediated and that no new risks had surfaced due to changes in the environment.	
Verify the policy requires risk assessments be completed at least every three years or whenever there is a significant change in the environment including, but not limited to, the following events.	
Introduction of new systems;	
Significant upgrades to existing systems;	
Retirement or disposal of systems;	
Physical relocation of IT assets;	
Introduction of new lines of business; and,	
Reorganization of the entity's management or business structure.	
Verify that supporting procedures for conducting risk assessments have been developed and formally documented. (See Table 5-4.)	
Conduct the risk assessment.	
Verify management approval of the risk assessment results.	
The approver should not be the individual responsible for completing the risk assessment or involved with the day-to-day operation of the assessed system.	
Retain evidence of this approval, within the document itself if possible.	
Identify corrective action for weaknesses identified during the risk assessment process. Include steps to mitigate residual risks.	
Re-perform the risk assessment, following established policies and procedures, every three years or whenever there is a significant change in the environment. Although this re-performance should assess all areas of risk, include particular focus on areas in which corrective actions have been implemented since the previous risk assessment. Focus scrutiny on new or modified systems and facilities.	
Verify relevant documentation and its content relative to the specified criteria for an assessment of potential risks and vulnerabilities of ePHI.	

- Risk assessments were not current. They were performed more than three years earlier and were not reviewed and updated to reflect the changes in their environments.
- Not all potential areas of risk were addressed. Processes did not include all applicable areas or systems. Some organizations did not maintain an accurate inventory of systems which stored, processed and transmitted ePHI, or they did not properly identify the applicability of components of the organization (i.e., business uses). In some cases, risk assessments were performed without consideration of HIPAA standards.

A recommended course of action for exercising management oversight of the risk assessment process is outlined in Table 5-3, while Table 5-4 outlines high-level procedures for conducting a risk assessment.

TABLE 5-4: Key Activity—Develop Supporting Procedures for Conducting Risk Assessments.[6]

Procedures	✓
Identify the systems which store, process, or transmit ePHI.	
Identify components of the organization which handle ePHI and the physical location of IT assets containing ePHI and gain understanding of the business uses of ePHI.	
Develop procedures outlining the following steps:	
Identify the criticality of the system and its data.	
Identify threats to the system.	
Identify vulnerabilities on the system.	
Analyze existing controls and those planned for implementation.	
Identify the probability that vulnerabilities may be exploited.	
Identify the impact of a successful threat exercise.	
Assess the level of risk.	
Identify additional controls to mitigate identified risks.	
Document the results of the risk assessment.	

MANAGEMENT VERIFIES STAFF EXPERIENCE AND QUALIFICATIONS

Performance Criteria: Standard §164.308(a)(3) Workforce Security—"Implement policies and procedures to ensure that all members of its workforce have appropriate access to electronic protected health information, as provided under paragraph (a)(4) of this section, and to prevent those workforce members who do not have access under paragraph (a)(4) of this section from obtaining access to electronic protected health information."

Granting and modifying user access was one of the top security issues identified in the initial twenty audits of the OCR pilot program (November 2011 to December 2012) assessing the HIPAA privacy, security and breach notification performance of covered entities. Action steps for verifying criteria and procedures for hiring and assigning roles are presented in Table 5-5.

TABLE 5-5: Key Activity—Verify the Establishment of Criteria and Procedures for Hiring and Assigning Tasks.

Management Action Steps	✓
Verify staff members have the necessary knowledge, skills, and abilities to fulfill particular roles, e.g., positions involving access to and use of sensitive information.	
Review formal documentation and evaluate the content in relation to the specified criteria.	
Confirm documentation demonstrating management's verification of the required experience/qualifications of the staff (per policy).	
If the organization chose not to fully implement this specification, verify documentation of the rationale.	

MANAGEMENT AUTHORIZES USER ACCESS

Performance Criteria: Standard §164.312(c)(1) Integrity—"Implement policies and procedures to protect electronic protected health information from improper alteration or destruction."

Authentication/integrity was one of the top security issues identified in the initial twenty audits of the OCR pilot program assessing HIPAA privacy, security and breach notification performance. Management action steps for verifying procedures for authorizing user's access are presented in Table 5-6.

TABLE 5-6: Key Activity—Verify Procedures Addressing User Access Authorizations.

Management Action Steps	✓
Verify access control procedures are in place.	
Obtain and review policies and procedures and evaluate the content in relation to the specified criteria to determine whether formal procedures over access control exist.	
For a selection of new hires, verify user access authorization forms to determine that access is approved per management's requirements.	

MANAGEMENT VERIFIES THE QUALIFICATIONS OF THOSE WITH EMERGENCY ACCESS TO EPHI

Performance Criteria: Standard §164.312(a)(2)(ii) Access Control—"Establish (and implement as needed) procedures for obtaining necessary electronic protected health information during an emergency. Identify a method of supporting continuity of operations should the normal access procedures be disabled or unavailable due to system problems."

Specific action steps for verifying emergency access procedures are listed in Table 5-7.

TABLE 5-7: Key Activity—Verify the Establishment of an Emergency Access Procedure.

Management Action Steps	✓
Determine whether and how access to initiate the emergency access process is limited to appropriate personnel.	
Obtain and review a list of individuals with access to initiate the emergency access procedures.	
Obtain evidence indicating whether individuals have the qualifications and training over ePHI, per management's established policy or process.	

MANAGEMENT IDENTIFIES AUDIT TOOLS

Performance Criteria: Standard §164.312(b): Audit Controls—"Implement hardware, software, and/or procedural mechanisms that record and examine activity in information systems that contain or use electronic protected health information."

Management action steps for identifying audit tools are listed in Table 5-8.

TABLE 5- 8: Key Activity—Verify Selection of Tools for Auditing and System Activity Reviews.

Management Action Steps	✓
Verify that systems and applications have been evaluated to determine whether upgrades are necessary to implement audit capabilities.	
Obtain and review documentation of tools or applications identified by management to capture the appropriate audit information.	

MANAGEMENT RETAINS DETAILS OF SECURITY INCIDENTS

Performance Criteria: Standard §164.308(a)(6) Security Incident Procedures §164.308(a)(6)(ii)—"Identify and respond to suspected or known security incidents; mitigate, to the extent practicable, harmful effects of security incidents that are known to the covered entity; and document security incidents and their outcomes."

Incident response was one of the top security issues identified in the initial twenty audits of the OCR pilot program beginning in November 2011. Management action steps for developing and implementing procedures for security incident response and reporting are presented in Table 5-9.

TABLE 5-9: Key Activity—Verify Development and Implementation of Procedures to Respond to and Report Security Incidents.

Management Action Steps	✓
Verify that policies and procedures exist regarding identifying, documenting, and retaining a record of security incidents.	
Verify that policies and procedures are in place to ensure security incidents are identified and documented, and that evidence is retained.	
Verify that security incidents have been identified and documented and management retained detailed evidence of the incidents.	
Verify that the results of post-incident analysis are used to update and revise security policies and controls.	

MANAGEMENT VERIFIES DISPOSAL OF ePHI

Standard §164.310(d)(1): Device and Media Controls—§164.310(d)(2)(i) "Implement policies and procedures to address the final disposition of ePHI and/or the hardware or electronic media on which it is stored."

Media reuse and destruction was one of the top security issues identified in the initial twenty audits of the OCR pilot program. Action steps for verifying methods of disposal are presented in Table 5-10.

CONCLUSION

This chapter featured ten management oversight activities referenced in the HIPAA Security Rule, the HIPAA Audit Program Protocol, summary reports from HIPAA Compliance Reviews in 2008 and 2009 and security issues identified in the initial OCR audits which began November 2011. Many of the audit procedures in the HIPAA Pro-

TABLE 5-10: Key Activity—Verify Methods for Final Disposal of ePHI.

Management Action Steps	✓
Determine how the disposal of hardware, software, and ePHI data is managed.	
Review formal policies and procedures and evaluate the content relative to specified criteria regarding the disposal of hardware, software, and ePHI data.	
Sample evidence to determine whether the entity had oversight policies and procedures addressing how management verifies that disposal policies are carried out.	

gram Protocol are directed to management. The expectation is that management is knowledgeable and plays an active role in the information security program. Protection of assets is a management function and digital assets are no exception.

REFERENCES

1. U.S. Department of Health & Human Services. Office for Civil Rights. The security rule. Available at: www.hhs.gov/ocr/privacy/hipaa/administrative/securityrule/securityrulepdf.pdf.

2. U.S. Department of Health & Human Services. Office for Civil Rights. Audit program protocol. Available at: www.hhs.gov/ocr/privacy/hipaa/enforcement/audit/protocol.html.

3. Centers for Medicare & Medicaid Services. Office of E-Health Standards and Services. HIPAA compliance review analysis and summary of results. 2008. Available at: www.hhs.gov/ocr/privacy/hipaa/enforcement/cmscompliancerev08.pdf.

4. Centers for Medicare & Medicaid Services. Office of E-Health Standards and Services. 2009 HIPAA Compliance Review Analysis and Summary of Results. September 22, 2009. Available at: www.hhs.gov/ocr/privacy/hipaa/enforcement/cmscompliancerev09.pdf.

5. To help entities implement risk assessments, CMS provided additional guidance through paper six of the security series "Basics of Risk Analysis and Risk Management." Although this approach is not required, it defines steps to address the key tenets of an effective analysis of risk. Entities are expected to analyze their environment and assess potential risks and vulnerabilities which may affect the confidentiality, integrity and availability of ePHI. The risk assessment process lays the groundwork for entities to build their policies and procedures around addressing these risks.

6. Section 3 of NIST SP 800-30, "Risk Management Guide for Information Technology Systems" provides guidance on the steps to conduct an effective risk assessment. Additionally, "Basics of Risk Analysis and Risk Management," a part of CMS's security series, provides risk assessment guidance for covered entities to improve their level of compliance with the Security Rule. For guidance regarding the process of identifying criticality, NIST has developed SP 800-60, "Guide for Mapping Types of Information and Information Systems to Security Categories", which outlines steps to categorize the data on the system and information system itself, and Federal Information Processing Standards (FIPS) Publication (Pub) 199, "Standards for Security Categorization of Federal Information and Information Systems" which outlines steps to categorize the information system.

CHAPTER 6

Information Security Regulations

By Susan Gatehouse

Information security has become, bar none, one of the most formidable components of running a healthcare organization today. Hospitals, clinics, and medical practices are charged with heavily safeguarding fluid data, while still retaining immediate access rights for healthcare professionals and their patients.

Operating a public or private sector healthcare facility in the United States comes with mandatory data security measures. The measures are intended to protect a wide range of information and data from accidental loss, misuse, or intentional breach. While the regulations are far reaching, they are not customized to each sub-organization or individual operating structure. Healthcare enterprises should still individually assess their operating procedures and system mechanics for ways to safeguard their data beyond the scope of its mandatory compliance measures.

This chapter will provide a comparative overview of legislative acts, including the Health Insurance Portability and Accountability Act of 1996 (HIPAA), the Federal Information Security Management Act of 2002 (FISMA) and the Health Information Technology for Economic and Clinical Health Act of 2009 (HITECH), as well as private sector standards, such as the International Organization for Standardization (ISO 27000) and the Payment Card Industry Data Security Standard (PCI DSS).

Herein you will find a description of each of these entities thereby developing a cursory understanding of where security overlaps or gaps are present, as illustrated through a comparative table.

The advent of technology has introduced a wealth of opportunity for information management, along with its share of growing pains to the medical industry. Breaches and data loss account for billions of dollars in lost revenue and reputational harm. The federal government enacted legislation that mandates government agencies institute specific data-protective practices. Influential organizations in the private sector also developed data security initiatives based on their own bodies of study and expert-driven recommendations.

Even though these mandates are prescribed to by the majority of healthcare organizations' medical facilities, human fallacy, adept hackers, natural disasters, and technological malfunctions all contribute to the continued data compromises we hear about in the news each week.

LEGISLATIVE ACTS

HIPAA

HIPAA was the first national health privacy law to provide standards on how healthcare providers, employers, clearinghouses or insurance providers collect and share healthcare-related information. It grants individuals the right to their health records and supersedes state law unless the state law offers more stringent patient privacy protection. Under HIPAA, state laws remain intact surrounding reports of disease or injury, child abuse, population statistics (birth and death records), treatment of minors, and public health concerns.

There are five titles to HIPAA. The first allows individuals to maintain health insurance coverage when they change employers. The second portion of HIPAA, the one we will concentrate on here, has five sections: (1) Standards for Electronic Transactions, (2) Unique Identifiers Standards, (3) Security Rule, (4) Privacy Rule, and (5) Enforcement Rule.

Let's examine the crux of the Privacy and Security Rules. The Privacy Rule governs the collection, use, storage, disclosure and disposal of protected health information (PHI) and individually identifiable health information (IIHI). It is intended to safeguard healthcare-based transactions from fraud or misuse and governs entities such as health plan providers, healthcare clearinghouses, hospitals, clinics, and dental practices. The law is also applicable to these providers' business partners, their subcontractors and third-party vendors. Providers are responsible for ensuring their affiliates understand and comply with HIPAA regulations.

The Privacy Rule was designed to protect people's health records, healthcare, and payments for healthcare in regard to all past, present, and future diagnosis and subsequent care. Healthcare facilities are responsible for protecting this information in all forms, including electronic, written, and verbal.

All providers who fall under HIPAA's governance must inform their patients of their rights through a written Notice of Privacy Practices. Providers are also responsible for implementing data security measures to ensure that only designated personnel have access to the "minimum necessary information" to accomplish their objective surrounding diagnosis, treatment, patient-permitted disclosure, or billing activities. Covered entities must designate a privacy official to oversee compliance, and the covered entity must provide its workforce with the necessary training to ensure it complies with data security protocols. Additionally, the covered entities must enforce all sanctions and establish a mechanism to field and respond to complaints. Figure 6-1 provides examples of such parameters.

The Security Rule effectively "enhances" the Privacy Rule. It offers specific safeguards surrounding electronic protected health information (ePHI) in three data spaces: administrative, physical, and technical.

The U.S. Department of Health & Human Services (HHS) Office for Civil Rights is responsible for enforcement of both the Privacy and Security Rule.

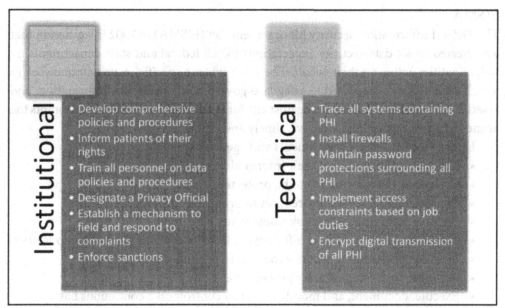

Institutional
- Develop comprehensive policies and procedures
- Inform patients of their rights
- Train all personnel on data policies and procedures
- Designate a Privacy Official
- Establish a mechanism to field and respond to complaints
- Enforce sanctions

Technical
- Trace all systems containing PHI
- Install firewalls
- Maintain password protections surrounding all PHI
- Implement access constraints based on job duties
- Encrypt digital transmission of all PHI

FIGURE 6-1: Sample Parameters for Both the Institutional and Technical Sides of Business.

45 CFR Parts 160 and 164

Modifications to the HIPAA Privacy, Security, Enforcement, and Breach Notification Rules under the Health Information Technology for Economic and Clinical Health Act and the Genetic Information Nondiscrimination Act; Other Modifications to the HIPAA Rules

ACTION: Final rule.

SUMMARY: The Department of Health & Human Services (HHS or "the Department") is issuing this final rule to: Modify the Health Insurance Portability and Accountability Act (HIPAA) Privacy, Security, and Enforcement Rules to implement statutory amendments under the Health Information Technology for Economic and Clinical Health Act ("the HITECH Act" or "the Act") to strengthen the privacy and security protection for individuals' health information; modify the rule for Breach Notification for Unsecured Protected Health Information (Breach Notification Rule) under the HITECH Act to address public comment received on the interim final rule; modify the HIPAA Privacy Rule to strengthen the privacy protections for genetic information by implementing section 105 of Title I of the Genetic Information Nondiscrimination Act of 2008 (GINA); and make certain other modifications to the HIPAA Privacy, Security, Breach Notification, and Enforcement Rules (the HIPAA Rules) to improve their workability and effectiveness and to increase flexibility for and decrease burden on the regulated entities.

DATES: This final rule is effective on March 26, 2013.

FISMA

The Federal Information Security Management Act (FISMA) of 2002 is legislation that was created to set data security expectations for all federal and state departments, as well as entities acting on their behalf. The act provides a specific security framework in which each agency is expected to safeguard government operations, information, and assets it creates, stores or accesses against any form of data breach or loss. It prompts the agencies to do so using cost-effective, timely and efficient means.

Under FISMA, federal departments and agencies are required to:

- Maintain an inventory of their information systems.
- Categorize the information to be protected.
- Implement policies and procedures to bring risk to an acceptable level.
- Perform recurring system risk assessments.
- Assess, evaluate, and refine information security controls on a continuous basis.
- Provide data handling security training to personnel and contractors.
- Establish business continuity procedures.
- Execute, document, and monitor security controls on a continuous basis.
- Report information security status annually.

HITECH

After organizations, agencies, and providers got a taste of HIPAA, they uncovered some inherent flaws in its policies—mainly that many of its regulations were ineffective and unenforceable. The Health Information Technology for Economic and Clinical Health (HITECH) Act of 2009 was designed in response to those concerns. We frequently see the two terms together in the compliance arena, often referred to as "HIPAA-HITECH."

The introduction of HITECH was met with strict enforcement, including hefty fines for those who did not adhere to its regulations. In fact, HITECH provides that state attorneys general are responsible for enforcing HIPAA laws and incentivizes its enforcement by making them eligible to retain the fees from fines that are levied.

The additions HITECH made to HIPAA's base regulations include a health data breach notification clause that requires healthcare providers to notify both patients *and* local authorities any time there is a potential data breach. HITECH introduced a training program for state attorneys general surrounding how to enforce HIPAA laws and collect and retain fines from violators. It also introduced a staggering 6,000 percent fine increase from HIPAA's initial fine structure, which now ranges between $25,000 and $1.5 million. Additionally, if a data breach reveals PHI of more than 500 individuals, the offending entity is required to notify the news media.

All of these changes resulted in strong incentives for businesses to encrypt their information for both data transmission and storage. Encryption ideally renders PHI unusable, unreadable, or undecipherable to unauthorized individuals and is designed to safeguard information that is accidentally or maliciously intercepted.

Strong data encryption practices allow healthcare providers, clearinghouses, and related covered entities and business associates to head off many potential full breach scenarios and can help these enterprises meet a host of cross-regulations and standards simultaneously.

Section 13402(e)(3) of the HITECH Act's breach notification interim final rule, which became effective on September 23, 2009, requires covered entities to provide notification of breaches of unsecured protected health information to both the affected patients and to the HHS. Smaller breaches must be annually reported to HHS, and business associates must notify the affected covered entity of breaches. Breaches that affected 500 or more individuals within one jurisdiction or state have two additional requirements. The breach must be reported to:

- HHS within 60 days rather than annually, and covered entities must provide this notification via the online form on the Office for Civil Rights (OCR) website.
- The news media by sending a press release to major media outlets without unreasonable delay and no later than 60 calendar days from discovery.

The HHS rule also includes guidance on how to determine when information is "unsecured," which means that the information is unreadable or indecipherable to unauthorized individuals. This implies encryption, which is covered in greater detail in Chapter 11.

There are also three exceptions as to when unauthorized access is not considered a breach. They are:

1. Any unintentional acquisition, access or use of PHI by a workforce member or person acting under the authority of a covered entity (CE) or business sssociate (BA) if such acquisition, access or use was made in good faith and within the scope of authority and does not result in further use or disclosure in a manner not permitted under the Privacy Rule.

2. Any inadvertent disclosure by a person who is authorized to access PHI as a CE or BA to another person authorized to access PHI as the same CE or BA, or organized healthcare arrangement in which the CE participates, and the information received as a result of such disclosure is not further used or disclosed in a manner not permitted under the Privacy Rule.

3. A disclosure of PHI where a CE or BA has a good faith belief that an unauthorized person to whom the disclosure was made would not reasonably have been able to retain such information.

There is also a stipulation that allows covered entities to determine the probability that PHI has been compromised. If it is determined through a risk assessment that there is no probability of access, then a breach notification may not be required.

Although encryption of electronic PHI (ePHI) is still an addressable implementation specification and not required within the HIPAA Security Rule, the inclusion of this "risk threshold" or "safe harbor" within the breach notification rule is driving encryption for ePHI in transit and at rest to become the prevailing practice among healthcare organizations.

PRIVATE SECTOR STANDARDS

ISO 27000

The International Organization for Standardization (ISO) 27000, published in 2005, models standards to help enterprises define, establish, institute, operate, monitor, maintain, and remediate Information Security Management Systems (ISMS). There are more than 1,000 certifications available within ISO worldwide, covering all organization types.

The ISO 27000 series identifies prerequisites for ISMSs to sustain a reasonable and proportionate level of system and procedural protections against data loss or breach. ISO standards are meant to instill operational confidence across businesses worldwide as the gold standard of data security, encompassing both their physical and electronic security practices, and procedures.

ISO comes from a non-governmental organization, and adherence by a business to ISO standards is strictly voluntary; ISO does not regulate, legislate or enforce implementation. Adherences to ISO standards can position businesses to become more technically sound, in terms of data protection, and lend a note of trustworthiness and value to their bottom line.

PCI DSS

Very few businesses operate strictly by cash or check payments. The vast shift to credit card, debit, prepaid, automated teller machine (ATM) or point-of-sale (POS) cards prompted the Payment Card Industry (PCI) Data Security Standard (DSS) to protect cardholders from fraud.

PCI DSS defines specific controls around accepting, processing and storing credit cardholder information in order to protect cardholders from internal or external exploits.

Figure 6-2 displays the six control objectives that break into specific requirements surrounding PCI DSS.

COMMON TECHNICAL SECURITY FEATURES

Legislative acts and private sector standards contain many of the same technical features. Each has principles and requirements as defined in prior chapters. For this section, we will review the overlaps and differences for technical security features.

Many healthcare industry regulations and standards carry requirements that either overlap or contradict one another. Overlapping standards can lead to wasted resources on redundant efforts, and contradicting regulations can leave administrators to disentangle conflicting directives while their security protocols remain vulnerable or exposed.

Because government and private industry modify standards and regulations on a continual basis, it becomes difficult for organizations such as those in healthcare, whose primary focus is not data security, to understand and comply with the ever-changing bodies of regulations that govern its data use practices. The overabundance of ever-changing responsibilities healthcare organizations face often serves to impede their progress, as well as their ultimate goals of compliance and information protection.

Compliance does not mean that an information system is entirely secure, but adequate protections and care often help a business meet its compliance objectives by default. This is certainly the prescription for future security models: implement strong, risk analysis focused security controls based on individual operating environs and done correctly, it will not only meet necessary compliance standards but account for any vulnerabilities that a strict compliance-based program could leave exposed.

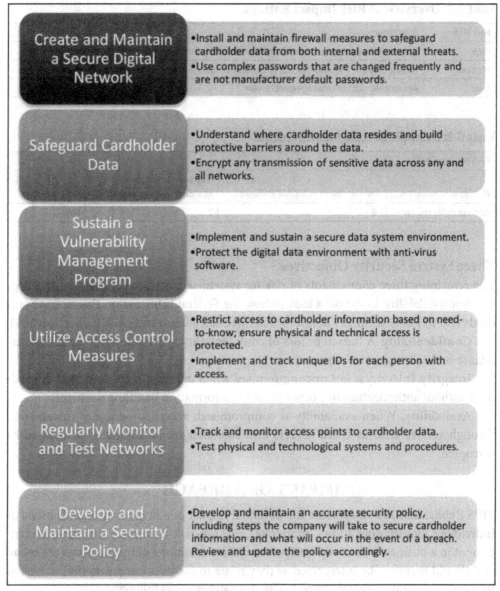

FIGURE 6-2: General Breakdown of PCI DSS Requirements.

For our discussion, the most common approach to security can be categorized into four groupings: risk categorization, confidentiality, integrity and availability.

The standard industry formula for categorizing risk is

$$\textbf{IMPACT x PROBABILITY = RISK}$$

As you can see in the risk equation, risk is calculated by the impact a data breach would have on a business multiplied by the probability that the risk would come to fruition. Risk measurement is an auditable control parameter, as depicted in Table 6-1 and Table 6-2. See also Appendix A.

TABLE 6-1: Overview of Risk Impact Ratings.

Risk Rating	Risk Impact
High	Undesirable and requires immediate attention; controls to be implemented immediately.
Medium	Undesirable and requires corrective action, but some management discretion is allowed.
Low	Acceptable, but with management review.

TABLE 6-2: Example of Risk Measurement.

Risk Measurement			
IT control parameters	Sample size of auditable instances	Number of instances non-conformity is observed	Compliant rate
Access rights review	10	2	80%

Three System Security Objectives

The remaining three components of risk for system security are confidentiality, integrity, and availability. Let's take a look at how the Federal Information Processing Standards (FIPS) Publication 199 defines these three categories per 44 U.S.C., Section 3542:

Confidentiality. A breach or loss of confidentiality is defined as the unauthorized release or disclosure of information.

Integrity. Integrity is lost or compromised when information is destroyed or modified without authorization or proper sensitive information handling protocols.

Availability. When availability is compromised, access to or use of information through venues such as client servers and customer-facing interfaces is delayed or disrupted.

IMPACT OF A BREACH

FIPS Publication 199 categorizes the potential impact of a breach on organizations or individuals by assigning a low-, moderate-, or high-risk rating to each relevant component in a business's observed risk posture. The definitions of these ratings are broad and should therefore be interpreted as they relate to the business enterprise, as well as in regard to overall national interest. The risk ratings are as follows:

Low-Risk Rating

An assigned low-risk rating means the loss of confidentiality, integrity or availability would have a minor or limited adverse effect on an organization's operations, assets, stakeholders and on individuals whose information it carries.

A limited adverse effect means that a breach would produce minor damage or financial loss to the organization.

Moderate-Risk Rating

A moderate-risk rating is assigned when the loss of any of the three key components of system security (confidentiality, integrity or availability) is projected to have a serious adverse effect on a business's operations, assets or on individuals or businesses whose information it handles. This is measured by the potential for significant damage, financial loss or organizational compromise short of life-threatening injuries or death.

High-Risk Rating

A risk is rated high when the confidentiality, integrity or availability of a business's physical or information assets could reasonably be expected to have a severe or catastrophic adverse effect. This includes major damage to organizational assets, finances, or catastrophic harm to individuals including life-threatening conditions or death.

High-risk ratings are marked critical and need to be adequately addressed immediately to protect lives, as well as the business's integrity, reputation, and posture.

SECURITY CATEGORIZATION APPLIED TO INFORMATION SYSTEMS

When determining the Security Category (SC), every information type that is resident on the information system must be taken into account. The highest applicable value (i.e., high water mark) is assigned to the information system, as compared to the three security objectives.

An information type's SC can be tied to both user and system information and is applicable to any sensitive information, regardless of form or expression (i.e., verbal, physical or electronic).

A security category is established by measuring the potential impact each security objective may have in relation to each particular information type. The most common format used to express an information system's SC where acceptable values for potential impact are low, moderate, or high is:

$$SC \text{ } information \text{ } system =$$
$$\{(\textbf{confidentiality}, impact), (\textbf{integrity}, impact), (\textbf{availability}, impact)\}$$

Free Security Tool

This enterprise-level tool can be downloaded at no cost to assist with managing and tracking security at all levels. Business models can be used to maintain system security and are available for download. Comparatively, the available free model makes from-scratch systems seem comparatively expensive and timely. Consider first utilizing existing documents and procedures surrounding industry best practices and then consider supplementing additional areas with customized solutions: http://demo.openfisma. org/auth/login.

CHAPTER 7

Security Policy Development

By Judi Hofman, CAP, CHS, CHSS, and
Michele T. Kruse, MBA, RHIA, CHPS

No other documentation shows an organization's commitment to information security like its information security policies and procedures. Policy development is critical to ensure consistency and order in the organization. Without policies, staff would rely on their own, possibly limited, knowledge and experiences, resulting in a free-for-all with no one knowing what the others were doing. This is most apparent in the area of information security. Not only is there a lack of understanding by most people in the area of technology, but also about the risk to the organization and the ever-changing regulations surrounding healthcare technology. To minimize risk, it is imperative that policies and procedures are developed and staff is well trained in their meaning and objectives.

Policies define the rules specific to a practice or a technology. They state required actions expected and emphasize desired results. These rules should be based upon best practice, industry standards and organizational requirements to reduce risks. For instance, an Internet acceptable use policy defines the expectation for employee use of the Internet on a facility computer. A backup and storage policy defines the systems, frequency, and storage requirements. Adherence to the rules can usually be measured and/or verified.

Policies help in the defense of an organization against possible lawsuits and also document the standards or requirements necessary for regulatory or accrediting agency mandates. They arose as supporting documentation to reflect the degree of compliance the organization takes toward their business practices. Therefore, it is critical that employees are trained on applicable policies and routinely directed to those policies. This is particularly evident with acceptable use policies, which direct behavior. It is also important to define disciplinary actions associated with failure to comply, especially with these types of policies.

Policies also support the culture of the organization. Policies should be linked to the organization's mission, vision and values. They should be a direct by-product of the Information Security Plan and its objectives as they define the controls needed to implement the plan. Consideration should also be given to the effect of policies on the organization's current infrastructure and any legacy systems. If an exception must be made because of the inability of a legacy system to adhere to the policy, it should be noted.

Policy Content

Security policies contain the standard policy language for the organization and should be consistently communicated with other policies. Policies must be concise and direct, leaving little room for interpretation. They should be written at a sixth- to eighth-grade reading level.[1] However, if the policy is technical in nature and intended for a technical audience such as network engineers, the language should be in the terminology that is expected.

Policies should define the information or resources to be protected, and balance should be struck between that protection and the impact on operations, especially in clinical areas. Policies should not be overly restrictive or present difficulty in compliance. Otherwise staff will either ignore the policy or develop workarounds.

Policies should define who should comply, and contain the following elements:

Regulatory definition. This may be shown to note in the header information the regulation, accrediting standard, or other external mandate driving the policy. This is helpful in mapping the policy for auditing purposes, as well as documenting to the reader that this is a required policy for compliance.

Unfamiliar definitions. There are many definitions in the area of information security with which most staff, especially those in clinical areas, are unfamiliar. Defining information security terms assures everyone is speaking the same language. For instance, an encryption policy might define the terms *proprietary encryption*, *symmetric cryptosystem*, and *asymmetric cryptosystem*. Policies regarding protection of data may include definitions of terms such as *protected health information (PHI)*, *personally identifiable information (PII)*, *confidential information*, and *sensitive information*.

Guidelines. Those practices which are suggested but not mandatory are considered guidelines and are often found in policies and procedures. An acceptable use e-mail policy may include guidelines for format and appropriate language/tone. An acceptable use mobile device policy may include how to care for the device.

Organizational position or expectations. This is a documented position that may not be driven by regulatory or other external mandates but is the position or stance taken by the organization. For instance, the Internet may be only used for business purposes; or attachments may not be downloaded from personal e-mail accounts.

Policy and Procedure Management

Policies and procedures are an organization's attempt to set technical standards and define expectations of the workforce in order to maintain consistency (quality) and a unified approach for security.[2] However, there is an implicit assumption that simply putting these policies and procedures in place will cause good things to happen.[2] As Peter G.W. Keen pointed out in *The Process Edge* (1997), the "process paradox" in an organization can decline even as processes improve. Recommendations from Gartner Inc., is that organizations focus on two principles:[2]

1. Improve service and business performance.
2. Put in place just enough processes.

Again, if no foundational policies are provided or developed by management, employees will create their own processes with no support.

Focus on Service and Business Performance Improvement

Remember the end goal is not to only have a document to refer to, but to be able to gauge the meaning of "successful" tangible outcomes. These outcomes will increase the quality, efficiency and effectiveness of the services being delivered to drive business performance improvement.[2] For example, the policy may set the following objective: "Create new user accounts prior to an employee's first day on the job by obtaining new hire employee lists from Human Resources." This is a good business practice and it improves security. If an employee has been set up to access the network immediately after completing the new hire orientation, it is unnecessary for them to "share" another employee's user ID and password while waiting for the provisioning team to set up their access.

Put in Place Just Enough Process

Organizations can overburden themselves with policies and procedures that do not add value to the end users. Process-mature and process-capable organizations have just enough control and management to ensure compliance.[2] Organizations that have 5,000 policies and procedures in their document center leave themselves open to the risk that not all workforce members will know them or abide by them.

Policies and Procedures

Policies are rules that govern the activities of processes in an organization are a statement of expectations and are the rules of engagement. Procedures, on the other hand, represent an implementation of processes and should evolve over time as new tools emerge, new processes are designed, and the risks associated with an area change in response to internal or external environmental changes. Policies and procedures should exhume openness and transparency of the organization and are intended to be a means to an end.[2] Even if regulatory standards are addressable, prevailing practice across the industry must be considered.

Policy foundation and structure is essential to the development of an effective security program. Organizations do not have to reinvent the wheel when policies and procedures are created. Choose a foundational standard, such as NIST or ISO, and map the risk gaps identified from the standard to build the policy base. This will ensure that the security policy architecture is sound and well supported.

THE FOUR 'Cs'

Base the policies and procedures on the four 'Cs'.

Complete

The policy and procedures must be complete but with minimum verbiage to get across to the end user the actions required of them. Policies and procedures must also be factual and accurate. They must be periodically checked against the foundational standard and/or regulations they refer to. Clear roles and responsibility of management to the policy must be documented and communicated. Policies and procedures must have affective control processes in place that allow the controls to be tested in an audit with documented evidence.

Compliant

Document owners should be the policy and procedure content experts and must be readily available to interpret and resolve problems or answer questions of their policy or process.

The policies and procedures must meet the regulatory obligation they reference, again, with measures and documental evidence. This is where plagiarism is acceptable—quote regulations directly. For example, when referring to the HIPAA Privacy and Security Rule, great care must be taken in meeting the requirements in policy language.

§ 164.316 Policies and procedures and documentation requirements.

A covered entity must, in accordance with §164.306:

(a) <u>Standard: Policies and procedures.</u> Implement reasonable and appropriate policies and procedures to comply with the standards, implementation specifications, or other requirements of this subpart, taking into account those factors specified in §164.306(b)(2)(i), (ii), (iii), and (iv). This standard is not to be construed to permit or excuse an action that violates any other standard, implementation specification, or other requirements of this subpart. A covered entity may change its policies and procedures at any time, provided that the changes are documented and are implemented in accordance with this subpart.

(b)(1) <u>Standard: Documentation.</u>

(i) Maintain the policies and procedures implemented to comply with this subpart in written (which may be electronic) form; and

(ii) If an action, activity or assessment is required by this subpart to be documented, maintain a written (which may be electronic) record of the action, activity, or assessment.

(2) <u>Implementation specifications:</u>

(i) <u>Time limit (Required).</u> Retain the documentation required by paragraph (b)(1) of this section for 6 years from the date of its creation or the date when it last was in effect, whichever is later.

(ii) <u>Availability (Required).</u> Make documentation available to those persons responsible for implementing the procedures to which the documentation pertains.

(iii) <u>Updates (Required).</u> Review documentation periodically, and update as needed, in response to environmental or operational changes affecting the security of the electronic protected health information.

The authority to enforce the policy must also be clear. Support for policies should be evident from the top down. Management must actively be referring to policies and procedures relevant to their workforce. If referred to throughout the workday, the culture of policy and procedural acceptance is established. An organization cannot fully mitigate a risk with policies. Policy judgment might have to be made, again with support of the document owner or manager of the division.

Current

Conduct robust review and assessments to assure that policies and procedures are current and working. Do not include names or dates that can become outdated. The policy owners must identify affected workforce members and involve them in creating new policies or revision to existing policies.

Within the HIPAA Audit Program Protocol, which used by the OCR by its auditors, is a common "Audit Procedure" that pertains to any standards, policies, procedures, plans, or other forms of documentation:

> Determine if the covered entity's formal or informal policy and procedures have been updated, reviewed, and approved on a periodic basis.

Policies should be specific, measurable controls that have evidence-based documentation against their foundational risk gap analysis. The policy must mitigate or minimize the gap identified.

Current policies and procedure owners must support the development and training of the workforce members as appropriate. This includes identified expert departmental or corporate staff to which the workforce can turn for guidance in implementing the policy or procedure.

Policies and procedures are living documents that must be monitored and updated on a regular basis. How often a procedure or policy is renewed can generally depend on the regulation that the organization is mitigating.

Best practice does not support a policy writing party on the same day that the Office of Inspector General (OIG), Office for Civil Rights (OCR), or The Joint Commission arrive at a facility. This is a very risky way to manage policies. Further best practices are to only make electronic policies or procedures accessible in a pdf format to avoid "tweaking" of the document and to maintain clear version control. During an agency investigation, the burden of proof is up to the organization to provide the metadata to determine if the policy submitted to them was actually the one in place when the incident occurred.

An evaluation (technical or nontechnical review) of existing security controls may indicate a deficiency or need to revise or update policies and procedures.

Consistent

Policies and procedures must represent a consistent, logical framework for organizational action. The organization must support the policy statements and implement the procedures in a fair and equitable manner across the enterprise.

Procedures should be tied to a policy or policy statements. This explicit relationship between policies and procedures will help the organization tie the two to its strategic goals and objectives, as well as to its mission, vision, and values.

Consistency between the reported practice against the procedure or policy needs to be monitored. Evidence of practice monitoring to determine whether the practice is being followed as outlined in policy can help support practices when the organization is under regulatory investigation or credentialing scrutiny. Map policies and procedures against federal law and state law.

CONCLUSION

There are many fundamental standards by which organizations can base their policies and procedures. Do not let the framework overburden the organization with excessive policies and processes. This could discourage compliance by the end users or set out undue risk to the organization. Keep in mind the means to the end when writing policies and procedures. When referring to a specific security framework, use agency recommendations, such as the HIPAA Security Rule Audit Program Protocol and the specific guidance pertaining to policies.

Many templates and tools are available to help document policies and procedures. If using an official document retention product, confirm the functionality to archive and control versioning. Policy statements must support process standards. Consistent format and language processes for the development is critical. Combining policies and procedures in a predefined mapping system will help to ensure that end users have consistent access to documents needed to complete their work.

REFERENCES

1. Campbell NJ. *Writing Effective Policies and Procedures: A Step By Step Guide for Clear Communication*. New York: AMACOM;1998, 95
2. Mingay S, Bittinger S. Don't Just Implement CMMI and ITIL: Improve Services, Research Note G00136578. Stamford: Gartner, Inc., December 2005.

CHAPTER 8

The Concept of Security Controls

By Kim E. Sassaman, CISSP

Implementation of information technology security controls is how the Security Program is put into operation; these are the components that ensure policies are being enacted and enforced. The controls are also components of the framework that challenge threat attempts to exploit technologies or people. These controls are the front-line mechanisms that protect information assets, alert security teams, and provide assurance.

What is a security control? A control is any administrative, management, technical or legal method that is used to manage risk. Controls are safeguards or countermeasures. Controls can include practices, policies, procedures, programs, techniques, technologies, guidelines, and even organizational structures.

Controls are implemented based on the organization's risk methodology. By going through a risk assessment, the risk analyst will identify what control types should be implemented. For some organizations, regulations such as HIPAA or even contractual requirements will define what baseline controls should be implemented.

Operational controls are domain-specific and are utilized to implement the processes of the security program. The control definitions as used at Presbyterian Healthcare Services are as follows:

Organizational
- Individuals assigned to fulfill functional roles with specific duties and responsibilities.
- Committees and forums that serve as platforms for discussion and publicizing of information security issues.

Physical
- Fences and walls that create physical security perimeters.
- Doors and gates that control physical access to the security perimeter.

Technical
- Hardware devices such as firewalls, intrusion detection systems (IDS) and intrusion prevention systems (IPS) or IDS/IPS, web application firewalls, anti-malware systems.
- Software products.

Procedural
- Run books, standard operating procedures, checklists, punch lists, guidelines in place, hardening scripts.

Governance
- Information security tasking reports.
- Metric reports.

Example of operational controls: a role (organizational) uses a device (technical) following a standard operating procedure (procedural) to complete a task (duty) on a schedule (governance). Or a security engineer uses a SIM following the run book to create a list of active threats that appears every morning at 8:00.

According to the Government Accountability Office (GAO), "The control environment sets the tone of an organization, influencing the control consciousness of its people. It is the foundation for all other components of internal control, providing discipline and structure. Control environment factors include the integrity, ethical values, and competence of the entity's people; management's philosophy and operating style; and the way management assigns authority and organizes and develops its people."[1]

The following are common control types:

Organizational controls. These are the functional roles, or positions, that exist. For example, a security engineer would be considered an organizational control. These controls tend to be actors of other control types and execute against policy.

Physical controls. These controls include doors, gates, badges, card readers, various physical access control components or any physical object that is implemented to protect information or the assets that contain information.

Technical controls. These are the controls that most IT departments are most familiar with, as these are deployed technologies such as firewalls, intrusion detection systems, etc. These technologies enforce policies and provide for alerting and monitoring to provide assurance that risk is being managed.

Procedural controls. Standard operating procedures are another format for control. They ensure consistency and predictability, such as providing a consistent manner for system access via a user access management process.

Governance controls. These are the committees that directly oversee or are reported to regarding the execution of the various processes and policies that the organization has implemented. They can provide direction, funding, or visibility for issues that arise and play a crucial role in the success of your security program.

Security controls are needed in all aspects of life. An example of a physical security control that most individuals use on a daily basis is the lock on your house or car. These locks ensure that only the person authorized (owner) has access to their house or car if they have the correct key in their possession. A common weakness with this physical control is that the lock can be penetrated by a wily lock pick, or your keys can be presented by another owner, but the general concept is this: he who has the key has access. Imagine your house or car without a lock. What would prevent people from helping themselves to your belongings? This is important to keep in mind when you think of your security program and the various controls that you need to deploy. It is critical to not let yourself feel overwhelmed with the number of controls needed; instead, take the risk approach previously discussed.

When deciding which controls to deploy or not to deploy, the decision should first be documented as part of a risk analysis or assessment. Perhaps the organization wants to embrace social media. Once you realize that there are secure and practical ways to enable the organization, you put the effort through a risk assessment, which identifies what data types will be exposed, what controls are currently in place to manage risk and then identify, within a risk treatment plan, what controls need to be deployed to reduce risk to an acceptable level. This needs to be thoroughly vetted and documented to ensure that if someone asks why you didn't do x or implement y, you have defensibility. Perhaps the business did not want to spend thousands of dollars on the solution you proposed because they believed the mitigating controls (other controls that already reduce risk) were adequate. In that scenario, swallow your pride and record the decision. Having a governance team sign off on the risk acceptance can at times lead to further discussion or a second evaluation of the risk.

Control types as previously listed need to be tied to control objectives. Control objectives are very specific implementations of a control type. For example, ISO 27002 specifically provides guidance on how to implement access control. Without defining the control objective and meeting a minimum guideline, we could deploy generic user names and simple passwords, but if our policies stipulate these requirements, then our control objective should be specific to that policy. For instance, your policy might state that you will use passwords that are eight characters long, upper case, numbers and symbols. Your control objective for passwords would ensure that passwords are implemented to a minimum baseline that your policy stipulates. Control objectives are also leveraged by auditors when auditing your controls. If you have not defined your control objectives, then they will be more than happy to provide you with their opinion of the control objective. In general, the control objective is a statement of the desired result or purpose to be achieved by implementing the control.

So what controls should you implement? Well, considering we are in healthcare, your control objectives should map directly to the HIPAA Security Rule. The following is a list of the safeguards (controls) that you need to address:

Administrative Safeguards
- Security Management Process (§ 164.308(a)(1))
- Assigned Security Responsibility (§ 164.308(a)(2))
- Workforce Security (§ 164.308(a)(3))
- Information Access Management (§ 164.308(a)(4))
- Security Awareness and Training (§ 164.308(a)(5))
- Security Incident Procedures (§ 164.308(a)(6))
- Contingency Plan (§ 164.308(a)(7))

- Evaluation (§ 164.308(a)(8))
- Business Associate Contracts and Other Arrangements (§ 164.308(b)(1)).

Physical Safeguards

- Facility Access Controls (§ 164.310(a)(1))
- Workstation Use (§ 164.310(b))
- Workstation Security (§ 164.310(c))
- Device and Media Controls (§ 164.310(d)(1))

Technical Safeguards

- Access Control (§ 164.312(a)(1))
- Audit Controls (§ 164.312(b))
- Integrity (§ 164.312(c)(1))
- Person or Entity Authentication (§ 164.312(d))
- Transmission Security (§ 164.312(e)(1))

If you are looking for a security framework similar to ISO 27002, which provides guidance for implementing various controls, we would recommend reviewing NIST 800-66, "An Introductory Resource Guide for Implementing the Health Insurance Portability and Accountability Act (HIPAA) Secure Rule".[2] In the following chapters, we will cover the various control types that need to be implemented in healthcare to ensure a HIPAA-compliant environment. When choosing to implement controls, one should always be aware of their obligation to legal and regulatory requirements. For instance, you find out that the HIPAA Security Rule states that you should address encryption. If you conduct your risk assessment and the organization decides against it, you should also make them aware that the HITECH Act provides a "safe harbor" provision, exempting organizations from reporting data breaches if encryption is implemented and it meets federal standards—FIPS 140-2. Furthermore, you can also share with them the penalties assessed on other organizations for failure to implement prevailing practices. Documenting why controls are chosen and implemented will be the key.

REFERENCES

1. United States Government Accountability Office. Accounting and Information Management Division. Federal information system controls audit manual. Vol. 1: Financial statement audits. Available at: www.gao.gov/special.pubs/ai12.19.6.pdf.

2. Scholl M, Stine K, Hash J, Bowen P, Johnson A, Smith CD, Steinberg DI. An introductory resource guide for implementing the Health Insurance Portability and Accountability Act (HIPAA) Security Rule. NIST Special Publication 800-66 Revision 1. National Institute of Standards and Technology. October 2008. Available at: http://csrc.nist.gov/publications/nistpubs/800-66-Rev1/SP-800-66-Revision1.pdf.

CHAPTER 9

Access Control

By Brian Evans, CISSP, CISM, CISA, CGEIT

Healthcare organizations have faced the challenge of managing user access for decades now. Information technology departments are often unable to handle the manual processes, complex tasks and excessive administrative overhead needed to effectively manage user identities. In addition, regulatory requirements have added increased external scrutiny on access management processes. These standards and requirements coupled with increased business needs have led many healthcare organizations to grant user access to information resources not actually needed rather than to determine what specific rights are minimally required.

According to the National Institute of Standards and Technology (NIST), "Access control is concerned with determining the allowed activities of legitimate users, mediating every attempt by a user to access a resource in the system."[1] Since healthcare systems and applications contain confidential information, the goal of access control is to allow access by legitimate users and devices and disallow access to all others. Legitimate or authorized users may be employees, physicians, vendors, contractors, patients or visitors. Legitimate or authorized devices are those whose placement on the network is approved in accordance with organizational policy. Access should be authorized and provided only to those users whose identity is established, and their activities should be limited to the minimum required for business purposes.

Access control has two different dimensions that are sometimes in conflict with one another. While the primary objective for applying access control is restricting access to information, usability is an equally important feature. In most industries, the default rule is to deny access when in doubt. For healthcare, the rule is typically to allow access when in doubt. Protecting patient privacy is important, but the most important goal is patient care delivery and safety, which is contingent on users having access to information. Restricting access or providing the wrong access leads users to find work-arounds, such as password sharing in obtaining the information they need to get their jobs done. Ultimately, access control is a balance between confidentiality and availability. This is what makes access control in healthcare so challenging.

ACCESS CONTROL POLICY

An access control policy is necessary because it is generally impossible to address a challenge or accomplish a complex task without a document providing direction for doing so. An access control policy serves as that document and ensures the proper principles are applied. An access control policy reduces the risk of a data breach or security incident by providing direction to the workforce in supporting the confidentiality, integrity and availability of data. It also provides legal protection by specifying to users exactly how access to data should be managed.

An access control policy can be required by third-party vendors or business associates as part of their due diligence process if confidential data or network connectivity is involved. An access control policy also indicates senior management's commitment to maintaining the confidentiality, integrity and availability of data, which allows the workforce to do a more effective job of securing information assets.

Lastly, one of the most common reasons why healthcare organizations create an access control policy is to meet regulatory requirements and standards. The Payment Card Industry Data Security Standard (PCI DSS) and HIPAA require, in some form, a documented access control policy.

The third standard in the HIPAA Security Rule's Administrative Safeguards section is Workforce Security, which requires a covered entity to: "*Implement policies and procedures* to ensure that all members of its workforce have appropriate access to electronic protected health information (ePHI), as provided under (the Information Access Management standard), and to prevent those workforce members who do not have access under (the Information Access Management standard) from obtaining access to electronic protected health information."[2]

The fourth standard in the Administrative Safeguards section is Information Access Management, which requires a covered entity to: "*Implement policies and procedures* for authorizing access to ePHI that are consistent with the applicable requirements of subpart E of this part (the Privacy Rule)."[3]

The first standard in the HIPAA Security Rule's Technical Safeguards section in Access Control requires a covered entity to: "*Implement technical policies and procedures* for electronic information resources that maintain ePHI to allow access only to those persons or software programs that have been granted access rights as specified in §164.308(a)(4)(Information Access Management)."[4]

Although healthcare organizations have the latitude to define and interpret these policies and procedures to meet their particular needs, they must balance a respect for the privacy rights of their patients with what is reasonably possible to do, given the organization's resources and limitations. When drafting or updating policy documentation, healthcare organizations must also take into account the HIPAA Audit Program Protocol[5] published by the Office for Civil Rights (OCR) at the U.S. Department of Health & Human Services (HHS). The protocol contains audit procedures pertaining to the HIPAA Security and Privacy Rule and federal breach notification requirements that are audited by the OCR, as outlined in the American Recovery and Reinvestment Act (ARRA) of 2009.

An access control policy should describe the rules for the workforce that need to be enforced, and detail the allowable uses and the consequences of noncompliance. The following are core components expected for an access control policy:

- Authorizing and modifying a user's right of access to information resources.
- Granting levels of access based on business need.
- Approving and communicating levels of access.
- Defining roles and responsibilities that correlate with job functions.
- Defining procedures for disabling access for voluntary and involuntary terminations.
- Monitoring to determine whether access to ePHI is terminated.
- Defining technical access capabilities such as read-only, modify, and full-access.
- Establishing and assigning unique user IDs.
- Defining procedures for creating generic and system IDs and the approval forms for each.
- Establishing procedures for access during an emergency.
- Reviewing and verifying access rights periodically.
- Establishing bans on attempting to break into accounts, crack passwords, or disrupt service.
- Determining consequences of noncompliance.

An access control policy establishes standards for what is permitted or denied. It helps create consistency across the organization. In this way, risks are avoided and penalties are outlined for failure to adhere to the rules within the policy. A policy also identifies the roles and responsibilities of everyone impacted by access controls. The policy should be clear enough and inclusive enough to be easily implemented and followed. It is also important that the policy be flexible enough to encompass and accommodate a wide range of data and many different systems, activities and resources. Users should generally receive a copy of the policy and appropriate training, signifying their understanding and agreement with the policy before being granted access.

ACCESS CONTROL ADMINISTRATION

Access control administration is about assigning and revoking permissions for authorized users. The goal of access control administration is to identify and restrict access to any information resource to the minimum required for work to be performed. There are generally three events that trigger the need for administrating access control:

- Hiring a new user.
- Transferring or promoting a user where the job function and/or place of work changes.
- Terminating a user.

Healthcare organizations need to have an effective process to administer access control, which should include:

- Assigning users and devices only the access required to perform their required functions.
- Updating access rights based on personnel or system changes.
- Reviewing users' access rights periodically at an appropriate frequency based on the risk to the system or application.

- Designing appropriate acceptable-use policies and requiring users to agree to them.

Unfortunately in healthcare today, access control administration is not typically automated and is still mostly a manual process. The following is a common scenario found in assigning permissions to a new user:

- A manager completes an access request form (either paper or electronic) stating the type(s) of access needed.
- The form is distributed to the IT department and other application owners where the access is created.
- The new user is granted access to a set of systems and applications that are part of the permissions for his/her role.
- If an existing employee changes job functions or place of work, this triggers the need to complete another access request form.

Information resources need to be accessed by users in order for work to be performed. Access beyond the minimum required exposes the organization to a loss of confidentiality, integrity and availability. Management and system and application owners need to diligently evaluate access privileges on an ongoing basis to prevent unwarranted access. Access rights should be based on the needs of the user to carry out legitimate and approved activities. Policies, procedures, and criteria need to be established for both the granting of appropriate access rights and for the purpose of establishing those legitimate activities.

Access control administration consists of four processes:

1. A provisioning process to add new users to the information resource.
2. An authorization process to add, delete or modify user access to systems, applications, directories, files, and specific types of information.
3. An authentication process to identify the user during subsequent activities.
4. A monitoring process to oversee and manage the access rights granted to each user.

The provisioning process establishes the user's identity and anticipated business needs for information and information resources. New employees, outsourcing relationships, and contractors may also be identified, and the business need for access determined during the hiring or contracting process.

During provisioning and thereafter, an authorization process determines user access rights. In certain circumstances the assignment of access rights may be performed only after the manager responsible for each accessed resource approves the assignment and documents the approval. In other circumstances, the assignment of rights may be established by the employee's role or group membership and managed by preestablished authorizations for that group. Business associates or partners, on the other hand, may be granted access based on their relationship with the organization.

Deprovisioning is a key function of access control. Deprovisioning ensures that accounts are systematically disabled or deleted and privileges are revoked when users leave the organization. Good security practice recommends that accounts be disabled quickly to prevent possible attacks by disgruntled users, but not deleted in case it becomes necessary to audit activities associated with the account.

Privileged Access

Privileged access refers to the ability to override system or application controls. Authorization for privileged access should be tightly controlled and good security practice includes:

- Identifying each privilege associated with each information resource.
- Implementing a process to allocate privileges on a need-to-use or an event-by-event basis.
- Documenting the granting and administrative limits on privileges.
- Finding alternate ways of achieving business objectives.
- Assigning privileges to a unique user ID apart from the one used for normal business use.
- Logging and auditing the use of privileged access.
- Reviewing privileged access rights and allocations periodically.
- Prohibiting shared privileged access by multiple users.

User Account Reviews

Although technically feasible, user accounts do not typically terminate or update automatically. Many job changes can result in an expansion or reduction of access rights. When these job events occur, organizations should take particular care to promptly revise and update the access rights for users who have access to confidential information. Therefore, periodic reviews or recertification of access rights is necessary. Periodic reviews are a useful control to test whether the access termination and updating processes are functioning properly because gaps do occur. Healthcare organizations should review access rights on a schedule commensurate with risk, but annually is becoming the accepted practice.

Passwords

Passwords are the most common authentication mechanism. Passwords are generally made difficult to guess when they are composed of a large character set, contain a large number of characters, and are frequently changed. However, since hard-to-guess passwords may be difficult to remember, users typically take actions that weaken security such as writing passwords down. Any information resource must balance the password strength with the user's ability to maintain the password as a secret. When the balancing produces a password that is not sufficiently strong, a different authentication mechanism should be considered.

The PCI DSS provides specific requirements regarding password complexity.[6] These requirements include the following:

- Change user passwords at least every 90 days.
- Require a minimum password length of at least seven characters.
- Use passwords containing both numeric and alphabetic characters.
- Maintain a password history that blocks individuals from reusing any of their last four passwords.
- Do not allow an individual to submit a new password that is the same as any of the last four passwords he or she has used.

Users should select a password as the following examples illustrate:
- Choose small words and combine them (i.e., "Always!4Give").
- Use transliteration (i.e., foTOgraph$4U for "photograph for you").
- Interweave characters (i.e., 3!ihrOrnSes for "three iron horse").
- Substitute synonyms (i.e., #1jaVa*rest for "first coffee break").
- Substitute antonyms (i.e., sart'T1!dark for "first stop light").

Users should not select a password that meets these requirements:
- Containing personal details such as a relative's name, birthday, license plate or common character sequences (i.e., 123456).
- With only one word in any language, slang, dialect, jargon, etc. (can combine dictionary words).
- Composed of repeating the same character (i.e., aaaaa) or keyboard scale (i.e., asdfghj).

Passphrases are one alternative to passwords as a consideration. Due to their length, passphrases are generally more resistant to attack than passwords. But the length and character set are important controls for passphrases, as well as passwords.

Passwords that are either not changed or changed infrequently are considered significantly more vulnerable. These passwords are appropriate in information resources whose data and connectivity is considered low risk or employ effective compensating controls such as physical protections, authentication and auditing/monitoring.

Another use of passwords is with a challenge/response process. Challenge/responses uniquely identify the user by matching knowledge on the information resource to knowledge that only the resource and user share. If the information resource's challenge question(s) matches that entered by the user, the user is authenticated. Examples include:
- What was your high school mascot?
- What was your first pet's name?
- What was the make and model of your first car?

The strength of challenge/responses is the lack of disclosure about the secret, the difficulty in guessing or discovering the secret, and the length of time that the secret exists before it is changed. The strength is typically assured through configurations that enforce the password policy. This minimizes the chance of implementing a weak challenge question such as "What is your favorite color?" Authentication systems should force changes to challenge questions on a schedule commensurate with risk. NIST does provide a draft guide on passwords.[7]

Token Solutions

A token is a physical device, such as an ATM card, smart card, or other device that contains information used in the authentication process. Token solutions typically authenticate the token and assume that the user who was issued the token is the one requesting access. One example is a token that generates dynamic passwords after a set number of seconds. When prompted for a password, the user enters the password generated by the token. The token's password-generating function is identical and synchronized to that in the information resource, allowing the information resource to recognize the password as valid. This method is two-factor authentication, using both something the user has and something the user knows and is stronger than single-factor authentication such as a user ID and password. Similarly, an ATM card is a token with a magnetic strip on the back of the card containing a code recognized in the authentication process. However, the user is not authenticated until he or she also provides a PIN or shared secret. These methods can allow an organization to authenticate the user as well as the token. The strength of this type of authentication rests in the frequent changing of the password and the inability of an attacker to guess the password at any point in time.

There are a few primary weaknesses in token systems, which include:

- Theft or loss of the token during delivery to the user or while in the possession of the user.
- Ease of successfully forging any authentication credential that unlocks the token.
- Reverse engineering or cloning of the token.

Each of these weaknesses can be addressed through additional security controls. Token theft or loss generally is protected by policies that require prompt reporting and cancellation of the token's ability to allow access, and monitoring of token delivery and use. Additionally, the impact of token theft is reduced when the token is used in two-factor authentication. For instance, the password from the token is paired with a password known only by the user and the information resource. This pairing reduces the risk posed by token loss, while increasing the strength of the authentication mechanism. Forged credentials are protected by the same methods that protect credentials in non-token information resources. Protection against reverse engineering requires physical and logical security in token design. For instance, token designers can increase the difficulty of opening a token without causing irreparable damage, or obtaining information from the token either by passive scanning or active input/output.

Biometrics

Biometrics verifies the identity of a user by referencing unique physical (human) or behavioral characteristics. A physical characteristic can be a fingerprint, iris, or facial pattern. A behavioral characteristic can be the unique pattern of key depression strength and pauses made on a keyboard when a user types a phrase. The strength of biometrics is its uniqueness of the physical characteristic selected for verification, since no two fingerprints, irises, or faces are the same. This method is similar to a token in that it can be two-factor authentication, using both something the user is (such as a fingerprint) and something the user knows (like a password). Biometric technologies assign data values to the particular characteristics associated with a certain feature. For example, the iris typically provides many more characteristics to store and compare, making it more unique than facial characteristics. Unlike other authentication mechanisms, a biometric authenticator does not rely on a user's memory or possession of a token to be effective.

Provisioning is a critical process for the use of biometric authentication. The user's physical characteristics must be reliably recorded. Reliability may require several samples of the characteristic and a recording device free of lint, dirt, or other interference. The device must be physically secure from tampering and unauthorized use.

When provisioned, the user's biometric is stored as a template. Subsequent authentication is accomplished by comparing a submitted biometric against the template, with results based on probability and statistical confidence levels. Practical usage of biometric solutions requires consideration of how precise information resources must be for positive identification and authentication. More precise solutions increase the chances a person is falsely rejected. On the other hand, less precise solutions can result in the wrong person being identified or authenticated as a valid user (i.e., false acceptance rate).

Weaknesses in biometric systems relate to the ability of an attacker to submit false physical characteristics or to take advantage of flaws to make the system incorrectly report a match between the characteristic submitted and the one stored. An attacker might submit a copy of a valid user's thumbprint to a thumbprint recognition system. One control against this attack involves ensuring a live thumb was used for the submission. That can be done by physically controlling or monitoring the thumb reader to ensure no tampering or fake thumbs are used.

Attacks that involve making the system falsely deny or accept a request take advantage of either the low degrees of freedom in the characteristic being tested or improper system tuning. Degrees of freedom relate to measurable differences between biometric readings, with more degrees of freedom indicating a more unique biometric. Facial recognition systems, for instance, may have only nine degrees of freedom while other biometric systems have over one hundred. Similar faces may be used to fool the system into improperly authenticating an individual. Similar fingerprints and irises, however, are difficult to find and even more difficult to fool a system into improperly authenticating.

Attacks against system tuning also exist. Any biometric system has rates at which it will falsely accept and reject a reading. The two rates are inextricably linked because in any given system, improving one worsens the other. Systems that are tuned to maximize user convenience typically have low rates of false rejection and high rates of false acceptance. Those systems may be more open to successful attack.

NETWORK ACCESS

Network security requires effective implementation of several control mechanisms to adequately secure access to information resources. Many organizations have increasingly complex and dynamic networks stemming from the growth of distributed computing. Healthcare organizations should evaluate and appropriately implement those controls relative to the complexity of their network.

Healthcare organizations should start by mapping and configuring the network to identify and control all access points. Network configuration considerations include the following actions:

- Identifying the various applications and systems accessed via the network.
- Identifying all access points to the network including various telecommunications channels (i.e., wireless, Ethernet, frame relay, dedicated lines, extranets, Internet).
- Mapping the internal and external connectivity between various network segments.
- Defining minimum access requirements for network services (i.e., network access policy).
- Determining the most appropriate network configuration to ensure adequate security and performance.

With a clear understanding of network connectivity, healthcare organizations can avoid introducing security vulnerabilities by minimizing access to less-trusted domains and employing encryption for less secure connections. Organizations can then determine the most effective deployment of protocols, filtering routers, firewalls, gateways, proxy servers, and/or physical isolation to restrict access. Some applications and business processes may require complete segregation from the corporate network (i.e., no connectivity between corporate network and credit card processing operations). Others may restrict access by placing the services that must be accessed by each zone in their own security domain or Demilitarized Zone (DMZ).

An effective approach to securing a network involves segmenting or dividing the network into logical security domains. A logical security domain is a distinct part of a network with security policies that differ from other domains, and perimeter controls that enforce access at a network level. The differences may be far broader than network controls, encompassing personnel, host and other issues.

Security domains are bounded by perimeters. Typical perimeter controls include firewalls that operate at different network layers, malicious code prevention, outbound filtering, intrusion detection and prevention devices, and controls over infrastructure services such as Domain Name Service (DNS). The perimeter controls may exist on separate devices or be combined or consolidated on one or more devices. Consolidation on a single device could improve security by reducing administrative overhead. However, consolidation may increase risk through a reduced ability to perform certain functions and create a single point of failure.

Internally, networks can host or provide centralized access to mission-critical applications and information, making secure access an organizational priority. Externally, networks can integrate organizational and third-party applications that grant authorized users access to their confidential information. Failing to restrict access properly can increase operational, reputation and legal risk from threats, including the theft of confidential information, data alteration, system misuse, or denial-of-service attacks.

OPERATING SYSTEM ACCESS

Healthcare organizations must control access to system software within the various network clients and servers, as well as stand-alone systems. System software includes the operating system and system utilities. The computer operating system manages all of the other applications running on the computer. Common operating systems include Microsoft Windows, Novell Netware, IBM zOS, OS/400, AIX, and Linux. Application programs and data files interface through the operating system. System utilities are programs that perform repetitive functions such as creating, deleting, changing or copying files. System utilities also could include numerous types of system management software that can supplement operating system functionality by supporting common system tasks such as security, system monitoring, or transaction processing. Healthcare organizations need to understand the common vulnerabilities and appropriate mitigation strategies for their operating systems.

Healthcare organizations should secure operating system access by:

- Securing the devices that can access the operating system through physical and logical means (i.e., the system administrator should only log in using the system console).
- Updating the operating systems with security patches.
- Restricting and monitoring privileged access.
- Securing access to system utilities.
- Logging and monitoring user or program access and alerting on security events.

System software can provide high-level access to data and data processing. Healthcare organizations should restrict privileged access to sensitive operating systems. While many operating systems have integrated access control software, third-party security software is available as an alternative or additional level of security. Network security software can allow organizations to improve the effectiveness of the administration and security policy compliance for a large number of servers often spanning multiple operating system environments. Whether included in the operating system or as additional security software, the critical aspects for access control software include:

- Effective authentication methods to restrict system access to both users and applications.
- Limited number of users with access to sensitive operating systems with a minimum level of access required to perform routine responsibilities.
- Activated and utilized operating system security and logging capabilities.
- Filtered logs for potential security events and adequate reporting and alerting capabilities.
- Restricted access to sensitive or critical system resources or processes and the capability to extend protection at the program, file, record or field level.
- System administrators and security staff with adequate expertise to securely configure and manage the operating system.
- Locked or removed external drives from system consoles or terminals residing outside physically secure locations.
- Prohibited remote access to sensitive operating system functions, where possible, and strong authentication and encrypted sessions before allowing remote support.
- Segregated operating system access, where possible, to limit full or root-level access to the system.
- Updated operating systems with security patches and appropriate change control processes.

Application Access

Sensitive or mission-critical applications should incorporate appropriate access controls that restrict which functions are available to users and other applications with which they may interface. Healthcare organizations should control access to applications by minimally:

- Using authentication and authorization controls commensurate with the criticality of the application and its data.

- Logging access activities and security events.
- Monitoring access rights to ensure they are appropriate.

Some security software can integrate access controls for the operating system and applications. Such software is useful when applications do not have their own access controls or when the organization chooses to rely on the security software instead of the application's access controls. Organizations should understand the functionality and vulnerabilities of their application access control solutions and consider any identified issues in their risk analysis process.

Healthcare organizations should consider a number of concerns regarding application access control to include:

- Implementing a robust authentication method consistent with the criticality and sensitivity of the application such as two-factor authentication instead of relying solely on user IDs and passwords.
- Maintaining consistent processes for assigning new user access, changing existing user access, and promptly removing access on terminated users.
- Monitoring existing access rights to applications on a periodic basis to ensure users have the minimum access required for their jobs.
- Logging access, activities and events.

ROLE-BASED ACCESS CONTROL (RBAC)

Many healthcare organizations typically manage access rights individually, which can lead to inappropriate access levels being provisioned. By grouping users with similar access requirements under common access roles (i.e., physician, nurse, or social worker), then access can be more effectively assigned and managed. The key concept in RBAC is to define roles that correspond to job titles and responsibilities within the organization. Each role is associated with a set of access rights. Employees holding the same job within an organization are assigned to the same role. Thus, the number of roles is considerably lower than the number of employees in an organization. Having a common standard to use as a base specification is important to enable interoperability of different types of solutions. In response to this need, NIST proposed a standard for RBAC.[8]

The NIST RBAC standard presents a model that encompasses the most important features. Figures 9-1 and 9-2 illustrate a simplified view of this model.[9]

Permissions are a set of allowed functions on objects. An object may be an information element. A role is associated with a set of permissions such as a physician or nurse. Users are assigned a set of one or more roles. Therefore, the access rights for one user are defined by the set of roles currently assigned to that user.

Most applications claim to support RBAC. A majority of applications have chosen an approach based on the concepts of roles and responsibilities in combination with information, like place of work. The underlying assumption is that any specific role has a well-defined set of responsibilities and should allow users to perform these responsibilities.

To establish RBAC, organizations should start by working with each department/ unit to examine how users currently access confidential data. Document the list of job categories that require access to confidential data and the purposes and conditions

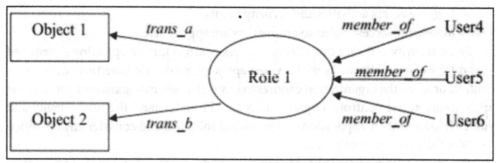

FIGURE 9-1: Role Relationships.

Department	Role / Job Title	Access to Information Systems			
		Application	Views	Privileges*	Internet Access
Patient Accounting	Clerk	Patient Care System	Billing	R/W	No
Scheduling	Clerk	Patient Care System	Scheduling	C/R/W	No
Lab	Lab Tech	Lab and Patient Care System	Order Entry	R/W	Yes
Nursing	Nurse	Patient Care System	Order Entry	R/W	No
Nursing	Manager	Patient Care System	Order Entry / Scheduling	C/R/W/D	Yes
Nursing	Manager	HR/Payroll & Timekeeping	Timekeeping	R/W	Yes
Administration	Office Manager	Patient Care System	Billing and Scheduling	C/R/W/D	Yes
IT Support	SysAdmin	All	All	C/R/W/D	Yes
Human Resources	Clerk	HR/Payroll & Timekeeping	Payroll	R/W	No

*Key: C = Create, R = Read, W = Write, D= Delete

FIGURE 9-2: Sample Role-Based Access Control Matrix. *From Tom Walsh Consulting, LLC, used with permission.*

under which confidential data are needed. Some healthcare organizations are documenting this using a grid approach:

- List all categories of users on one axis.
- List categories of confidential data on the other axis.
- Make check boxes and notes regarding special conditions in each cell where those users need access to specified categories of confidential data.

Compare findings of what information is currently made available to the various users with what they need to know. Do they have access to more health information than they really require? If so, is it reasonably possible to segregate the needed information in a way that gives them only what they need? It may not always be possible or feasible to restrict all extraneous health information beyond what is needed. However, the organization's goal should be to restrict access to what is needed.

Once this exercise is performed, the foundation for a minimum necessary policy and procedure is established, as well as the role definitions required for RBAC. For example, consider a social worker who examines confidential data as part of evaluating elderly patients for possible placement in a long-term care facility. Using the minimum necessary principles, the organization would determine what the social worker needs in order to perform this function such as information about the patient's current condition, needs for long-term care, basic demographic information, and insurance resources. De-identified data would not meet the needs of this social worker.

The organization then compares these needs to the social worker's current access and determines whether it is reasonably possible to limit access to only a subset of the confidential data. It may not be practical to restrict certain subsets of information from the social worker. However, the organization should use the results of the analysis to define what portions of confidential data a social worker may typically use in performing this function. The social worker role would be established in the application adhering to this analysis and restricting access to confidential data out of the scope of the function being performed.

REMOTE ACCESS

Many healthcare organizations provide employees, contractors, vendors, and others with access to the organization's network and information resources through external connections. Those connections are typically established through the Internet or private communication lines. The access may be necessary to remotely support the organization's systems and applications or off site operations.

The HIPAA Security Rule[10] requirements for access control do apply to users who telecommute or have home-based offices, assuming the users have access to ePHI. Healthcare organizations allowing users to telecommute or work out of home-based offices and have access to ePHI must implement appropriate safeguards to protect the organization's data. The HIPAA Security Rule's information access management and access control standards specifically require healthcare organizations to implement policies and procedures for authorizing access to ePHI and technical policies and procedures to allow access only to those persons or software programs that have been appropriately granted access rights.

This is important because remote access can provide an unauthorized user with the opportunity to compromise information resources. As a result, healthcare organizations should establish a policy and procedure restricting and managing remote access to include identifying all remote access devices operating in their environment. Controls for remote access should include:

- Disallowing remote access to users by policy and practice unless a business justification exists.
- Requiring management approval for remote access.
- Regularly reviewing remote access approvals and rescinding those that no longer have a business need.
- Configuring remote access devices based on industry standards and/or product specifications to include automatic logoffs.
- Patching, updating, and maintaining all software on remote access devices.

- Enabling encryption to protect data in storage and transit.
- Logging remote access activities, analyzing them in a timely manner, and addressing any anomalies.
- Securing remote access devices against malware.
- Periodically auditing the access device configurations and patch levels.
- Restricting remote access through network segmentation.
- Centralizing Internet access to provide a consistent authentication method and ensuring network traffic has appropriate perimeter protections and network monitoring.
- Establishing a two-factor authentication process for remote access (i.e., PIN-based token card with a one-time random password generator).
- Disabling remote access when the need no longer exists.

HEALTHCARE REGULATIONS IMPACTING ACCESS CONTROL

Most regulations in place today require healthcare organizations to know who is accessing certain information, what they are doing with it, and be able to prove what happened in an audit. Regulations have tremendous influence and impact on the healthcare industry.

For example, the U.S. Food and Drug Administration (FDA) established requirements for electronic records and signatures under Part 11 of the U.S. Title 21 Code of Federal Regulations (21 CFR Part 11).[11] The regulation became effective in 1997 and enforced in 2000. To be compliant, an organization must define and implement procedures and controls to ensure the authenticity, integrity and the confidentiality of electronic records. It includes some of the following requirements:

- Verify the identity of each user before providing any credential.
- Maintain secure audit trails.
- Store records in a protected database.

21 CFR Part 11 is high level and does not provide strict recommendations. However, it does provide the basic principles for proper computer use.

The HIPAA Security Rule requires organizations to appropriately manage their access control, provisioning, and other aspects of security inherent in IT systems. It also prescribes limiting access to individual healthcare information to the minimum necessary to perform job duties. This means authenticating users with unique IDs. However, most healthcare organizations have not reached an adequate level of maturity in meeting this requirement. Beginning in 2003 and every year since, user access has been a top five issue in investigated privacy cases closed with corrective action by the OCR.[12]

The HIPAA Privacy Rule complements the HIPAA Security Rule's Access Control standard.[13] The Privacy Rule minimum necessary use standard requires providers to "identify those persons or classes of persons, as appropriate, in its workforce who need access to protected health information to carry out their duties; and for each such person or class of persons, the category or categories of protected health information to which access is needed and any conditions appropriate to such access." Minimum necessary does not apply when a treatment relationship exists, but is subject to verification of the identity and authority of anyone attempting to access ePHI.

The Payment Card Industry Data Security Standard (PCI DSS) has a total of 12 requirements.[14] "Requirement 7: Restrict access to cardholder data by business need-to-know" mandates that organizations restrict access by ensuring adequate steps are taken to prevent unauthorized users from accessing cardholder data. Some of the specific requirements in this section include the following:

- Assign access to individuals based upon their job function, and limit their access to the minimum required to complete their jobs.
- Use an authorization form for each privilege assignment that specifies the privileges required and includes management sign-off.
- Use an automated access control system that follows access restrictions and denies any activity that is not explicitly allowed.

"Requirement 8: Assign a unique ID to each person with computer access" governs the use of unique identifiers for access to information resources in the cardholder environment. The goal of this requirement is to ensure that strong authentication identifies each user so that they may be held accountable for their actions. Specific requirements in this section include:

- Using unique identifiers for all users so there are no group or shared logins to any system in the cardholder environment.
- Using two-factor authentication for all remote access.
- Locking out users for at least 30 minutes after six incorrect login attempts and logging out sessions after 15 minutes of idle time.
- Encrypting passwords during transmission and storage.
- Implementing formal procedures for addition, modification and deletion of accounts, password resets and first-time passwords.
- Revoking access immediately for terminated users and those that have been inactive for 90 days.

CONCLUSION

Healthcare is one of the most information intensive industries in society today. The paper-based medical record is becoming a thing of the past, and as all the information about a patient is being put into electronic form, the risk scenario changes. Access control is a key feature of healthcare information resources because it ensures information is accessible only to authorized users. As such, access control protects the patient's right to privacy, while ensuring users get access to the right information at the right time in order to be able to provide the best possible treatment for their patients. As a result, it becomes increasingly important to have sound and sufficient controls in place to manage access to this information.

REFERENCES

1. Hu CTC, Ferraiolo DF, Kuhn DR. Assessment of access control systems. NIST Interagency/Internal Report (NISTR) 7316. Available at: www.nist.gov/manuscript-publication-search.cfm?pub_id=50886.

2. 45 CFR Parts 160, 162, 164. Available at: www.hhs.gov/ocr/privacy/hipaa/administrative/securityrule/securityrulepdf.pdf.

3. Ibid.

4. Ibid.

5. U.S. Department of Health & Human Services. HIPAA Audit Program Protocol. Available at: www.hhs.gov/ocr/privacy/hipaa/enforcement/audit/protocol.htm.

6. PCI Security Standards Council. Documents library. Available at: www.pcisecuritystandards.org/security_standards/documents.php.

7. Scarfone K, Souppaya M. Guide to enterprise password management (draft): Recommendations of the National Institute of Standards and Technology. NIST. Available at: http://csrc.nist.gov/publications/drafts/800-118/draft-sp800-118.pdf.

8. National Institute of Standards and Technology. Role-based access control (RBAC) and role-based security. Available at: http://csrc.nist.gov/groups/SNS/rbac.

9. Ferraiolo DF, Kuhn RD. Role-based access controls. 15th National Computer Security Conference. Baltimore, MD. 1992: 554-63. Available at: http://csrc.nist.gov/rbac/ferraiolo-kuhn-92.pdf.

10. 45 CFR Parts 160, 162, 164. Available at: www.hhs.gov/ocr/privacy/hipaa/administrative/securityrule/securityrulepdf.pdf.

11. U.S. Food and Drug Administration. CFR-Code of Federal Regulations Title 21. Available at: www.accessdata.fda.gov/scripts/cdrh/cfdocs/cfcfr/CFRSearch.cfm?CFRPart=11.

12. U.S. Department of Health & Human Services. Top five issues in investigated cases closed with corrective action, by calendar year. Available at: www.hhs.gov/ocr/privacy/hipaa/enforcement/data/top5issues.html.

13. U.S. Department of Health & Human Services. The Privacy Rule. Available at: www.hhs.gov/ocr/privacy/hipaa/administrative/privacyrule/index.html.

14. PCI Security Standards Council. Documents library. Available at: www.pcisecuritystandards.org/security_standards/documents.php.

CHAPTER 10

Network Security

By Buddy Gilbert, CCNA

Network security is the epitome of evolution and change. Network security may seem expensive to maintain and challenging to manage, but the expense and reputation damage an organization can endure recovering from a data breach can pale in cost comparisons. Just do a web search on "most expensive network security breaches." These companies/organizations have experienced first hand the nightmares no one hopes to endure, and they provide valuable information to help everyone develop better techniques to protect themselves. In addition, we must understand how important it is in the healthcare industry to keep the information flowing. The dependencies on technology have grown, in a short time, from a novelty to a critical part in staying competitive in the industry. Leaving security unattended at any level is not an option. We must never forget that fast, accurate, dependable information does make a difference in the care we provide to every patient.

With all the publicity security issues receive, it is hard to believe we still find resistance from some people. Yet I still hear things like, "I think this security stuff is overkill and way too much trouble." "Why can't I get to my systems from anywhere, anytime, and from any device?" "Are all you security people on some kind of power trip?" "All you ever say is NO." "Can you do this for me, just this once?" You would be surprised how many times I hear these kinds of questions/statements. The truth is that most do not have any idea how much planning, time, and effort is spent trying to get to the proverbial "YES." I have personally lost track of how many times the IT department has worked nonstop for 24 hours plus trying to keep things safe—recovering from security incidents or patching operating systems because of identified exploits, while staying as transparent to the end users as possible. Most IT people in healthcare are very passionate and dedicated about what they do and take their job very seriously. It's really easy to do when we keep in mind that we are not just supporting a device, we are supporting a *clinician* who provides care to important people (our patients). When we fully understand this concept, it really makes it easy to do the right thing even when we are getting beat up for slowing down a project because we are trying to fully test a new technology. Conceptually, being on the bleeding edge of new technology seems really cool and exciting, but when reality strikes during implementation and it's your blood on the floor, the coolness can quickly turn bitter cold and after you lose a couple of digits from frostbite, you have a tendency to become more cautious. In a healthcare environment, the tried and proven methods should be in place in the most critical areas; where you can afford to implement new technology, make sure detailed expectations are proper communicated. In this chapter, we will break down components of the building blocks of a secure robust network. The principles, in most cases, can be applied to any size network. The best place to begin is where network security got its start, the Internet edge.

Internet Edge/DMZ Block

The Internet Edge/DMZ Block has uplink connections to the Internet and downlink connections to the core through the firewall, with a combination of security hardware and software strategically placed to secure the perimeter. To draw an analogy, the DeMilitarized Zone (DMZ) gets its name from a border area between nations where military action is prohibited. In network terms, the DMZ is an area of the network housing Internet-accessible devices such as Virtual Private Network (VPN) devices, secure file transfer, e-mail, front-end web services, server load balancers (SLB), or anything that needs direct access from the Internet.

Even though the devices in the DMZ are outside the enterprise network, they should still have adequate protection using Access Control Lists (ACL) or stateful firewall inspection along with an Intrusion Detection System/Intrusion Prevention System (IDS/IPS) monitoring. IDS/IPS systems signatures should be automatically updated, at a minimum, daily. The DMZ should also have dedicated packet-capturing capability, allowing administrators to quickly gather information to confirm possible attacks or breaches. Additionally, dedicated packet-capturing capability can be used to understand normal data flow and thus establish a baseline for comparison when an attack is suspected. (See Figure 10-1.)

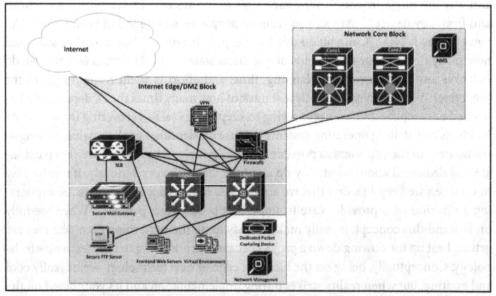

FIGURE 10-1: Components of the Internet Edge/DMZ Block Should Be Physically Separated from Internal Network Equipment.

Firewalls

Firewalls have been around for more than 25 years. The first firewalls were basic compared to today's deep packet inspection standards, but packet filtering still has a place in the layered security approach. Most routers support packet filtering. This feature can be used for intranet segmentation and on the perimeter to block traffic before it gets to the firewall. Packet filtering uses a list of permit and deny statements based on the source/destination IP address/subnet, protocol type, or Transmission Control Protocol/User Datagram Protocol (TCP/UDP) port number. The list is referred to as an Access Control List (ACL). The packet is compared to each line in the ACL until a match is found. If no match is found, an implicit deny at the end of the list will disallow the packet.

As firewalls developed, stateful packet inspection was the next step. ACLs are applied along with information about connections. The stateful firewall also keeps up with those who initiate the connection, allowing more efficient rule sets. State tables are created when the first packet of a conversation passes through the firewall. With TCP the first packet (synchronize packet) has the SYN bit set and triggers a new connection. After the session is fully established with a (synchronize acknowledgement packet) SYN-ACK and an (acknowledgement packet) ACK (referred to as the three-way hand shake), traffic can efficiently traverse the firewall. The stateful firewall also keeps up with connections of other protocols like UDP and Internet Control Message Protocol (ICMP), but usually tears down the connection only after a timeout is reached from not receiving a reply. Although stateful firewalls have some limit application awareness, a need for more application protection has arisen because of the sophisticated hacks from organized cybercriminals. These groups of bandits can hide anywhere in the world, and they have unlimited time and resources. There is nothing sacred to these thieving scoundrels; they will pillage and plunder your grandmother's life savings or your children's identity without a second thought. The only way to combat the cybercrook is for the good guys to unite and educate.

Deep Packet Inspection (DPI) can be very beneficial to the enterprise network security. It gives the administrators more insight into everything entering and leaving the network. Time is of the essence when dealing with fast-spreading infections or data leakage. Some application firewalls have the ability to learn and baseline an application, allowing administrators a better understanding of the rule sets needed to protect the application. Each level of firewall still has its place in the network—it just depends how deep you want or need to go into the IP packet, and there is a bigger expense associated with the deeper you go.

There is some controversy surrounding DPI at the Internet Service Provider (ISP) level. Concerns have arisen because of laws passed like the Communications Assistance for Law Enforcement Act (CALEA). Laws like CALEA were originally passed for telecommunication, but because of the explosive growth of Voice over Internet Protocol (VoIP), government agencies needed the ability to quickly set up TAPs (Traffic Access Points) to monitor Internet traffic. Some feel that this gives big brother too much visibility into private information and gives them access to all traffic on the Internet. Because of our awareness that anyone can eavesdrop when traffic leaves the safety of the enterprise perimeter, we now use Virtual Private Networks (VPN), Secure Socket Layer (SSL), and Secure File Transfer Protocol (SFTP) to encrypt communication. Firewalls protect us from the openness of the Internet, and encryption allows us safe passage through the Internet.

Secure File Transfer Protocol (SFTP)
SFTP is a good solution when you do not need the complexity of VPN, but need to move files between trusted entities. The SFTP server should be in the DMZ with the proper password policies, file retention policies, and standard DMZ protection. Files can be accessed, managed, and transferred from a central location.

Virtual Private Networks (VPN)
With the availability of high-speed Internet access, using VPN has become a standard way for individuals and autonomous networks to communicate. Encrypted connections can be established without worries of eavesdropping in transit over the Internet.

When designing the VPN connectivity, license costs and sizing for the web-based SSL access, VPN client-based access, and Local Area Network-to-Local Area Network (LAN-to-LAN), and IPsec tunnels should be considered. The more encryption, the more resources used. To ensure affordability, smaller networks can bundle VPN and other security features with the firewall, while larger networks should keep them separate, allowing for flexibility and easier administration.

SSL Clientless VPN
Web browser-based VPN allows users safe connections regardless of the operating systems (OS). Java or Active-x plug-ins can be pushed to the user device, allowing IPsec like network layer connection back to non-web applications.

LAN-to-LAN IPsec Tunnels
Organizations can use LAN-to-LAN tunnels to connect, allowing specific communication through encrypted tunnels utilizing exiting corporate Internet connections.

E-mail Security
The ability to detect outbound transmissions of protected health information (PHI) intentionally or unintentionally is as important as protecting against inbound e-mail threats. The e-mail security appliances can be load balanced for flexibility and ease the pain of administration during maintenance.

Network Core Block
The Network Core Block connects everything together. In the past, we built redundancy for equipment failure; as the network community gained experience, it made sense to have physical separation between redundant devices. There is a cost associated with the amount of distance, but sometimes just having the equipment on opposite sides of the room can make a big difference with minimal cost (leaky ceiling or small containable electrical fire). There are many philosophies about the best way to build a core network, but it really depends on specific individual needs and scale. If you stick to the principles of "fast and dependable" for the network core, the rest will work out. Fast means streamlining connectivity and segmenting all traffic entering the core with layer three connections to all devices. Layer three connections allow traffic to flow to the

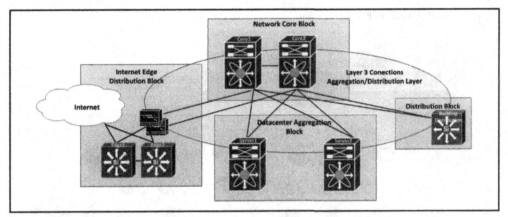

FIGURE 10-2: Redundant Layer 3 Core Configuration.

core on individual segments/broadcast domains and with fully redundant core switches coupled with equal cost redundant paths, you can eliminate any single point of failure insuring dependability. Figure 10-2 shows the relative connectivity of the core devices to the rest of the network.

Data Center Aggregation Block

The Data Center Aggregation Block has uplink connections to the core and down-link connections to network appliances, high-demand systems, and server access switches. The Data Center Aggregation Block is the core of the data center and should be designed with maximum flexibility, throughput and reliability in mind. With the explosive growth of the virtual environment, special considerations should be made when designing because of the ability to move applications around within the data center. The capability to quickly add capacity to any part of the data center network is very important.

All critical servers should have redundant connection, whether they are active/active or active/standby. When possible, the redundant connections should be to different server access switches, permitting undisruptive application access during network upgrades.

Appliances and high-demand systems such as Server Load Balancers (SLB), high performance firewalls, packet-capturing devices, network management, high-end servers, Internet Small Computer System Interface (iSCSI) storage and backup servers should be connected to the data center core to maximize throughput and to reduce traffic on the server access switch links. (See Figure 10-3.)

The ability to automatically notify administrators when thresholds are exceeded and redundant components fail should be a part of any Network Management System (NMS) installation and is especially critical in the data center; when testing failover, saturated links, and undetected failed components could spell disaster and cause extend unexpected outages.

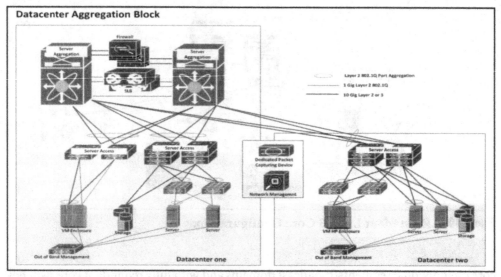

FIGURE 10-3: High Availability Is Essential in the Data Center.

Virtualization

Virtualization of servers and desktops is growing at an alarming rate, from a network perspective. I have personally witnessed over a thousand virtual desktops that have sprung up overnight, and considering they have the ability to move virtually anywhere within the data center, the appropriate design will quickly need adjusting. This kind of growth and on-the-fly change can really test the network infrastructure. For the data center network to endure, it must be as flexible as possible. The ability to add bandwidth to any part of the network quickly and without application disruption should be part of the data center design.

CLOUD COMPUTING

The National Institute of Standards and Technology (NIST) definition of cloud computing is as follows:

Cloud computing is a model for enabling ubiquitous, convenient, on-demand network access to a shared pool of configurable computing resources (e.g., networks, servers, storage, applications and services) that can be rapidly provisioned and released with minimal management effort or service provider interaction. This cloud model is composed of five essential characteristics, three service models, and four deployment models.

Essential Characteristics

On-demand self-service. A consumer can unilaterally provision computing capabilities, such as server time and network storage, as needed automatically without human interaction with each service provider.

Broad network access. Capabilities are available over the network and accessed through standard mechanisms that promote use by heterogeneous thin- or thick-client platforms (e.g., mobile phones, tablets, laptops, and workstations).

Resource pooling. The provider's computing resources are pooled to serve multiple consumers using a multi-tenant model with different physical and virtual resources dynamically assigned and reassigned according to consumer demand. There is a sense of location independence in that the customer generally has no control or knowledge over the exact location of the provided resources but may be able to specify location at a higher level of abstraction (e.g., country, state, or datacenter). Examples of resources include storage, processing, memory, and network bandwidth.

Rapid elasticity. Capabilities can be elastically provisioned and released, in some cases automatically, to scale rapidly outward and inward commensurate with demand. To the consumer, the capabilities available for provisioning often appear to be unlimited and can be appropriated in any quantity at any time.

Measured service. Cloud systems automatically control and optimize resource use by leveraging a metering capability at some level of abstraction appropriate to the type of service (e.g., storage, processing, bandwidth, and active user accounts). Resource usage can be monitored, controlled, and reported, providing transparency for both the provider and consumer of the utilized service.

Service Models of the Cloud

Infrastructure as a Service (IaaS). The capability provided to the consumer is to provision processing, storage, networks, and other fundamental computing resources where the consumer is able to deploy and run arbitrary software, which can include operating systems and applications. The consumer does not manage or control the underlying cloud infrastructure but has control over operating systems, storage, and deployed applications; and possibly limited control of select networking components (e.g., host firewalls).

Platform as a Service (PaaS). The capability provided to the consumer is to deploy onto the cloud infrastructure consumer-created or acquired applications created using programming languages, libraries, services, and tools supported by the provider. The consumer does not manage or control the underlying cloud infrastructure, including network, servers, operating systems or storage, but has control over the deployed applications and possibly configuration settings for the application-hosting environment.

Software as a Service (SaaS). The capability provided to the consumer is to use the provider's applications running on a cloud infrastructure. The applications are accessible from various client devices through either a thin client interface, such as a web browser (e.g., web-based e-mail), or a program interface. The consumer does not manage or control the underlying cloud infrastructure including network, servers, operating systems, storage or even individual application capabilities, with the possible exception of limited user-specific application configuration settings.

Deployment Models

Private cloud. The cloud infrastructure is provisioned for exclusive use by a single organization comprising multiple consumers (e.g., business units). It may be owned, managed, and operated by the organization, a third party, or some combination of them, and it may exist on or off premises.

Community cloud. The cloud infrastructure is provisioned for exclusive use by a specific community of consumers from organizations that have shared concerns (e.g., mission, security requirements, policy, and compliance considerations). It may be owned, managed, and operated by one or more of the organizations in the community, a third party, or some combination of them, and it may exist on or off premises.

Public cloud. The cloud infrastructure is provisioned for open use by the general public. It may be owned, managed and operated by a business, academic, or government organization, or some combination of them. It exists on the premises of the cloud provider.

Hybrid cloud. The cloud infrastructure is a composition of two or more distinct cloud infrastructures (private, community or public) that remain unique entities, but are bound together by standardized or proprietary technology that enables data and application portability (e.g., cloud bursting for load balancing between clouds).

Application service providers have been around for a long time. The services have developed and are maturing into what is now referred to as cloud computing. Small businesses can use features of the cloud and have some of the flexibilities of larger businesses without having to maintain IT staffing. Medium to large companies can do some preliminary testing and development without having to buy additional infrastructure. Cloud services should add some immediate value, making your job easier. For example, open annual enrollment that requires enormous resources for a short time; that is, resources that can quickly be added in the public cloud without disrupting day-to-day business operations or take away local Internet bandwidth. Non-mission critical applications are also a good fit for the public cloud.

Securing the cloud is still a big concern. The lines between hardware, OS, networking, storage, dedicated, and shared resources are blurred. It's bad enough when it's a private cloud, but we are in the early stages of trusting public cloud providers. As cloud computing grows in popularity, you can count on the cyber criminals to target and exploit any weaknesses they can uncover. When looking for public cloud service providers, make sure they have a good security record, and when building a private cloud, implement your standard security policies. It's difficult trying to determine if the public provider has adequate facilities and back policies but if you happen to pick a hosting site that has violated federal laws, like copyright infringement, the provider can be shut down for an undetermined amount of time, and it can be painful for a business to lack access to their data. When using cloud services, make sure you have very clear language about compliance by the provider (HIPAA, PCI, etc.), data ownership, backups, security, migration of data, logs/audit trails, and a clear termination clause. If a company goes bankrupt, you need assurances you can get to your data; if you want to change providers, you need to know your data are in a usable format when you receive them and all other copies of your data will have been destroyed (production, development, disaster recovery, business continuity, and backup).

It will be interesting as we watch this technology evolve and the creativity unfolds. Some public cloud providers are collaborating with bandwidth providers, allowing dedicated, on-demand bandwidth to the cloud service as a creative way to meet customer need. When deciding what cloud technology to use, the best advice is never try

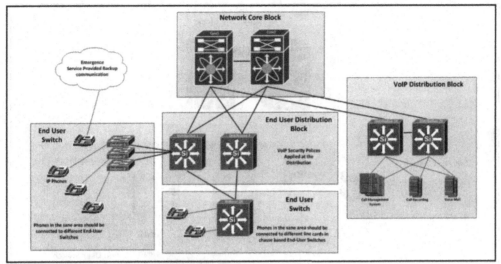

Figure 10-4: VoIP System Should Be Designed to Be as Stable as Legacy Voice Systems.

to make a round peg fit into a square hole, and when looking for solution, determine the technology that best fits the needs of the problem you are trying to solve. Know everything might not belong in the cloud.

Voice over IP (VoIP) Distribution Block

The VoIP Distribution Block has uplink connections to the network core and downlink connections to the call management system, voicemail system, call recording system, and other voice application servers, and services.

The legacy voice systems have set very high standards for uptime. The challenge for VoIP is to meet the uptime expectations of legacy systems and provide additional flexibility and features. When placing the phones, consider dispersing them over different access switches for phones in the same area. This will help reduce the end users' pain when hardware fails and allows some normal communication until the problem can be resolved. In a healthcare environment, voice communication is critical; emergency backup systems/plans should be in place, reviewed and tested regularly.

ACLs can be applied at the various distribution blocks to protect VoIP components. Any VoIP security policies should be thoroughly tested before implementation. (See Figure 10-4.)

End User Distribution Block

The end user distribution has uplink connections to the network core and downlinks connection to user access switches. End user distribution devices are used for segmentation of end user devices and for applying security policies using ACLs to the segments when needed. We will go into more detail about segmentation of end user devices in the "Network Segmentation" section later in the chapter.

Processing capability should be considered for the lifetime of the distribution device. If you plan to use the equipment throughout its entire lifecycle, you should plan for plenty of growth for the processor, bandwidth, and flash storage. Similar methods

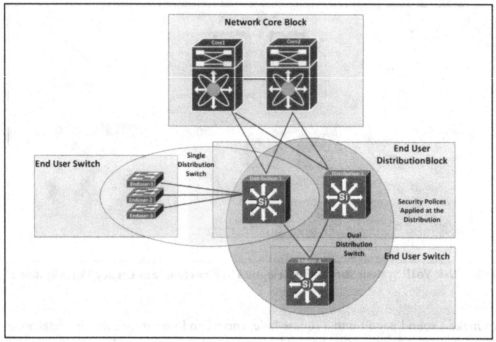

FIGURE 10-5: Redundancy Can Be Built into the Same Chassis or in Separate Chassis.

of redundancy can be applied at the distribution, as they are at the core, or you can use a single chassis with redundant power supplies and processors within the same chassis. (See Figure 10-5.)

End User Access Block

The end user access block has uplink connections to the distribution and downlink connections to the end user devices and Wi-Fi access points (AP). The APs and access switches are used as a direct connection to end user devices. Today most hospital equipment can benefit from network connectivity for monitoring or uploading relevant information for quick access. (See Figure 10-6.)

Because of the large number of these devices and device types, there should be a user tracking system in place to quickly identify the location of a device when an infection or problem is detected. With the extensive wireless and VoIP installations, just turning off an Ethernet port is no longer the standard method for mitigating violators. Management systems, specific techniques, and policies must be put in place to promptly identify and properly remove infected devices from the network without interfering with uninfected devices.

Not all internal attacks come from infected devices and may not be malicious. There is an enormous amount of bandwidth available in today's network environment. When you combine this with the ever-growing processor capability present in the end device, unintentionally bringing down critical systems is an evident risk. It can be something as simple as mistakes like swapping the IP address with the default gateway on a device that can cause equipment on the same subnet to behave oddly. In larger networks, without proper system logging, documentation, and tools, this type of misconfigured device

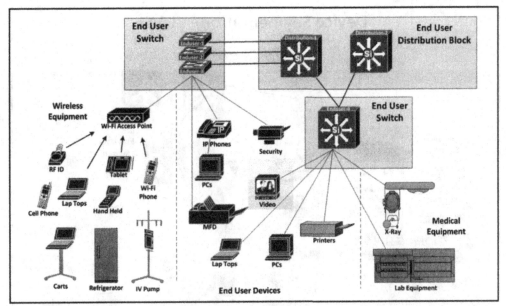

FIGURE 10-6: Baseline Traffic Patterns and the Relationship of Devices Throughout the Network.

can be difficult to find. The same holds true with a misbehaving device that is spewing erroneous traffic like large amounts of Domain Name System/Dynamic Host Control Protocol (DNS/DHCP) requests, saturating resources at every hop along the way.

Locking down Media Access Control (MAC) addresses to an Ethernet port is one way to reduce the user's ability to move or exchange devices without network administrators' knowledge. It takes effort to set up, but can save a lot of pain later when trying to track rogue devices. Please do not forget to turn off all ports that are not in use.

NETWORK SEGMENTATION

It is becoming necessary to have more granularity in the segmentation of users and devices to effectively manage security on the internal network. Traditionally, parallel vendor networks were installed for segmentation, using low- to mid-range equipment. In larger networks, users can take advantage of connecting to existing enterprise class, network equipment that has sufficient redundancies already in place. By using proper segmentation with ACLs, strict policies and rule sets can be applied to individual segments allowing application and administration access only to the specific required communication. (See Figure 10-7.)

Examples of Segmentation

Medical subnets. Because of FDA certification, medical systems, or biomedical devices can lag substantially behind security patch cycles, especially Windows OS. Systems can be segregated, permitting additional layers of protection from the standard populating using ACLs, substantially reducing risk from internal compromised devices. Biomedical devices are at a higher risk than standard user population devices and may need protecting from them as well.

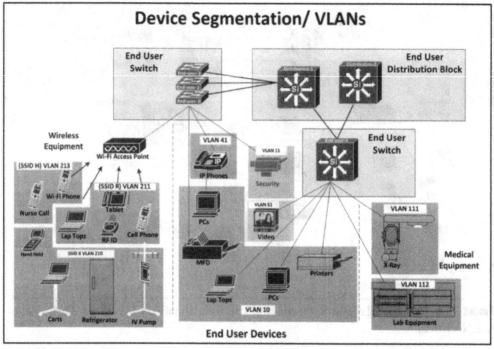

FIGURE 10-7: Group Devices According to Specific Needs and Requirements.

User group subnets. Groups of users that need the same type/level of access. This is especially helpful for groups of users that administer the network, mainframe, e-mail, databases, etc. Access applied to a group helps to efficiently manage change.

Restricted subnets. Groups of users that need the same type of restriction. This works well for public user access within your organization. They may have access to the Internet only and be denied access to all internal systems.

Specialized subnets. Used for network equipment management, VoIP, physical security systems (badge readers for doors), video (surveillance cameras), PCI, and out-of-band management, these systems usually have very specific and/or very restricted access. These devices can require more attention because of the Windows-based OS that requires patches and virus software updates after the approval process. Whenever possible, use internal servers for the updates, and only allow specific access to servers using ACL, even if you go outside of your network for the updates.

Server subnets. Used to allow only specific access to applications on the servers. Best set up behind a data center firewall.

WIRELESS SECURITY

Wireless connectivity, how hard could it be? You can go to your local electronics store and buy an AP, connect it to the Internet, then you and all of you neighbors can surf the web.

One of the biggest problems with wireless in an enterprise network is improper AP installation by someone just wanting to use their wireless device. Users can innocently serve up your internal network to anyone walking by just by plugging in a consumer grade AP to your network. Wireless rogue detection should be part of your wireless security strategy, along with a couple of hand-held devices to track down the most elusive rogue devices. An array of other wireless tools are needed to help manage air space due to the enormous amount of interference found in the healthcare environment. This is including but not limited to wireless sniffers, spectrum analyzers, and site survey equipment.

Some of the same security principles can be applied at the wireless local area network (WLAN) as the local area network (LAN). Proper segmentation based on access and security policies should be put into place. Wireless is a shared media, the same way devices on hubs use to share bandwidth. This is why it is so important to adhere to nothing less than Wi-Fi Protected Access 2 (WPA2) for mission-critical devices. Most APs have a limited number of Service Set IDs (SSID) they are capable of broadcasting. When laying out the WLANs, use the SSIDs wisely.

Many devices used in the healthcare setting have smaller processors and can have problems handling broadcasts sent out by many SSIDs.

Bring Your Own Device (BYOD)

BYOD has become a very important subject. It means much more than employees paying for their own devices they use at work. There is a real benefit to allowing use of devices that employees are comfortable with to access the information needed to increase productivity. The challenge is allowing employees and visitors the freedom to bring their own devices while maintaining controls to ensure security and prevent data loss. Another challenge is not only the number of the devices allowed, but how many types of devices and how quickly they change. If an organizations does agree to support mobile devices, for now, it involves only a short list and use only when they are on the internal Wi-Fi. In order to get to the next level, a minimum security baseline must be established that identifies any device connecting to the network and authenticating both user and device. There is also the complication of mixing corporate and personal data on the same device. Because of HIPAA, PCI and others, as well as compliancy, coupled with the need to protect corporate data, a requirement for a business partition is a good solution, allowing a remote wipe of corporate data without harming personal data. The IT department does not want to be responsible for wiping out Dr. Mike's family photos. Connecting mobile users to a back-end Virtual Desktop Infrastructure (VDI) is also a good solution, which is to never allow any data to be stored on the mobile device.

Some would say that smartphones can do it all—make calls, provide instant messaging, access the Internet, run applications, take pictures, make videos, etc. The reality is that most people will have multiple devices (laptops, tablets, e-readers and smartphones), and they will all need connecting. What this means for the internal Wi-Fi, along with service providers is that the number of devices is increasing, and we have to stay ahead of the curve with connectivity volume and security. It is estimated that mobile traffic will increase more than five times from 2012 to 2015.

I think we all know where BYOD will end up—"I need to connect to everything, anytime, from anywhere, with any device."

Installation and Decommissioning Network Equipment

Security should be considered through the entire lifecycle of a network device. Standards should include security policies for network devices, specific configuration examples and a security template for removing unnecessary services and factory default configuration settings not needed for the intended application of the devices. You should also have a checklist and a senior staff member sign off on the newly installed device to finalize the installation. The same diligence should be taken when decommissioning equipment. See **Installation Checklist 10-1** and **Decommissioning Checklist 10-2**.

INSTALLATION CHECK LIST 10-1

1. Load proper code version /operating system (OS)— network devices sent from the factory rarely have the specific code version that the organization has standardized for a particular type of equipment. It is much easier to keep up with security alerts when all like equipment are running the same versions.

2. Load security template— it is a good idea to have a well thought-out security template that enforces all security policies and disables factory settings used to easily compromise systems. (See **List 10-3**.) Be careful when upgrading code; it can change security settings.

3. Document—properly document devices for future reference. Keep a good list of active inventory, along with end-of-support dates. Update network diagrams.

4. Add equipment to Network Management Systems (NMS)—systems used for alerting, auditing, logging, and poling for historical baselines. NMS are a critical part of keeping the network secure.

5. Sign off/validate—have a senior network staff member sign off on all new installations. Make sure all unused ports are disabled, security templates have been installed and uplinks/downlinks are configured properly.

6. Make a backup copy of the network equipment configurations, and make sure the backup is stored off site.

DECOMMISSIONING CHECK LIST 10-2

1. Archive configurations for future reference if any issues or questions come up after replacement of decommissioned equipment.

2. Remove all configurations from device—make sure all copies of the configuration have been removed from the Nonvolatile Random Access Memory (NVRAM). and all flash memory. It is a good idea to format the flash memory after deleting the configuration files. Know where files are stored on your systems, especially pre-shared encryption keys.

3. Remove decommissioned devices from documentation—clean up documentation. Remove from databases and lists.

4. Remove decommissioned devices from all NMS—clean up after yourself. Don't forget the Domain Name System (DNS), Terminal Access Controller Access-Control System (TACACS), and logging devices. It is much easier to clean up as you go rather than expecting someone else to figure it out afterward.

5. Get rid of the decommissioned devices as soon as possible—if you are using them for a trade-in or selling them to a third party, be careful that you don't keep them laying around too long. They're too easy to redeploy in an emergency situation and, besides, you don't need them taking up your valuable space.

LIST 10-3: NETWORK EQUIPMENT SECURITY TEMPLATE

1. Time stamp local system logging—helps to correlate logs when working on problems.
2. Encrypt passwords—denies over-the-shoulder eavesdropping for passwords.
3. Auto configure—disable if not in use.
4. Setup authentication, authorization, accounting (AAA)—allows proper user access, levels of access, time of access, duration of access, and auditing of all changes after access.
5. Change all factory default passwords—factory settings can be used for unauthorized access to equipment. Just doing a web search on "default password list" should convince you.
6. Error-disable—if your device has an error disable feature, make sure you set up a timed auto recovery. If you have a problem like a spanning-tree misconfiguration that error-disables multiple ports on multiple devices, auto recovery is a much faster way to recover than physically visiting each device and manually enabling error-disabled ports.
7. Daylight Savings Time (DST)—set up clock for proper Greenwich Mean Time (GMT) offset and DST variables.
8. HTTP/HTTPS/Telnet access—disables all access to the network devices that are not in use. Command Line Interface (CLI) should only be allowed with Secure Shell (SSh).
9. Administrator access—set up Access Control List (ACL) to only allow specific subnet or individual administrators' IP addresses to have direct CLI or Graphical User Interface (GUI) access.
10. External logging—set up an external logging server. For example, a Syslog server or event log management system to aggregate syslogs from all network devices is preferable to a server that is not directly accessible to anyone except the information security officer because hackers try to obtain system administrator access and then delete the event logs to hide their activities.
11. Simple Network Management Protocol (SNMP)—change all default SNMP read-write community strings.
12. Message banner—a message banner should state very specifically that unauthorized access is prohibited. Refrain from using words like "welcome" or from disclosing information that will be useful to an intruder or hacker.
13. Set up console access—when all else fails you must be able to access the equipment through a console port.
14. Idle timeout should be set to clear connections that are not being used (20 minutes should be long enough).
15. Access using Secure Shell (SSH)—enabling SSH access allows encrypted communication to network devices.

16. Time Protocol (NTP)—keeping all device clocks synchronized helps with logging and the timing of network issues.
17. Off site access—all access from off site should be handled through a Virtual Private Network (VPN) connection.

NETWORK ATTACKS AND COUNTERMEASURES

A stable network infrastructure is the foundation of a secure network. Building the network with scalability, flexibility and the right level of redundancy can be a double-edged sword when trying to deal with predictable traffic flow. Take the time to baseline, and understand the data flow in your network.

Keeping accurate, easily accessible, and up-to-date documentation can accelerate the time it takes to explain problems to others who are trying to help. Understanding how things fit together in today's complex environments, when seconds can make a difference, is not something that can be put off. The days of keeping your network diagram on a dry erase white board are no longer acceptable at any level. There are a variety of excellent tools available to help with the documentation. Take the time to select the right tool for the job. Using automated tools can help reduce human error.

Keeping everyone engaged and informed with a formal change management process is a part of a stable environment. Change management should have an official approval and communication process that describes the reason for the change and includes a detailed test plan, areas/things affected, time frame, resources needed, benefits, level of risk and a back-out plan. Coordinating changes for the organization can help alleviate extended outages caused by one group taking down a resource at an inopportune time for another group. When implementing information security, you will always search for a balance between security and access. At one end of the spectrum is a closed network that can only be accessed on site and/or over highly encrypted communication, with very tight physical restrictions as seen in military installations. At the other end, you will see open access from anywhere to anything like a public wireless network at Starbucks. You must take the time to understand where in the spectrum your policies fall. In most cases, you will find yourself at different levels in different parts of your network.

Anytime you look at the perimeter network traffic, you will see someone or something trying to penetrate your defenses. If your organization understands that security is everyone's responsibility, you are way ahead of most. Educated users are the best first line of defense. Information security is not about any one thing that will protect your network, it is instead about every part of the layered defense giving you end-to-end protection. Everything discussed in this chapter is a part of the countermeasure. It is not as much about the specific attack; a new one will be created to replace the one you stopped today. It is more about being prepared for the unexpected.

ADDITIONAL RESOURCES

1.　　Herzig TW. *Information Security in Healthcare: Managing Risk.* Chicago: HIMSS, 2010.
2.　　Armerding T. The 15 worst data security breaches of the 21st century. CSO. Available at: www.csoonline.com/article/700263/the-15-worst-data-security-breaches-of-the-21st-century.

3. Wikipedia. Communications assistance for law enforcement. Available at: http://en.wikipedia.org/wiki/Communications_Assistance_for_Law_Enforcement_Act.

4. Porter T. The perils of deep packet inspection. Symantec. Available at: www.symantec.com/connect/articles/perils-deep-packet-inspection.

5. Nesser P. An appeal to the Internet community to return unused IP networks (prefixes) to the IANA. Nesser & Nesser Consulting. February 1996. Available at: http://tools.ietf.org/html/rfc1917.

6. Congdon P, Sanchez M, Aboba B. RADIUS attributes for virtual LAN and priority support. Hewlett-Packard Co. and Microsoft Corp. Available at: http://tools.ietf.org/html/rfc4675.

7. Mell P, Grance T. The NIST definition of cloud computing: Recommendations of the National Institute of Standards and Technology. Special publication 800-145. NIST. September 2011. Available at: http://csrc.nist.gov/publications/nistpubs/800-145/SP800-145.pdf.

8. Balint B, Griggs P. IUP IT Services. Cloud computing: Best practices for public, private or no cloud at all. [video] Available at: www.brighttalk.com/channel/499.

9. InfoWorld. Cloud computing deep dive. *InfoWorld*. February 2012. Available at: www.infoworld.com/sites/infoworld.com/files/cloud-deep-dive0212.pdf.

10. Cisco. Cisco bring your own device: Device freedom without compromising the IT network. July 17, 2012. Available at: www.cisco.com/en/US/docs/solutions/Enterprise/Borderless_Networks/Unified_Access/byodwp.pdf.

CHAPTER 11

Use of Encryption

By Brian Evans, CISSP, CISM, CISA, CGEIT

The rise of malicious attacks from insiders and outsiders and the turn from nuisance hacking to profit-driven hacking has dramatically increased the likelihood of vulnerabilities being exploited in damaging ways, reducing the margin of error on technical controls. Failures of information security routinely make headlines and involve increasingly costly response efforts. As a result, information security is now a board-level concern, which has focused the interest in a variety of technical solutions.

One technical solution has become a critical component to every healthcare organization—encryption. According to the HIPAA Security Rule, "Encryption means the use of an algorithmic process to transform data into a form in which there is a low probability of assigning meaning without use of a confidential process or key."[1] Encryption technologies are used to store and transfer data in a secure format, ensuring its protection against compromise or unauthorized access. The U.S. Department of Health & Human Services (HHS) references stored data or "data at rest" as data residing in databases, file systems, and other structured storage methods; and "data in motion" as data moving through a network, including wireless transmission.[2] While encryption may not be suitable for every situation, healthcare organizations need to have a solid business case for not deploying them.

HHS designated encryption as an addressable implementation specification to provide additional flexibility in complying with security standards. Therefore, it is not a HIPAA requirement to encrypt electronic PHI (ePHI). However, the Health Information Technology for Economic and Clinical Health (HITECH) Act's breach notification rule contains a Safe Harbor provision,[3] exempting organizations from reporting data breaches that are encrypted in compliance with specific National Institute of Standards and Technology (NIST) guidelines,[4] which are as follows:

- The Special Publication (SP) 800-111 Guide to Storage Encryption Technologies for End User Devices describes the strengths and weaknesses of various file and file-system encryption methods. This document illustrates data storage problems and the ways various mechanisms work to protect data.
- The SP 800-52 Guidelines for the Selection and Use of Transport Layer Security (TLS) Implementations, SP 800-77 Guide to IPsec VPNs, and SP 800-113 Guide

to SSL VPNs describe how to use virtual private networks and encrypted channels to protect transmitted data.

REGULATIONS AND STANDARDS

Under the Technical Safeguards section, the HIPAA Security Rule lists encryption twice, both as an addressable implementation specification. The first entry, §164.312(a) (2) (iv) Encryption and Decryption, is intended to ensure that encryption is appropriate for storing and maintaining ePHI at rest. The second entry, §164.312(e) (2) (ii) Encryption, is intended to ensure that encryption is reasonable and appropriate for ePHI in transmission. Since the Security Rule states that addressable specifications are required in any situation where their implementation would be "reasonable and appropriate," then the reason must be documented and equivalent security measures must be implemented if the situation is not reasonable. However, NIST states "For all federal agencies . . . all of the HIPAA Security Rule's addressable implementation specifications will most likely be reasonable and appropriate safeguards for implementation, given their sizes, missions, and resources."[5]

The HITECH Act's breach notification rule stipulates that healthcare organizations, health plans, other healthcare service providers and their business associates are required to issue notifications to federal authorities, as well as those affected if protected health information (PHI) is breached.[6] As of October 1, 2012, the Office for Civil Rights (OCR) had posted 498 total breaches of PHI affecting 500 or more individuals.[7] A majority of these breaches originated from laptops, desktops, servers, backup tapes, hard drives, e-mail, CDs and other portable electronic media accounting for 76 percent, or 381, of the total. These data breaches could have been avoided if encryption was employed. The increasing prevalence of mobile devices and peripherals will make the likelihood of breaches even higher.

HHS has identified encryption and destruction as acceptable methods for rendering ePHI unusable, unreadable, or indecipherable to unauthorized individuals. So, if encrypted data are lost or stolen, then the incident is not even considered a data breach. This avoids the potential fines and penalties associated with breaches, as well as the costs of investigating and notifying affected individuals.

Federal and state regulations are increasingly emphasizing encryption capabilities, specifically those tied to breach notifications. Besides the HIPAA Security Rule and HITECH Act, there are two other external drivers impacting encryption requirements in healthcare today. They originate from Meaningful Use (Stage 1 and 2) and the Payment Card Industry Data Security Standard (PCI DSS).

Under Meaningful Use Stage 1, two of the requirements pertain to encryption,[8] which are as follows:

- General encryption. Encrypt and decrypt electronic health information in accordance with the standard specified in § 170.210(a)(1), unless the Secretary determines that the use of such algorithm would pose a significant security risk for Certified EHR Technology.
- Encryption when exchanging electronic health information. Encrypt and decrypt electronic health information when exchanged in accordance with the standard specified in § 170.210(a)(2).

Healthcare organizations can use any encryption algorithm identified by NIST as an approved security function in Annex A of the Federal Information Processing Standard (FIPS) Publication 140-2.[9] The electronic health record (EHR) applications should support encryption features including its databases, servers and individual workstations. When data are exchanged between EHR applications, encryption should be used.

Under Meaningful Use Stage 2,[10] one objective is to "Protect electronic health information created or maintained by the Certified EHR Technology through the implementation of appropriate technical capabilities." The measure of this objective is a risk analysis, which has changed slightly from Stage 1, with one notable addition that highlights encryption:

"Conduct or review a security risk analysis in accordance with the requirements under 45 CFR 164.308(a) (1), *including addressing the encryption/security of data stored in Certified EHR Technology* in accordance with requirements under 45 CFR 164.312(a) (2) (iv) and 45 CFR 164.306(d) (3), and implement security updates as necessary and correct identified security deficiencies as part of the EP's [Eligible Professional] risk management process."

As part of Stage 2 Meaningful Use, encryption of data at rest should be considered an addressable control. As such, healthcare organizations need a process by which they evaluate whether the control is reasonable and appropriate and would likely contribute to protecting ePHI. If the control is deemed reasonable and appropriate, then it must be implemented. However, if the decision to encrypt data at rest is not reasonable and appropriate, then there must be documentation as to why it is not reasonable and appropriate, and an equivalent, alternative measure must be implemented. This makes it increasingly difficult for any organization to justify not encrypting ePHI under the "reasonable and appropriate" stipulation.

This provision is not an encryption mandate, but determining reasonableness is more about whether or not the organization can execute the requirement consistently and effectively than the cost of hardware, software, or the complexity of encryption implementation. Given that the majority of reported breaches to date have been the result of lost or stolen devices containing unencrypted data, and the increasing mobility of data itself, it will be difficult for organizations to find alternative measures that can match the level of protection offered by encryption solutions.

PCI DSS requires sensitive information to be encrypted during transmission over public networks and end-user messaging technologies because it is easy and common for a malicious individual to intercept and/or divert data while in transit.[11] Additionally, PCI DSS has encryption as one of the primary approaches for rendering credit card data unreadable anywhere it is stored, including on portable digital media, backup media and in audit logs. There is also a standard established for point-to-point encryption (P2PE) used to secure payment card information.[12] P2PE is a security technique that provides encryption of cardholder data from the point of interaction all the way to the payment processor. Interaction is the initial point where cardholder data are read from a credit card, generally from the keyboard where manual entry is made or the card reader itself.

Although complying with regulations and standards like PCI DSS actually promotes security, healthcare organizations have the challenge of complying with more than one regulation or standard, with overlapping or occasionally contradictory requirements. As security-related regulations and standards multiply and become more prescriptive, healthcare organizations face the prospect of being mired in multiple compliance efforts and losing focus on real security objectives. Organizations need to realize that while compliance does not necessarily lead to security, good security most likely meets the "due care" principle underlying most regulations and standards. The only reasonable solution in the long run is to rationalize security controls and processes so that compliance with applicable regulations and standards becomes a by-product of security.

ENCRYPTION POLICY

Every organization needs a policy that sets out how users can access, use, store, transmit and e-mail information. A policy can drive and shape training and technical decisions when it comes to encrypting data at rest and in transit. But before investing in encryption technology, it is important for healthcare organizations to start with a risk analysis. This will provide insight into the encryption controls that currently exist, any gaps and overall risk rankings and help identify where and what types of encryption solutions or controls are needed. Once the risk analysis is complete, develop an encryption policy and procedure, spelling out what is needed to enable encryption not only from a compliance perspective but a risk management perspective as well. For example, the policy should require that all e-mail containing confidential information be automatically encrypted.

Based on the HIPAA Audit Program Protocol,[13] elements to consider include but are not limited to

- Type(s) of encryption used.
- How encryption keys are protected.
- Access to modify or create keys is restricted to appropriate personnel.
- How keys are managed.

Mobile Devices and Peripherals

Deploying encryption where there is a high risk of data loss or theft is the best place to begin. One of the largest risks for exposed confidential information comes from mobile devices such as laptops, tablets and smartphones and peripherals such as USB drives, thumb drives, memory sticks, CDs, and DVDs. In today's mobile generation, the ability to protect data is an issue that encryption handles well. Encryption does not prevent an unauthorized individual from gaining access to a mobile device or peripheral, but it does prevent access to the information it stores. Rendering stolen or lost data useless is an important aspect in securing information and one of the basic building blocks of an effective information security program.

With the emergence of low-cost, highly portable devices of varying shapes, sizes, and configurations, organizations should extend the same encryption practices regardless of cost, resources, or unique platforms. With the upsurge of smartphones and tablets, many employees are using their own devices as well. These devices need to be verified so that the data can be encrypted before the organization puts itself at a higher level of risk.

There are basically two approaches available for securing data stored on mobile devices and peripherals: purchase devices with built-in encryption or add encryption to the devices by using a third-party software product. Both are effective options. However, built-in hardware encryption may result in better performance and be more user-friendly. Heightened awareness surrounding mobile device security issues has increased the demand for built-in and add-on encryption. As a result, vendors have a number of products available to help meet this demand. SanDisk, Lexar Media, IronKey, McAfee, Checkpoint, and PGP are just a few vendors offering encrypted solutions for mobile devices and peripherals that meet the FIPS 140-2 encryption standards.

There are encryption solutions available at no cost as well. Microsoft's Encrypting File System (EFS) is part of the Windows XP operating system and BitLocker Drive Encryption provides built-in whole-disk encryption on the Windows 7 operating system. Other encryption solutions can be downloaded and installed for free such as TrueCrypt. Third-party compression utilities such as 7Zip and WinZip offer built-in encryption that allows secure packaging of data files for transport.

Regardless of what vendor or encryption option is considered, organizations need to realize that mobile devices and peripherals are becoming a large part of the overall operation and need to be protected with encryption. With the multitude of affordable encryption options available, it becomes increasingly difficult for organizations to allow confidential data onto unencrypted mobile devices and peripherals. Ultimately, healthcare organizations are putting themselves in an unnecessary position of risk without encrypting their data on mobile devices and peripherals. NIST has published recommendations to improve the security of mobile devices in SP 800-124, Rev 1, Draft Guidelines for Managing and Securing Mobile Devices in the Enterprise.[14]

Wireless Networking

Most wireless local area networks (WLANs), or Wi-Fi networks, provide network connectivity primarily for computing devices. For patients and visitors, Wi-Fi networks provide convenient Internet access from laptops and smartphones. For clinicians and administrators, Wi-Fi networks provide access to networks and databases from workstations on wheels (WoWs), tablet computers, handheld mobile computers, smartphones, and other computing devices. The healthcare environment naturally lends itself to wireless networking, given the inherently mobile nature of physicians, nurses and other clinicians who move from bedside to examining room in delivering patient care.

While Wi-Fi networks are exposed to many of the same risks as wired networks, they are vulnerable to additional risks as well. Wi-Fi networks transmit data through radio frequencies and are open to unauthorized users unless protected. Unlike wired networks, unauthorized monitoring and denial of service attacks can be performed without a physical wire connection.

Additionally, unauthorized devices can potentially connect to the network, or connect to other wireless devices. Without proper Wi-Fi security in place, an unauthorized user could use intercepted Wi-Fi packets to gain access to the wired network and view confidential information transmitted over the air.

Wi-Fi security threats are mitigated through good security practices. The foundation of strong security is the Wi-Fi Protected Access Version 2 (WPA2). WPA2 provides both access control and transmission controls for communications traveling across the network. WPA2 creates fresh session keys on every association. The benefit is that the encryption keys used for each device on the network are unique and specific to that device, ensuring that all communications sent over the air are encrypted with a unique key.

WPA2 should be used on every device that supports it. Devices that do not support WPA2 should be segregated onto a different Wi-Fi network Service Set Identifier (SSID). The SSID is the public name of a wireless network. Sharing or mixing devices of varying levels of security on the same SSID is not recommended. Similarly, devices from visitors, as well as devices brought in and used by employees but not managed by the organization, should be on a different SSID as well.

WPA2 offers considerably more protection than the older standards such as Wired Equivalent Privacy (WEP) and Wi-Fi Protected Access (WPA), both of which can be compromised quickly. WPA2 uses the Advanced Encryption Standard (AES) for data encryption and is FIPS 140-2-compliant. WPA2 provides healthcare organizations with a high level of assurance that their data will remain protected and that only authorized users can access their Wi-Fi networks.

From a regulation and standard perspective, the portion of the HIPAA Security rule that is primarily applicable to Wi-Fi devices and networks is section 164.312, which lists technical safeguards for access control[15] "Ensure that only authorized users can gain access to ePHI" and transmission security "Implement technical security measures to guard against unauthorized access to ePHI that is being transmitted over an electronic communications network." The PCI DSS prohibited the use of WEP as a security control as of 30 June 2010. It recommends that WPA2 be used with a minimum 13-character random passphrase and AES encryption.[16] NIST has published recommendations to improve the security of wireless networks in SP 800-153 Guidelines for Securing Wireless Local Area Networks (WLANs).[17]

HIPAA Security and PCI DSS should be taken into account when buying new wireless-enabled equipment. Not every bedside monitoring device or wireless intravenous pump has the capacity to encrypt at the WPA2 level. Work with the biomedical equipment vendors on getting the highest encryption level possible because they are behind in providing the latest wireless technology.

DATABASE ENCRYPTION

Healthcare organizations have traditionally overlooked the practice of database encryption as a viable protection method despite the increasing number of data breaches and importance of regulations and standards impacting databases. This is also in spite of the fact that most major database vendors have a built-in transparent data encryption (TDE) solution to include Microsoft's SQL Server, Oracle's 11g and InterSystems' Caché databases. The financial services industry has embraced TDE for years, but it has not been equally adopted in healthcare. According to the PCI DSS Requirement 3.4, credit card data should be unreadable anywhere it is stored and should never be stored as clear text, which includes in databases.

The most cited reason for avoiding database encryption is that it might slow down critical business processes. Although performance overhead can be a legitimate concern, this can vary widely and can be reduced by using dedicated hardware encryption. Platforms running TDE, for example, can average about a 5 percent performance hit when encrypting database files, which is hardly noticeable to the average user. Results may vary based on the nature of the data in the database and the applications accessing it. Testing in a customized environment will determine if database encryption impacts performance.

There are three basic approaches to encrypting database data:

- File-level encryption
- Column-level encryption
- Application encryption

File-level encryption. Healthcare organizations concerned about unauthorized access to database files should use file-level encryption, which is the most transparent form of database encryption. Database files are encrypted completely at the storage level using a hardware or software encryption tool on the server or network appliance. The files are decrypted when accessed by the database management system or other authorized users. File encryption protects against direct unauthorized access or theft of database files, but it does not protect the database if it is accessed through an authorized channel such as an SQL injection attack. Remote and mobile databases containing confidential information should use file encryption. Database files should be encrypted on servers or file stores when the physical security of the storage medium cannot be guaranteed which includes backup data.

Column-level encryption. Healthcare organizations concerned with the database administrator and other users accessing sensitive data should consider column-level encryption. Fields within the database are encrypted based on their column. So, only authorized users can see the decrypted results. Unauthorized users see a scrambled or blank result, which is known as data masking. For example, if the "Social Security number" column is encrypted, authorized users running queries see the numbers, while other users that run the same query see only blank data or truncated data. Column-level encryption protects against unauthorized access or theft of database files, or unauthorized access to column data by an authorized database user. Performance hits from column encryption vary based on the structure of the database and query structure.

Application encryption. Data are encrypted by the application before it is stored in the database. Database queries return encrypted data that they can only be decrypted by the application. Key management and access management is handled by the application, or by an external cryptographic engine through an application-programming interface. Application-level encryption can be difficult to manage, difficult to program and varies widely in the applications that offer it. However, it ensures that the data are encrypted from acquisition to storage.

Column-level encryption and most forms of application encryption offer the protections of file encryption, and they can restrict authorized users from seeing restricted data without compromising these users' ability to otherwise use the database. For example, column-level encryption can separate database administration and security administration functions.

Database encryption is an effective tool but only as a component of an overall comprehensive information security program. The appropriate encryption strategy should be applied in combination with overall security practices and database access controls. Once again, conducting a risk analysis will provide a good understanding on the appropriateness of database encryption.

Secure Sockets Layer

Secure sockets layer (SSL) technology continues to be an essential component of web-based operations. Healthcare organizations increasingly rely on the Internet to reach their patient population with online patient records and bill paying. With this increase in web traffic, along with transmission of confidential information, SSL is no longer just a nice-to-have capability, but an absolute necessity. At the same time, Internet security threats are escalating every year. Readily available Internet session hacking tools like Firesheep pose a serious security threat to online operations. To combat these threats, organizations should implement SSL for all Internet traffic.

Simply encrypting login and checkout pages is no longer sufficient. Healthcare organizations should expand the use of SSL to cover the entire user session, which better protects themselves and their patients against security threats. This allows SSL to encrypt not only the sensitive components of the application such as the login page, but the entire application surface area. In addition to using SSL, the strength of encryption is also important. NIST has issued a security notification, SP 800-131A Transitions: Recommendation for Transitioning the Use of Cryptographic Algorithms and Key Lengths, which advocates that organizations stop using 1024-bit keys between 2011 and 2013. It also advises against the use of 1024-bit keys beginning in 2014.[18]

Additionally, leading browser vendors such as Microsoft's Internet Explorer will start requiring websites to use 2048-bit keys to protect browser users. These browser vendors require certificate authorities (CA) to ensure that certificates issued with a key size smaller than 2048-bit will expire before December 31, 2013. This means that browsers like Internet Explorer will refuse to access websites that do not have keys with minimum lengths. Doubling key size from 1024-bit to 2048-bit certainly offers twice the strength. However, the SSL processing power required with 2048-bit keys is also greater than what is required for 1024-bit from an infrastructure standpoint.

For these reasons, healthcare organizations need to properly plan for the migration from 1024-bit to 2048-bit to secure their applications and application data, and to ensure their infrastructure can support larger key sizes or risk performance and availability impacts to their operations. This means organizations need to adopt new SSL infrastructure specifically designed for stronger SSL to maintain application performance and availability.

The following are key steps to take in preparing for 2048-bit SSL certificates:

- Inventory each infrastructure element terminating SSL traffic, and determine if it has the processing capacity to support stronger levels of encryption.
- Conduct an audit of SSL certificates currently in use and renew the ones expiring soonest.
- Evaluate current SSL performance requirements of the network and applications.
- Design an infrastructure to meet both present and future requirements.

- Test less mission critical applications to gain familiarity with the technology and understand the new performance demands.
- Measure end-user application performance before, during and after the transition to 2048-bit SSL.

E-MAIL ENCRYPTION

One of the many challenges faced by healthcare organizations is the need to exchange information securely. Compliance drivers like the HIPAA Security/HITECH Acts and PCI DSS all but mandate e-mail encryption. Case in point, the Transmission Security standard in the HIPAA Security Rule states: "Implement technical security measures to guard against unauthorized access to electronic protected health information that is being transmitted over an electronic communications network."[19] The only way to effectively meet this standard is to encrypt e-mails that contain confidential information. Another driver is the flurry of data breach reports of lost mobile devices containing unencrypted data, which often include e-mails. The HITECH Act's notification provision applies only to breaches involving unsecured information whether the data are in motion or at rest. E-mail and any associated attachment files sent unencrypted are typically copied to several servers in transit. The data on those servers are usually backed up on tape or disk. Therefore, any organization sending confidential information over the Internet needs to encrypt it. Yet, the adoption of e-mail encryption has been slow. On January 30, 2012, Forrester Research issued a white paper stating that only 33 percent of companies surveyed indicated that they had implemented e-mail encryption.

There are several e-mail encryption options available:

Desktop-to-Desktop
E-mail is encrypted at the sending desktop and remains encrypted until it is decrypted at the receiving desktop. At no point is an e-mail unencrypted during the transmission of the message. Technically, this can work well. But it has several disadvantages:
- Managing the keys can be burdensome.
- Keys are no more secure than the desktops themselves.
- Because users can store e-mail encrypted with their personal key, management can lose control over these records, finding it difficult if not impossible to decrypt messages deleted by employees or to access e-mail of terminated employees.

Server Level or Gateway-to-Gateway
This approach uses similar technology to desktop encryption, but performs the encryption and decryption on a server rather than on a desktop client. This is different from the desktop approach in several ways.
- There are fewer keys to manage.
- Users are not burdened with key management.
- Messages are encrypted over the Internet between organizations but can be decrypted within the organization.
- E-mail is stored on the servers of sending and receiving organizations and remains under their control.
- Management retains control over its records.

- Virus checking and content filtering are possible.
- Applications can use gateways to send or receive messages.
- "Trust" is established at the organizational level rather than the individual level.

E-mail is encrypted between gateways, but not within the sender's or recipient's organizations. Administration is simpler, user burden is reduced, and organizational control over e-mail is retained. A potential drawback is that identification occurs at the organization level rather than the user level. For most business purposes, however, establishing "trust" at the organizational level should be sufficient. With this approach, business associates have to trust each other to manage their communications securely.

Secure Web Mail or Gateway-to-Web

In this approach, the sender posts a sensitive message to a secure website using an encrypted transmission. An unencrypted e-mail points to an obscure website, which is then sent to the recipient. The recipient accesses the sensitive message at the website using a secured session. The recipient uses an ID and password to access the secure session. The password is provided through a separate contact such as a telephone call or through self-registration by the recipient. E-mail is encrypted between the gateway and web portal, but not within the sender's or recipient's organizations.

This approach has the following advantages and disadvantages:

- The recipient only needs a Web browser and Internet access.
- Users and organizations do not need to manage keys (beyond those used for session security).
- Messages cannot be sent, read, or managed through existing e-mail systems.
- Messages reside on the provider's server and can be removed at any time by the sender.
- Messages cannot be downloaded, stored, or managed by the recipient except by cutting and pasting the text or saving the HTML page.
- Users must manage IDs and passwords for each individual they e-mail.
- User identification, nonrepudiation, and proof of receipt may not be fully supported.
- Virus scanning and content filtering cannot be performed when viewing and downloading due to the use of SSL sessions.

This approach has the noted disadvantages compared to approaches that preserve integration with existing e-mail systems. On the other hand, its main advantage is that such systems are not needed. This approach is the best alternative for business-to-client secure Internet e-mail. Some of its disadvantages are reduced where many of the recipients (i.e., patients) will conduct secure Internet e-mail with only a few users (i.e., physicians). It also works reasonably well where one party (i.e., physicians) conducts secure Internet e-mail with many others (i.e., patients). The process in which many parties conduct secure Internet e-mail with many other parties does not work as well.

Cisco Systems, McAfee, Symantec, ProofPoint, Trend Micro, Microsoft, Google, Secure Computing, IronPort, ZixCorp, and Tumbleweed are just a few vendors offering e-mail encryption solutions. Some vendors are also integrating their technology with inbound traffic protection by combining their message encryption products with anti-spam and antivirus solutions.

DATA BACKUP TAPES AND DISK-BASED BACKUPS

Healthcare organizations continue to use backup tapes as a means for data recovery. Encryption is an option in most backup packages, but they are not typically used. One reason appears to be that once a backup process is established and working, there is not enough incentive to add another layer of complexity potentially impacting how quickly data can be recovered. Another reason is that it may not make sense to turn encryption on globally because all the backup data are not confidential and resulting in an unnecessary increase in computing needs and time to complete backups.

On September 14, 2011, the Defense Department's TRICARE healthcare program had backup tapes stolen from the car of a business associate who was responsible for transporting them between facilities. About 4.9 million patients were affected.[20] This was the largest breach reported to OCR since the HIPAA breach notification rule mandated under the HITECH Act took effect in September 2009.

In today's world of heightened awareness about data breaches from backup tapes and the ever-increasing regulatory landscape, healthcare organizations should modify their backup practices to ensure confidential information cannot be accessed by unauthorized parties. This means making the security of backup tapes, regardless of location or type of storage device, an integral part of the overall recovery process.

Data encryption is the most effective way to ensure that only authorized users have access to confidential information, whether it is stored or transported internally or externally. When information on a tape is encrypted, it is unreadable without the key. Though it is difficult to reconstitute the information on an unencrypted backup tape without the precise hardware, software and system components, it can occur. Encryption of the data on backup tapes is the only effective means of making certain that others cannot read the information on the tapes in the event they are lost or stolen.

Encrypting backup tapes is generally not cost prohibitive. There may be server overhead, as well as staffing requirements to support key management and protection, but the cost is small in comparison to the risk of having confidential information fall into the hands of unauthorized users.

There are several options for implementing encryption that can balance backup objectives with the need to protect confidential information. These include

Application data encryption. Under this solution, an application writes the data to the hard drive in an encrypted format. Therefore, the backup software copies encrypted data. Data compression techniques cannot be used once the data have been encrypted. With the lack of compression, more media and a longer backup window are required.

Storage software/backup software encryption. Most backup software includes an option for encryption. This provides the benefit of low impact on infrastructure changes, but may not be the right choice for high-volume data encryption. Adding a step to the backup process may increase the time needed to successfully complete the backup, prohibit the use of compression, and potentially increase the media required to complete the backup. Increasing amounts of data and increasing backup windows can impact the success of the backup process.

Appliance model. Appliances promise a high throughput, low-impact configuration, allow use of compression and require lower management overhead. These devices are either a physically attached device or the combination of a device and agent software.

Combination approach. Backup data are sent in an encrypted form over the network to a secure disk vault. Then, this encrypted information is moved to a backup tape for off-line secure storage.

Regardless of the method, the data will eventually need to be unencrypted. An encryption key can be a simple password or a highly complex string of random characters. Different users will require specific keys to access data, making key management central to any encryption solution. Successful key management should include a backup plan that is compatible with other leading solutions in case strategies change.

Another alternative to consider beyond backup tape encryption is a disk-based backup solution. Disk-based solutions offer non-linear writing and reading, faster restore times and an overall easier backup process. They do not require sensitive handling like tapes. Off site backups do not require the physical transportation of media, which can slow down the Recovery Time Objectives (RTO) because tapes need to be a safe distance from the primary site of operations to the current backup storage facility site.

The random access nature of disk drives enables the instant merging of incremental backups. Contrast this with tape, where multiple incremental backups are often spread across multiple tapes and are likely to be far from the start of the tape. The Redundant Array of Inexpensive Drives (RAID) configuration of the disks in a backup appliance allows for redundancy and increased throughput by backing up and restoring multiple clients simultaneously. So, when a file or an e-mail needs to be restored, finding and restoring it can be done in a matter of minutes without sorting through any number of tapes.

Disk-based backups reduce the backup windows in two ways. First, random access and higher reliability of the disk media means more incremental backups can be leveraged per full backup. Full backups can be scheduled much less frequently, or selected to coincide with an expected lull in operations (i.e., over the weekend). Since incremental backups typically need to save a small fraction of the total data, most backup windows become much shorter. Second, multiple devices can be backed up simultaneously with disk-based backup, which results in higher throughput.

Research has found that as many as 70 percent of tape recovery attempts fail. Disk-based solutions benefit from very reliable commodity disks. There are no tapes to misplace, or robotics to jam and recalibrate. Disk drives are self-contained and less sensitive to environmental conditions, so they can be reliably used for a longer period of time in more diverse environments.

CONCLUSION

Healthcare organizations have realized it is not possible to protect everything, so they must prioritize what to protect. The measures should be proportionate to the threat, and the cost should not exceed the value of the asset being protected. There is no doubt that encryption protects confidential information during storage and transmission. It serves as part of a defense-in-depth strategy and provides important functionality to reduce the risk of intentional and accidental compromise.

Healthcare organizations need to create a sustainable culture of information security by supplying executives with the requisite information necessary to make trade-off decisions between encryption and other business priorities. Since encryption is a safe harbor provision in the eyes of the law, healthcare organizations should do all they can to achieve it. By taking steps to implement encryption, healthcare organizations and their business associates can reap the operational benefits while avoiding potential fines and penalties associated with breaches that might result from regulatory action, as well as the costs of investigating and notifying affected individuals.

REFERENCES

1. HIPAA Security Rule Appendix A to Subpart C of Part 164-Security Standards: Matrix §164.304 Definitions.

2. 74 FR 79. April 27, 2009. Available at: www.hhs.gov/ocr/privacy/hipaa/understanding/coveredentities/federalregisterbreachrfi.pdf.

3. 45 CFR Parts 160 and 164. Available at: www.hhs.gov/ocr/privacy/hipaa/understanding/coveredentities/hitechrfi.pdf.

4. National Institute of Standards and Technology. Special publications (800 series). Available at: ttp://csrc.nist.gov/publications/PubsSPs.html.

5. National Institute of Standards and Technology. Special Publication 800-66. An introductory resource guide for implementing the Health Insurance Portability and Accountability Act (HIPAA) Security Rule.

6. U.S. Department of Health & Human Services. Breach notification rule. Available at: www.hhs.gov/ocr/privacy/hipaa/administrative/breachnotificationrule/index.html.

7. U.S. Department of Health & Human Services. Breaches affecting 500 or more individuals. Available at: www.hhs.gov/ocr/privacy/hipaa/administrative/breachnotificationrule/breachtool.html.

8. 42 CFR Parts 412, 413, 422, et al. Available at: www.gpo.gov/fdsys/pkg/FR-2010-07-28/pdf/2010-17207.pdf.

9. National Institute of Standards and Technology. FIPs publications. Available at: http://csrc.nist.gov/publications/PubsFIPS.html.

10. http://www.ofr.gov/OFRUpload/OFRData/2012-21050_PI.pdf.

11. Payment Card Industry Security Standards Council. Data security standard: Navigating PCI DSS. Available at: www.pcisecuritystandards.org/documents/navigating_dss_v20.pdf.

12. Payment Card Industry Security Standards Council. Solution requirements and testing procedures: Encryption, decryption, and key management within secure cryptographic devices. Available at: www.pcisecuritystandards.org/documents/P2PE_%20v%201-1.pdf.

13. U.S. Department of Health & Human Services. Audit program protocol. Available at: www.hhs.gov/ocr/privacy/hipaa/enforcement/audit/protocol.html.

14. Souppaya M, Scarfone K. Guidelines for managing and securing mobile devices in the enterprise (draft): Recommendations of the National Institute of Standards and Technology. NIST. Available at: http://csrc.nist.gov/publications/drafts/800-124r1/draft_sp800-124-rev1.pdf.

15. 45 CFR 160, 162, AND 164. Available at: www.hhs.gov/ocr/privacy/hipaa/administrative/securityrule/securityrulepdf.pdf.

16. PCI Security Standards Council. Information supplement: PCI DSS wireless guidelines. August 2011. Available at: www.pcisecuritystandards.org/pdfs/PCI_DSS_v2_Wireless_Guidelines.pdf.

17. Souppaya M, Scarfone K. Guidelines for securing wireless local area networks: Recommendations of the National Institute of Standards and Technology. NIST. Available at: http://csrc.nist.gov/publications/nistpubs/800-153/sp800-153.pdf.

18. Barker E, Roginsky A. NIST Special Publication 800-131A. Transitions: Recommendation for transitioning the use of cryptographic algorithms and key lengths. Available at: http://csrc.nist.gov/publications/nistpubs/800-131A/sp800-131A.pdf.

19. 45 CFR 160. 162, and 164. Available at: www.hhs.gov/ocr/privacy/hipaa/administrative/securityrule/securityrulepdf.pdf.

20. Tricare. Proactive steps taken to address data breach. Available at: www.tricare.mil/breach.

CHAPTER 12

Managing Mobile Devices

By Mark W. Dill, Brian Evans, CISSP, CISM, CISA, CGEIT, and Tom Walsh, CISSP

Innovative technologies have paved the way for mobile devices to integrate into healthcare operations. These devices have acted as a catalyst for improving efficiency, productivity, and availability. While many healthcare organizations are using this technology, they typically have not considered the overall risks or governance implications associated with mobile devices. As a result, the growth of mobile device use has created one of the top security concerns for every healthcare organization.

Mobile devices (as used within the context of this chapter) can be defined as having personal computer-like functionality, or "smartphones", which include laptops, netbooks, tablet computers and personal digital assistants (PDAs), providing the user with the opportunity for seamless communication and/or information storage whether in the office or elsewhere. The communication capabilities use wireless networks to communicate via phone, e-mail, or text.

The opportunity to leverage the benefits of these devices and improve efficiency and physician satisfaction is significant. The argument for their use is compelling. Information security professionals must find a way to maintain the necessary balance between protecting confidential information and device usability for organizations and patients to reap the rewards of innovation.

The consumerization trend has hit IT as an unstoppable force, as 821 million smartphones and tablets were purchased worldwide in 2012 and will pass the billion mark in 2013, according to Gartner, Inc. Mobile devices account for 70 percent of total devices sold in 2012.[1] The consumerization of IT assets will challenge the healthcare market space.

Mobile device usage within healthcare organizations falls into three common use cases.

Internal—clinical. Access to a multitude of clinical information at the point of care can make a remarkable impact. For example, the ability for a radiology image to be displayed on a mobile device while in the company of the patient facilitates a better patient education experience. The ability of today's handheld mobile devices to interact, zoom, rotate, and focus in on an area of the image can provide a better level of understanding.

TABLE 12-1: Text Messaging and E-mail via Mobile Devices.

E-mail—Most organizations allow PHI to be sent through internal e-mail because it is considered secure. However, these same organizations also allow web access to e-mail. If I send you an e-mail with PHI, I may think you are in your office working on your computer, when in reality, you could be on any computer, laptop, tablet, smartphone—anywhere—checking your corporate e-mail via a web browser. Forget about the MDMS—we're talking PHI anywhere! What happens if the user does a "print screen" or saves an e-mail attachment to their smartphone? What are the risks here?

Text messages—Text messaging is quickly replacing pager use. Texting questions about a patient's care is more common than "paging" the doctor with a question. Is text messaging secure? What mobile device do they use? Is there an audit trail or record of this? How can we rely on the identity of the message sender, especially if the device was not locked? Where is the message stored? If there was an adverse outcome with the patient, could the personally-owned device become part of a litigation hold? Are users aware of this?

The Joint Commission and Text Messaging

"It is not acceptable for physicians or licensed independent practitioners to text orders for patients to the hospital or other healthcare setting."

"This method provides no ability to verify the identity of the person sending the text and there is no way to keep the original message as validation of what is entered into the medical record."

The Joint Commission (November 2011)

Another example is showing or discussing a lab result. This can be done bedside with a mobile device rather than requiring the patient to walk to a PACS workstation, moving a computer on wheels over to the patient or supplying the lab result on paper. In some organizations, text messaging has replaced pagers. However, this can be a risky practice. Table 12-1 outlines some considerations for using text messaging and e-mail with mobile devices.

External—clinical. Mobile devices play a critical role in home healthcare, and now there is a real prospect for mobile devices to eliminate some of the health disparities by reaching underserved and remote populations. Patients located in rural and remote areas can use their mobile devices, such as iPads or tablets, to link with clinical specialists working in larger urban areas where more healthcare service options are available. For example, a parent might use their smartphone to record their child having a seizure to send it to a caregiver or show while at a doctor appointment as proof of what their child is experiencing.

Internal—non-clinical. Business process improvement and patient experience can be enhanced through mobile devices. For example, patient transportation can use mobile devices to access web apps to improve their efficiency by determining the location of staff and who is closest to the next patient. Another use case is for medical residents. Residents can do rounds or gain access to their graduate medical education curriculum, exam criteria, textbooks online, and drug interaction calculators with their iPads, thereby boosting their productivity.[2] Mobile devices can assist with onboarding of new physicians by providing them with all policies and awareness content conveniently delivered on mobile platforms. This facilitates faster learning with a higher retention level.

The opportunities presented to healthcare by the variety of mobile devices and platforms are as great as the challenges to secure them. Organizations should view this as a golden opportunity to make information security a business enabler. However, to proceed responsibly, organizations will need to analyze the risks of organizationally-issued, personally-owned and rogue devices and then apply reasonable controls. Who knows—the next super app might be one created for healthcare on a smartphone or tablet. This chapter will help healthcare organizations by outlining the key issues and recommended controls to manage the risks of using mobile devices.

TRENDS

Mobile devices have pervaded business as well as private life and offer an unprecedented degree of flexibility and a convenient alternative to laptops or computer workstations. Convenience and new patterns of work have even led to a degree of dependency on mobile devices. According to Gartner, mobile phones will overtake PCs as the most common web access device worldwide by 2013.[3]

Market demand. Apple's iPad has remained the sales leader for the past few years, but has gradually lost market share to Android devices. This trend will continue as Android tablets surpass that of the iPad in the first half of 2013, says Sameer Singh, an analyst with mergers and acquisitions consulting group, Finvista Advisors.[4] Cost pressures, however, may require healthcare organizations to consider alternatives. It may also depend on which platforms offer the best ability to innovate with software development. Inexpensive, rapidly developed, innovative and securely coded platforms will be the key to adoption success.

Although the use of Apple products is prevalent in healthcare, most IT departments have Microsoft-certified technicians with limited experience or Apple certification. How can healthcare organizations support and secure devices such as iPhones, iPads, or MacBooks if organizations don't have the expertise to support them? It is important to ensure IT departments are staffed with qualified individuals with the capabilities of supporting all technologies within their environment.

Using personally owned devices. Users initially purchase a mobile device for their own reasons but later want to use their device for business purposes as well. With the wide selection of consumer devices available today, users often have better equipment at home than they do at work. In the past, users snuck their personal mobile devices into the organization rather than risk having them banned if they asked the IT department for permission. Users who are not allowed to use what they consider cutting-edge mobile devices will inevitably see IT as behind the times and a barrier to their success. Because users don't want to carry two mobile devices with them—one for business use and one for personal use—IT departments are sometimes confronted by users who say, "I have this mobile device to do my job so make it work!" Many organizations even encourage this practice by reimbursing users for using their personal device to conduct business. This topic is covered in more detail in the section entitled "BYOD."

THREATS

There are several specific "reasonably anticipated" threats an organization should consider for mobile devices. Table 12-2 highlights the most common threats.

TABLE 12-2: Threats.

Threat Name	Impact
Theft or loss	High
Unauthorized access to confidential information	Med—High
Malicious code (virus, worm, spyware, etc.)	Med
Electronic eavesdropping or interception of wireless transmission	Med—High
Hardware failure due to mishandling or physical damage (for example, dropped or smashed)	Low

These may not be the only threats organizations will face, but they should consider how they will mitigate the risk of these threats first.

If an organization is investigated by the Centers for Medicare & Medicaid Services (CMS), the Office for Civil Rights (OCR), or the Office of the Inspector General (OIG) as a result of a breach, the first likely request will be to produce its HIPAA-required IT risk analysis and risk management plan. The second request of the investigator may likely be "show me where you assessed the risk for the root cause of the breach," and in this case, the risk of theft or loss. Organizations will be held accountable for the risk mitigation measures chosen to address this potential threat based on the likelihood and harm rating assigned to the threat.

The Department of Health & Human Services (HHS), CMS, OIG, and OCR have already established the likelihood and harm ratings for theft and loss of mobile devices, based on the root cause analysis of other breaches reported to HHS. A majority of the breaches reported to HHS that affected more than 500 patients have been caused by theft or loss; mostly from the theft or loss of laptops, tablets, smartphones and portable media.[5]

The likelihood for loss is high and the magnitude of harm is high as well, when PHI is stored on the device. This yields a high overall risk rating, and it is incumbent upon an organization to manage this risk to a reasonable level. While many controls can achieve this, the most important control organizations will likely consider is encryption for the data stored on and transmitted to and from the mobile device. Adding effective authentication to the device and its remotely accessed app or database often provides an encryption key to unlock the data and make them available to the user. This can make the device virtually impossible to access if or when it gets lost or stolen. Encryption could be considered a "get-out-of-jail-free-card" for breach notification if it is applied on all mobile assets using built-in or commercially purchased tools. The Health Information Technology for Economic and Clinical Health (HITECH) Act's breach notification rule contains a "Safe Harbor" provision,[6] exempting organizations from reporting data breaches that are encrypted in compliance with specific National Institute of Standards and Technology (NIST) guidelines.[7] Healthcare organizations are challenged with encrypting every device with PHI primarily out of concerns for the

- Cost of hardware and software;
- complexity of built-in encryption; and
- separate purchase, configuration and implementation of an encryption solution because some devices may not come with encryption.

Mobile device protection will become a primary task for organizations of all sizes. Risks posed by mobile devices are best dealt with using both network-level and device security. IT departments have to adapt to a changing environment and apply network security technologies such as VPNs, firewalls and intrusion detection/prevention systems to safely meet user demands for information access. Network security technologies can monitor the behavior of mobile devices and the use and flow of data while connected to the organization's network. Additionally, audit trails, sufficiently strong algorithms, and key management are important for mobile device security.

BYOD

BYOD stands for bring your own device to work. It implies an organizationally sponsored program allowing a worker to use their personally owned device (laptop, tablet, smartphone, etc.) to synchronize and access the organization's e-mail, calendar, and sometimes, even the network.

BYOD is largely a consumer-driven trend. While this is a worker "satisfier" for many reasons, some of the most common drivers for healthcare organizations are

- Increased worker efficiency.
- Decreased costs in capital, connectivity and IT asset acquisitions for enabling an increasingly mobile workforce.
- Improved, competitive hiring advantages for being "employee friendly."

Decisions about what to allow workers to access or store with their personal device (i.e., documents, spreadsheets, files, e-mail, applications, etc.) should be part of the BYOD program. The benefit for workers is the expectation that they can use their personal device. BYOD programs can be credited for enabling innovation within an organization, and the value proposition is engaging. If organizations have not started yet, a conversation with other organizations, more mature in their BYOD implementation, can provide a more realistic view when trying to confirm "reasonable expectations" for this program.

The flip side of the value equation remains the question of "How can this asset class be reasonably secured?" Minimum security standards are often enforced within BYOD programs including the operating system and application version levels, specific patch levels, antivirus packages with current pattern files, etc. Network Access Control (NAC) and Mobile Device Management (MDM) solutions can be deployed to interrogate organizationally issued and BYOD devices at connection or login time to ensure they meet minimum security standards and suggest or require remediation before being "trusted" on the network to perform any function. Although there are a variety of security solutions available, healthcare organizations should choose BYOD security options based on their risk tolerance level.

Challenges with BYOD

Many organizations are a hybrid environment: some smartphones and mobile devices are organizationally owned while others are personally owned with different strategies, policies and tools. IT departments will struggle as they try to support users due to the variety of products and models. Therefore, IT departments may want standardization; however, the personal nature and rapid evolution of devices make platform standardization extremely difficult. There are too many operating systems, devices and hardware platforms to expect security management agents to exist for every device and for every agent to act the same way. IT departments will have to come to the realization that managing employee-owned devices will be a challenge. They cannot configure them nor can they use tools like URL filtering when the employee is working on a personally owned device over a personal network. As a result, layered security should be standard practice and the primary focus should be on securing the data, avoiding the loss or theft of the device and the response if it does happen. Application firewalls and data loss prevention (DLP) solutions are becoming more commonly coupled with up-to-date network security-based policies.

Also, there is the issue of "ownership." The use of any mobile device encompasses a legal relationship and obligations that must be taken into account. In partial or full BYOD situations, legal obligations may arise from the fact that parts of the mobile device and its information are beyond the control of the healthcare organization. Additionally, the organization's retention policy should be reviewed to determine whether it appropriately applies to mobile devices. By the portability of mobile devices, healthcare organizations should be aware that a device may be subject to the retention requirements of several jurisdictions. A retention policy review should address:

- What type of retainable information is being stored on mobile devices.
- How this information is being archived in a BYOD environment.
- How users may be archiving data.
- How information is deleted from the mobile device and archival backups.
- How information is secured and preserved on mobile devices when required by legal orders.
- How information is efficiently extracted from mobile devices when required by court order or regulatory requirements.

Other mobile device ownership challenges include:

- Multiple manufacturers, devices and operating systems.
- Different carriers—T-Mobile, Verizon, AT&T, Sprint, etc.—with different plans, rules, capabilities, etc.

One way to address these challenges is by requiring BYOD users to agree to a set of rules outlined in a contract or user agreement. Table 12-3 outlines the key elements for a BYOD user agreement.

While BYOD may be seen as an enabler, it has also introduced a number of new risk areas. These risks need to be balanced with the advantages of mobile device use, taking into account the security needs of the individual, as well as the healthcare organization.

MOBILE DEVICE MANAGEMENT (MDM)

Mobile device management (MDM) is a tool that an IT department uses to gain oversight and some control of mobile devices used in the organization. MDM tools provide a one-console view into the devices and the users connecting to the network. MDM enables IT departments to manage mobile devices by applying a set of policies to ensure compliance, such as:

TABLE 12-3: BYOD Contract Elements.

Paragraph Title	Criteria
Title	Decide if this is an agreement or contract for BYOD devices
Purpose	Establishes the criteria of authorized use of wireless and/or wired use of named assets (iPhones, iPads, Android Devices, etc.)
Scope	Specifically, what assets are covered in this agreement (i.e., iPhones, iPads, Android, etc.) and which operating system versions? How many assets is each person permitted to enroll?
Eligibility	Define who is eligible to participate in the program (everyone, only management, physicians, hourly vs. salaried workers)
Support	**Hardware**—Who will perform break/fix services? What is the procedure to request this service? How will you ensure that your list of vendors will sign a Business Associate Agreement (because they may be exposed to you or your hospital's e-PHI)? What if the vendors agree to "reset" the device before providing their break/fix services—is that good enough? What if the device is fixable but it's damaged just enough that it cannot be reset—do you still surrender it with all its data? If you supply the password for the device, is this a breach? Will you supply or recommend a support contract with each device? **Software**—Which software packages as-delivered (by your vendor, carrier or IT team/MDM software) is fully supported? Who is responsible for making updates available in the app store vs. who is responsible for performing the software updates on the mobile device? **End-User Support**—Who does the end user contact with general questions? At what point is the end user solely responsible to solve a unique problem? Will you inform the user that they may not jailbreak or root a device once it's in the BYOD program? Will your MDM tool alert the IT team that a device has been jailbroken or rooted? **Limitations**—What types of support services will you announce as "best effort"?
Responsibility	What policies will you announce that each worker is responsible for following as they use this mobile device(s)?
Applications	**White List**—Will you manage an organization-specific "App Store" where approved applications are offered? Will they be free? When should users expect to have to pay out of pocket for apps? **Black List**—Will your IT team reserve the right to "black list" applications that are known to be malicious, infected, or that do not function with integrity?
Obtaining Approval & Enrollment	**Enrollment**—If you decide on a paper-based approach to this agreement, consider announcing that formal enrollment is required. Consider informing the reader of the kinds of information that may be required (name, department, cost center, etc.). **Process**—Describe the process for enrollment—Does anyone have to approve? Will this be a manual or automated process? Will the end user do all the work or will your IT department take possession while they inspect and install the MDM software—then make sure it works? Will this agreement be paper-based and wrapped in the box (requiring a signature before it's authorized, or will you use a click-through agreement?). If you use a click-through, will you pause to reinforce the most important points and require the reader to click "I agree" before proceeding? Would you use e-mail to request and authorize? Who is responsible for tracking the agreement and asset's status in this process?
Reimbursement	Detail what the payment plan is—who pays for the device, the data usage plan, the service contract, the apps in the app store vs. downloaded apps. Detail what will or will not be covered via reimbursement or stipend. Will the organization or individual pay for accessories? Who will pay for a lost or stolen device?

TABLE **12-3:** *Continued.*

Paragraph Title	Criteria
Security	• **Jailbreak**—How will you handle "jailbroken" or "rooted" devices? • **Lost or Stolen Devices**—What is the process/timing for reporting lost or stolen devices? Is it immediate or within a specific time limit? What is the one number you want the end user to call when they report? • **MDM settings**—What features of your chosen MDM software suite should be turned on? • **Wipe conditions**—Under what conditions will the IT department wipe the device? Will any attempt be made to wipe only organizational data vs. personal data? What will the organization's liability be if you accidentally erase someone's personal data (by accident or purposefully)? • **Device reset rules**—Under what conditions will the device be reset to factory and/or post MDM settings? • **Data backup**—Who is responsible for backing up the content on their device? Where will you instruct them to do this—to their work PC, the organization's network or a cloud-based service? Will you expect the end user to encrypt this backup or use on-boarding tools? What is the strength of backup encryption? Is this strength strong enough to meet regulatory requirements if the data goes into a public or private cloud? What if the cloud provider will not sign even a pared down Business Associate Agreement (BAA)? Is encrypted PHI still PHI when it's stored in a cloud? Who manages the encryption keys? Who holds the password to unlock the encrypted data? Will the end user be required to supply this password for e-discovery or litigation hold? • **Disclaimer of Personal Loss**—Is the BYOD service offering provided as-is without any warranty? What liability does the hospital have if personal data loss occurs? • **Camera use limitations**—Will you advise the customer to follow the hospital's Privacy and/or Camera policy to maintain patient privacy? • **Bluetooth accessory limitations**—Bluetooth is inherently insecure but useful. What will your policy be about using accessories such as keyboards? Will you advise the reader that privacy and security cannot be maintained when using these devices or will you *attempt* to forbid them? • **e-Discovery/Litigation Hold**—When will the user be required to hand over their device (and to whom) if this device becomes the target of an e-discovery and/or litigation hold? • **Handling sensitive data (e-PHI, SSN, credit card, etc.)**—Will you allow any sensitive data on a mobile device? If yes, how much? If not, what about e-mail, calendar events, pictures? For Payment Card Industry (PCI) compliance reasons, what will you advise the user about using this device with services such as Square for collecting credit cards at point of sale? • **Physical security recommendations**—Since each circumstance might be different and not all rules apply at all times, what reminders (to avoid loss or theft) will you provide to this user?
Acceptable Use	You could reference other acceptable use of technology/information policies here—set the expectation that the same rules for computer workstations and laptops apply (or not) with mobile devices.
Related Policies	List the privacy, security, and/or other HR or related policies with a reminder that "your use must comply with HIPAA" and other pertinent regulations and standards.
Sanctions	Describe what could or will happen if the reader does not comply with policy (accidental vs. purposeful).
Signature	Capture the readers' receipt of, understanding of, and/or agreement to abide by the terms of this agreement/contract.

- Automated device provisioning—The ability to enroll an organizationally issued or personally owned device and apply the policies or settings chosen to control risk.
- Device lock—The ability to lock the device after a period of inactivity.

- Remote wipe—The ability to remotely remove data from the device if the device is reported as lost or stolen.
- Encryption—The ability to render data unusable to unauthorized users.

There are several important advantages to these tools over something as simple as ActiveSync[8]—which many organizations with Microsoft Exchange for their e-mail system use to control these devices. Depending on the MDM used, organizations could erase personal data stored on the device if a wipe or kill command is issued to include contact lists, e-mails, pictures and other data or files. To overcome this, some MDM vendors create a partition (sometimes called a "sandbox") to isolate organizational data from personal data. However, this usually requires a second set of passwords, PINs or some other form of authentication that is not user friendly. Therefore, a one-size-fits-all security solution does not exist. Table 12-4 outlines some of the features to consider when looking for an MDM solution.

Besides enforcing the policy through technical controls to minimize the risk of breaches, some MDM tools provide detailed audit logs, which can be valuable if there is a breach. An MDM can provide an audit trail, making it easier to determine what data was transferred and stored on a mobile device. Not using some type of MDM could be interpreted by regulators as not implementing the same reasonable and prudent safeguards commonly used in the industry. (In legal terms, this is also known as the *prevailing practice*.)

While securing mobile devices is important, end-user experience with the platform must remain engaging in order to enable broad and innovative use. Therefore, when considering MDM solutions, validate what the differences are (security and experience) between a containerized (sandboxed) and non-containerized approach through a vendor comparison evaluation. Organizations will need to decide which option is best suited for their environment based on the risk tolerance level. Table 12-5 lists some of the MDM vendors.

DATA STORAGE

Device storage can be broadly subdivided into three major categories: permanent internal storage using flash read-only memory (ROM) or similar, hard disks or solid state drives (SSD) and removable random-access memory (RAM) units. These include common types of memory cards used in a variety of mobile devices.

Permanent Storage

While ROM, by its nature, is not easily accessible to change, internal storage on a hard disk should be treated just like any other storage medium. Security managers should apply the same criteria to mobile storage disks as they would to laptop, desktop computer and other storage media. Additional encryption steps and proper segregation of system components from user data are recommended for mobile devices due to their higher level of exposure.

Removable Storage and Devices

Most mobile devices allow for the insertion or connection of removable storage units, such as external hard disks, USB thumb drives and slot storage cards. In addition,

TABLE 12-4: What to Look for in an MDM Solution.

Feature Name	Capabilities/Characteristics
Policy Enforcement	Provides the ability to monitor, restrict or filter: • Eligible devices (and number of devices permitted per person). • Operating systems (OS) versions, applications allowed, data allowed, what access is permitted for noncompliance (just e-mail, e-mail and browsing vs. sensitive data and applications), etc. • Ability to detect/alert or disallow devices that have been tampered with (jailbroke - Apple devices) or rooted (Android and Widows smartphones). • Eligible applications and websites (what you are allowed to run or visit vs. what you cannot)—plus the IT alerts (for monitoring or auto-block capabilities). • Data plan usage including unauthorized international usage. • Data co-mingling (between organizational content and personal) and where it is allowed to be transferred to (i.e., Data Loss Prevention [DLP]). • End user features such as file tagging; the ability for end users to specify what is "theirs" vs. what is "yours." • Boundaries—what you are allowed to do when your asset doesn't meet the standards or you have violated the usage rules.
Compliance	Provides the capabilities to meet your regulatory and/or security policy requirements such as: • Personal firewalls and antivirus software (for platforms that can support this software). • Password rules (length, complexity, expiry, re-use, etc.). • Screensaver (device is locked after *x* minutes of inactivity). • Wipe—Completely (all device data) vs. Selective (only hospital data)—implies the ability to perform this function remotely. • Encryption for data at rest (on-board storage and/or removable memory) and data in transit via Virtual Private Network (VPN) connections to the hospital network. • Alternative authentication mechanisms such as digital certificates. • Audit trails and reports for validating who did what/when. • Archiving of messages generated via IM, SMS, chat, etc.
Sandboxing	Provides the ability to "containerize" (a.k.a. run in a sandbox) applications and data to protect and isolate hospital data and applications from personal data and applications. This containerization can achieve a superior security result by providing a boundary around application/data behavior to ensure such things as: • The operation system cannot be corrupted. • Data is not permitted to be copied where it does not belong. • Data is encrypted inside the application—so even if the device is compromised, an unauthorized user cannot access the data. • Data is separated (personal folder vs. corporate folder, for instance). In this approach, proprietary applications for e-mail, calendar, contacts and browsers, for instance, replace the native apps (the ones supplied with the device) which will have to be authenticated separately in addition to authenticating to the device. The user's experience with the proprietary applications is often perceived as "diminished" or "requiring too many extra steps." This is simply a tradeoff between end-user experience and security. This solution is appropriate for highly regulated environments.
Asset Management	Provides the ability to inventory assets and know who "owns" which assets and/or what their settings were at time of loss or theft, for instance; this is the evidence which may be needed to protect the organization's interests in a lawsuit.
Software Distribution & Updates	Provides the ability to alert the user that updates are available or push the update automatically to the device (security fixes, operating system/application bug fixes or new features). Also may provide a private, organizational application store and backup/restore/encryption capabilities (to a local PC, network shared drive or the cloud, etc.) Some tools provide file sharing and file collaboration tools.
Platform Administration	Provides the IT Department the tools necessary to automate the administrative and reporting tasks associated with managing the fleet of mobile devices.

Source: Gartner, G00230106 Critical Capabilities for Mobile Device Management, August 8, 2012.

TABLE 12-5: MDM Software Vendors.

If you conduct an Internet search on the term "MDM software vendors," within the first several pages of your search you will the following vendors, among others (listed alphabetically) that provide MDM solutions:

- AirWatch
- AmTel
- Boxtone
- Dialogs Smartman Device Management
- Exitor DME
- FancyFon
- Good Technology
- IBM
- LANDesk
- McAfee/Intel
- Mobile Iron
- SAP
- Sophos
- Symantec

external appliances may be connected to the device, ranging from headsets on a smartphone to independent devices in cars such as Ford Motor Company's Sync technology. External storage and directly connected devices or appliances should be evaluated consistent with their functionality and their corresponding risk. Security managers should inventory externally connected devices and develop individual security controls for them. These should be aligned with business requirements, given that the use case may be restricted to a few users. Examples include

- Connecting a device to a computer via USB.
- External secure digital (SD) storage card inserted in a smartphone.
- External loudspeakers attached to a tablet PC over the air.

While the potential number of device combinations is unlimited, security managers should follow a series of verification steps to identify the business need, as well as the technical effort to harden the device or combination of devices. Just because something is possible does not mean it is needed from an organizational point of view. Other use cases may be business essential, but they may carry a high-risk exposure and the effort to manage it may be cost prohibitive. As an example, an over-the-air transmission of confidential information to a physician's smartphone may be essential, but the risk of compromise, cost, time, and effort to protect this transmission may prohibit its use.

Retention and Archiving

Organizational and patient data are subject to retention and archiving requirements. Depending on the nature and context of the data, management faces a number of retention periods. Therefore, healthcare organizations will need to decide whether or not information should be stored on mobile devices. If stored information is allowed, then a decision needs to be made regarding the types of information potentially stored on mobile devices and their relevant minimum retention periods.

Organizations should have a retention policy guiding users on their obligations to retain information and securely delete it when there is no obligation or business requirement to keep it. For example, some organizations have configured their MDM to wipe any e-mail older than five days from a smartphone to limit their exposure and risks.

IT departments should review their organization's retention policy and determine whether its provisions are appropriately applied to mobile devices. This review should include assessing

- Whether the organization understands what type of retainable information is being stored on mobile devices.
- How this information is being archived by the organization and in the BYOD environment and how the user may be archiving data.
- How information is deleted from the device and archival backups.
- Whether procedures are in place to secure, preserve and efficiently extract information on mobile devices when required by eDiscovery legal holds, court orders or regulatory requirements.

VIRTUALIZATION

To keep data from being stored on devices, organizations are relying more on virtualization technology, which allows data to be securely accessible to authorized individuals, at any time from any place. Virtualization turns "physical" resources into "logical" resources. Think of it in terms of an item in the display window of a store. The item can be seen and a store employee can move it around, but it cannot be removed from the store. A common form of this in healthcare is a Citrix solution, which allows access to patient information on any device using a web portal.

Virtualization keeps the data stored in a secure location. Users are simply "renting" or using the processing capability applications provided, as well as the storage capability that leadership or the IT department has deemed appropriate. If a session is compromised through malware or error, then the user's session will end, the host computer will discard the flawed session and re-load the standard image for that session to provide the next user the same consistency as desired. Additionally, virtualization can restrict storage in data centers, so the data are still beneficial to users but never leaves the organization's network environment.

TRANSMISSION

Mobile devices predominantly rely on wireless data transmission, except for the few cases when they are physically connected to a laptop or desktop computer. These transmissions create a risk of unauthorized network connectivity, especially when using WLAN/WiMAX or Bluetooth at close proximity. As a newer transmission protocol, near field communication (NFC) increases the risk of unauthorized connectively because it enables mobile devices to transmit data over very short distances, such as a few inches, mainly intended for transmitting payment data. It allows mobile devices to establish radio communication with each other by touching them together or bringing them into close proximity. Mobile devices frequently use unsecured public networks and the large number of known attacks on WLAN and Bluetooth make this a significant risk.

CLOUD COMPUTING

NIST defines cloud computing as a model for enabling ubiquitous, convenient, on-demand network access to a shared pool of configurable computing resources (e.g., networks, servers, storage, applications and services) that can be rapidly provisioned and released with minimal management effort or service provider interaction.[9] The trend toward cloud computing will continue as healthcare organizations try to manage growing IT infrastructure and costs.[10] Some of the top IT benefits are lower operating costs and increased data center efficiency.

In some vendor cloud environments, mobile device operating systems and apps are shifting their processing capability provided by cloud technology and reducing the possibility of direct interaction between the mobile device and other computing devices. This leads to storage, processing and use of confidential information in cloud technology rather than on devices owned and controlled by the end user. Examples include the synchronization of office data, calendar files and e-mails through various cloud services.

Healthcare organizations should carefully analyze the technical characteristics and terms of use for any cloud solution for mobile devices. It may be necessary to disable or prohibit the use of cloud services, or discourage the use of the mobile device altogether. The Apple iCloud and Google Play are examples of cloud services mandated by manufactured products. Protection strategies include:

- Encrypt data. Protect confidential information before moving it to the cloud technology by encrypting it or ensure the cloud vendor encrypts the data.
- Remove and reconfigure. Provide specific user requirements that force them to remove the cloud service from the mobile device.
- Disengage or prohibit. Do not allow devices with certain mandated consumer cloud services by excluding those devices from BYOD.

TAKING ACTION

Getting Started

The important first steps for healthcare organizations to take are as follows:

- Leverage existing security where possible. Organizations should extend existing security to mobile devices that include:
  - Authentication and access control technologies such as VPN solutions and Citrix.
  - Lifecycle management process for apps includes inventory, reporting and controlling of apps on mobile devices and addresses provisioning, updating and deleting apps.
  - Antivirus and protection from malicious code.
  - Assessments to inspect and validate policy compliance on mobile devices.
  - Data loss detection and prevention controls.
  - Secure communication protocols such as 3G wireless, IPsec or TLS/SSL.
- Implement a baseline of safeguards and controls for mobile devices, both organizationally owned devices and personally owned devices, listed in Table 12-6.
- Create a mobile device policy. Table 12-7 lists some recommended content to include in a policy.

TABLE 12-6: Safeguards and Controls for Mobile Devices.

Minimum Controls (Core)	Recommended Controls (Advanced)
Mobile Device Management (MDM) To enforce security policies.	**Data Loss Prevention (DLP)** To monitor, prevent, and/or detect inappropriate transfer or storage of confidential information.
Encryption (enforced by the MDM tool) To protect data at rest (stored within the device's internal memory) and in-transit.	**Network Access Control (NAC)** To ensure that only trusted mobile devices gain access to your network, applications, and data (See note #3).
Virtual Private Networking (VPN) For securely connecting to the network remotely.	**Multi-Factor Authentication (for remote access)** To ensure the identity of the device and user (See note #4).
Authentication To prevent unauthorized access (See note #1).	**Advanced Persistent Threat Protection** For detecting and blocking ultra-silent spyware designed to steal data.
Antivirus (when available) To prevent malicious code (See note #2).	**Monitoring** To understand usage trends, check devices, and users' compliance with written and digital policies.
Policies, Procedures and Standards To define management's expectations and influence user behavior.	**Notes:** 1. A password, a PIN, a pattern or biometric to unlock the device.
Education and Awareness To educate and make users aware of their responsibilities.	2. Some mobile device operating systems are so tightly controlled by the vendor that antivirus tools won't work; they cannot properly interact with the operating system.
User Agreements or BYOD Contracts To legally obtain users' buy-in and limit the organization's liability.	3. "Trusted" means that the mobile device's security settings and controls meet the organization's baseline standards.
Audit Logs To hold users accountable for their actions.	4. Soft tokens have a broader appeal than hard tokens. New solutions that allow the phone to be used as a token are appealing. Also, a federal advisory committee was promoting multi-factor authentication for clinicians and other caregivers involved with electronic health information transactions that represent a high risk.
Remote Wipe To remotely wipe (sanitize) the device so that confidential information cannot be accessed in the event the device is lost or stolen.	

- Create user agreements or contracts. Table 12-8 lists several websites where organizations may find sample BYOD policies and contracts.
- Employ MDM. MDM can manage devices, ensure antivirus software is enabled, confirm that screen locks are active and give IT wiping capabilities to remotely remove specific apps and files from compromised devices without affecting a user's personal data via partitioning (i.e., BYOD).

TABLE 12-7: Recommended Policy Content.

Policy Considerations
A mobile device policy should, at a minimum, require users to have:
1. Power-on password or owner authentication.
2. Automatic time out or locking of the device after a predetermined period of inactivity (e.g., 10 minutes).
3. Encryption of confidential information stored on the device (Note: Some older versions of smartphones did not encrypt or it was weak).
Some other considerations include:
• Setting the memory to automatically erase after ten unsuccessful logon attempts.
• Keeping the storage of confidential information on the smartphone to the minimum necessary. For example, consider purging any e-mail that is older than five days from the phone; e-mail is still available through the e-mail account.
• Requiring users to store important files or critical data on a network drive rather than downloading them to the smartphone or consider view only data.
• Requiring users to sign an agreement or acknowledge their responsibilities as part of the process for allowing them access via a mobile device.
• Removing all business-related information from the mobile device before trading in the device or sending it off for repair.
• Disallowing users to download unsigned apps. These are usually "free" apps that circumvent the existing security controls inherent in the mobile device, which may allow the unsigned app access to a mobile device's root file system. This is also referred to as "jailbreaking" (Apple) or "rooting" (Android).

TABLE 12-8: Sources for BYOD Policy and Contract Samples.

Vendor/Document	URL
For Free	
HIMSS *Sample Mobile Device User Agreement*	www.himss.org/content/files/MS04_Sample_Mobile_Agreement_Final.pdf
Good *BYOD Document Construction Series*	www1.good.com/support/training-ps/byod-policy
Mocha5 *Bring Your Own Device Programs: Policies and best practices for success*	www.mokafive.com/resources/analyst-reports-and-white-papers.php
SANS *Security Policy for the use of handheld devices in corporate environments*	www.sans.org/reading_room/whitepapers/pda/ security-policy-handheld-devices-corporate-environments_32823
CIO Council *A Toolkit to Support Federal Agencies Implementing Bring Your Own Device (BYOD) Programs*	www.scribd.com/doc/103702838/A-Toolkit-to-Support-Federal-Agencies-Implementing-Bring-Your-Own-Device-BYOD-Programs
Network World *(A sampling of BYOD user policies)*	www.networkworld.com/news/2012/040212-byod-policies-257751.html
For Subscribers	
InfoTech Advisor *BYOC Acceptable Use Policy*	https://www.infotech.com/user/login?login_redirect=%2Fmycontent
Gartner *Toolkit: Mobile Device Policy Template*	www.gartner.com

TABLE 12-9: HIMSS Mobile Security Toolkit.

HIMSS Mobile Security Toolkit
"The HIMSS Mobile Security Toolkit assists healthcare organizations and security practitioners in managing the security of their mobile computing devices."
"This Toolkit will help you understand the security risks and issues associated with incorporating mobile devices into your organization, and how to develop mobile security policy implementations for corporate and personally owned devices. It contains resources with tips on securing your wireless network, smartphones and other mobile devices."
www.himss.org/asp/topics_pstoolkit_mobilesecurity.asp
Some of the topics that you will find at the link below include: • Considerations for Employee-Owned Mobile Devices   • Sample Mobile Device User Agreement   • Mobile: How to Say 'Yes' Securely   • Security Challenges BYOD Presents   • BYOD: Get Ahead of the Risk
www.himss.org/asp/topics_FocusDynamic.asp?faid=652

- Educate users. It is important to provide user education on mobile device risks and take the time to explain why certain security controls are required and how these controls protect both the user and the organization. Users should also be educated on the mobile device policy itself. Without that clear understanding, security controls may be viewed as a barrier and users will find convenient workarounds. It is also important to educate users on their own liabilities. With the enforcement rules for HIPAA, individuals can be held liable for their actions, especially if they knowingly violated policies or regulatory requirements where PHI was compromised. (See Table 12-9 for an example.)

CONCLUSION

It seems that each healthcare organization is competing to find ways to improve patient outcomes, physician satisfaction and reduce costs by applying innovative ways to improve healthcare delivery and operations. Mobile devices offer some highly valued benefits in this space because they can be a catalyst for improving efficiency and productivity. However, these benefits can be realized only if organizations manage the technology effectively for both value and risk. Many organizations have chosen to embrace the use of personally owned mobile devices in the workplace, sometimes without considering the business risk or the governance implications associated with personally owned devices. Organizations need to strike a balance between the benefits mobile devices offer against the additional risks. Once benefits and risks are understood, organizations should employ a governance framework and policies and implement safeguards and controls to ensure security policy changes are understood and implemented to prevent unauthorized access to or loss of confidential information.

In this chapter, we addressed some of the challenges from using mobile devices in healthcare, some of the common threats and vulnerabilities, and recommendations to mitigate the risk. There is no silver bullet to address all of the risks. Policy, user agreements, awareness, encryption, effective authentication and audit trails are just some of the basic safeguards and controls needed. To help executive management make informed business decisions, organizations need to conduct a thorough risk analysis and get executive management to sign off on it. Part of managing risks includes actively partnering with your users of mobile devices and getting involved in the early stages of mobile app development and/or procurements to ensure that any new application meets business needs and security requirements.

Ensure that an effective incident response plan is in place. Organizations cannot stop the proliferation of mobile devices in the workplace. Therefore, it is important to embrace them with an appropriate plan of action.

REFERENCES

1. Gartner. Gartner says 821 million smart devices will be purchased worldwide in 2012: Sales to rise to 1.2 billion in 2013. Available at: www.gartner.com/it/page.jsp?id=2227215.

2. Perez I. iPad programs up resident productivity. *Chicago Maroon*. November 5, 2010. Available at: http://chicagomaroon.com/2010/11/05/ipad-program-ups-resident-productivity.

3. Gartner. Gartner highlights key predictions for IT organizations and users in 2010 and beyond. January 13, 2010. Available at: www.gartner.com/it/page.jsp?id=1278413

4. Whitney L. iPad will lose market dominance to Android next year, says analyst. Cnet. November 13, 2012. Available at: http://news.cnet.com/8301-13579_3-57548900-37/ipad-will-lose-market-dominance-to-android-next-year-says-analyst.

5. U.S. Department of Health & Human Services. Breaches affecting 500 or more individuals. Available at: www.hhs.gov/ocr/privacy/hipaa/administrative/breachnotificationrule/breachtool.html.

6. 45 CFR Parts 160 and 164. Available at: www.hhs.gov/ocr/privacy/hipaa/understanding/coveredentities/hitechrfi.pdf.

7. National Institute of Standards and Technology. Special publications (800 series). Available at: http://csrc.nist.gov/publications/PubsSPs.html.

8. ActiveSync is probably one of the most widely used programs for controlling mobile devices because it is free for Exchange e-mail clients.

9. Mell P, Grance T. The NIST definition of cloud computing: Recommendations of the National Institute of Standards and Technology. NIST. Available at: http://csrc.nist.gov/publications/nistpubs/800-145/SP800-145.pdf.

10. PriceWaterhouseCoopers. Top health industry issues of 2012. Available at: www.pwc.com/us/en/health-industries/publications/top-health-industry-issues-of-2012.jhtml.

CHAPTER 13

Application Security

By Joseph Dalton and Ander Hoaglund

When thinking about launching an application security (AppSec) program it is vital to consider the breadth, depth, and adversarial nature of the discipline. AppSec includes elements of many other branches of security, governance, risk management, compliance, systems and security engineering, quality and development. Application security incorporates multiple levels of protection from the minutiae of coding methodologies, user interfaces and communication protocols to the macroscopic organizational risk, cost modeling, and compliance implications. This comprehensive nature of AppSec requires analysis and action from all levels of an organization and across many job functions. As such, this makes the successful deployment of an AppSec program difficult.

DEFINING APPLICATION SECURITY

Application security is broadly defined as securing an application. Taking a deeper look at what goes into an application we begin to get an idea of the scale of the subject and understand that no one individual can be responsible for application security; just about every individual in an IT environment will play some role, and it is easier to define application security in terms of their job functions. An AppSec program has different implications to a developer than it does to a system administrator. This chapter will examine three general aspects of application security: software security in the development lifecycle, secure coding practices and operational application security. Each of these aspects accurately defines application security, but covers only their portion. In lieu of devising a comprehensive definition here, we will address each of these aspects. While topics covered within other chapters are not discussed here, application security elements of those topics may be mentioned to help broaden understanding. The chapter has been organized in a bottom-up approach in order to assist readers without application development experience in understanding general development concepts prior to integrating these concepts into an overarching approach to application security. Lastly, this chapter is meant as a primer for further study and not as a comprehensive work. The topic is simply too broad and covers so many technical roles that there now exist several texts— and over 1,000 pages—devoted to just the *components* of application security, much less the entire subject.

Engineering Secure Code

The science of software development is relatively new; in its infancy compared to any of the more established sciences, and has only recently been added to the curriculum in schools.[1] Building a secure application is not an easy feat, especially considering the ever-growing number of languages, techniques, platforms, libraries, databases, run-time environments, and frameworks. Then add the complexity of the different operating systems, network configurations and protocols. Furthering the difficulty is the requirement to examine the interplay between objects outside of the view or control of the application developer, making it essentially an emergent property of a complex system. With all these factors to account for, the act of securing an application might seem insurmountable; however, there are some tools, general principles and practices designed to help minimize the difficulty and make it easier to build considerably safer and higher quality applications. Framing each tool, principle or practice within the software development lifecycle (SDLC) should facilitate understanding of their appropriate application and how all the pieces fit together.

Software Development Lifecycle

An SDLC is a process to plan, organize and manage software creation. Most methodologies base their structure on the systems development lifecycle and have their own advantages, disadvantages and distinct lexicon, but each SDLC contains similar engineering elements. Generally, the traditional process is divided into phases, each covering one or many of these topics: Requirements Gathering, Design, Implementation, Testing and Deployment phases. Whether the process is cyclical or linear, each phase has specific requirements and generated artifacts. This general methodology works well for tangible system development; however, software is a special case. Software flaws are not easily visible fundamental defects in production, which would be obvious in a physical object and would remain invisible for years. These defects may only come into view at the moment of exploit, which is far too late for correction. To address this shortcoming in traditional SDLC, security focused elements have been added to the standard SDLC, targeting the underlying need for incorporation of security processes. These elements have been drawn from Microsoft's Secure Development Lifecycle (SDL) and the Software Security Framework[2] adding security tools and processes or artifacts at each step in the SDLC.

Training Phase

Microsoft's SDL suggested the addition of a pre-training phase, focusing all members of a software development team (not only developers) on the newest techniques, best practices and security requirements associated with their work.[3] Training is critically important because the divide between security personnel and developers is far too wide. Developers have little to no exposure to security concepts and their education process has little to no emphasis on security. Until recently, classes in secure coding practices were not offered. To ensure a knowledgeable development team, training should be done at least annually and should cover technical topics such as secure design, security architecture, secure coding, threat modeling, security testing, privacy, and secure user interfaces.

Gather Requirements/Determine Objectives

Requirements gathering starts the traditional software development lifecycle and can be either the initial starting point of the project or in the case of iterative project management, simply the beginning of a new iteration. Techniques utilized in traditional requirement gathering, such as brainstorming, interview and document analysis, may need to be augmented to ensure the collection of security requirements. These additional techniques should involve a review of both compliance standards and internal policy.[4,5] Pushback from managers concerning the schedule or developers chomping at the bit to begin coding can be addressed (at least in part) by pointing out the significant fiduciary advantage delivered from spending extra effort in this phase; the cost associated with handling defects not found in this phase of the lifecycle can be up to 15 times the cost of the entire endeavor.[6]

Design

Starting any project with a good foundation is essential, and the same can be said in the realm of software security. Gary McGraw states in his book, *Software Security* (Addison-Wesley Professional; 2006) that 50 percent of all vulnerabilities can be attributed to architectural design flaws within an application. Taking this into consideration, any operations targeting this phase of the SDLC can greatly benefit the security posture of an application. The benefits of this process are two-fold. First, it allows developers the opportunity to leverage the knowledge of security professionals and, second, has the added benefit of keeping security in the forefront of people's minds. In practice, the review should target any potential security risks to the application with regard to the environment in which it will reside. Risk areas reviewed should include input validation, authentication, authorization, data classification and storage, cryptography, error handling, and auditing.

Implement/Develop

Secure implementation requires the appropriate use of secure coding practices and frameworks. The procedures implemented in this phase include tool-based code review,[1] peer code review,[8] dynamic code review[9] and risk-based security testing (security unit testing).[1] A detailed description of secure coding techniques is included in the "Software Development Security" section of this chapter.

Code review is a process of validating elements of a program in order to find and document defects within that code. Code review, whether done through an entirely manual process or with the aid of review tools, requires an understanding of the software security and potential software bugs associated with the specific technologies utilized, as well as enough knowledge about the policy requirements to be able to frame the review findings. Because "at the end of the day we are not securing code for the code's sake, but for what the code or application is protecting: the money, the business intelligence, the good stuff that gives business an edge or the data which equates to financial and capital assets."[10]

Verification/Test

Application and security testing against requirements is the most important component in the removal of software defects, specifically as done in the penetration test.[1,11] Testing and evaluation allows for an examination of an application's performance under real-world—and potentially sub-optimal—conditions, offering software developers (and any other participant in the software lifecycle) the ability to truly assess the security of their application. By employing the same techniques hackers would use to break into the application in the same environment, penetration testers can help to ferret out any lingering security shortcomings prior to release. Additionally any penetration testing must be clearly solution-focused, emphasizing (for the sake of development and security team harmony) that there are no "Us vs. Them" differences. However, if the software to be tested is not mature enough to gain a benefit from penetration testing, emphasis should instead be focused on code review and architectural risk analysis.[1]

Deployment/Release

Public consumption of code is done in this phase. In the case of linear models, this phase is focused on fixing bugs, compared to iterative models where planning for new features may be included. The security techniques housed on this phase consist of any operational elements of information security and are outside the purview of this chapter.

Common Development Threats

Examining known threats gives developers ideas of where they need to focus their efforts to preemptively fix application security holes.[12] While the specifics of risk assessment were covered in Chapter 4, it is still necessary to articulate the most common development security threats (see Appendix B). One method of approaching this is described in Microsoft's S.T.R.I.D.E. system. This approach divides the AppSec threats into six general classifications (Spoofing, Tampering, Repudiation, Information disclosure, Denial of service, and Elevation of privilege).

Spoofing is the impersonation of another user or service. Users should not be able to impersonate other users. This can be avoided by employing techniques that ensure users are who they say they are. HIPAA discusses four requirements that pertain to this threat: use of unique logon, automatic logoff, credentials (biometric, passwords and PINs), and how authentication will be handled in emergency situations.

Tampering is the unauthorized alteration of data. Ensuring the use of appropriate authorization and tamper-resistant protocols can mitigate this risk. HIPAA discusses the inclusion of digital signatures and check sums.

Repudiation is a system's difficulty in tying activities to the appropriate users. Ensuring activates are tied to a specific user can be addressed with digital signatures, timestamps, and effective logging. HIPAA discusses the use of audit trails; however, the specifics of implementation are left to the organization.

Information disclosure is the likelihood that data are released inappropriately. This can be mitigated with proper authentication and encryption. HIPAA discusses encryption both in terms of what to do to store the data and what is required to transfer it.

Denial of service covers the likelihood that a system can be made unavailable. HIPPA has no requirement that discusses denial of service.

Elevation of privilege describes increasing the permissions or trust on a system. A mitigation strategy is to ensure that applications are designed to operate using the principle of least privilege, which states that no one should have more rights than is necessary to perform the required operation.

This simple idea can be hard to implement, but is extremely effective in securing not only your application but also the system it resides on.

SOFTWARE DEVELOPMENT SECURITY

Ensuring the protection of protected health information (PHI) is becoming increasingly difficult, especially as the public's desire for constantly available information increases. This changes the way healthcare handles data, placing a greater focus on using distributed and web-based applications. Greater availability also means there is an increase in the risk of data being impacted.

In this section, we will examine secure coding best practices and development threats discussed throughout the literature. Best practices offer developers the ability to keep a conceptual list of what is required without the need to memorize the most recently trending security information. A checklist of HIPAA technical requirements will also assist both administrators and developers to grasp what is minimally required for applications, which handle PHI. It is also recommended that developers understand the most common threat vectors affecting the environments their application will reside in.

Secure Coding Best Practices

The various security groups have a slightly different take on what is most important when securing code. Some commonalities exist, but there are some areas and perspectives that are unique to each list of best practices. Compiling lists from these sources allows a more complete understanding of the best of the best practices. In order to collect a comprehensive set of application security minimums, the authors reviewed and compiled the best practices from the computer emergency response team (CERT), the Open Web Application Security Project (OWASP) and McGraw's 10 steps to secure software. This was concatenated with the NIST Engineering Principles for Information Technology Security and the OWASP Secure Coding Principles, a fairly comprehensive list of application development best practices. Finally a list of six principles from a 2005 article by Marcus Ranum was added. The resulting list of secure coding practices is presented in Table 13-1.

DATABASES

Databases are integrated aggregations of data usually organized to reflect logical or functional relationships among data elements.[13] Databases are commonly thought of as repositories of data from web applications or enterprise-level software packages, but it is currently common to see small lightweight databases included in applications. The topic of database security is one that touches application security; however, it is handled quite differently. Databases are themselves applications whose interactions tend to be

TABLE 13-1: Secure Coding Practices.

Software Best Practices	Description
Keep things simple	Complexity makes debugging painful, so simplicity is your friend.
Defense in depth	Layer security through both physical and logical methods.
Be reluctant to trust	This means be skeptical of: • Services. • Inputs and data from other systems. • Targets of outputs (so sanitize data). • Infrastructure. • Minimize internal systems utilized. • Transmission methods. • Default deny everything you don't specifically require.
Operate under least privilege	Give only the minimum permissions required to perform a job.
Separate duties	Minimize the impact of a breach by compartmentalizing sections of code and creating clear lines of trust.
Fail and recover securely	Lower the likelihood of issues by ensuring software failure occurs in a secure manner.
Don't rely on obscurity	You can't assume because you hid something, it can't be found.
Identify and correct issues early	Finding and correcting shortcomings in code early in a process can result in significant decrease in cost later in the lifecycle.
Minimize the application attack surface	Reduce the number of ways applications can be attacked.

indirect in nature, while applications are the primary vehicle of user interactions with databases. Databases also contain specific security features of their own and, therefore, can be considered a special class of application.

An Initial Database Primer

Basic table structure and SQL (Structured Query Language). Understanding how databases work is essential to grasping how to protect them. An easy way to conceptualize databases is to liken them to libraries. The same way rows, shelves and books comprise the organization of a library, tables, columns and rows make up a database. So, if you were looking for a line from a specific book in the library, you would look up the location of the book in the library index or card catalog and get a code describing where that book is housed. After finding that row, you would skim the codes of a few books on each shelf until you found the shelf containing the code range of the book—then you would specifically hunt for it. Once discovered, the book is opened and the contents read.

In reality, it would not be possible to simply browse through a database to find what we want like we did in this example. We would need to give the database a set of instructions to have it return the information we would want from the book and to do that, we would use a SQL statement. SQL is the language used to interact with databases, allowing us to add, retrieve, move and alter information stored within.

Views access control. One of the harder concepts in the domain of database development is the idea of a view. A view is a stored SQL statement, which presents or transforms the data held in a table, meaning that where the data in the table changes, the data in the view also changes. The advantages of using views is that views are different objects from the table they reference, so different permissions can be assigned to both a table and a view containing the same information. Controlling access in this method is called view-based access control.

Stored procedures. When you think about the workhorse of a secure database, stored procedures should be at the forefront of your mind. This is a way to collect and encapsulate pieces of code that allow users to perform actions in a database without having access to the database itself or the underlying data they are affecting. Much in the same way views are different objects from their underlying data, stored procedures offer developers the ability to allow users permissions to specific pieces of code without allowing them access to the code itself. This is a way of allowing users to interact with the database but limiting what actions they can take. Additionally stored procedures allow developers to ensure parameterization of variables at the database level, which is one method for preventing SQL injection attacks. Views and stored procedures offer a layer of abstraction between the user and the database. Essentially, they are ways of allowing users to interact with the database without letting them directly access the tables.

Communication. A method of communication must exist between the application and the database. In larger applications, the database resides on a remote computer in the network. When the user interface of the application and database are separated, they communicate through the use of listeners. Listeners are services that run on the server and act as the ears of a database. They wait and listen for connections, then filter or pass received instructions onto the database. Listeners can be configured to communicate with specific devices or IP ranges, so only authorized computers can initiate a connection. However, listeners are themselves services that are susceptible to exploitation, so they must be hardened against attack.

Database Security Techniques

As mentioned earlier, databases are special classifications of applications. They act as both an application and a highly configurable network resource. They can afford certain additional protections to the data they house, but only if they are configured (hardened) and programmed correctly to resist security threats. Hardening guides targeting your database can be used to augment any threat analysis, but are not a replacement.

Common threats plaguing database programmers are SQL injection and improper connection string password storage. Connection strings are stored connection parameters. These parameters are passed to the database to set up and authenticate a connection. To mitigate this threat, be sure to encrypt the connection string before storing it. SQL injection is another common development threat to databases. SQL injection is the act of inserting SQL commands into a database through some intermediary process, for example, through a web form. Injection can be mitigated through the use of parameterization, length and type checks.

Software Selection

Whether purchased from a third party or built in-house, assessment of the software should be required. This process should focus on more than the glossy brochures, salesman's pitch and assurances of the development staff. Inclusion of software assessment professionals at every level of the software development lifecycle is critical to ensure the product utilized by the staff meets at least the minimum security requirements. The approach to addressing software purchased from third parties differs slightly from that of software developed in-house. Techniques for assessing in-house developed software were covered in the software development lifecycle section of this chapter.

When you are purchasing software remember the old saying, *caveat emptor* (let the buyer beware). The purchase of software is something that should not be taken lightly. By its very nature, software has the potential to cause a great deal of headaches for users, security personnel and administrators. These costs can build over time to far exceed the monetary cost of the application. When deciding on a purchase, it behooves you to take your time, perform a thorough examination and get all the sales agreements in writing, especially when the product will greatly impact your business.[14] When interviewing sales staff, it is essential to question their implementation of secure programming practices. Questions you could ask to get a sense of their program might include:

- What application development security certifications do your application development staff hold, when were they issued and what are their certification numbers? Certifications are not required to produce good secure code, but sales staff with knowledge of security may indicate a security-focused culture. Example, when securing software development certifications, include GSSP (application development), GWEB (web development) and GWAPT (penetration testing), all of which are from SANS Institute, a company specializing in information security research, training, and certification. Research any certifications you are not familiar with and, for high value software purchases, contact the governing body to validate the certification.
- What were the results of your last:
  - Risk assessment
  - Security audit
  - Penetration test
  - Code review
    - Did a third party perform the review?
    - Can you have a copy of all or part of these documents, and can you contact the reviewing party? When discussing this with the sales staff, a confident and open organization might share some of their results.[14] In cases where a vendor will not make the result public or simply has not done an audit, it maybe worth considering having your own audit performed. The cost of the audit must be compared to the value the application might have to the organization.
- What secure coding practices do you utilize? Look for the use of best practices, secure libraries, security-focused staff, code auditing, active penetration testing, etc.
- What security controls are required or prohibited? Red flags might include items such as the application needs root level access or the application does not support secure sockets layer (SSL) communication
- What secure libraries do you utilize? If they are willing to give you the names of the code libraries they use, look them up and see how secure they are.

- What is the support plan for this application moving forward?
  - What is your patching schedule? A regular scheduled patching schedule is preferred, divided between major and minor releases.
  - Do you support software source code escrow? Software escrow is an agreement in which a software vendor agrees that if they choose to no longer support their application, the application source code will be released to the purchaser in order to allow other support avenues to be pursued. Keep in mind that the escrow contract should not only include the initially purchased package but subsequent patches and builds.

Cloud Software

Assessing software or services based in the cloud requires more attention than simply purchasing software to run in your own environment. You would try to assess the software in the same way, but there are additional points that must be evaluated. First a majority of cloud applications do not have any components that run in your own local environment; they are accessed through the Internet or by connecting your network to theirs via tunnel. This means you must take into consideration how the information is being transported between these two endpoints. Second, since the endpoint for your data is going to be in a datacenter outside your control, it is important to assess the security of their datacenter. This means asking all the same security questions of the vendor as you would if you were assessing the security of your own datacenter.

CONCLUSION

Understanding the complex and nuanced world of application security is not an easy feat for experienced programmers and software engineers, and doubly so for those without software development experience. It is a domain of knowledge spanning several disciplines, emphasizing both big picture ideas and minute procedures. Despite these difficulties or maybe due to them, application security is a growing domain that deeply needs our attention. With this growth, it is becoming increasingly necessary for the workforce to understand the world of AppSec. The required level of understanding may not rival that of the developers, but it should at least include the basic lexicon and conceptual understanding of what developers, administrators and evaluators face.

Application security from the point of view of a manager can be boiled down to this:

- Know the security requirements for each application.
- Communicate your expectations to your developers and explain the rationale and benefits of adding security in early on.
- Make sure your development teams are actively involved, with security as a portion of their SDLC.
- Ensure that programmers know how to use best practices.
- Tie security to the idea of quality.
- Perform threat assessments and penetration testing against applications.
- Ensure any databases are hardened and use good development processes.
- Be sure applications you are planning to purchase address security to your satisfaction, and don't be afraid to ask hard questions.

REFERENCES

1. McGraw G. *Software Security: Building Security In*. 1st ed. Westford, MA: Pearson Education; 2006.

2. McGraw G, Chess B. n.d. Software [in]security: a software security framework: working towards a realistic maturity model. Informit.com. Available at: www.informit.com/articles/article. aspx?p=1271382. Accessed December 9, 2012.

3. Staff M. n.d. Microsoft security development lifecycle (SDL). Msdn.Microsoft.com. Available at: http://msdn.microsoft.com/en-us/library/windows/desktop/cc307748.aspx. Accessed December 9, 2012.

4. Hubbs BL. n.d. Assessing vendor application security—a practical way to begin. Sans.org. Available at: www.sans.org/reading_room/whitepapers/application/assessing-vendor-application-security-practical_1370. Accessed November 25, 2012.

5. Morana MM. n.d. Application security guide for CISOs-OWASP. Owasp.org. Available at: www.owasp.org/index.php/Application_Security_Guide_For_CISOs. Accessed December 2, 2012.

6. Tassey GPD. The economic impacts of inadequate infrastructure for software testing. Nist.Gov. Available at: www.nist.gov/director/planning/upload/report02-3.pdf. Accessed November 24, 2012.

7. OWASP Secure Coding Practices Quick Reference Guide. January 1, 2010. OWASP Secure Coding Practices Quick Reference Guide. Owasp.org. Available at: www.owasp.org/images/0/08/OWASP_SCP_Quick_Reference_Guide_v2.pdf. Accessed December 3, 2012.

8. Cohen J, Teleki S, Brown E. n.d. *Best Kept Secrets of Peer Code Review*. (J. Cohen, ed.). smartbear.com.

9. Dowd M, McDonald J. Schuh J. *The Art of Software Security Assessment: Identifying and Preventing Software Vulnerabilities*. 1st ed. Boston: Addison-Wesley; 2007.

10. Code Review and the SDLC n.d. Owasp.org. Available at: www.owasp.org/index.php/Code_Review_and_the_SDLC. Accessed December 9, 2012.

11. van der Stock A, Lowery D, Rook D, Cruz D, Keary E, et al. n.d. OWASP CODE REVIEW GUIDE. Owasp.org. Available at: www.owasp.org/images/2/2e/OWASP_Code_Review_Guide-V1_1.pdf. Accessed November 24, 2012.

12. Hernan S, Lambert S, Ostwald T, et al. Uncover security design flaws using the STRIDE approach. Msdn.Microsoft.com. Available at: http://msdn.microsoft.com/en-us/magazine/cc163519.aspx. Accessed September 10, 2012.

13 Slade R. (2009) *Official (ISC)² Guide to the CISSP CBK*. 2nd ed. Boca Raton, FL: Taylor & Francis Group; 2007.

14. McKerchar R. (2012, March 16) Practical IT: how to assess a third-party provider's security (part 1). Naked Security. Available at: http://nakedsecurity.sophos.com/2012/03/16/how-to-assess-a-third-party-provider-security. Accessed September 9, 2012.

CHAPTER 14

Information Security Operations

By Darren D. Dannen, CISSP

In early 2010, I was a manager of the infrastructure for a large physician group in Minnesota. As part of my daily activities, I logged onto a system server. On this particular day, I got a unique file error message. It was a simple pop-up message stating that a file was missing on the main hard drive. I looked over the system and found that there was increase of use resources, but nothing else that I could determine.

At the time, I was not that worried yet; with over 18 years of experience, I had seen many instances of systems that had issues, but that were not security events. When I logged in into another system, I had the same issues, an error message and an increased of use of resources—I started getting worried.

What I had just started to notice was that my organization and my team was under attack. One of my staff visited a web page that infected his system with a Trojan virus whose purpose was to capture accounts and steal personal data. That virus also scanned the local network, attempting to infect other systems.

By the time symptoms started to show, the organization had about 50 servers that were infected. My team was in the middle of an attack, and we were uncertain of the situation, the impact of the attack and the consequences. We were at war! For the next 36 hours, my team investigated, isolated, and removed the infection, on little or no sleep.

Lucky for us, the systems that were infected contained no customer personal data, and we were able to isolate the infected systems. We could verify that no customer data were compromised. We were also lucky we could contain and remove the virus without impacting operations. It could have been *a lot* worse. The headlines are filled with organizations that are attacked and have data compromised.

In early 2011, the anti-security group Anonymous got angry when Aaron Barr, at the time the chief executive officer (CEO) of HB Gary Federal, alluded to plans to reveal the identities of several Anonymous members at the Security B-Sides Conference. In retaliation, the group compromised the systems of both HB Gary Federal and sister firm, HB Gary Inc. Anonymous then copied and made public thousands of private HB Gary documents, including e-mail.[1]

This experience taught me that all information professionals are at war, a defensive war where individuals and groups are attempting to access or disrupt your organization; a war in which IT professionals need to keep important services operating, guard transactions from losses or delays and keep data out of hackers' reach on a daily basis. But this is a unique war, one in which the velocity, veracity, and volume of attacks are increasing at a dramatic rate and, therefore, protecting networks is one of the most critical security challenges facing information professionals today.

A century ago, the United States discovered that technology could be the key to victory. Since then, there has been a steady stream of new weaponry, new technologies, and new ways to attack. It is helpful to see Internet cyber attacks as the latest in a long line of technological advances that have changed warfare and provided new military capabilities. We have only begun to explore the uses of this new capability, and as the world becomes more dependent on networks and computer technology, the value and effect of these cyber attacks will grow.[2]

In any war, one of the greatest needs for the participants is to gain the information or data needed to make critical decisions. One of the major hindrances is the natural tendency in times of crisis for information to be distorted. Military professionals call it the "fog of war." Fog of war is the uncertainty in situational awareness experienced by participants in fast-pace operations.

War is an area of uncertainty; three-quarters of the elements on which all action in war is based is bound up in a fog of uncertainty to a greater or lesser extent. The first thing needed to address this situation is a fine, piercing mind to feel out the truth with the measure of its judgment.

I experienced this first-hand during the aforementioned viral attack for which we, my team and I, had inadequate situational awareness. We did not know what was happening, how the virus was spreading or even what systems were infected. Most of my staff worked hard but not very effectively, I must admit. We were working hard, but not solving problems and the main reason was the lack of certainty about the information concerning the nature of the attack. We were in the middle of the fog of war and we were not prepared!

So how do you counter the fog of war in information technology? The best way to accomplish this is through effective operational planning. Operational planning is leveraging related, currently owned technology investments to efficiently and effectively defend important information assets and developing data collection processes and procedures so staff knows what to do during incidents. Good organizational planning will prepare the staff and the organization for cyber attacks, will clear the fog of war and in essence, will build effective security operations. This chapter will focus on how to do successful planning that will build effective Information Security Operations. This will be accomplished through three basic planning phases: strategic, tactical and operational. This chapter will not necessarily provide specific actions or directions but will provide guidelines and principles for the planning that will allow an organization to be prepared and have effective information security operations.

STRATEGIC PLANNING:
ALLOCATING THE RIGHT RESOURCES

The first phase of successful information security operations planning is strategic planning—protecting the right data with the right resources. Strategic planning is an organization's process of defining its strategy or direction and making decisions about allocating its resources to pursue this strategy. The first major question to ask for operational strategic planning is this: what is Information Security Operation's purpose? The U.S. *National Information Systems Security Glossary* defines "information systems security" as the "protection of information systems against unauthorized access to or modification of information, whether in storage, processing or transit, and against the denial of service to authorized users or the provision of service to unauthorized users, including those measures necessary to detect, document, and counter such threats."[3] Information Security Operations include the processes and procedures that enable data protection on a daily basis. The planning for that operations process must resolve around how systems and data can be protected and how the organization will respond when attacked. Basically, strategic planning is asking the question, "What do we *do*?"

The best method to address that question is through good risk analysis and management. There are several books and a chapter in this book that deal with this topic. It is an important aspect for the planning process to assure that the correct resources are allocated to protect the data that need to be protected according to risk, either accepted or mitigated by business decisions. When cyber attacks happen, information professionals need to have the resources and knowledge to respond and protect what is important. But what is more important, because all organizations have limited resources, is that the business leaders, and not IT need to determine what to protect.

An effective way to manage risk is to collaboratively work with business executives and leaders to help IT departments determine some key operations security planning questions, such as:

- What is it important or not important to protect?
- What needs to be monitored?
- When/how do we respond?
- When do you call staff in for assistance (Escalation Procedures)?
- What data/systems do you isolate?

Risk management is a process for identifying, assessing and prioritizing risks to data and IT systems. Once the risks are identified, the organization will create a plan to minimize or eliminate the impact of negative events through a decision process with the executives of the organization, because they ultimately are responsible for making decisions on risk mitigation. The executives should determine what information assets are important to protect based on business needs and then how IT should respond. Good risk management allows the use and allocation of resources within the organization to optimize operational security.[4] When planning, regardless of size, the organization must determine what to protect before an attack happens. You will not have time to determine this during the attack.

The first principle of information security operations is to focus on the business. Individuals within the information security community should forge relationships with business leaders and show how information security can complement key business and risk management processes. They should adopt an advisory approach for information security by supporting business objectives through resource allocation, programs and projects. High-level enterprise-focused advice should be provided to protect information and help manage information risk, both now and in the future.[5]

Additionally, when an organization is performing strategic planning, there are other key components that are important for information security operations that should be addressed.[6] The general key components of *strategic planning* include an understanding of the vision, mission, values and strategies involved. The two that I will focus on are vision and values. *Vision* is what the organization wants to be or how it wants the world in which it operates to be. Within information security, it is the idealized view of what is attempting to be accomplished compared to what the business is trying to accomplish. Does the security operations' vision match the organization's vision? In my case, working for an organization that is part of an education institution, where freedom of speech and innovation are highly important to the organization and is highlighted in the organization's vision, the security operations needed to incorporate that vision within the planning. While many of the staff and physicians are not happy with some of these controls and security operations, we actually have fewer technical restrictions than other healthcare organizations due to that overall vision. The organization may be willing to accept additional risk or utilize different controls that some IT professionals may not like.

One example is to allow physicians to use e-mail systems other than our highly restricted messaging system. To mitigate the risk in allowing physicians to use other systems for business, the organization implemented a policy that no protected health information (PHI) can be included in messages, even when or especially as the other system is out of the organization's control. Management was willing to implement a policy instead of highly restrictive technical controls, while business leaders were willing to take some additional risks or implement fewer strict controls because of the overall vision. The vision for security operations—what to monitor, manage and respond to— have to align to the vision of the organization; residual risk must be accepted by the business leaders.

Another key component of the strategic planning for security operations, if it is to be successful, is that the planning must consider the values or culture of the organization. I have seen many security professionals who do not take into account the culture or values of the organization when planning security operations. The values should be assessed internally and externally; the internal assessment should focus on how members inside the organization interpret information security operations and the external assessment, which includes all of the businesses' stakeholders, offers a different perspective. The purpose of the culture assessment is to get a picture of how to integrate information security operations into the normal operations of the organization. Considerations include:

- Who should champion the operations?
- How should the team respond?
- What other types of communications should be used and other resource utilized?

The discrepancies between these two assessments can provide insight into the effectiveness of the security operations and planning and next steps.

There are other good general information security principles that I have used after a risk management process to help me determine what resources to allocate to protect which information asset. As example, listed next are three principles I usually consider.

Principles of easiest penetration. An intruder must be expected to use any available means of penetration and will likely use the easiest. In security operations, do not forget the human factor and that all aspects of information security need to be assessed and reviewed.

Principle of adequate protection. Assets must be protected only until they lose their value and be protected to a degree consistent with their value. In operations, respond according to their value. Can an organization afford to monitor every device? Should the organization monitor devices to the same degree if one contains no data?

Principle of weakest link. Security can be no stronger than its weakest link. Whether it is the power supply that powers the firewall, the operating system under the security application or the human who plans, implements and administers the controls, a failure of any control can lead to a security incident.

These principles can assist you in planning information security operations and ensuring good security fundamentals. Are your security operations protecting the right data at the right time with the right resources?

TACTICAL PLANNING: A STRUCTURE THAT WORKS

The second phase of successful information security operations planning is tactical planning; building a security operations structure that works. Tactical planning or tactics are the techniques for using resources in combination for identifying and stopping an attack. Tactics are specific actions that you take to implement your strategy, or specifically define the action items or structure to get the work done. An information security tactical plan is basically a roadmap for the staff on what they need to do and when they need to do it that fits within the strategic plan.

Tactical planning for security operations is the process of building a structure that can respond and the techniques to reduce the impact of incidents; both are highly important for security operational planning. First, the structure, in any size organization, is based on defining the roles that are important so that the staff knows their specific role and what to do and when to do it. Some of the roles may be filled by different people or the same person, but the important fact is that the structure needs to be in place so effective information security operations can take place. These are the roles that all organizations need to define:

Chief Information Security Officer (CISO). The person ultimately accountable for Information Security Operations, including strategic advice and metrics analytics. As the primary interface between the security function and the organization, the CISO is responsible for information security operation's resources and that activities are aligned to support the overall strategy of the business.

Security manager. The other person ultimately responsible for Information Security Operations, including the responsibilities for metrics-gathering and incident response oversight. The manager supervises the day-to-day security operations, putting in place the people, tools, processes and reporting needed to achieve effective information security operations.

Security guru. The subject-matter expert used for conducting triage, investigation, and thorough research.

Security analysts. The person(s) responsible for the day-to-day monitoring, investigations, alerting, device configuration management, vulnerability management and, potentially, the first responders to an attack. Security analysts are on the front lines of security operations. They constantly monitor the environment for signs of trouble and often the first point of contact and respond to any suspected attack that begins to affect business operations.[7]

Even in relatively small organizations, information security operational function roles and responsibilities need to resemble some variation of what has been described. The key responsibility for planning is to translate the roles and responsibilities to your organization's requirements and implement the required internal structure to make sure the different roles and responsibilities are being utilized. Considerations include:

- Does your organization have a security team or is this outsourced?
- Does the regular network IT staff have some of these responsibilities or are all responsibilities owned solely by those with specific security roles?
- Who is ultimately responsible and accountable for information security operations?

This may include just one or two people handling all of the tasks, with a focus that is limited to the most urgent or critical activities. Large organizations may have a sizable team of dedicated security operation personnel, each with a specialized area of expertise, as depicted in Table 14-1.

Beyond developing roles and responsibilities, it is important for tactical security planning to include the development of techniques. There are two aspects of techniques every organization needs to address in their planning. The first aspect is training. No staff person can be effective without the appropriate training. Luckily, there are many resources for training including computer based training, on-the-job training, workshops, webinars and formal training classes. The important thing is for the organization to implement a formal, approved training plan that prepares the staff for possible

Table 14-1: Roles and Responsibilities in Information Security.

Within the HIPAA Audit Program Protocol, released in June of 2012, are several audit procedures pertaining to roles and responsibilities, including:

- Determine that the roles and responsibilities of the Security Official have been clearly identified in a job description.
- Inquire of management as to whether the roles and responsibilities of the assigned individual … are properly documented in a job description and communicated to the entire organization.
- Inquire of management as to whether staff members have the necessary knowledge, skills, and abilities (KSA) to fulfill particular roles.
- Obtain and review relevant job descriptions and evaluate the content in relation to the specified performance criteria and determine that roles and responsibilities are defined and correlate with job function.
- Obtain and review documentation demonstrating that management verified the required experience/qualifications of the staff.

Management has a responsibility for assuring the assigned individuals have the necessary skills and that their responsibilities are clearly defined and documented.

Source: http://www.hhs.gov/ocr/privacy/hipaa/enforcement/audit/index.html.

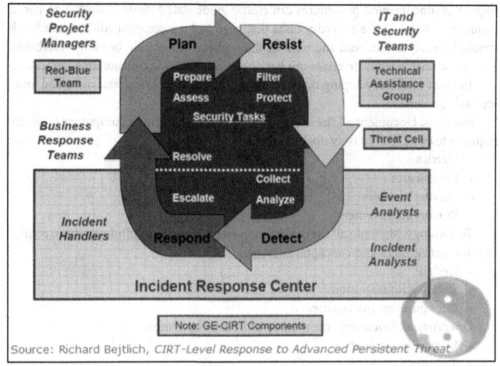

FIGURE 14-1: Security Incident Lifecycle.

security incidents. The major areas of training should follow security incident lifecycle, as depicted in Figure 14-1:

Plan. This area involves what specific training the entire staff including both operations and security personnel should have so that they understand the threats likely to be faced and understand its current state. Specifically, this training should prepare the staff to design an effective, practical and information security architecture.

Resist. The staff should be trained on specific tactics and procedures that will be used to improve the overall information security of the organization and resist or reduce breaches, as well as the impact of breaches.

Detect. Since it is unreasonable for an organization to be able to resist all intrusion attempts, the staff will need training in detecting security compromises. The training involves how staff will collect and analyze data to determine when an investigation is warranted.

Respond. Once a breach has been detected, the organization will need to mobilize resources to respond; this training includes specific training in forensics, communications, and evidence collection.

The training plan should consider the information security skills that maximize the staff's effectiveness for operations.

The second aspect of developing techniques is for organizations to develop an IT security or Stand Operating Procedure handbook. The processes and procedures in such a handbook act as a bridge between technology and the staff. For example, when a staff person is working on a possible incident and has little time to contact experienced staff or outsource security experts, he or she will have a set of procedures to help dictate next steps. Well-documented procedures can clearly guide staff actions in both high-paced incidents but also in the everyday tasks that need to be accomplished. The handbook should be easily found, read and used by the staff but also should be easily searchable. The best format in which to create this handbook is a wiki-type collaborative application.

To assist you in developing that handbook, there are generally four main and fourteen sub-processes.[8]

Business. Document all the administrative and management components that are required to remain effectively operational.

- Metrics
- Compliance
- Disaster recovery
- Process improvement

Technology. Maintain all the information related to system administration, configuration management and conceptual design.

- Design
- System administration
- Configuration management

Operational. Document the mechanics of daily operations.

- Event management
- Training
- Daily operations

Analytical. Encompass all activities designed to detect and better understand malicious events.

- Reporting
- Incident management
- Intrusion analysis
- Subtle event detection

Both training and process/procedure development are important for the organization for planning the tactics for your Information Security Operation function. Does your organization have the structure defined for Information Security Operations?

OPERATIONAL PLANNING

The third phase of successful Information Security Operations planning is operational planning; the daily tasks that need to get done. A security operation is a term that describes a range of activities with the intended purpose of protecting information assets. In some organizations, the tasks to accomplish that purpose may be split among several teams or departments on an ad-hoc basis but also the tasks could be combined for one security team. The daily activities are designed to keep security systems working optimally so that information assets are protected, yet operate without disruption to the business. The five basic functions to plan for in information security operations are:

1. Vulnerability management
2. Device management
3. Monitoring
4. Threat analysis
5. Incident response

The first functional area of operational planning is vulnerability management. Identifying unpatched systems, weak passwords and a misconfiguration basically strengthens your security posture and gives you an accurate picture of security vulnerabilities. One of the first steps that hackers use to exploit your system is to determine if any of external and if possible internal systems are vulnerable to scanning. Vulnerability management is the function in which the organization has a formal process of first patching systems but also a process to detect current vulnerabilities. Key assessment questions to ask include:

- Does your organization have a formal process to patch systems? If the application cannot be patched, how will the vulnerability be mitigated?
- Does the organization scan the network for vulnerabilities?

In turn, the organization can stay one step ahead of hackers who might want to exploit those vulnerabilities, and of auditors who will hold you accountable for protecting the infrastructure in a compliant manner.[7]

The second functional area is information system device management. Information system device management increases the accuracy of threat detection and decreases vulnerabilities. Keeping firewall policies up-to-date, hardening systems, tuning the rules for an Intrusion Prevention Systems (IPS) and Security Information and Event Monitoring Systems (SIEM) enables the organization to improve the detection of valid attacks but also reduces vulnerabilities. When the technology that is deployed is doing its job, it reduces the number of events and also reduces staff time spent investigating false positives. This function is the one of the most challenging for an organization to accomplish because it does not have an immediate impact on improving operations. And, if an organization neglects device management, the organization will lose their situational awareness and experience more of the fog of war.

The third functional area is monitoring, which provides an early warning for possible events and helps to mitigate when there is an attack. This includes verifying that security systems are working properly, checking various communication channels for automated alerts that may require follow-up and scanning for other indicators, such as an unexplained spike in network traffic that may signal that an attack is underway. Monitoring is highly important because it is in monitoring where the organization sees events, indications that there may be in trouble, and hopefully, prevents the attack before it becomes a security incident. It is better to know when a valid attack is occurring rather than being notified later when it is too late.

One aspect of operational planning that is often neglected is threat analysis; assisting in what to look for and how others are responding. Many resources are available to help an organization to keep track of newly discovered threats; how organizations are being exploited and what possible steps to mitigate have been developed. There are several resources such mailing lists: the Computer Emergency Response Team (CERT); the SANS Institute, which specializes in information security research, training and certification; and the Department of Homeland Security's Cyber Security Alerts. Additionally, the function of threat analysis should be based on specific research tailored to specific systems and applications of the organization. Threat analysis is analyzing and developing steps to counter information security threats. This analysis is the process of gathering information about the organization and threats (hackers, viruses) and more importantly, processing that information based on the risk assessment to determine any indications or warnings for the organization. It is a blend of defense but also espionage or intelligence.

The information generated can help provide a quicker response, more effective actions taken, longer term reduction of risk and a better prioritization for resources to protect information assets.

Another set of highly important tasks that need to be planned is how the organization responds to security incidents or Incident Management. The basic principle is that incident response must be planned and exercised or tested because rapid response mitigates or reduces the impact of attacks. The front line staff directs the response to attacks, taking immediate steps to alleviate the attack and isolate the impacted systems to contain the incident. The primary goal of incident response is to minimize the impact to the organization and return the organization to normal operations without harming future litigation through deletion or changing forensic data. In order to reach that goal, the organization must have developed the planning to assemble a team that can deal with the multiple facets of the incident in real-time. The procedures that should be included in the plan should cover six phases, Preparation, Identification, Containment, Eradication, Remediation, and Lessons Learned:

Phase 1: Preparation. In the middle of the "fog of war," when an incident has been revealed, knowing next steps could be difficult to determine. By establishing policies, procedures and agreements in advance, you minimize the chance of making disastrous mistakes. If needed, contact a security professional to develop what your organization should and could do in the preparation phase.

Phase 2: Identification. Identification involves determining whether or not an incident has occurred, and if one has occurred, determining the nature of the incident. The most important aspect of this phase is that everyone knows their role and responsibility in an incident.

Phase 3: Containment. During this phase, the goal is to limit the damage and magnitude of an incident in order to keep the incident from getting worse. One important aspect of this phase is to determine the risk of continuing operations compared to isolating the system. That decision will need to escalated and explained if needed. Another aspect that is important is to back up the system to new media; this is important for future forensic evidence of any illegal activity and for future lessons learned.

Phase 4: Eradication. This phase's goal is to ensure that the incident or problem is eliminated and the vulnerabilities that allow re-entry to the system are eliminated. An important aspect of this phase is to implement mitigation strategies to protect the data in the future.

Phase 5: Remediation. This phase's major goal is to make sure that the system is returned to a fully operational status or restored. An important aspect of this phase is that management is the decision maker for when or how that will happen.

Phase 6: Lessons Learned. This phase is important in identifying lessons learned that will prevent future incidents through a detailed incident report.

The end result goal of the process is to create changes to the organization in order that any given incident is not repeated.

Keeping organizational information assets secure in today's interconnected computing environment is a true challenge that becomes more difficult with each new "e" product and each new intruder tool. Most organizations realize that there is no one solution or panacea for securing systems and data; instead a multi-layered security strategy is required. One of the layers that many organizations are including in their strategy today is the creation of a Computer Security Incident Response Team.[9]

CONCLUSION

Every organization that connects to the global Internet is at war, war that is extremely fast moving and with multiple opportunities for IT professionals to encounter the fog of war, an experience in which there is uncertainty. This chapter argues that to prepare for this type of warfare, informational professionals need to prepare and plan. There are three basic planning functions:

1. Strategic planning: Allowing the business to allocate resources to protect and respond to information assets that are worth protecting.
2. Tactical planning: Building a structure, a staff, that can protect these information assets.
3. Operational planning: The daily tasks that need to get done.

If organizations and information security professionals implement these planning functions, then they can create an effective information security operation.

Author's Comment

I believe that information security as a profession is in a transition. Previously, information security was simply a matter of implementing a few tools such as a firewall, into the current environment with advanced hacking tools and techniques. With the increased sophistication of hackers and increase of vulnerabilities of systems, everything has changed and all organizations have to immediately adapt. There is an old saying in the military that we must prepare for the last war. Is your information security based on old assumptions? This transition is making all information professionals into security professionals. We need to view this as a new type of war. A positive for IT professionals is that the United States has been fighting this irregular war, an IT war, for more than 15 years and has learned lessons that we can use. While we do not need lessons in fighting a real war, we can learn from the planning and preparation that occur in this kind of war. That is what I have tried to do in this chapter—bring forward the lessons that I learned from my military service in Afghanistan to protect our data. I hope I have succeeded.

Editor note: Throughout the chapter, the author uses the war analogy to illustrate his points. Having served his country for one year in forward operations in Afghanistan, Mr. Dannen truly knows what war means.

REFERENCES

1. Goodchild J. CSO Security and Risk. May 14, 2012. Available at: http://www.csoonline.com/article/706400/10-hacks-that-made-headlines?page=1.

2. Lewis JA. Cyber attacks, real or imagined, and cyber war. July 11, 2011. Center for Strategic and International Studies. http://csis.org/publication/cyber-attacks-real-or-imagined-and-cyber-war.

3. Hayden MV. National Information Systems Security (INFOSEC) Glossary. www.dtic.mil: Available at: www.dtic.mil/cgi-bin/GetTRDoc?Location=U2&doc=GetTRDoc.pdf&AD=ADA433929.

4. Risk Management Standard. Available at: www.theirm.org/publications/documents/Risk_Management_Standard_030820.pdf. 2002.

5. Principles of Information Security Practitioners. www.isaca.org. 2010.

6. Mckeown M. *The Strategy Book*. Prentice Hall; 2012.

7. RSA White Paper-Creating an Effective Security Operations Function; 2008.

8. ArcSight - Building a Successful Security Operations Center; 2009.

9. Creating a Computer Security Incident Response Team: A Process for Getting Started. Available at: www.cert.org/csirts/Creating-A-CSIRT.html. 2002.

CHAPTER 15

Security Considerations in Technology Contracting

By Melissa Markey, Esq., and Margaret Marchak, Esq.

There may be some who question the need for an entire chapter on security considerations in healthcare technology contracts. The technology contract, however, establishes the parameters of the relationship between the vendor and the customer, and given the highly regulated nature of healthcare, one of the critical relationship issues is responsibility for data security. Failure to address issues of security may impact the relationship that the customer has with the vendor; more importantly, it can impact the relationship that the healthcare entity has with its clients and patients, as well as its relationship with regulators and enforcers of laws.

APPLICABLE LAWS

The number of laws that address the security and privacy of healthcare data is increasing, and that trend is expected to continue. The primary laws are briefly summarized next; however, it is important to remember that, as this is a dynamic area of the law, it is critical to update information and work with legal counsel who are experts in, and maintain currency with, these laws. It is also important to remember that laws may exist on *both* federal and state levels and that contracts may also impose additional voluntary standards or terms. The primary federal laws addressing the security of healthcare information and technology are as follows:

HIPAA/HITECH

The Administrative Simplification provisions of the Health Insurance Portability and Accountability Act of 1996 (HIPAA) include both privacy and security requirements. The U.S. Department of Health & Human Services (HHS) was required by this statute to adopt national standards for the security of electronic protected health information and did so in the regulation commonly known as the Security Rule, which is found at 42 U.S.C. § 1320d-2(d), 45 C.F.R. Part 160 and Subparts A and C of Part 164. The Security Rule requires those covered by it to adopt and implement administrative, technical and physical security safeguards. The Security Rule is technology-agnostic and is intended to be flexible and scalable to permit each covered entity (and its business associates) to adopt the security approach most appropriate, given the computing environment in question.

HIPAA was amended by the American Recovery and Reinvestment Act of 2009 in the Health Information Technology for Economic and Clinical Health (HITECH) Act provisions. HITECH was enacted to modify the HIPAA Security Rule, among other objectives, to require those covered by HIPAA to enhance the privacy and security protections for protected health information. One of the biggest changes to HIPAA in HITECH was the direct imposition of certain HIPAA obligations on business associates.[1] HITECH provides that the Security Rule applies to business associates and that they are required to comply with the regulations regarding implementation of administrative safeguards,[2] physical safeguards,[3] technical safeguards,[4] and policy, procedure and documentation requirements.[5]

As part of its rulemaking authority under HIPAA/HITECH, HHS issued in July 2010 a notice of proposed rulemaking (NPRM) to modify the HIPAA Privacy, Security, and Enforcement Rules. The proposed rule includes extending the applicability of certain of the Privacy Rule and Security Rule requirements to business associates, in accordance with the HITECH Act. A significant number of comments from the industry and privacy community were submitted in response, providing insight into the amount of interest, and varying perspectives, in this area. The industry had been waiting for the final HITECH rules to be published and after more than two years, the Omnibus Rule was released on January 25, 2013. (See 45 CFR Parts 160 and 164). This Omnibus Rule addresses the following four rules: Breach Notifications Interim Final Rule (IFR) (08/24/09), Enforcement and Compliance IFR (10/30/09), the HITECH Privacy/Security/Enforcement NPRM (7/14/10) and Genetic Information Non-discrimination Act NPRM (10/01/09). The date of release of the Omnibus Rule and the publication of this book did not allow enough time for an in-depth analysis.

Some vendors have used the HITECH Act's direct regulation, which imposes liability on business associates for violations of HIPAA, to argue against including provisions in business associate or other agreements that require the business associates to indemnify the covered entity for breaches of HIPAA caused by the business associate. The vendor may advocate that it is already responsible to the regulators for the violation and should not also be liable to the covered entity. However, the fact that a business associate is directly liable for compliance with certain HIPAA standards does necessarily eliminate the covered entity's potential liability for a breach caused by its business associate. A covered entity may choose to require the business associate to protect the covered entity from costs and losses due to the failure of the business associate to comply with the agreement.

As part of HITECH, the Federal Trade Commission (FTC) implemented a Health Breach Notification Rule at 16 CFR Part 318 to require vendors of personal health records (PHRs) and related entities and third-party service providers that are not covered under the HIPAA Security Rule to notify certain individuals when a security breach of health information occurs. As of the date of this chapter, very few notifications had been submitted to the FTC.

Federal Information Security Management Act

Title III of the E-Government Act of 2002, entitled the Federal Information Security Management Act (FISMA), was enacted to provide a comprehensive framework for information security controls over information resources that support federal operations and assets. Further, the act provides for the development and maintenance of minimum controls required to protect federal information and information systems. It requires each federal agency to have an agency-wide program to provide information security for its operations and assets, including those provided or managed by another agency, contractor, or other source. FISMA assigns certain responsibilities to the National Institute of Standards and Technology (NIST) to develop information security standards and guidelines for most federal information systems. Some of these requirements may be imposed upon a federal contractor to protect data received from the federal agency.

The Privacy Act of 1974

The Privacy Act of 1974, found at 5 USC 552a, applies only to federal agencies and governs the collection, maintenance, use, and dissemination of information about individuals that is maintained in systems' records by those agencies. The Privacy Act requires each federal agency to have an administrative and physical security system to prevent the unauthorized release of certain records. The Computer Matching and Privacy Protection Act of 1988 amended the Privacy Act to add procedural requirements for federal agencies to follow when engaging in computer-matching activities and to require those agencies to establish data protection boards to oversee their matching activities.

Gramm-Leach-Bliley Act

The Financial Services Modernization Act of 1999, also known as the Gramm-Leach-Bliley Act (GLBA) for its drafters, addresses a consumer's personal financial information held by financial institutions. The definition of "financial institution" is broad enough to cover the activities of some entities engaged in the healthcare industry. GLBA required the FTC to establish standards relating to administrative, technical and physical information safeguards for financial institutions subject to the FTC's jurisdiction. The FTC issued the Safeguards Rule under section 501(b) of GLBA to provide standards to ensure the security and confidentiality of customer records and information and to protect against threats or hazards, including unauthorized access, to the use of such information.

Payment Card Industry Data Security Standards

The Payment Card Industry Data Security Standard (PCI DSS) resulted from a collaboration of major credit card issuers seeking to strengthen protections for payment card data in January 2005. These comprehensive security standards include requirements for security management/policies/procedures, access controls, network architecture, applications, storage, transmission and testing as a recommendation for a minimum set of protective measures. Compliance with the standard is contractually required by the individual card payment companies for merchants that accept, transmit or store any cardholder data. A sample of these standards is in Table 15-1.

TABLE 15-1: Payment Card Industry Data Security Standards.

Merchants (organizations that accept credit or debit cards for payment) must manage and monitor their service providers to assure their PCI DSS compliance. Section 12.8 of the standard, requires:
12.8   If cardholder data is shared with service providers, maintain and implement policies and procedures to manage service providers, to include the following:
12.8.1 Maintain a list of service providers.
12.8.2 Maintain a written agreement that includes an acknowledgement that the service providers are responsible for the security of cardholder data the service providers possess.
12.8.3 Ensure there is an established process for engaging service providers including proper due diligence prior to engagement.
12.8.4 Maintain a program to monitor service providers' PCI DSS compliance status at least annually.

Recently, some states have codified some portions or all of the PCI DSS. Where a vendor is responsible for processing or storing credit card data, the agreement with that vendor should expressly require the vendor to comply with the PCI DSS and should provide the basis for the merchant to fulfill the obligations imposed on the merchant to monitor service providers' protection of the credit card data. A contractual requirement that the vendor obtain an evaluation of compliance with PCI DSS by a qualified external entity, and provide evidence of compliance with that requirement, may be useful.

Sarbanes-Oxley Act

The Sarbanes-Oxley (SOX) Act, enacted in 2002, applies to companies that are required to report to the Securities and Exchange Commission (SEC) in an effort to protect investors. These for-profit, publicly traded companies are required to protect certain financial data and maintain internal controls over such data, among other requirements. The information security provisions of SOX are generally found in Sections 302 (Responsibilities of the CEO and CFO for establishing and maintaining internal controls), 404 (Internal controls), and 409 (Disclosures of material events).

GENERAL CONTRACTING CONSIDERATIONS

There are two general schools of thought with respect to drafting contractual provisions for security. The first is the prescriptive approach, where the contract provisions spell out, in considerable detail, the required security measures. The contract may require the vendor to implement and maintain, for example, firewalls and antivirus software. The second is the results-oriented approach, where the vendor is obligated to take all reasonable and necessary actions to establish and maintain a secure environment that meets or exceeds relevant legal requirements and industry standards or best practices. Each approach has advantages and disadvantages, and which is best depends on the facts and circumstances of the situation.

The prescriptive approach provides a clear level of expectations and, assuming the healthcare organization has and exercises its audit rights, enables the organization to determine whether the vendor is complying with its contractual obligations. As threats and vulnerabilities change, it is inflexible, because changes to the standards would require amendments to the contract and may not provide protection against new dangers. The results-oriented approach has the advantage of providing flexibility to accommodate new threats and vulnerabilities, as well as new legal requirements and developing best practices. Where the vendor has particular expertise in hosting, it also shifts to the party with the greatest knowledge the responsibility for determining the most appropriate approach to security for that environment. Whether the vendor has performed in compliance with the contract standards may not be known with certainty until too late—after a breach has occurred. The decision about which approach to take in a particular contract, or how to create an effective hybrid approach, should be worked out between technology counsel and the security team during the early stages of the contracting process.

Software Contracts

For traditional software licensing agreements, the terms related to security primarily involve ensuring good title to the software, performance considerations, and that it does not contain code that either intentionally or inadvertently poses a threat to security. For these contracts, consider the following provisions:

Warranty of title. The vendor should warrant that the vendor owns all rights necessary to grant the rights of use granted under the agreement, and, to the extent third-party software is included, that the vendor has all rights necessary to grant rights, such as rights of use, in the third-party software. The vendor should also agree to defend, indemnify, and hold harmless the customer and its employees, officers, and users against any claims that the software has infringed a third-party's rights. The warranty of title and intellectual property infringement provisions serve similar purposes, but protect in different ways. The title warranty constitutes a special type of promise that the vendor holds all rights necessary to grant the rights provided in the agreement. The infringement indemnity protects the healthcare organization against the situation in which a third party actually brings a claim of infringement, ensuring that the vendor will be responsible for defending against the claim, and paying for any costs associated with the claim, including any damages that the claimant might receive.

The Uniform Commercial Code (UCC) Article 2 applies to the sale of goods. Each state has adopted the UCC in some form, although there are some variations from state to state. Many authorities have concluded that UCC Article 2 applies to the licensing of software. Therefore, unless disclaimed, the implied warranties of Article 2 may apply. These warranties include the implied warranty of title and the implied warranty of non-infringement. The implied warranty of title constitutes a warranty that the vendor owns the software that it is licensing; the implied warranty of non-infringement is a warranty that the software is free of rightful claims of infringement. Under the UCC, the infringement need not be proven to have breached this warranty; the mere fact that a party is able to bring a colorable infringement claim breaches the warranty and permits the software licensee to bring a claim. While these UCC warranties are valuable, they are often disclaimed by software vendors. Healthcare organizations should resist the vendor's attempts to disclaim these warranties, as it is reasonable to expect the vendor to warrant both as to ownership and as to non-infringement. Because the remedies differ from the indemnity, having both the warranty and the infringement indemnity is important.

Warranty of non-beneficial code. The vendor should represent and warrant that the software does not include any non-beneficial code. Non-beneficial code can include anything from counters or timers that are primarily intended for a purpose other than the proper operation of the software to viruses, "easter eggs,"[6] and other malware. Timers and counters that are intended to monitor the number of users should be disclosed and should not be permitted to shut down access to critical clinical applications. Any code which permits an entity other than the healthcare entity to control access to the software is a security risk and should not be permitted. Vendors may claim that the ability to shut down access is necessary to avoid violations of licenses that are limited to a certain number of users; however, vendors have adequate remedies for such license violations, namely, by imposing a fee for exceeding the number of licensed copies or potentially through a breach claim; the remedy should not impede the effective delivery of patient care.

Warranty of performance. The warranty of performance contributes to the contractual description of security by assuring the buyer that the software will perform as promised, or as described in the documentation. While the warranty of performance is important for many reasons, it can also play a role in security. The documentation should be reviewed to ensure that it addresses authentication and secure access appropriately. Authentication is a critical component of information security, as it is necessary to determining the integrity of information. Under the HIPAA Security Rule, covered entities and business associates are required to assign unique user identification and access control capabilities to ensure that the person accessing electronic protected health information (ePHI) is who he/she claims to be. Therefore, ensuring this is an important component of due diligence regarding the software. If flaws in the software later contribute to a data breach, the warranty of performance may have been breached, if the authentication, security, or other capabilities failed to perform as described.

Application Security
The vendor should be required to warrant that appropriate security measures have been incorporated into the application itself, that code is written in a manner which minimizes errors, and that vulnerabilities are minimized. An increasingly important concept is that of *security by design*, where security is a consideration throughout the development of the application. Securing the perimeter is insufficient; increasingly, there is no perimeter, as applications and data are accessed through mobile devices and the cloud. Therefore, the security of the application itself becomes increasingly important. Application security is covered in Chapter 13.

Access Controls, Audit Trails, and Logs
The capability of the software to restrict access to authorized personnel, and to record, display and print audit trails and logs are important security features. Under the HIPAA Security Rule, a covered entity must implement processes that limit access to ePHI to personnel who require such access to perform legitimate job functions. An important component of complying with this obligation is the ability of the software to limit access at an appropriately granular level.

Likewise, it is important for the covered entity to maintain audit trails and audit logs that track access to ePHI. Audit trails should be sufficiently detailed that the covered entity can identify which user accessed which record, when. It is best if the audit trail also discloses the period of time the record was accessed and the actions taken—for example, what was edited, whether it was printed, sent or downloaded or whether it was opened briefly and closed. Increased detail in the audit trail permits a more accurate picture regarding data access should issues arise. In selecting and contracting for software, healthcare organizations should evaluate the ability of the software to maintain audit trails and should ensure that audit trails are referenced in the documentation, which is referenced by the performance warranty. Healthcare organizations that perform research that generates data that will be submitted to the U.S. Food and Drug Administration (FDA) should also consider the requirements of 42 CFR Part 11. While the requirements of these regulations are not currently enforced against healthcare organizations, new purchases of software should be made with an eye toward compliance.

Breach Notification and Investigation

Under HIPAA, impermissible uses and disclosures of PHI may constitute breaches that must be reported to the U.S. Department of Health & Human Services; similarly, many states have enacted breach notification statutes. In some states, those statutes require notification only for breaches of healthcare information; however, in other states, any breach of personally identifiable information must be reported. Because the duty to notify is, under many of these laws, based on the state of residence of the affected individual, healthcare organizations are often confronted with the need to comply with the most stringent breach notification laws that apply to a particular incident.

Where a software or technology services vendor causes the breach, the healthcare organization is necessarily dependent on that vendor to some extent for the investigation and breach response; therefore, it is important to address in the contract breach response obligations. The agreement should specify when the healthcare organization should be advised of possible unauthorized use or disclosure of confidential information (Immediately? After some investigation indicates that a breach was likely? Only after the beach is confirmed?). Many healthcare organizations may want to participate in the investigation, to have the right to approve any notifications to patients/affected individuals and regulators and to approve or require mitigation efforts. If these issues are addressed early in the relationship and memorialized in the contract, decision-making, and response during the high-stress period immediately following a possible breach will be more streamlined and effective.

Mobile Applications

As mobile devices become more ubiquitous and medical applications more pervasive, the importance of the security of these devices and applications increases. Devices that were primarily developed for consumers may not have had a significant focus on security. As devices are used more for business applications and individuals are providing their own devices, the focus on security tends to be significantly enhanced, and third-party products to strengthen security become available. Mobile devices range from tablets to smartphones and include varying levels of capability. Regardless of the type of device, however, special care must be taken with respect to mobile device security. Several different characteristics of mobile devices contribute to the unique security concerns. Additional information is available in Chapter 12.

From the legal perspective, one of the challenges about mobile devices is finding the "contract" under which the security for mobile devices can be managed. In a "bring your own device," or BYOD model, the user holds the contract with the telecommunications vendor, which hosts the mobile device software and stores the data transmitted to and from the mobile device in the first instance. Mobile device users are increasingly using cloud services such as iCloud for storage, and when the user uploads the data from the mobile device, business information may be uploaded along with the user's personal information. This puts the business in the very risky position of possibly placing protected and confidential information in the possession of an entity (the telecommunications vendor or the cloud vendor) with which it has no relationship and no ability to control the dissemination of and/or retrieve the information and no ability to ensure the data are properly protected.

As this discussion illustrates, many of the issues and activity related to BYOD mobile devices occur outside of the healthcare entity—the action is between the user and the mobile device company, the telecommunications vendor or cloud vendor that stores the data. Therefore, the "contract," which must be used to control the risks related to this area, comprises the policies and procedures under which the user has the right to access the healthcare entity's data. A full mobile device management plan (MDM) is critical and should include enforceable policies that require:

- Access only to the data that the person requires to do their job.
- Use of a password to access the device.
- Locking of the device after a (short) period of inactivity.
- Immediate reporting if the device is out of the control of the individual.
- Remote wiping of the business content on the device if the device is out of the control of the individual, or terminated from employment.
- Access to the device for purposes of litigation hold compliance.

Mobile device management is covered in Chapter 12.

Outsourcing Contracts

When information technology services are outsourced, computing security services are often outsourced as well. However, regulators have sent a clear message—healthcare providers may delegate tasks, but the responsibility for compliance remains with the regulated entity. Even where the outsource vendor is a business associate of the covered entity, and thus directly regulated under HIPAA, the covered entity remains responsible for the security of protected health information (PHI) and for other personally identifiable information (PII), which is protected by other laws. More importantly, the patients who entrusted their information to the covered entity will look to the covered entity for protection of the data. Therefore, the importance of addressing security responsibilities in the outsourcing agreement is clear.

DUE DILIGENCE

The first step in addressing security issues in contracting begins with due diligence. In outsourcing your information technology services, you are entrusting some of your most important assets—data—to the vendor. The reputation of the vendor for customer service, security, and operational compliance is critical. Is the vendor known in the industry for vigorously protecting the security of data? Does the vendor view customer service as a critical component throughout the relationship, or do customers complain that vendor promises are not fulfilled as the contract is performed? Has the vendor previously suffered a data breach? If so, how was it handled? If the vendor is publicly traded, has it reported previous security incidents to the Securities and Exchange Commission (SEC)? Does your salesperson know the name of the information security officer, privacy official, and compliance officer? If not, the vendor may not view privacy and security as a priority.

Consider the vendor's financial condition. How long has the vendor been in business? Is the vendor adequately capitalized? Consider doing a search of financial statements to understand whether the vendor's equipment is encumbered or owned free and clear. While many businesses have financed equipment, vendors whose financial condition is precarious, or who are cash-poor, may cut corners on security. A financially vulnerable vendor who holds your data places your data in a vulnerable position.

The answers to your due diligence questions will help both with the vendor selection and in determining the importance of various contractual provisions. Caution should be exercised with a vendor whose financial condition is unstable, even if the software has attractive functionality. Consideration should be given to maintaining a copy of your data in your control, so that if the vendor goes out of business, your data remain available. A source code escrow provision may also be appropriate, if your technical staff is capable of maintaining the software if the vendor ceases operations. Finally, contract provisions providing the right to audit and monitor privacy, security, and operational compliance, and require vendor corrections of weaknesses identified, can help protect against vulnerabilities exposed through the due diligence process.

The Request for Proposal (RFP) or Request for Information (RFI)

When preparing the request for proposal/request for information for vendors, security issues should be considered. The RFP/RFI should expressly state any security requirements, including desirable security-related certifications, and specify applicable compliance standards. For healthcare entities, HIPAA and its related regulations establish the regulatory privacy and security floor; additional privacy and security standards may be established by state laws. Certain types of data, which are viewed as particularly sensitive, may be subject to additional protection under either state or federal law.

Publicly traded entities may also be subject to additional requirements under regulations promulgated by the SEC, and public-facing websites (i.e., those that are readily accessible by consumers) are subject to regulation by the FTC. The Federal Communications Commission regulates transmission of data via wired and wireless communication devices and may impose additional restrictions related to such transmissions. Legal counsel should be consulted to ensure that all applicable regulatory requirements have been considered, and the vendors who are bidding to be considered should be required to address how compliance with the various legal requirements is accomplished.

The RFP can also be used to set expectations regarding contractual provisions. A clear statement that certain contract provisions are mandatory, preferably including preferred language, can help set expectations early in the process. Among the contract provisions which might be included in this category are those addressed in this chapter, as well as others that are of particular importance to the entity. By including the contract provisions in the RFP, negotiations for the software agreement can be expedited, as the vendor will know your contracting expectations at the time of the RFP response. Those provisions should automatically be included in the software agreement.

Cloud Computing

Cloud computing is characterized by high flexibility, high agility, and low capital commitments for the data owner. When contracting for cloud computing services, the nature and scope of contract protections will vary based on the type of cloud (public, private or hybrid), the service model (Software as a Service, Platform as a Service, or Infrastructure as a Service), and the type of data in question. The type of cloud will influence the need for contractual protections, as that will determine the relative control over the security of the infrastructure held by each party to the contract—the cloud vendor and the owner of the data. The type of data to be held and processed in the cloud will also impact the contractual obligations; more stringent contractual provisions are necessary for sensitive and highly regulated data than are necessary for unregulated, less sensitive information.

There are several different types of cloud computing arrangements, or service models. Infrastructure as a Service (IaaS) is a utility computing model,[7] in which the cloud vendor provides the computing infrastructure—the data center, servers, base telecommunications capabilities, desktop virtualization, administration and support services—and the customer is responsible for all non-hardware related operations.

Platform as a Service (PaaS) is a model where the cloud vendor provides all of the services provided in IaaS, but also provides the operating system and storage and network capacity management. In PaaS, the cloud vendor is responsible for providing all assets and services other than the software applications and services related directly to those applications. Essentially, the customer has outsourced to the cloud vendor full data center operations, while retaining applications-level responsibilities, including maintenance of databases, patch administration, and similar activities.

Software as a Service (SaaS) describes an arrangement where the cloud computing vendor provides a complete package of software, hardware, and services to the customer. The cloud vendor is wholly responsible for the infrastructure, the operating systems, the background programs and the applications. All services are provided through, and the responsibility of, the cloud vendor. While in some cases the customer may retain Level 1 Help Desk services (typically to preserve the illusion, for the benefit of the end user, that the customer is the provider of the services), the assistance provided by the Level 1 Help Desk is typically limited and based on knowledge bases provided by the cloud vendor. Because higher level Help Desk services will be provided by the cloud vendor, it is likely that the vendor will be exposed to protected health information, and the contract should contemplate such exposure.

As the descriptions of IaaS, PaaS, and SaaS make clear, the relative degree of control over the environment, both hardware and software, vary significantly depending on the service model procured by the customer. In IaaS, the cloud vendor has control of the physical environment and hardware and, thus, should be contractually obligated to implement reasonable security controls over related risk areas. Because the customer has control over the operating system and applications, the customer must accept greater responsibility for security with respect to those elements. The opposite is true, however, for SaaS implementations, wherein the cloud provider should be contractually obligated to implement reasonable security controls for the entire environment.

Due Diligence

Similar to security in other outsourcing agreements, the first step in addressing security issues in cloud computing contracts begins with due diligence. The level of security required will vary based on the type of computing to be conducted and data stored in the cloud. While there is always a need for basic confidentiality, integrity, and availability, certain types of information and operations require higher levels of security. If the data or operations in question require higher levels of security, some vendors may not be appropriate. For example, most public clouds will not meet the security needs of companies and agencies that are using and storing highly sensitive data because public cloud security is often limited and public cloud vendors are typically unwilling to increase security due to cost. That does not mean, however, that cloud computing is completely impossible; there are company-specific cloud implementations (often called private cloud) and hybrid cloud implementations (a combination of models) that may meet those security needs.

Again, the reputation of the vendor for security and operational compliance is critical. The same concerns as discussed earlier under Outsourcing Contracts exist in the cloud computing environment. However, the nature of cloud computing presents additional risks that should be considered. One of the most important of these is the risk of distributed denial of service (DDoS) attacks. In these attacks, the vendor is flooded with incoming traffic, overloading the capability of the system to respond and bringing down system. Cloud computing vendors are particularly vulnerable to DDoS attacks, often because the cloud vendor itself or some of the co-located companies in the cloud may attract the attention of hackers, leading to an attack, and potential customers should understand the vendor's experience with and defenses against DDoS attacks. Similarly, the large amount of data located in a cloud computing environment poses an enticing target to identity thieves; once the security is penetrated, the thieves have hit a rich payload.

Cloud vendor financial condition is also important in the cloud computing context. One of the characteristics of cloud computing is that it is "pay as you go." Vendors must have excess resources standing by and ready for deployment at customer request. While many are using virtualization and automation to accomplish this, there are costs associated with flexibility, and a vendor needs to be financially resilient. While most outsourcing vendors are relatively large, there are many small cloud computing vendors, and many are relatively new companies. Therefore, another consideration is the vendor's experience with data centers and virtualization. Many of the benefits of cloud—flexibility, scalability, resiliency and redundancy, rapid deployment—will only be captured if the vendor has the knowledge and experience necessary to monitor and anticipate customers' needs. Talk to customers about their experience with the vendor. Ask questions about downtime and time to add resources. Explore customer service options and the vendor's response to unique customer needs. If you aren't comfortable asking questions of the vendor now, consider whether you are going to be able to communicate effectively if a dispute ever arises.

SECURITY BY OBSCURITY IS NOT SECURITY

Part of the due diligence is gaining an understanding of the cloud vendor's security approach. Security-related questions can be divided into categories of physical, technical, and administrative approaches to security. While the exact questions may vary based on the type of cloud, the type of data, and the scope of services offered, the following are examples of questions you might ask:

- What security measures are in place to protect the data center against unauthorized physical intrusion?
- Who would be permitted to access my data and under what circumstances?
- What are your procedures for terminating access to data or systems upon termination of an employee, or upon change of job duties?
- What are the processes to ensure that default passwords are changed and/or other access controls are implemented?
- What procedures exist to ensure configurations are properly set?
- What does your testing/patch process include?
- What is your encryption policy?
- How do you secure transmissions outside your network?
- Where will the data be stored? In the United States or other countries?
- Does the cloud provider:
  - Have cyber-insurance?
  - Have an audit certification of their information security program in compliance with the Statement on Standards for Attestation Engagements (SSAE) No. 16 Service Organization Control (SOC) 2 or 3, or equivalent audit (e.g. ISO 27001/2)?
  - Conduct (at a minimum) quarterly vulnerability scans and annual network penetration tests?
  - Use security monitoring and event log management to ensure the collection and secure storage of audit trails?
  - Review event logs periodically for anomalies?
  - Document changes following industry standard practices for configuration management and change control?
  - Employ redundant hardware components, load-balanced Internet connections with multiple service providers, and functioning firewalls?
  - Implement backup options and encrypt any removable or portable backup media?

⊃ Conduct business continuity and disaster recovery exercises on a regular, planned basis?

Some vendors may object to answering questions, arguing that security is weakened by revealing security measures. However, security by obscurity is not a good policy. The answers to the questions just given, and other similar questions, will not weaken the security of the system. They will allow the customer to evaluate whether security is reasonable. There may be some security details that may not be shared but, typically, the security official for the data center should be able to speak frankly with the security official for the customer about the security processes that will affect the customer's data.

External Security Certifications

For many years, the gold standard for security certifications for data centers was the Statement on Auditing Standards 70, commonly referred to as SAS 70, an auditing standard established by the American Institute of Certified Public Accountants (AICPA). AICPA intended SAS 70 to evaluate controls established on financial reporting controls by service organizations—those entities to which core functions had been delegated or outsourced, particularly the functions that are directly related to the financial reporting activities of the customers of the service organization. However, due to a lack of other reliable indicia of effective controls, SAS 70 became the measure for effective non-financial compliance and operational controls—a use for which it was never intended. Therefore, for report periods after June 15, 2011, SAS 70 was replaced, in part by SSAE 16 and in part by AT 101. Statements on Standards for Attestation Engagements (SSAEs) are promulgated by AICPA and describe the standards by which attestation engagements are to be conducted by professional accountants.

SSAE 16 describes the standards for reporting on controls at service organizations, particularly with respect to internal controls over the service organization's financial reporting. There are three different types of Service Organization Control (SOC) reports available—SOC 1, 2, and 3—which focus on different areas and levels of detail, depending on the nature and scope of risk assumed by the service organization. SOC 1 reports are based on SSAE 16; SOC 2 and 3 reports are based on AT 101, which uses the Trust Services Principles and Criteria for Security, Availability, Processing Integrity, Confidentiality, and Privacy. Just as with SAS 70, SOC 1 and SOC 2 reports may be either Type I ("snapshot" reports, based on reported information from management of the service organization, looking at a particular point in time) or Type II (a report on the effectiveness of controls based on management's description and observation of the systems in place over a period of time specified in the report).

An SOC 2 report is likely to be of significant interest to a potential or current customer in evaluating a data center. SOC 2 reports focus on controls related to confidentiality, integrity and availability of data and when a Type II report is obtained, results of tests evaluating protection against unauthorized access, accuracy of processing, compliance with the entity's privacy notice, availability of the data for appropriate use and compliance with generally accepted principles of confidentiality are reported. A SOC 2, Type II report helps demonstrate the ability of a vendor to protect a customer's data and helps the customer evaluate whether the vendor is able to deliver on the promises of uptime and availability, as well as security and confidentiality, which are critical when housing healthcare data.

An SOC 3 report is also based on the Trust Principles and uses the same criteria for testing as are used in a SOC 2 report. However, the SOC 2 report will include detailed information regarding the testing conducted and the results of that testing, as well as the auditor's opinion of the service organizations policies and operational capabilities; a SOC 3 report will not. SOC 2 reports are not intended to be shared with third parties; an SOC 3 report is. Therefore, the SOC 2 report includes significantly more sensitive information than does the SOC 3 report. A SOC 3 report may be obtained on only one of the categories (for example, focusing only on processing integrity), and a seal may be placed on the company's website.

When negotiating a contract for cloud-based hosting services or software, consider requiring the vendor to provide a report from an independent validation and review focusing on privacy and security compliance. The positive responses to the due diligence questions should be incorporated into the contract as continuing obligations; if there were negative responses, consideration should be given to requiring the cloud vendor to implement the safeguard within a specific period of time. This commitment should also be documented in the agreement.

Impact of Privacy and Security Laws on Cloud Computing Agreements

The privacy and security laws and regulations that apply to data depend, in part, on the type of data and the location in question. There are several different data protection legal and regulatory schemes, both local and national. Some data may also be subject to regulation by other nations, where the data have become subject to those laws due to residence (i.e., storage) in foreign jurisdictions. Determining which jurisdiction's laws apply can be difficult, and in cases where data have been collected, used, or stored in several different nations, qualified counsel should be consulted to ensure compliance with all applicable laws.

It is also important to remember that the most commonly considered privacy and security laws and regulations, such as HIPAA and the Canadian PIPEDA set a floor, rather than the ceiling, of requirements for data protection. Where there are other laws that are more protective of data, such as other federal or state laws, those more protective laws take precedence. For example, data related to certain alcohol and drug abuse treatment programs are subject to enhanced protection under 42 CFR Part 2, Confidentiality of Alcohol and Drug Abuse Patient Records. Similarly, many states have enhanced privacy laws for mental health and sexually transmitted disease records. Therefore, when contemplating security requirements for confidential data, it is important to consider the strictest privacy and security statutory and regulatory regimen applicable to the data to ensure compliance.

Other Laws

Other laws may also need to be considered. For example, hospitals may have peer review records that are used to evaluate the professional competence of caregivers and which, so long as they are properly protected, are privileged from discovery. It is important to consider whether permitting a third party to administer the data center and potentially access those records will affect that privilege, and to structure the cloud provider contract in a manner that minimizes the risk of losing the privilege. The same is also true for similar doctrines, such as the attorney-client privilege.

The cloud provider contract should also address the response to a request for records from a third party. State laws often grant to certain people the right to request records; for example, corporate records may be requested by shareholders and medical records may be requested by patients and their representatives. It is important to address in the contract the proper response to such requests by the data center. Often, the customer will want notice of and the ability to respond to such requests; however, because the laws granting the right of access often have time limits for such response, prompt notice is necessary. The contract should make clear the time requirement for providing notice, the person to receive notice and the obligation of the vendor to provide reasonable assistance in responding to the notice at no additional charge.

As more records are computerized, the need to access those records for purposes of litigation and investigation is becoming more common. In some cases, a simple printout of the records will suffice. However, in other cases, the electronic version of the record, including metatdata, is required. It may be possible, in some cases, to provide the electronic version on a CD; however, at times it is necessary to create an isolated environment that replicates the operating environment, as it existed at the time of the event in question, to preserve that environment. It also may be necessary to stop taking any steps that could destroy data, information or items that might be needed for the litigation or investigation. This can include suspension of automatic overwrites of data, deletions of e-mail, and rotations of backup media, as well as suspension of other processes. The process of protecting and preserving the data, information and material that is relevant to the investigation or litigation is called a *litigation hold*, and the process of providing the electronic version of data and information is referred to as *eDiscovery*. When the data or information that needs to be protected and preserved is in the custody of a cloud computing vendor, the customer needs the cloud computing vendor to cooperate with the customer to meet these obligations. The contract should include a provision that requires the vendor to cooperate with litigation hold and eDiscovery obligations and, when appropriate, provisions that permit access to and use/display of software in the course of litigation.

Disaster Recovery and Continuity of Operations
While some may not consider disaster recovery and continuity of operations a component of computer security, it is integral to two of the three basic security principles—integrity and availability. Considerations of disaster recovery and continuity of operations should be addressed early in the due diligence process of vendor selection. The request for information or request for proposal should solicit information regarding the vendor's disaster recovery and continuity of operations plans. This topic is covered in Chapter 16 in detail; our discussion will focus on the contractual issues.

Contractual commitments should include additional details including commitments regarding the obligation to maintain and implement, as appropriate, disaster recovery plans. The customer and vendor should reach a common understanding about when the disaster recovery plan will be triggered. Is the plan reserved for "smoking hole" situations, in which the data center has been reduced to a wholly non-functional facility? Or is the vendor amenable to triggering the disaster plan for lesser events which, while not completely rendering the facility unavailable, reduce capability to the extent that service levels cannot be met and the user experience is significantly impacted?

Consider also how a disaster is declared. Does the vendor wholly control the declaration of disaster, or does the customer also have a role in the declaration? Must all customers be affected? Is there a time component, requiring that the disruption be anticipated to persist for a specific period of time before it is considered a disaster? A clear understanding of the parameters of the declaration of disaster is important and should be addressed in the contract.

Also of importance is understanding the scope of disaster recovery services. The recovery point objective (RPO) is the maximum amount of data that may be lost in the event of a disaster and is based on the frequency with which data are backed up or mirrored (copied) to an alternative location. The RPO is based on the criticality of the data. Mission-critical data need to be backed up frequently, as the loss of data is poorly tolerated by the business operation. Some types of data, on the other hand, can be easily recreated and reloaded and can tolerate a longer RPO. Cost increases as the RPO is shortened; therefore, it is important to consider the RPO carefully. Not all data on a system need to have the same RPO, which permits prioritization of recovery of data. RPO should be explicitly addressed in the contract. Depending on the complexity of the cloud contract and the variability of the types of data stored, there may be several different RPOs, based on priority of the data.

The recovery time objective (RTO) is the duration of time a data service may be down due to a disaster. As with the RPO, cost increases as the RTO decreases. During the business impact analysis, it is important to consider carefully what can be tolerated. While RTO and RPO can (and should) be set forth in the contract, consider setting it forth in an exhibit or attachment that can be easily updated as appropriate.

An additional consideration for cloud contracts is the business continuity plan for the cloud vendor. While the disaster recovery plan focuses on how the actual infrastructure and data will be recovered and restored to functional status, the business continuity plan focuses on how the cloud vendor will restore its business operations including the help desk, standard information technology operations and other operational functions. While RTO and RPO requirements will address the restoration of customer-focused data and infrastructure, it is equally important to ensure that the standard cloud operations are restored promptly to avoid other operational complications.

Data Ownership

At times, a question may arise regarding the right of an SaaS or cloud vendor to use a customer's data for certain purposes. A contract provision expressly addressing data ownership is of less importance in a standard software license, as the software is resident in the customer's data center and the data remain under the control of the customer. As the custody and control of the data transitions to the SaaS or cloud vendor, however, the importance of clearly delineating ownership and rights to use customer data increases. This is particularly true given the growing emphasis on "big data"[8] and the development of benchmarking, evidence-based medicine and the learning healthcare system. The customer should carefully consider what uses the vendor legitimately may make of the customer's data, and spell out those uses clearly. If the vendor is permitted to use de-identified data for benchmarking purposes only, but not for development of new products, it is important to establish those parameters in the contract. Of course, the customer may decide that the vendor may only use the customer's data to perform under the service agreement and to comply with law; in this case, a carefully crafted ownership and limited rights of use clause is critical. Where a business associate agreement exists, it is important to align the provisions regarding data use in the agreement with those in the business associate agreement; the fact that HIPAA permits the business associate to use the data in certain ways does not necessarily mean that the covered entity must agree to those uses.

Geolocation of Data

Where the vendor will have access to sensitive data, the customer may want to specify limitations on the cross-border transportation of that data. Transmission of data beyond the boundaries of the originating country may trigger significant privacy and security consequences, including in some cases exposing that data to the jurisdiction of the laws of other countries, and therefore should be addressed in the agreement.

Non-beneficial Code

As discussed earlier under software licenses, a cloud computing contract should clearly prohibit the use of non-beneficial code by the cloud vendor. Of particular concern are the various types of malware and mechanisms which could be used to disable or prevent access to the software or system at the option of a party other than the customer. In the case of mission–critical software and systems, such code should not be permitted even for purposes of self-help, for example, in the event of non-payment. The vendor has other, sufficient remedies, and the risks posed to patient care are not acceptable if access to an electronic medical record, for example, is disrupted due to a payment dispute. This should be directly addressed in the contract.

Remote Access and Compliance with Security Policies

It is likely that the vendor will require remote access to the healthcare entity's systems from time to time to provide maintenance and support services. Any time a third party accesses the system, security issues must be considered. Because there may be either direct or incidental exposure to protected health information, a Business Associate Agreement must be executed. The underlying agreement should also require the vendor to comply with the healthcare entity's remote access and change control procedures, as well as other applicable security policies and procedures. These typically include policies related to access controls, authentication and acceptable use limitations. The customer should have the right to immediately suspend access and require the removal of any vendor personnel who violate these policies.

Risk Assessments

Risk assessments are a critical component of a healthcare entity's HIPAA security compliance and are required to obtain Meaningful Use incentive funding. Cloud computing vendors should be conducting risk assessments at least once a year, if not more frequently, such as when there are significant changes to the computing environment or when new threats or vulnerabilities are identified. The vendor should provide an executive summary of the risk assessment to the customer's security official and should work with the security official to identify and prioritize risk management and mitigation strategies. This contractual obligation should be included as part of the governance provisions.

Return of Data

Ensuring that the healthcare entity has a complete and accurate copy of the data is critical to ensuring the integrity and availability of the data. Customers should consider including in the contract a right to request a copy of their data at any time, in a format reasonably acceptable to customer. At the end of the engagement, it will be necessary for the vendor to return and/or destroy the healthcare entity's data, unless the return of that data is infeasible. If the return or destruction of data which is ePHI is infeasible, pursuant to the Business Associate Agreement, the vendor must continue to protect the data and may only use or disclose the data for the purposes that make the return or destruction infeasible. Typically, the healthcare entity wants the data to be returned to the entity. The contract should specify the format in which the data will be returned, or that the data will be returned in a format reasonably acceptable to both parties. When the data held by the vendor is the only copy of the data, there should be a time limit within which the vendor must make the data available to the customer, which is consistent with the need for that data in the conduct of business. Once the vendor has provided the data to the customer and the customer has confirmed that the copy of the data is usable, the vendor should destroy the data, unless the vendor has a legal obligation to retain a copy.

CONCLUSION

Among the many areas that must be negotiated when contracting for technology services and software, security is an essential consideration. In healthcare, ensuring that the appropriate expectations for security are addressed, from the initial request for information through the final contract, will help minimize regulatory risk and maximize patient and clinician satisfaction with the technology experience.

As this chapter illustrates, the scope and nature of security considerations vary based on the type of technology transaction; within the categories of transactions, further variations are seen based on the type of data, the software and hardware involved, and the risk tolerance of the organization. Early involvement of skilled technology counsel can help find the proper balance between functionality and protection for the institution, providing a secure environment while controlling cost and minimizing adverse user impact.

REFERENCES

1.   42 U.S.C. § 17931 (security provisions); 42 U.S.C. § 17934 (privacy provisions).

2.   164.308.

3.   164.310.

4.   164.312.

5.   164.316.

6.   An "easter egg" is a hidden feature programmed into software which is only revealed in response to an undocumented series of keystrokes. Easter eggs are often jokes, images, or other innocuous displays; however, there is concern that easter eggs could contain malicious code.

7.   Utility computing is the delivery of computing services and resources on a metered basis, similar to the delivery of power and other utilities.

8.   "Big data" can be defined as large, highly complex data sets that require high-power and large-memory computing capabilities. Often, the data come from disparate systems with incompatible data formats and structures, requiring normalization before manipulation and analysis of data can begin.

CHAPTER 16

Business Continuity and Disaster Recovery

By Tom Walsh, CISSP

You can spend years building a well-run health system, hospital, and/or clinic with a reputation for excellence and attentive patient care. And you can lose that reputation in just one day. A failure of information technology infrastructure or critical systems can lead to a catastrophic disruption in patient care, mangled medical records and business operations, and snarled billing.

Responding to such disasters hinges, for the most part, on what you do before disaster strikes. That means understanding your patient workflow, departmental dependencies, business operations, recovery capabilities, and strategies and preparing plans for sustaining clinical operations. The goal is to make system recovery seamless to your operations and as transparent as possible to patients and the public.

Healthcare, after all, is a critical component of our nation's infrastructure, and when a regional or other large disaster strikes, the public expects healthcare to be available. In fact, that may be—and in the public's view, certainly is—the moment it is most needed. Your ability to respond at such times may well define your organization for years to come.

The goal of good planning is to anticipate risks, understand the potential impact on patients, and on the business as a whole, and create procedures to carry you through the difficult times and to recover quickly and efficiently. Unfortunately, disasters come from many uncontrollable sources and at unpredictable times: tornados, hurricanes, earthquakes, fires, lightning strikes, power outages, equipment problems, and human error are a few. Among the possible impacts and risks:

- Inability to treat patients.
- Financial losses and lost revenue.
- An organization's credibility and reputation.
- Litigation.
- Penalties or fines for noncompliance.

To minimize these risks, appropriate response and recovery planning is vital. This chapter will provide you with some guidance on how to get started, things to consider, and information for creating plans to respond to information technology interruptions.

BUSINESS CONTINUITY PLANNING

The Business Continuity Plan (BCP) is the umbrella plan outlining what is needed and when by all hospital departments and personnel, including critical recovery support from the information technology department. Many hospitals have a Hospital Incident Command System (HICS) or something similar, which serves as the hospital's BCP. The plan outlines predetermined responses to disastrous events or incidents caused by other types of threats in order to:

- Protect human life.
- Maintain services to patients.
- Provide accurate patient information.

The recovery of information technology operations in a disaster is best driven by a separate, but related, Disaster Recovery Plan (DRP). Although similar in many ways, a DRP focuses on information technology and is a component of the BCP, whereas a BCP covers a broader range of response and recovery objectives across all departments in the organization.

Preparing these plans, of course, can be a long and complicated process. It pays to know you have the necessary resources and support to write these plans. Together, they outline response and recovery tasks, set priorities, and assign responsibilities for getting the work done, all while ensuring coordination and reducing confusion. Here are three important issues to consider before getting started:

- Get senior management support and approval. Writing, exercising, and maintaining any plan requires significant resources—resources that could be spent doing something else. Planning for "What if…" scenarios that hopefully will not happen may not be a priority to anyone except for those delegated with the responsibility for creating the plan. Therefore, consider having management's approval and support documented in an e-mail or memo endorsing the creation of the plan and its importance. No one in management wants to face the public, patients, or workers after a disaster strikes to explain why there wasn't a well-defined recovery strategy outlined in a plan. Because executives and officers are potentially culpable for not allocating the necessary resources to ensure the continuity of business (duty of care), they also should have an active role in determining an appropriate recovery strategy.
- Develop a risk-based approach. It makes sense that a sound plan would be based upon reasonably anticipated threats, rather than trying to write a plan to address every conceivable threat. Those that are not familiar with this process may argue, "How can I create a plan when every time there is a disaster, it could be different?" Different levels of emergency call for different responses. It is a good idea to conduct a Hazard Vulnerability Analysis (HVA) to identify threats (both internal and external) that may cause a significant disruption and prioritize the likelihood of a threat. Once threats are identified, current controls or safeguards to address each threat can also be assessed. While the threats may be different, in many cases the emergency procedures and recovery process will be the same. Table 16-1 is an example of an HVA.
- Keep the plans mission and business focused. Those writing the plan must have an in-depth knowledge of the priorities of the whole healthcare system, hospital,

TABLE 16-1: An Example of a Hazard Vulnerability Analysis (HVA).

Hazard Type	Hazard	History	Probability	Impact	Rank
Acts of Nature	Earthquake	H	H	H	High
Environmental	Data Center Failure	M	M	H	High
Environmental	Fire	L	L	H	Medium
Environmental	Utility Failure: Electric (< 72 hrs)	M	M	L	Medium
Human Acts	Hazardous Chemical Spill	L	L	H	Medium
Environmental	Utility Failure: Telecommunications	L	M	H	Medium
Acts of Nature	Pandemic (outbreak of disease)	L	M	H	Medium
Human Acts	Behavioral Emergency	H	M	L	Medium
Environmental	Utility Failure: Water	L	L	H	Medium
Environmental	Utility Failure: Sewer	L	L	H	Medium
Environmental	Utility Failure: O$_2$ & Medical Gases	L	L	H	Medium
Acts of Nature	Extreme Heat / Cold	M	L	M	Medium
Acts of Nature	Flood	L	L	H	Medium
Human Acts	Hostage / Abduction	L	L	M	Low

TABLE 16-2: Lessons Learned from Hurricane Katrina.

Hurricane Katrina, which struck the Gulf coast in 2005 and killed more than 1,800 people, tested recovery plans in ways few, if any, had anticipated. Among lessons learned from that tragic event are:
- Communications outages can make it difficult to locate missing personnel and communicate with family or other loved ones.
- Access to, and reliable transportation into, restricted areas is not always available.
- Lack of electrical power or fuel for generators can render computer systems inoperable.
- Obtaining replacement supplies as initial stocks are exhausted can be difficult.
- Food and water can be difficult, or impossible, to obtain, especially early on.
- Large amounts of cash to pay for critical supplies and services may be needed.
- Mail service can be interrupted, possibly for months.
- Payments from patients and insurance companies take far longer than normal, putting a strain on the cash flow necessary for business operations, including payroll, which impacts the workforce who may also be dealing with the same challenges listed above.

or clinic. A patient-centric workflow approach is a good start. That's one reason a Business Impact Analysis is such an important step. (See Table 16-2.)

BUSINESS IMPACT ANALYSIS

A Business Impact Analysis (BIA) is the foundation upon which you can build your disaster recovery strategy and perhaps portions of the business continuity plan. The analysis will determine patient care and business operation needs so that logical and effective choices can be both planned for and made in the midst of an emergency. Without this analysis, the organization runs the risk of underestimating the resources required to respond to a disaster or business disruption. What follows is a brief look at the role of a BIA.

Key Objectives of the BIA

- Identify the critical resources required to minimally maintain business operations in the wake of a disastrous event.
- Estimate the operational and financial impacts caused by the loss of an information technology resource as it relates to the functioning of the organization.
- Determine business recovery objectives and assumptions.
- Establish an order or priority for restoring business functions and the information resources that support those functions.
- Facilitate planning strategies.

Critical Questions

- What is the impact to patient care?
- How much downtime can each department or business unit sustain before it has a significant impact on patient care and/or business operations?
- What are the information technology systems that support those mission-critical operations?
- If a department or business unit generates revenue, then on average, what is the hourly or daily revenue generated?
- How is data or information received and processed?
- What are the dependencies?
- Who and what are key employees, vendors, workflows, supply chain, etc.?

Analysis of Data

- Determine the recovery point objective (RPO), or the goal for recovery of data and operations, for each department or business unit (How much data loss is acceptable?)
- Assess any gaps with current backup capability and the RPO stated by the departments.
- Determine the recovery time objective (RTO), or the maximum allowable downtime, for each department or business unit.
- Identify the vital information and records needed for patient care and hospital operations and how they will be made accessible during an interruption of information technology services.

Getting Started

Before getting started on the BIA, you'll need a draft project plan and an executive sponsor. Without executive sponsorship, you may face a difficult time in getting participation in the data gathering process because of the many other competing priorities.

An inventory of applications and systems should be created and the BIA project scope will determine which of the applications or systems will be included and their "ownership." Ownership implies the name of an executive who oversees the department or departments that most heavily rely on the application for running their operations and is ultimately responsible for making risk-based decisions on the application or system.

A brief memo or e-mail should be sent to your organization's management team from the BIA project sponsor explaining:

- What is a BIA?
- Why are we doing a BIA?
- Who is conducting the BIA and who needs to participate in the process?
- How will the data be collected?
- When will the interviews take place?
- Where will the interviews take place?

Or the memo could explain fewer details, but require participants attend a short kickoff meeting or teleconference call to explain the whole process and what is expected of them. This is also the time to provide to the participants the BIA questionnaire form and a list of the in-scope applications or systems to each department or business unit. The questionnaire should be completed by someone in the department that is knowledgeable about business processes, workflows, and applications or systems used by the department.

Next, you will need to schedule a time to meet with each participant and review their completed BIA questionnaire during the interview. This typically takes between 30 and 45 minutes, unless the questionnaire was not filled out in advance—then the interview will probably take at least one hour. After the interview, it is recommended that you summarize the findings of the interview and send that summary back to the attendee to validate that you have the correct restoration order and the maximum tolerable downtime. Sometimes after an interview, the participants may go back to their department and consult with others regarding their answers. The summary affords them the opportunity to change their mind.

Data Analysis

The results of the BIA will provide your organization with an idea of the order in which information systems are needed (restoration priority) in such a way that the greatest good is provided to the organization. Besides a written report, a matrix in the form of a spreadsheet or table could be used to list the departments (or business units) in the first column and applications needed, ordered by priority for the remaining columns. The cell at the intersection between a department name and an application or system would show a number, which indicates restoration priority as identified by that particular department. The cell can be colored or shaded to indicate the criticality based upon the recovery time or maximum tolerable downtime for that application or system as identified by the department. For colors, a key can be used to help to match colors and recovery times. Table 16-3 is an example. In this simple example, the critical applications are shaded in gray. The rows and columns are rearranged so that the most critical applications are listed in order from left to right across the top of the matrix and the departments are listed in order of restoration priority in the first column from top to bottom. This matrix should be reviewed and approved by your executive management team. In some cases, priorities may be changed, especially when department directors view the matrix and can compare their department against others.

For some departments, there may be several applications or systems that need to be restored in a short period of time, perhaps four hours or less, while for other depart-

TABLE 16-3: A Simple Example of a BIA Summary Matrix.

Department	RTO	Telephone/Pagers	Clinical Information System	PACS	Laboratory Information System (LIS)	Pharmacy System	ER System	Cath Lab System	Network drives (File and Print servers)	Internet	E-mail
Intensive Care Unit	1 hr	2	1						3	5	4
Surgery	1 hr	1	2			3			4	6	5
Radiology	2 hrs	2	1	3					5	4	6
Lab	2 hrs	1	2		3				4	5	6
Pharmacy	2 hrs	1	2			3			4	5	6
Emergency Department	4 hrs	1	3	4		5	2		8	6	7
Medical/Surgical Units	4 hrs	3	1			2			5	6	4
Cardiology	4 hrs	3	2	4		5		1	6	7	8
Dietary Services	4 hrs	1	2						3	4	5
Admitting (Patient Access)	8 hrs	1	2						4	3	5
Respiratory Care	8 hrs	2	1			3			6	4	5
Environmental Services	1 day	1							2	4	3
Finance	2 days	2	1						5	3	4
Billing & Patient Accounting	2 days	1	2						5	3	4
Human Resources	2 days	1							4	3	2
Facilities Maintenance	3 days	1							4	3	2

ments their top restore priorities may be a day or more. In other words, the results of the BIA must reflect both priority and the recovery time (or maximum tolerable downtime) for each application or system used by each department. Having the data collected and displayed on a single spreadsheet or table gives everyone the "big picture" as to what needs to be recovered and the order of recovery by department(s) depending upon a particular application or system to sustain their mission or role within the organization.

For each application or system listed on the matrix, you need to verify the current capabilities from your IT staff for meeting the RPO and RTO. Inevitably, there will be gaps.

BIA Report

As you research and write your BIA report you will uncover much of the information senior management will need to evaluate funding and the recovery strategy that best fits the needs of the business. After completing the BIA and determining the business needs and priorities after a disaster or emergency strikes, you can identify gaps between expectations and existing systems, define workable downtime strategies, address EHR accessibility, and review the real costs associated with a disaster.

The cost of full redundancy for all systems is impractical, but you can identify gaps in what is possible under current conditions and the expectations of management and departments. Those gaps can help justify improved systems or significant changes in the system configurations—like a change to a remote or virtual system. As an example of a significant gap that senior management may wish to close, consider a BIA that identifies multiple departments requiring a recovery time of a critical system at four hours. If the backup system can deliver only 48 hours of turnaround, a significant gap exists between expectations and reality.

Justification for a strategy may be based upon the costs associated with a real disaster. While it is straightforward to see disaster costs in structural damage, equipment replacement and so on, other measurable costs may include:

- *Lost revenue from missed charges, delays in billing and collections.* The BIA should include the average daily revenue generated by each department so that level of risk is known. Contingency plans for entering data should address such issues and, hopefully, can lessen the impact. Some outpatient and elective-procedure patients may choose another provider if procedures are postponed for safety reasons.

- *Emergency purchases.* Disasters often create shortages of needed supplies. Hospitals should plan for the possibility of paying premium prices for needed goods and supplies in a crisis.

- *Workforce expense.* Overtime expenses and temporary labor for specialists or consultants can add to labor costs in a crisis, particularly for smaller operations that may not have the opportunity for extensive cross-training. The displacement of workers to recovery sites can increase support costs for travel or lodging.

- *Insurance.* Annual expenses may include business interruption insurance.

- *Penalties, late fees, missed discounts.* When a crisis causes you to be late with payments to other businesses, you can be assessed penalties or late fees, and you may miss discounts you are accustomed to for early payments. To avoid tax penalties, a hospital may need to apply for a tax forms submission extension.

- *Legal.* The United States is a litigious nation. A hospital may face malpractice claims and lawsuits resulting from health and safety issues for both patients and for the workforce. A point of exposure for a hospital would be whether the organization could be shown to be negligent through inadequate disaster planning and action.

- *Regulatory compliance.* The likelihood that the federal government would impose a penalty on a hospital for violations of HIPAA during a crisis is low. In 2008, the government issued a rule suspending some HIPAA requirements in a disaster situation. Still, executives remain potentially culpable for not allocating sufficient resources.

Some intangible costs include:

- *Productivity and morale.* Difficult working conditions, a lack of access to information and tools and a shortage of supplies can frustrate physicians, clinicians and other workforce members. This can have a direct impact on productivity, but it also can affect morale with an impact on daily operations.
- *Reputation.* Long-term disruptions can be embarrassing. In a regional disaster, patients often are more understanding of the difficulties of operating a hospital and running a business. But, as for all situations, there also may be a limit. And any internal disruption, such as a broken water pipe, will be met with less tolerance. Patients don't want to hear, "Our system is down today."

Whether tangible or intangible, the challenge is to quantify the impact of a business disruption to help justify a recovery strategy.

RECOVERY STRATEGIES

Thanks in part to the federal government's efforts, information technology systems are more central to patient records and care, and to business operations, than ever before. When systems fail, doctors and caregivers are left blind without access to patients' records. At the same time, much of the critical equipment directly related to patient care and monitoring also is electronic and/or digital, making time a critical factor in recovery. This has been accompanied by dramatic changes in the technology used to support mobile access, remote access, data storage, backups, voice communications and other critical information technology infrastructure systems. The rapid pace of change in information technology only adds to the challenges of developing a sound recovery strategy.

It is important that any recovery strategy adequately accounts for two concepts regarding recovery time which are determined while conducting a BIA:

1. **Recovery time objective (RTO).** This is the maximum tolerable downtime or interruption that a department could handle before the impact would be unacceptable to either patient care or business operations. Depending on the department, that time frame can range from minutes to days. Table 16-4 illustrates a few sample RTOs for some hospital departments. You will need to establish your own based on your BIA.

2. **Recovery point objective (RPO).** This is the maximum tolerable period for which access to information technology data can be compromised. Seen from another point of view, RPO is the age of data that must be recovered from backups in order for normal operations to resume. It is important to note that the RPO should be determined for each department and activity within the BIA, and that the existing method for system backup and recovery should not determine any RPO. Rather, these systems should be planned to deliver the necessary RPOs.

Too often, the current recovery capability is not good enough to meet the business needs and, unfortunately, meeting the desired RTO and RPO can be very expensive. When the RTO is four hours or less, it necessitates a failover strategy. A failover strategy implies there is an alternate location or secondary data center where the recovery occurs. However, many healthcare organizations are struggling; they lack the funding necessary to upgrade and maintain their existing data center or server room. Because

TABLE 16-4: Sample RTOs for Some Hospital Departments.

Hospital Department	RTO
Intensive Care Unit	1 hr
Surgery	1 hr
Radiology	2 hrs
Lab	2 hrs
Pharmacy	2 hrs
Emergency Department	4 hrs
Medical/Surgical Units	4 hrs
Cardiology	4 hrs
Dietary Services	4 hrs
Admitting (Patient Access)	8 hrs
Respiratory Care	8 hrs
Environmental Services	1 day
Finance	2 days
Billing & Patient Accounting	2 days
Human Resources	2 days
Facilities Maintenance	3 days

IT is an overhead department, data centers in rural or small community based hospitals are generally located in basements or other high-risk locations near sewer and water lines, placing them at greater risk for an internal disaster that can threaten the entire business. For clinics, a server room might be located in a utility closest or in some other location that does not provide adequate protection from physical and environmental threats. It's like parking a collection of beautiful handcrafted, luxury vehicles in an old, decrepit barn—not a good way to protect an expensive investment. However, the costs for upgrading an older data center to meet today's standards for resiliency and high availability required to meet business needs is difficult and expensive to achieve. Add to that the costs for creating a secondary data center for disaster recovery. It may be cost prohibitive for most healthcare organizations to continue with this type of support and recovery strategy. Therefore, information technology departments of all sizes are forced to rethink the traditional "we need to do it ourselves" approach (maintaining their own redundant hardware and secondary data center) and explore options where applications are remotely hosted and are accessible at any time through remote private clouds and virtual environments. The future hospital information technology professional may be called on to manage information technology systems and vendors, rather than "do" information technology with internal staff. Here are some considerations that make remote hosting worth considering:

- Buying equipment, software licenses, and maintaining multiple Internet service providers is expensive. Vendors buy equipment with built-in resiliency and lease multiple network lines that are shared by many customers, making it an affordable option because they spread the cost across multiple businesses.
- Maintaining a data center along with its utilities is one of the largest overall information technology expenses. Remote hosting vendors have built Tier III

and IV data centers, probably far more resilient than any data center in use by many healthcare organizations. Again, the vendors spread the disaster-resistant data centers' costs across multiple clients.

- Keeping pace with hardware, operating system, and software upgrades is time consuming and fraught with risk. Remote hosting is a way to transfer that risk to vendors who are responsible for patch management and updating their equipment.
- Remote hosting may avoid the same regional disastrous situation faced by a healthcare organization. Even if a disaster plays havoc across a wide region, as what typically happens in a hurricane, earthquake, or tornado, data still can be secure and accessible from another location through the Internet.

If remote hosting is not an option for your organization, then some of the sound, foundational things you need to consider for building your recovery strategy include:

- Standardizing data storage and backup. Storing critical data on a storage area network (SAN) and having that SAN replicated to another SAN in another location is one way to control where different types of information get stored and backed up. Table 16-5 offers some options and considerations concerning data availability and backup options.
- Conducting a risk analysis for the data center or server room and implementing safeguards and controls to address the threats that result in the highest risks to the organization.
- Standardizing the software and the hardware to a few common platforms. This makes it easier to maintain and less expensive in the long run. One of the reasons why Southwest Airlines is a low-cost, profitable airline is because it only uses the Boeing 737 aircraft in its fleet. Dealing with multiple vendors adds administrative costs and makes it more challenging to recover systems in a disaster.
- Virtualizing as many applications as possible to eliminate the number of physical servers while increasing the high availability of applications. Virtualization increases the recovery time in a disaster.
- Leasing equipment rather than purchasing it. The vendor providing the equipment handles the maintenance of the equipment. The lease may include options to refresh or update the technology. An additional benefit: the vendor assumes responsibility for proper disposal of equipment at the end of its useful life.
- Eliminating single points of failure. Instead of housing all of information technology in a single data center, consider using space at another location as an alternate data center. Split equipment between two locations. For example, instead of having two network core switches in the same data center (sometimes they are even located in the same rack) consider placing one of the core network switches in an alternate location. Use the alternate location for the secondary SAN and for servers hosting the test or training environments. Virtualized severs could also be housed in the alternate location and could be used as print and file servers or as failover systems. As hardware is upgraded for some of the critical systems such as the electronic health record, consider moving the older hardware to the alternative site where it could be used for recovery. The downside to this strategy is that it doubles the hardware and increases the operational

TABLE 16-5: Data Availability and Backup Options.

Are daily backups still an acceptable practice? Many organizations are moving away from daily backups to other strategies that ensure the quick availability of data. Listed below are some of those strategies:

Synchronous Mirroring

Consider synchronous mirroring where data is written to multiple disks in real time. Because the disks contain identical information, they are considered to be mirror images of one another. With synchronous replication, a write operation must complete on both disks before the application driving the transaction will move to the next step.

Asynchronous Mirroring

Asynchronous mirroring is a less expensive alternative to synchronous mirroring. With asynchronous replication, transactions are duplicated on a primary server in real time, but are then transferred to a secondary system only at predefined intervals. Replication can then be performed in two steps: first to a site in the same geographic area, then to a remote site or archival facility. Because asynchronous replication does not have high bandwidth requirements, it can be applied over long distances without performance degradation. However, it does not offer the same real-time recovery capabilities as synchronous replication.

Point-in-Time Copy

Point-in-Time copying replicates only changed data. Snapshots of data on a storage system are periodically replicated to a remote system at pre-defined time intervals. The frequency of the snapshot depends on the tolerance for data loss. This type of replication is often performed as transactions in databases.

Electronic Vaulting

Electronic vaulting (e-vaulting) can be accomplished either as an online backup and recovery service provided by backup service providers or as a set of products that enable an organization to manage its own internal data protection. E-vaulting solutions automate the backup process and eliminate the need for full backups because incremental changes are frequently sent to a remote server. Each time a backup occurs, the software looks for files that have block changes, and then locates those changed blocks, compresses and encrypts them, and sends them over the wire.

Whether you are installing backup systems yourself or using a vendor, you should have a formal backup plan for each application and information system that defines the backup strategy and process. Make sure that the backup strategy and plan can achieve both the needed RTO and RPO. A periodic test should be conducted to prove the plan will meet the business needs.

Reprinted with permission from Brian Evans Consulting, LLC

expenses associated with maintaining two data centers or server rooms. There is a huge expense in duplication of fiber runs to a secondary network core switch. Also, older hardware may not be able to adequately support the application and that is probably why the hardware was originally being replaced.

- Purchasing insurance to cover the organization's losses during a business interruption. Just remember that over time, the money spent on paying premiums could have been spent on addressing the issues.

Recovery strategies should be built around resiliency and recovery speed. Getting there means that anything an organization can do to implement a resilient system that can prevent a business interruption in the first place is more desirable than reacting after one has occurred.

Regardless of the recovery strategy, a disaster recovery plan will still need to be written. Parts of the plan could be developed and used even if there is no definitive recovery strategy. For example, creating contact information and call lists for employees and vendors, process steps in declaring a disaster, and recovery steps or checklists used for restoring applications and systems could be done even if there is not a well-defined strategy.

FORMATTING AND WRITING THE DISASTER RECOVERY PLAN

A Disaster Recovery Plan (DRP) is the documented, systematic approach to recover and restore information technology systems in the order and priority required to support patient care and business needs as defined in the BIA. As you prepare your plan, there are some formatting and writing concepts that can help make the content more understandable and easy to use:

- *Consider legibility.* A plan must be easy to read. Use a common, easy-to-read (no specialty fonts or scripts) font with a type size of least 12 points. Rule of thumb: Can you easily read the plan in a dark room with just a flashlight for illumination? You should bold critical text like phone numbers and contact information.

- *Be concise.* A common error is the belief that the "bigger the binder, the better the plan." Being thorough does not mean addressing every possibility or scenario. Consider this: In a crisis, will people take the time to sift through a plan in a huge binder? Probably not. The last thing you need in a crisis is a novel. Checklist formats provide faster access to information and, thus, faster response times by team members. Checklists allow you to gather a lot of information into a quickly read format. It is the "Goldilocks Zone" of plan writing—not too short, not too long, but just right. Table 16-6 is an example of a checklist approach.

- *Be specific.* Provide specific instructions, again, preferably in a checklist format for such actions as evacuation, shutting down equipment, alternate workflows and processes, and stopping and resuming business practices. Think of the plan as a sort of cookbook with ingredients and directions that can lead even inexperienced team members through critical processes. In a disaster, after all, the best trained, or most knowledgeable, person may not be available when needed.

- *Create appendices.* Information subject to frequent changes should be placed in appendices at the end of the plan. For example, the names and contact information for senior management and incident response team members can be easily updated in an appendix without any impact on the main plan itself. Other information you may want to place into appendices: department call lists, organizational charts, inventories, vendor contact and contract information, and other external organization information.

- *Use an electronic version for distribution.* Sure, keep a paper copy, or two, in a binder for those times when all power is out and all access to electronic equipment is compromised (just make sure you know where they are and that they are up-to-date). But consider an electronic version, probably a PDF, for basic distribution. Even in the most dire of emergencies, laptops with batteries usually are available for at least a short time. Store a copy of the plan on encrypted USB memory sticks and distribute them to key stakeholders. Mobile phone numbers, IP addresses, and vendor account information are just some of the examples of

Table 16-6: Sample Checklist Approach for DRP Content.

A simple checklist can be used within a plan rather than lengthy paragraphs. For example, the SAMPLE checklist below could be used within a disaster recovery plan for conducting a damage assessment.

✓	Task	Date & Time	Name	Status / Notes
	Take photographs of the damages for insurance purposes			
	Determine the impact to departments affected by the interruption or disaster			
	Uncover the cause of the interruption or disaster and/or type of damage (e.g., water, fire, power outage, electrical surge, etc.)			
	Coordinate with Facilities or Plant Operations and contractor engineers on the extent of the damages			
	Structure:			
	Walls			
	Ceiling			
	Floor			
	Door(s)			
	Windows (if applicable)			
	Electrical:			
	Transformers			
	Power distribution panels			
	UPS			
	Lights, switches, outlets, etc.			
	Environmental:			
	HVAC and air handling			
	Fire suppression			
	Determine if and when the Data Center and related work area will be safe for employees			
	Report assessment findings to the emergency response team and executive leadership			
	Assist with filing insurance claims			

Note: *The Chief Financial Officer (CFO) will handle all questions regarding insurance and will coordinate any claims.*

the sensitive or confidential information that may be contained in the plan. For that reason, the electronic copy of the plan should be either password protected at a minimum or encrypted to prevent unauthorized access in the event a USB memory stick is lost or stolen.

Plan Structure

There are plenty of business continuity planning and disaster recovery templates available on the Internet. You can conduct research and write your own plans around a template. The key is to find the right template to match the size and complexity of your organization and one that is applicable to your healthcare environment. Just be sure to think independently and add in any situations that may be unique to your operation and to cover needs defined by your BIA. In general, most plans will follow an outline similar to the one that follows:

- Scope and overview.
- Incident or disaster detection.
- Initial response—Plan activation.
- Notification.
- Assessment and situation analysis.
- Recovery.
- Emergency operation procedures.
- Restoration to back-to-normal operations.
- Plan administration and maintenance.
- Exercising and testing.

A sound plan includes more than assignments and activities during a disaster. It also outlines staff training, exercises, and systems tests, and plan administration and other factors that come into play before, during, and after a disaster. Additionally, the plan will define:

- *Command structures.* You will want to be able to clearly and concisely answer the two most common questions asked in a disaster situation: "Who is in charge?" and "What can I do to help?" Make these decisions early on and address them in the plan. Clearly identify an incident commander, with a clear process for succession in the role. In general, the first person on the scene with the highest level of authority, or the most seniority, by default assumes the initial leadership role. That person remains in charge until willingly replaced by someone with more authority or seniority. A common mistake is to assume that certain key individuals always will be available to take charge.
- *Responsibilities.* Plans should outline roles and responsibilities of responding team members in an easy-to-read format like a bulleted list. The duties should be clear and mutually exclusive—without overlap.
- *Testing and drills.* Retirement and personnel turnover may mean that those who at one time knew a work-around and what to do when there was a system outage may no longer be employed. Staff with less seniority may not even be aware of the downtime procedures or contingency plans for their department, let alone the organization as a whole. Budget cutbacks may make such drills difficult to perform, and limited versions may be conducted instead. For many hospitals, their HICS or BCP were originally created at a time when information technology was not as critical to patient care and business operations as it is today. Therefore, drills or plan testing should include interruptions to information technology which may impact telecommunications as well as data communications.

Define Disaster

Not every business or information technology disruption is a disaster. Some emergencies are bigger or more difficult to deal with than others. A recovery plan should take this into account and provide guidance that can be applied to various scenarios. Perhaps you are dealing with a power outage. Perhaps there is some damage to information technology equipment. Perhaps there is widespread damage to the hospital building and safety has become an issue. The plan needs to clearly define when a disaster should be declared, as opposed to an emergency or other, lesser disruption. That is why there

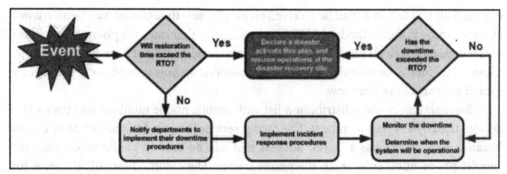

FIGURE 16-1: Sample Scheme for Declaring a Disaster.

needs to be a set of criteria for determining what constitutes a disaster and escalation of procedures is needed in every recovery plan. For any incident that creates some level of emergency, you can assess the damage to equipment, the threat to safety and the need for salvage. From a business perspective you may wish to evaluate the impact on facilities, procurement and logistics. As an example, Figure 16-1 conveys a possible scheme for declaring an emergency and what would constitute an appropriate escalation to emergency status of a lesser event. Your plan also should include who has the authority to declare a disaster-level event.

Bear in mind, as well, that any emergency also can invoke a number of business and regulatory requirements, ranging from HIPAA rules to workers' compensation and such things as documenting damage for insurance purposes. In the last case, it's a good idea to assign someone to take pictures of the damage immediately. It is surprisingly easy to forget this task in the crush of an emergency, but it is of vital importance in protecting the business against loss.

Communication Strategies

Nothing less than a revolution has occurred in interpersonal and business communications in the past few years. The digital era of cellular phones and smartphones has made friends, family and co-workers more accessible than ever. However, in a disaster the technology also may introduce challenges that require creative solutions beyond the traditional calling tree to mobilize staff resources in a crisis.

As an example, I was working at a hospital near Los Angeles in 2008 when a magnitude 5.4 earthquake struck. Within minutes, cell phones, as well as land lines, stopped working. It wasn't because the systems were knocked out by damage, however. All the systems simply were overloaded from the volume of calls. Given that most disaster recovery plans are based upon an organization's ability to quickly contact the right personnel, what can be done when there is no dial tone and no cell phone access?

One possible answer is text messaging. This was one of the lessons learned after Hurricane Katrina struck in 2005. Those who stayed behind and worked in New Orleans area hospitals found that even when cell phones did not have the signal strength for voice communications, text messages—which use less bandwidth—were getting through.

The California earthquake gave me a chance to test this approach—with a twist. Unable to reach my family in Kansas by phone, I sent a text message to my son, using e-mail. This was not an e-mail he received on his phone—though that may be an answer at times, too—it was a standard SMS text message so that my son's phone alerted him to the message's arrival. The hospital where I was working did not have such steps in its Hospital Incident Command System, but instructions on how to send a text message by e-mail are part of the plan now.

Hospitals can create a distribution list with mobile phone numbers and the carrier service used by key staff members. The carrier service is needed to send a text by e-mail because each carrier has a ".com" address that can be used in combination with the mobile phone number to reach the phone owner. The common e-mail addresses for text messages can be found on the Internet and by contacting the major carriers.

Application and System Recovery

During the BIA process, an inventory of applications and systems was created. Use this inventory as guidance for creating documented recovery processes. Because these recovery processes will be unique for each application and system, they should be listed in the Appendices section of the DRP or kept in separate files or documents, but included with electronic copies of the plan or paper copies. There is no reason to expand the DRP to hundreds of pages just to incorporate all of the technical recovery details for each application and system. These are important so the plan should at least reference the name of the file and where they can be found, or provide a hypertext link. Just remember that in a disaster, the network file servers may not be available; therefore, it is suggested that copies of those recovery procedures be kept in other locations as well.

Evaluation

One of the most important steps in creating a disaster plan is to evaluate it. Does it address all aspects of business and information technology recovery, including public response? Does it provide sufficient guidance for personnel on what to do and on how and when to do it? Is it clear and concise with adequate detail? Has an outside, impartial party reviewed the plan? Will it be helpful for responding to internal business interruptions as well as regional disasters?

The first self-evaluation for any plan will take place while you are writing it and immediately after finishing it. Table 16-7 provides a checklist for assessing recovery plans. You can use this checklist to guide the initial plan creation. Then, you can revisit the plan annually to see if conditions have changed or new procedures are needed. Management doesn't like surprises and, over time, things do change.

Plan Maintenance

Once a plan is in place, it needs to be more than a document on a shelf or some bytes on a flash drive. It's a living document that needs to be reviewed regularly and maintained to ensure it is up-to-date. In our mobile society, changes in personnel or changes in phone numbers and contact information for personnel are regular occurrences. Beyond annual reviews or tests of the plan, it is important to update the appendices containing contact information for key personnel regularly and frequently. This is one of the reasons that distributing the plan in an electronic format is recommended. Updating plans on paper can be burdensome.

TABLE 16-7: Checklist for Assessing Recovery Plans.

Evaluation Criteria	Status
Was a business impact analysis (BIA) conducted and signed off by key stakeholders prior to developing business continuity and disaster recovery strategies and plans?	
Does the plan specify the meaning of "disaster," include a flow chart, or define the triggers for declaring a disaster and activating the plan (including who has the authority to activate the plan)?	
Does the plan include emergency evacuation procedures?	
Does the plan heavily depend on telephone and cell phone communication systems working?	
Do response team members know where to report for duty following the activation of the plan?	
Are there provisions in the plan for addressing the situation when family members accompany an incident response team member when they report for duty?	
Is there a checklist of emergency preparedness items (equipment, tools, and supplies) that incident response team members are expected to have when responding to a disaster or an incident?	
Are there at least one or two copies of the plan in paper format, with at least one copy at the alternate recovery site?	
Does the plan address how communication with employees, patients, physicians, and business partners will be maintained?	
Are there instructions, directions, and/or maps for moving and restarting operations at an alternate recovery site?	
Does the plan prioritize the order for restoring information systems?	
Does the plan describe critical system dependencies such as interfaces or network connectivity?	
Does the plan describe the location and instructions for obtaining access to media and vital records kept in an off site storage facility?	
Are lists of equipment, tools, or supplies necessary for salvaging electronic equipment in the plan?	
Are there provisions in the plan to empower employees to make emergency purchases of needed equipment and supplies?	
Have contracts with vendors been written that specify expected service level agreements for emergencies such as quick shipments and preauthorized purchase agreements?	
Does the plan provide instructions for hiring temporary workers and/or redeployment of staff?	
Are there samples of paper documents or forms, which are used in the absence of information systems, included with the plan?	
Is the public spokesperson for the organization identified in the plan?	
Are there prewritten scripts for communications with the public and news media?	
Has the plan been exercised or tested within the last year?	
Does the plan require a post-disaster debrief meeting to evaluate the plan's effectiveness?	
Has the contact list of employees and vendors been validated for accuracy?	
Is there a link between change control process and the disaster recovery plan?	
Has the plan been reviewed by an impartial third party?	

Consider having the plan reviewed and updated at least annually. Choose a time of the year when things may be a little slower, such as the holiday season in December. Remember to provide training to key staff and management on any new changes to the plan.

Training

An untested plan is just a fantasy. Only when a plan is exercised and/or tested will some of the deficiencies in strategy and planning be discovered. A good plan will have

TABLE 16-8: HIPAA Security Rule Requirements Pertaining to Business Continuity and Disaster Recovery Planning.

§164.308(a)(7)(i)	Contingency plan
§164.308(a)(7)(ii)(A)	Data backup plan (Required)
§164.308(a)(7)(ii)(B)	Disaster recovery plan (Required)
§164.308(a)(7)(ii)(C)	Emergency mode operation plan (Required)
§164.308(a)(7)(ii)(D)	Testing and revision procedures (Addressable)
§164.308(a)(7)(ii)(E)	Applications and data criticality analysis (Addressable)

provisions for creating scenarios and ground rules to be followed when conducting evaluation and testing. Be sure that a debriefing of personnel in every department is included as part of any post-event evaluation. There is no better way to improve and perfect a plan.

Information about when and how to exercise or test the plan can be listed toward the back of the plan. It should include the training requirements, and cross-training needs for incident response team members. For some, training may involve rescue and salvage operations. Additionally, each department should train its employees on downtime procedures and the location of the department's contingency plan. All employees should be trained to be familiar with such organizational-level procedures as the code system within the hospital.

Aside from being a common industry practice, periodic testing and revision of the plan is needed to meet the addressable implementation specification of the HIPAA Security Rule: §164.308(a)(7)(ii)(D) Testing and revision procedures. Table 16-8 lists the applicable HIPAA Security Rule Requirements pertaining to business continuity and disaster recovery planning.

DEPARTMENTAL CONTINGENCY PLANS

Departmental contingency plans, often called downtime procedures, are temporary workarounds for providing patient care and maintaining business operations when the information technology systems affecting the department are down. This can be a planned outage or some unplanned event. Such plans should be based on the information gathered in researching the BIA. This is an important part of the information needed by senior management because the time required for restoring the systems must be factored into the gap analysis between recovery expectations and current capabilities. Departmental contingency plans:

- Identify applications and information systems used by the department. Many departments may not fully realize the number of applications or information technology systems they use.
- Determine the criticality of those applications and systems.
- Describe manual or workaround procedures to offset the loss of information systems.
- Outline escalation procedures for prolonged downtimes.

- Define how data captured on paper can be entered into systems when the interruption is over, with an eye to preventing data synchronization and integrity issues.
- Contains test procedures to test the integrity of data once information technology systems are restored.

The EHR Accessibility Dilemma

Access to previous lab tests, vital statistics and other information is a critical part of patient care. How long can physicians and clinicians go without access to such patient information? In some cases even 30 minutes of downtime can be unacceptable. This is especially true as healthcare organizations become increasingly digital. Paper backups may no longer be available or possible. Requirements of these departments will be spelled out in contingency plans based on the BIA.

The critical nature of these departments means that EHR systems, in particular, need either to be replicated or have frequent backups and resilient availability. That makes them expensive and harder to justify. But it also factors into management's thinking about how critical systems need to be protected.

SUMMARY

A sound business continuity plan provides an overall umbrella for organizational response to disasters while providing care for patients. A disaster recovery plan on the other hand, addresses the systematic recovery of information technology services in the event of an internal or external disaster affecting the data center. By conducting a business impact analysis first, the recovery priorities and time for information technology services are identified. Recovery strategies based upon the BIA assures that the needs of the business will be met and departments will continue to perform their mission. Contingency plans or downtime procedures assure that departments can continue to operate during planned or unplanned interruptions of information technology services. Regardless of the type, plans should be written in a concise, easy-to-read format and use checklists whenever possible. Plans need to be reviewed, tested, and updated periodically. If you follow these steps, then you'll be prepared for those rare occasions when the, "what if…" happens.

Three Tornados, Three Stories of Recovery

In March 2007, a one-mile-wide tornado that left a path of death and devastation 38 miles long, destroyed the 143-bed Sumter Regional Hospital in Americus, GA. Immediately, hospital officers turned the First Baptist Church into an ER/triage center. The hospital used an online web to communicate with patients, families, physicians, employees, and the public. For months, the hospital operated out of tents before moving into modular buildings, and in January 2012, saw the birth of the first baby in the new Phoebe Sumter Medical Center.

Greensburg, KS, was destroyed on May 4, 2007, by a tornado that literally flattened 95 percent of the town, including the 25-bed Kiowa County Memorial Hospital. Sixty-eight hospital employees lost their homes. The hospital brought in a medical mobile unit from Olathe, KS, almost 300 miles northwest of Greensburg. For months, the hospital operated out of tents provided by the Air National Guard in Topeka. The last time those tents had been deployed was for Hurricane Katrina. Operations were moved into modular buildings by December. And a new, environmentally green 15-bed hospital was up and running by May 2010.

St. John's Regional Medical Center, a 370-bed facility that is part of the Mercy system, was one of the casualties of the giant EF-5 tornado that devastated Joplin, MO, on May 22, 2011. The hospital resumed operations working out of tents. Electronic health records were back online within days once Internet connectivity was established because the records were remotely hosted on the other side of the state in the Mercy corporate data center in a suburb of St. Louis.

These stories demonstrate how resiliency and resolve are central in protecting important community resources like healthcare. And they provide insight into the sorts of risks hospitals and communities across the nation can face. Facing those risks, however, takes more than resolve. It requires foresight, planning, and preparedness, which, in itself, requires a willingness to identify priorities and make choices.

In all three stories, the leadership determined that the hospital would rebuild from scratch. Disaster recovery planning is a critical component of the survival of any organization in the aftermath of disaster.

CHAPTER 17

Change Control and Change Management

By Michelle Bigelow

Two network engineers, we'll call them Jim and Bob, were discussing an issue related to one of our medical record production servers. There appeared to be a memory problem. So, together, they worked out the technical requirements for physically changing out the memory and decided to proceed that evening.

At one point, Jim asked Bob if he thought there would be any negative impact from the change. Bob responded, "No, it's just a memory stick." That evening the memory was swapped out, and everything appeared to be back online and running normally.

When the workforce began to log into the system the next morning, however, they immediately began to experience issues. Soon, the entire system was unavailable. The impact on the organization was tremendous as work ground to a halt, impacting patient care and business operations. This became a huge embarrassment for the IT Department and later created trust issues.

Bob became the butt of a running joke. Any time someone wanted to make a change and described it as a "small" change, the change was referred to as "just a memory stick." Even when Bob left the organization several years later, he was given a T-shirt that read: "It's just a memory stick." All in good fun, but Bob and all of us learned a valuable lesson from that memory stick. The primary lesson we learned—changes must be appropriately managed to reduce the overall risk to the business. We needed a proactive process through which we could consistently manage changes, because overconfidence or underestimating even a simple system change can have a profound enterprise-wide impact. It only takes one oversight to create chaos. This story demonstrates how a well-structured change management program could have prevented a significant business interruption.

INTRODUCTION

Change, basically, is any adjustment, modification or enhancement to the computing and networking environment. *Change control* is a formal process used to ensure that changes to an application or system are conducted in a systematic, controlled, and coor-

---

Information Technology Infrastructure Library or IT Infrastructure Library (ITIL)

ITIL was developed by the Office of Government Commerce (United Kingdom) and has become the worldwide de facto standard in Service Management. The goal of ITIL is to improve the quality of IT service.

As it pertains to this chapter, the key ITIL Service Management Processes include:
- Incident Management
- Problem Management
- Release Management
- Change Management
- Configuration management

All of which are somewhat inter-related.

FIGURE 17-1: IT Infrastructure Library.

dinated manner. When done correctly, effective change control helps ensure quality services by:

- Reducing unauthorized changes, which could introduce other flaws into the system.
- Reducing prolonged downtimes or interruptions due to the change being carelessly implemented.
- Improving communications between IT and the user community.
- Maintaining system integrity.
- Managing changes in a systematic manner.
- Monitoring and evaluating the overall effectiveness of changes.
- Determining a pattern or tracking trends (e.g., server xyz has endured 16 changes over the last four months, and it is time to evaluate the server for possible decommission).

Change management is a standard method and set of procedures for handling changes within the IT environment to help minimize risk to the business. Change control is a component of the more comprehensive discipline of change management. Change management is one of the components of the Information Technology Infrastructure Library (ITIL),[1-4] addressing people, process, and technology. (Note: "ITIL" and the "IT Infrastructure Library" are registered trademarks of the United Kingdom's Office of Government Commerce (OGC)—now part of the Cabinet Office.) Figure 17-1 includes additional information about ITIL.

Most organizations already have some type of change control process in place when it comes to making changes to their major applications. For hospitals, it would be their electronic health record; for clinics, it's their electronic medical record (EMR); and for clearinghouses and payer organizations, it is the claims processing systems. For many of these systems, the vendor will drive the change control process.

Change control should also be followed when making changes to other applications and systems, including infrastructure components. This includes such hardware as desktops, laptops, servers, network devices and so on. This would include pushes for updating workstations on the network. It also includes operating systems (including upgrades, patches and service packs), major applications and software, interfaces, telecommunications and networking equipment. Unfortunately, this is an area where many IT departments are not as well-disciplined, as noted in the memory stick story. Therefore, this chapter will review the basic fundamentals of change control that should be followed for all changes in your IT environment. Worth noting at this point, not all changes will have the same risks or impacts. Changes that are determined to have a lesser risk may still go through change control, but would not have to follow all of the steps outlined in the chapter.

Getting Started

Each organization will customize their process based on the unique attributes of the organization. It is okay to start small and build it out as you go. Processes can be overwhelming. You know your own organization, the pace at which work gets done and the resources available. It is better to develop an abridged change process than none at all. Start talking to your IT staff and to the business about this new process and how important it is to the success of the business. This is an important step because buy-in by department heads, upper management and other key business leaders is a key element in making change successful.

Effective change management allows IT professionals to respond to and align with business needs and goals while maximizing value, reducing incidents and disruptions, and avoiding the inefficiency and cost of re-doing work.

The important first step is to create the standardized set of procedures. This may vary in detail from site to site, but the general structure and order normally would follow this pattern:

- A change is requested.
- The change is reviewed.
- The change is either approved for testing or denied.
- An approved change request is tested.
- The change is documented.
- The change is scheduled.
- Information about the change is communicated to all affected parties.
- The change is implemented.
- The change is evaluated.
- The change control database is updated.

Figure 17-2 is a flow diagram that illustrates a simple change control process.

Requesting. Requests for change can come from users, system administrators, IT staff, or application and system vendors to resolve a problem or issue. Requests can involve the replacement or upgrade of software or hardware, or resolve problems or results from a change in business requirements or operational needs. Regardless of the source or reason, a standardized form can organize requests and obtain the necessary information to help evaluate and process the request. The change requests form could be an actual paper form or an intranet web application. Figure 17-3 is an example of a change control request form.

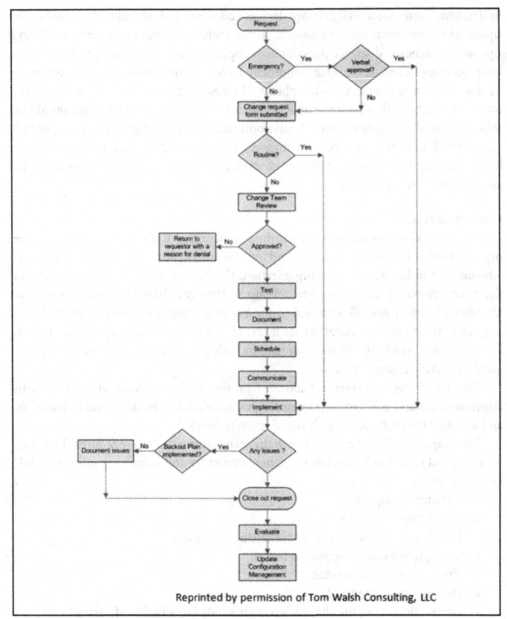

Reprinted by permission of Tom Walsh Consulting, LLC

FIGURE 17-2: Flow Diagram of a Change Control Process.

Each request must be dated and fully documented with the requestor's name, title, department and contact information. Each request also should include a brief description (a sort of title) of the change and a detailed description that reflects the type of change (hardware, software, operating system, etc.) and a requested date for implementation. The justification, or reasons, for the change are part of the request as well as the possible impact if the change is not implemented. All requests are normally sent to the IT Help Desk or to an e-mail address. Once received, the request is usually assigned a number (manually or automatically) and scheduled for a review.

Change Request					
Number:			Date needed by:		
Date:			Priority:		
Requested by:			Approval:		
Phone:			Status:		
Short description:					
Description: *(Includes the reason why a change is being requested (justification) and possible impact if the change is not implemented.)*					
Names of affected application(s) or system(s):					
Risk: *(impact and risks to both the business and to systems)*					
Impact:			Risk:		
Resources:					
Resources Required:					
Plans:					
Test Plan:					
Implementation Plan:					
Backout Plan:					
Communications Plan: *(Includes user awareness and updating of user documentation such as training manuals)*					
Documentation needing updating:					
Schedule:					
Planned start date/time:			Actual start date/time:		
Planned end date/time:			Actual end date/time:		
Approval:					
Implemented by:			Issues?		
Successful (Y/N):			Backout plan used (Y/N):		

Reprinted by permission of Tom Walsh Consulting, LLC

FIGURE 17-3: Sample of a Change Request Form.

Changes come in all shapes and sizes. Standard change management methodology talks about problem management, service continuity, security management and capacity/demand management. These processes are part of what make up your change management. Changes will occur from all of these processes and must be vetted carefully to ensure high success rates with minimum disruption to the business.

Reviewing. Once a request is entered into the system, both the business and technical risks and impacts of the change should be assessed. This can be done through categorizing changes as critical, moderate, routine or emergency (unplanned needs). Within any category of change both the risk and the impact also can be assessed as high, medium, or low. Figure 17-4 is an example.

Type of Change	Risk	Impact
Significant (or Critical)	High	High
	High	Medium
	Medium	High
Moderate	High	Low
	Medium	Medium
	Low	High
Routine	Medium	Low
	Low	Medium
	Low	Low

(<u>Note:</u> "Emergency" is not listed as a change type)

Figure 17-4: **Risk Categories and Impact Matrix.** *Reprinted by permission of Tom Walsh Consulting, LLC*

When reviewing a change, some of the factors to consider include the criticality of the information resources affected by the change; the number and nature of departments affected; resources required to develop, test and implement the change; other systems or departments that are dependent on the system being changed and potential issues (such as the likelihood of failure) that could arise and the cost of implementing the change. It often helps if a functional test plan is developed and presented as part of the initial request.

Approving. Approval processes can vary by the nature of the organization, but it is a good idea to create a team, led by a chairperson or change manager, that meets on a regular basis. The team is responsible for ensuring that the change is properly documented and technically feasible. The team should be prepared to approve, deny or defer a request and to present reasons for each, as needed, in addition to documenting the reviewing/approval authority with names, titles and contact information. Figure 17-5 provides some tips for creating a change control team.

Testing. This involves analysis in a test environment that closely simulates the actual production environment to confirm that the change will work. As you know, no IT department should test changes in the production environment. Testing procedures should track the name or names (and title, department and contact information)

Tips for Creating a Change Control Team

Name

There are a variety of names used to describe the group of people regularly involved with change control. Here are a few examples:

- Change Control Committee (CCC)
- Change Approval Board (CAB)
- Change Review Board (CRB)
- Change Advisory Team (CAT)

Membership

Your change team should be comprised of a cross-functional group of IT managers. Additionally, the membership at a particular meeting may also include the individual requesting the change and other support staff as needed to help explain and clarify the requested change to the committee. The chairperson leads the team and schedules the time and locations for the meetings.

Frequency of meetings

Most organizations hold weekly, one-hour change control meetings for evaluating requested changes. The length of the meeting depends on the number of changes and the complexity of the requested changes.

Scheduling

If approved, the change request is assigned to the appropriate team to test and later implement.

Project Management

If the organization is large enough, there may be a Project Management Office (PMO) that coordinates the change. The PMO coordinates resources, allocates time for the appropriate staff, monitors the progress of the change and may even coordinate with the end users who may be affected by the change.

FIGURE 17-5: Tips for Creating a Change Control Team. *Reprinted by permission of Tom Walsh Consulting, LLC*

of those responsible for the testing. The configurations against which the change was tested also should be documented.

Occasionally, additional hardware or software is needed before a change can be tested.

Remember to purge real patient identifiers from the test environment once the testing is completed.

Documenting. Results from testing are documented, including the creation of end-user and support documentation. Make allowances, as well, for user education and training, user documentation updates, manuals and quick reference guides. Depending on the type of change and the level of risk, documentation presented to the team may include results from functional tests, including user feedback and acceptance. Such documentation also should include validation that security controls will not be harmed, a communication plan for the roll-out of the change and a back-out plan should something go wrong with the implementation.

Scheduling. With the oversight and approval of the team, the date and time for scheduling the implementation of the change can be set. This should include the estimated time to implement the change and the anticipated duration of system downtime. Most organizations plan to implement changes after hours and on the same day of the week or month to help maintain consistency. Most organizations plan their changes for the middle of the week for several reasons. One, if there is an issue with a change, it is usually easier to get support from internal or external sources during a weekday than on a weekend. Two, many government holidays fall on a Monday. Three, the middle of the week may be less hectic than right before or right after a weekend.

In addition, project management will result in changes and require careful coordination around project tasks and schedules. Remember, your goal is to develop a central process in which all changes are submitted for consideration, planned for and approved in a standardized fashion.

Communicating. Notify your IT Help Desk (or equivalent) and all users and managers who may be affected by the change. Be sure to let them know the anticipated duration of the system outage so that contingency plans for operating during the downtime can be invoked. Many operations provide weekly notifications of changes and post a change calendar on an intranet site or self-service portal.

Implementing. Moving the change from the test environment into the production environment (software) or installing new hardware involves implementing the change steps as previously determined. As before, you should document actions and results from the implementation procedures and record the names, titles, departments and contact information of those responsible for the implementation.

Your change control process should include escalation procedures in the event that there is some difficulty in implementing the change within the allotted time. In those cases, implementers should be prepared to follow the back-out procedures and to document that process if required.

Evaluating. After the change has been implemented, you should closely monitor the change, especially within the first few hours to assess whether problems were encountered, including from the users' perspective. Monitoring will assure that the change met its performance requirements.

On the technical side, you can evaluate the success of the process by noting the actual start time of implementation and the completion time, or the duration of system downtime. Note whether the procedure occurred as planned, if problems were encountered or whether back-out procedures were implemented, and provide a description of what went wrong or what might improve the process.

Gather input from the users. What was the impact of the downtime? Did their downtime procedures work? Also, gather information on whether the change is performing as anticipated and whether the user documentation is sufficient and practical.

Updating. Maintain a configuration management database, and update it in a timely manner for each change. It is important that information related to the change is retained. Many organizations also use the database to create an archive, or history, of changes for a quick look at changes over time.

Emergency Changes

Occasionally, there is a need to bypass the normal change management process and implement an emergency change immediately. Changes that are categorized as "emergency" are those that are usually made to respond to an imminent threat or major business interruption. Your change management policy and process need to account for emergency changes and define how they will be handled. Because this bypasses the normal change control review process, emergency changes should be rare exceptions and are not to be used as a substitute for improper project planning. However, documentation about the change should still be required, even though the issue has been addressed and the change has been completed. This should be done as soon as possible, typically completed no later than the close of the next business day.

Asset Management and Change

Among the key elements in managing and tracking changes are the connections between your assets or attributes and your changes. As you develop your process, you will want to determine how a change can be linked to a configuration item, or CI. Examples of configuration items include laptops, printers, applications, routers, servers, etc. This gives you the ability to analyze hardware or software that has experienced changes and determine such things as whether more capacity is needed, if a piece of hardware is troubled, whether it's time for a software upgrade, etc. An ideal situation would be to attach a CI to a change in your change control tool, but if that is not feasible it can be tracked within your asset or configuration management system. An updated configuration management database will be extremely helpful for disaster recovery, especially when trying to restore new or replacement applications and systems to their original configuration prior to the disaster. You don't want to leave this up to memory.

Policy Considerations

Any organization that will undertake change control and change management procedures would benefit from a formal policy that outlines expectations for requesting, monitoring, implementing and evaluating changes. That policy could specify many of the steps outlined in this chapter and include such things as who may submit changes, how changes are approved and the level of change, risk or cost that would require upper management involvement. The policy should establish an appropriate mix of IT, management and user involvement for a team, or similar body.

Metrics

Effective change management requires continuing assessment of changes and the organization's ability to adopt the next wave of changes. No change management program goes completely according to the plan. A solid decision-making process and accurate information ensure that business leaders are staying well informed and making necessary adjustments to promote a successful change process that drives business results. Measuring helps identify underlying causes and promote trending. For example, a change report that reveals multiple changes to a server in recent months might flag technicians to analyze the server for certain types of failures, or take it out of service to reduce the risk of sudden downtime. Measurement also helps demonstrate where a thoughtful change management process has improved the operation of, or reduced disruption to, the business.

Measurements should be linked to business goals, cost, service uptime and reliability. There are certain key performance indicators associated with change management. These include but are not limited to:

- Number of changes implemented that meet customer requirements.
- Benefit gained as a value for improvement compared with the cost of operating a change process.
- Reduction in the number of disruptions to the business.
- Reduction in the number of unauthorized changes.
- Reduction in the backlog of change requests.
- Reduction in the number of emergency fixes.
- Reduction in the number of failed changes.
- Average time to implement based on change type.
- Incidents resulting from changes.

A variety of tools exist to assist an organization with change metrics or your change tool itself may contain a means to run meaningful reports and scorecards that demonstrate the gained value in running a change management program.

Culture

No one likes change. One of the most difficult aspects of implementing a change management program is helping IT staff understand the value in having such a process. We all know technicians who come to the table with a Wild West mentality that can hurt the organization, the IT department and the technician's own credibility. It is important to help staff see the value in change management and to provide some level of training. Planning, approving, and developing documentation, ultimately, will make them more successful in their jobs.

Making IT staffers "change advocates" and early adopters of the process will continue to encourage other staff and even colleagues on the business side who may previously have been accustomed to requesting changes in the hallway from their favorite IT staff member. They, too, will see the value of a fruitful change control once they understand how business disruptions and risks can diminish.

As you implement your change process, you likely will still see staff put through changes without approval. This often is a case in which a staff member needs more training on just what constitutes a change and what the procedures are for submitting a change. It also is not uncommon to see changes go through as "routine" when they are really minor or moderate in nature. It is the job of IT leadership—and of a team, or similar body—to make sure the change types have been properly categorized and scheduled. Some organizations have found it helpful to have upper management, such as the Chief Information Officer (CIO), show support for the change control and change management process. This helps reinforce the importance for change management. After all, when things do go wrong, it is usually the CIO who is held accountable for the business interruption.

CONCLUSION

How we manage changes determines the impact on our businesses. There are a variety of components involved in making your change management process a success. You must understand the purpose of a change, the goals behind a change and the desired outcome. With that you can begin to build your process.

As you develop your change process, you will want to think about the overall process strategy in your IT department and how the parts interconnect. A change control process is relevant to the whole lifecycle of service management on strategic, tactical, and operational levels. A solid change management process will deliver a service to the business that will result in reduced errors and disruption to the business and faster, more efficient implementation of changes.

Finally, Figure 17-6 is not meant to be a test of your vision. It is an illustration of the actual change control process used at the University of Minnesota Physicians. This diagram was created as a means to control the workflow within the Service Desk tool for the change control process. This diagram illustrates that there is much more complexity in practice as compared to the simple diagram in Figure 17-2.

REFERENCES

1.   Office of Government Commerce (2007). *Service Transition*. IT Infrastructure Library v3. (Edition: 1). The Stationery Office (TSO). ISBN-10: 0-11-331048-X. ISBN-13: 978-0113310487.

2.   Office of Government Commerce (2002). *Planning to Implement Service Management*. The Stationery Office (TSO). ISBN 0-11-330877-9.

3.   Office of Government Commerce (2001). *Service Delivery*. IT Infrastructure Library. The Stationery Office (TSO). ISBN 0-11-330017-4.

4.   Office of Government Commerce (2000). *Service Support*. The Stationery Office (TSO). ISBN 0-11-330015-8.

Note: The books referenced above are available at: www.best-management-practice.com.

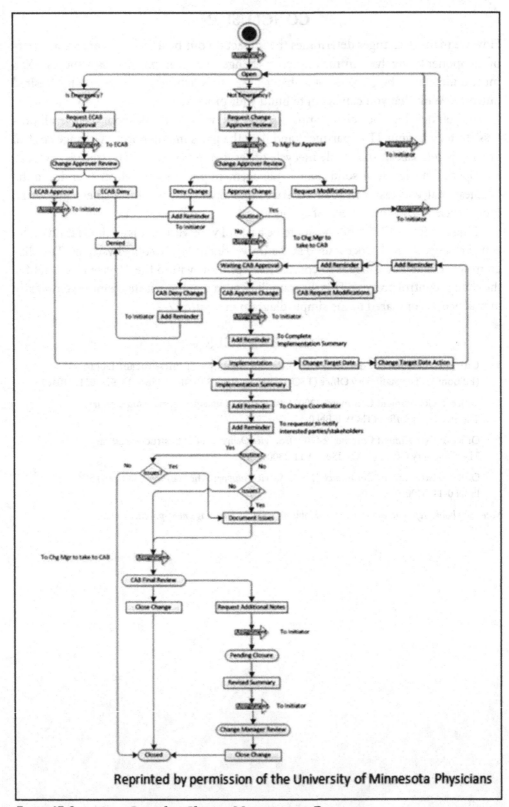

Reprinted by permission of the University of Minnesota Physicians

FIGURE 17-6: A More Complex Change Management Process.

CHAPTER 18

Testing Your Technical Controls

By Tom Walsh, CISSP, and Dennis Henderson

During the risk analysis project, interviews are conducted where initial control settings are assessed. The individuals participating in the interviews identify which controls they believe are implemented and their current settings. However, the only way to be absolutely certain that the controls are in place as stated is to do an actual test or evaluation of the control.

Evaluation is the review of systems, people and policies to validate that information security policies (and some privacy policies) are being enforced through the use of administrative and technical controls. Evaluation can identify vulnerabilities and track remediation efforts. The adequacy of existing safeguards and controls also may be tested.

Perception, Policy, Practice

Here is an example of how an evaluation validates policy. Let's say that your organization's password policy states that "Passwords must be a minimum of seven characters in length, incorporate complexity rules (comprised of both alpha and numeric characters and at least one capital letter) and be changed at least once every 180 days." However, when you do an evaluation on a particular application or system, you discover that the minimum password length is set to five, no complexity rules are enforced and passwords do not expire. As part of the control analysis process for risk analysis, the system administrator told you that the passwords followed organizational policy. Clearly there is a gap between the administrator's perception of the current control setting, policy and the current practice.

In general, controls should be risk-based or compliance-based. Therefore, the primary criteria for evaluating the adequacy of controls would be:

- Risk—Controls are measured against an acceptable level of risk, which should already be documented in the risk analysis for the particular application or system.
- Compliance—Controls are measured against some published standard. The standard could be your internal published policies or an external, regulatory requirement.

Sometimes both compliance and risk need to be assessed together. For example, the HIPAA Security Rule was made to be flexible and scalable; it doesn't always provide the specific controls settings. How do you evaluate the addressable HIPAA Security Rule implementation specification: §164.312(a)(2)(iii) Automatic Logoff? The rule specifies the need for automatic logoff but, as such, does not specify the inactivity time interval in minutes. Instead the rule states: "Implement electronic procedures that terminate an electronic session after a predetermined time of inactivity." Therefore, each entity has to implement the logoff based upon their risk acceptance level.

HIPAA Security Rule Requirements

The HIPAA Security Rule has the implementation specification: §164.308(a)(8) Evaluation, which requires covered entities to:

> Perform a periodic technical and nontechnical evaluation, based initially upon the standards and implemented under this rule and subsequently, in response to environmental or operational changes affecting the security of electronic protected health information, that establishes the extent to which an entity's security policies and procedures meet the requirements of this subpart.

The security safeguards specified within the HIPAA Security Rule are divided into three sections: Administrative, Physical, and Technical Safeguards. The Technical Safeguards pertain to applications, systems and networks that process and/or store protected health information (PHI). This chapter will focus on the steps that you should take to periodically validate and evaluate the technical security safeguards of applications, systems and network equipment.

TESTING APPLICATION AND SYSTEM SECURITY CONTROLS

The review of application or system security controls includes but is not limited to:

- Procedure for access control (authorization, establishment, modification and removal).
- Authentication control or method(s) used (user ID/passwords, token, biometric, badge, etc.).
- If passwords are used for authentication, password management practices in comparison to the organization's written policy.
- Remote access control and procedure for granting access to support staff and vendors.
- Automatic logoff time setting (Example: Logoff set to trigger after 10 minutes of inactivity).
- Identification of all generic user IDs associated with the application/system and the rationale for using generic user IDs.
- Account lockout after a predetermined number (such as three or five) of unsuccessful logon attempts.
- Automatic suspension of user accounts after a predetermined period of inactivity. (If the user has not logged into the application or system for several months, it may mean that the user account is no longer needed.)

In June 2012, the Office for Civil Rights (OCR), the organization for enforcement of the HIPAA Security Rule, released its HIPAA Audit Program Protocol. The protocol outlines the Audit Procedures that are used by OCR auditors. Using the protocol as a guideline, you should be evaluating some technical control settings within applications that store PHI based upon the Audit Procedures. Because the audit protocol is updated periodically, you should check the following website for the most current criteria.

http://www.hhs.gov/ocr/privacy/hipaa/enforcement/audit/index.html

FIGURE 18-1: The HIPAA Audit Program Protocol.

- Audit capability for tracking user activities.
- Tool(s) used for running audit reports of user activities.
- Data backup plan (type of backups created and frequency).
- Integrity control(s) in place to prevent the unauthorized alteration or deletion of data.

To successfully evaluate application or system controls, you'll need the help of the system administrator and in some cases, a database administrator. Security controls are validated through tests and/or demonstrations. The system administrator is usually asked to log in and produce screen captures as proof of security control settings. For example, you might ask, "Please show me the system settings for the minimum password length."

Because a review of controls can be subjective based upon the individual performing the review, it is recommended that controls be reviewed using some predefined criteria. The *HIPAA Audit Program Protocol* (see Figure 18-1 for more information) can be used as an objective way to evaluate security controls as compared to the HIPAA Security Rule.

Access Controls

Access controls are used for limiting the number of individuals who can access patient information and determine their privileges within an application or system. Examples of privileges, what users can do, include read only, edit, create, etc.

One of the important purposes for reviewing the access controls is to ensure patient privacy. The system administrator should produce a list of the user IDs, user names, and their current access rights or privileges. Managers and directors should periodically review this list to determine:

1. Is the user access still needed? This is especially important for nonemployees who will not be in your HR/Payroll system.
2. If the access is still needed, are their access rights or permissions appropriate?

If possible, the list should also indicate the last time the user logged into the application or system. For example, if the user has not logged in during the last 60 days, does the user still need access?

Applications that access PHI should have effective policies and procedures for:

- Establishing new accounts.
- Reviewing user accounts.
- Creating unique user IDs (other than service accounts—exceptions should be documented).
- Managing inactive accounts (Note: Some applications will not allow an account to be deleted).

As previously mentioned in this chapter, the HIPAA Security Rule does not specify any technical parameters, such as password complexity or inactivity time interval, so each entity has to implement the controls based upon their risk acceptance. Common sense would lead you to implement more stringent security controls where there is a greater risk. For example, the automatic logoff time interval may be set to 10 minutes in clinical or public areas where patients, family, and visitors are present, since there is a greater risk of unauthorized access. In contrast, a longer time interval such as 30 minutes may be appropriate in departments or areas that have limited employee access and no access by the general public. When evaluating the adequacy of the controls, risk-based methods should be used to match proper security controls with risk.

Some system controls can be programmed to automatically disable inactive accounts, thus eliminating the need for a manual review of inactive accounts; for example, automatically disabling a user account when the last logon was more than 60 days. However, if the application or system lacks this ability, then the system administrator should conduct a manual review of inactive user accounts.

If the application is used in critical patient care areas, it probably should have emergency access procedures that need to be tested. Emergency access procedures, often referred to as "break glass" procedures, are required by the HIPAA Security Rule and for vendors to implement within a certified electronic health record (EHR) under Meaningful Use. Not all organizations, departments or applications will have a need for emergency access procedures.

Audit Controls

Most applications create audit logs of transactions and user activities. The evaluation of audit controls would include validating some of the following:

- Do audit trails include sufficient information to establish what events occurred (type of event, when the event occurred, etc.)?
- How frequently are audit logs reviewed?
- Are any automated tools used to help analyze audit log data?
- How long are audit logs maintained?
- Are audit logs sent from the application to a secure, centralized audit log server?
- Are off-line audit log archives encrypted and/or stored in a physically secured area to preserve their integrity? (**Note:** Audit logs may be used as evidence; therefore, they must be protected against unauthorized access and tampering. When hackers break into systems, typically they first attempt to obtain system administrator privileges and then use those privileges to take control of the audit logs. By controlling the audit logs, the hacker can erase any log entry that may provide clues into their hacking activities.)
- Are all activities of system administrator and other privileged user activities logged?
- Are system administrators restricted from accessing the audit logs to prevent altering?

Audit logs should be reviewed on a periodic basis. If you only examine audit logs when there is a problem, then you are not practicing good security. To be more proactive, audit logs need to be monitored as close to real-time as possible. Even better are technical tools such as intrusion detection systems, which automatically monitor activities in real-time and send alerts to notify an administrator at the first indication of an incident or a problem. These tools require some tweaking to reduce the number of false alarms.

Third-party auditing tools can be used to review the audit logs of several different applications and systems, reducing the time and effort required to review audit logs. Audit tools can also be used to automatically:

- Sift through the volumes of audit data, determining unexpected or inappropriate events.
- Spot patterns of inappropriate behavior, such as snooping.
- Correlate logs from multiple systems relating to the same event.
- Create reports based upon predetermined criteria.
- Notify a manager or system administrator when the tool detects suspected behavior.

Web Applications

Because of their ease of use and development, the majority of applications being developed are web applications. Most healthcare organizations purchase their applications, as opposed to developing them themselves. Applications that are written in-house are usually web applications. For many organizations, web applications are the most vulnerable component of their information technology infrastructure. These applications pose greater risks from outside attacks because they allow public traffic, often from the Internet, to communicate with database servers. To reduce risk to web applications, many organizations have software code reviews performed and conduct application level scanning of their web applications.

Assessment tools for web applications usually scan for SQL (Structured Query Language) injection, cross-site scripting and many other types of vulnerabilities. Anything that can be done to secure web applications will reduce organizational risks. There are security companies that specialize in conducting code review of web applications. Much like having someone else proofread your work, consider using one of these organizations to assess your web code. Those individuals who developed the code oftentimes are not aware that their coding practices may work perfectly, but are unsafe and subject to attack.

Besides the code itself, the server, operating system and operational practices need to be assessed for risk. Check for password strengths, especially for the system administrator accounts. Vendor defaults should have been changed before any system connects to the network and especially before go-live.

Applications and systems may need to be reassessed or evaluated especially after:

- Significant changes occur to the application or system (hardware and/or operating system).
- Newly discovered vulnerabilities that would impact the system's security.
- Reported information security incidents uncover new risks.

In the Preamble to the HIPAA Security Rule, it states:

> In this final rule, we require covered entities to periodically conduct an evaluation of their security safeguards to demonstrate and document

their compliance with the entity's security policy and the requirements of this subpart. Covered entities must assess the need for a new evaluation based on changes to their security environment since their last evaluation, for example, new technology adopted or responses to newly recognized risks to the security of their information.

TESTING

As long as there have been networked computers, hackers have been trying to break in. Fortunately, network perimeter defense has greatly improved over the years, forcing the attackers to become more sophisticated. And yet, hackers keep finding new ways to bypass security defenses. Additionally, the time between the discovery of vulnerability and a targeted attack against it is decreasing, thanks in part to how quickly news travels among professional hackers. Hackers today are also more targeted in their attacks with a specific objective in mind. Money and political agendas are the two primary motivators for targeted attacks. Conducting active testing on a regular basis has become the new norm of due-diligence security. Most often, the active testing is done through the use of some type of scanning tool because these scanning tools:

- Identify the vulnerabilities; sometimes using the Common Vulnerabilities and Exposures (CVE) number (See Figure 18-2 for additional information).
- Rank the vulnerabilities by risk.
- Provide mitigation techniques to respond to each identified vulnerability.
- Specify the URL or web links to known "fixes" to address the vulnerability.

Prior to conducting the active testing of computer systems, a security specialist usually does "reconnaissance" work to discover, through public means, as much information as they can that may be useful to an attacker about the organization's network and systems. The reconnaissance step may also uncover confidential information about an organization that has leaked out and is publicly available. Sources for obtaining this reconnaissance information include:

- Domain registration information (Whois lookup for domain ownership information, IP address management, rank, traffic, point of contact for the domain, etc.).

Common Vulnerabilities and Exposures (CVE) is a dictionary of common names (i.e., CVE Identifiers) for publicly known information security vulnerabilities. NIST maintains the Comprehensive CVE vulnerability database that integrates all U.S. Government publicly available vulnerability resources.

National Vulnerability Database (NVD) – "NVD is the U.S. government repository of standards based vulnerability management data represented using the Security Content Automation Protocol (SCAP). This data enables automation of vulnerability management, security measurement, and compliance. NVD includes databases of security checklists, security related software flaws, misconfigurations, product names, and impact metrics." NVD is the U.S. government repository of standards based vulnerability management data. This data enables automation of vulnerability management, security measurement, and compliance (e.g. FISMA). Source: http://nvd.nist.gov/

Other sources for keeping updated on vulnerabilities and fixes include:
- @RISK (from SANS www.sans.org/newsletters/risk)
- Bugtraq (www.securityfocus.com/archive/1)
- US-CERT (www.us-cert.gov)

FIGURE 18-2: Common Vulnerabilities and Exposures (CVE).

- The organization's website.
- Internet search engines.

Vulnerability Assessments or Scans

Vulnerability scanning of both your external facing systems and internal network identifies weaknesses that could potentially be used by hackers to compromise your systems or gain access to sensitive information. Scanning usually identifies the level of exposure and can also reveal missing patches and security updates. Typically, a network vulnerability assessment is conducted in two separate phases: external network and internal network. Normally, a firewall is the device that separates the two types of networks. The internal network scanning project may be further divided by subnets or the type of sub-network, for example, the internal wireless network.

An external scan includes selected devices residing outside of the internal, local area network. These devices include, but are not limited to:

- Router(s)
- Firewall
- VPN devices
- Mail server
- Web servers
- Load Balancers
- Systems and/or servers located in the DMZ. (A DMZ, or De-Militarized Zone, is a network segment between an organization's trusted internal network and an untrusted, external network such as the Internet.)

The results of a scan of the network should be documented in a report that includes the identification of vulnerabilities, a ranking of their severity (typically on a scale of 1 to 5 [with 5 being the highest level of severity]), recommendations for reducing risks to an acceptable level and the prioritization of remediation efforts. Final reports should also provide recommendations of products and estimated costs for reducing and managing risks to the network and web servers. See Figure 18-3 for some evaluation report writing tips.

The following are some high-level tips for preparing a concise report. The written report should:

- Be written as objectively as possible; state facts while avoiding assumptions and feelings.
- Provide evidence and support for both findings and recommendations.
- Cite other references or sources to support a finding or a recommendation.
- Be based upon common industry practices to improve the overall security and privacy posture, reduce risks, and for industry and regulatory compliance.
- Be written in an easy-to-read font.
- Include an executive summary as the first page of the report and be no longer than two pages in length.
- List highest risk items or compliance issues first in the report and the lower risks or priorities near the end of the report.

The evaluation report is a direct reflection on the individual writing the report. However, report writing sometimes can be challenging for an information security professional. That is why you should have your report reviewed carefully by someone else with good technical writing skills to check for spelling and grammar errors. An executive's attention can be distracted if your report has errors or is poorly organized.

FIGURE 18-3: Tips for Evaluation Report Writing.

Any vulnerability that places the organization at great risk should be reported immediately, rather than waiting until the written report is ready. Less severe vulnerabilities may be reported at the time of the delivery of the final report.

The findings or vulnerabilities should be correlated to the Common Vulnerabilities and Exposures (CVE) naming convention. There are many reliable public and federal government sources for updates on newly discovered vulnerabilities and exploits. These sources usually offer the security patches, fixes or recommendations to defend against an attack by addressing the vulnerabilities.

A regularly occurring (e.g., bi-annual, quarterly, monthly) process using specialized scanning tools and techniques that evaluates the configuration, patches and services for known vulnerabilities should be employed. During this phase, a second round of vulnerability scans is conducted. These scans will focus primarily on the areas of weakness identified in the initial scan to determine if risks have been reduced to an acceptable level. The regular period of scanning can also reveal new vulnerabilities that did not exist in previous scans, as well as new systems that have come on the network since the last scan.

Virtual private network (VPN) connections are another conduit and, hence, a threat to PHI. Access to VPNs should be controlled diligently and evaluated as well. An evaluation of the VPN system would include reviewing the current policies and processes used to establish and administer the VPN and review the technical design to identify weak points.

Wireless Networking Evaluation

Wireless networking is just another means of access to PHI. The primary difference between wired and wireless is that with wired, you can only connect to the network for the length of network cable you have. If you keep your network cables and ports secured, then connectivity via the wired network can only occur where you physically allow it. Wireless networking, on the other hand, can occur anywhere that both the access point and the client can talk to each other. This may be possible outside the control of the company's security border—a parking lot, for example. To reduce risk from wireless access to PHI, best business practices recommend:

- Use Certificates and Domain Credentials. This will greatly reduce the chance that someone who is not part of the organization will be able to connect to the wireless network.
- Have wireless security assessments performed by an outside agency to determine if wireless signals propagate excessively far from the area of coverage.
- Use the latest encryption and authentication methods to reduce the chance of eavesdropping.
- Use equipment that can detect rogue access points and unauthorized attempts to connect to the wireless network.

Penetration Tests

A penetration test, as the name implies, is another method of evaluating the security of a system or network. By emulating a hacker, a security professional uses many of the same automated tools that a hacker would use to attempt an intrusion or attack. It is sometimes referred to as a "white-hat hack" or "ethical hacking." However, unlike a real hacker attack, great care is taken to prove that weaknesses and vulnerabilities exist and could be exploited without disrupting critical services. This is especially important in hospitals where systems must be available 24 x 7. The test process involves an active analysis of the system for weaknesses and then an attempt to circumvent the security controls intended to protect applications and systems.

There are two schools of thought regarding penetration testing:

1.   Overt testing: Let your network team know in advance when the test will be conducted, just in case any problems are encountered so they can recover disrupted services more rapidly.

2.   Unannounced testing: Making the test a secret to determine if detection systems were able to register and alert the network engineers of a possible attack. It is also a way to test your organization's incident reporting and response procedures.

Generally, unless your security program is very mature, it's better to inform your staff of testing. No want wants to be awakened in the middle of the night by being alerted to a possible attack, only later to find out it was planned but kept secret by management.

Depending on your credit card environment, annual network penetration tests are also required for your cardholder data environment as required in the Payment Card Industry Data Security Standard.

THINGS TO CONSIDER FOR ACTIVE TESTING

Vulnerability scanning and penetration testing can be intrusive and could have an unfavorable impact on the applications and systems being scanned. Care must be taken when conducting a scan. You want to avoid interfering with or disrupting the normal operation of applications or systems. That is why scanning and penetration testing are normally performed by either an IT technician or by a third-party vendor and conducted at a time when it will have the least impact on users. Because of the level of skill required and the risks associated with active testing, you may want to outsource this work to a third-party vendor. Figure 18-4 lists some suggestions for writing a Request for Proposal with an outside security firm.

Firewalls may affect your scanning results because they may react to the vulnerability scanning or tools used for the assessment as a possible hostile attack, thereby blocking access, which is what they are designed to do. While the actions of a firewall may prevent a successful attack, a real vulnerability should not be ignored simply based on the fact that the firewall will prevent the attack. Efforts to truly remediate vulnerabilities should be undertaken to the point where they are either remediated or compensating controls are in place to reduce risk. If compensating controls are used, they should be documented as exceptions and tested regularly.

For more information, refer to The National Institute of Standards and Technology (NIST) Special Publication 800-42, *Guideline on Network Security Testing*.

Scope

Determine boundaries by identifying which systems will be in the scope of work. For example, will your organization's electronic health record (EHR) be included or excluded from the scans?

Qualifications

The vendor should use credentialed professionals to conduct the scans and penetration tests. A Certified Information Systems Security Professional (CISSP) should either serve as the project manager for the engagement and/or be the person conducting the scans and tests.

Deliverables

The vendor should provide a report that clearly identifies the vulnerabilities found and the level of severity of each vulnerability. For each of the vulnerabilities identified within the report, the vendor should provide information on available patches or fixes. The report of findings should include a short executive summary written for the non-technical executive members of management. The vendor should be prepared to make a short oral presentation of their findings.

Proposal Format

An RFP should describe how the vendor must submit their proposal. In addition, the RFP should include:
- Scope of work
  - Services that will be provided.
  - An outline of the process (project plan) to be used in providing those services.
  - Identify the tools to be used for vulnerability scanning.
  - Determine the range of IP addresses of network devices, servers, and workstations to be scanned.
  - Methodology used for performing vulnerability scans, penetration tests, and measuring results.
- A schedule for the engagement
  - Projected dates when the vendor would be available.
  - Determine the appropriate day and time to begin the remote scan.
  - Expected delivery of the final reports (number of days from the start of the project).
- The deliverables
  - A brief description or sample of the reports.
- An itemization of total costs
  - Pricing should be based upon the vendor conducting the initial assessment and possibly conducting the follow up scan of the network after remediation activities have occurred.
- Qualifications of vendor staff
  - The names of the personnel assigned to the project and their qualifications and certifications.
- Vendor's strengths or specialties
  - Explain what differentiates your organization from other security companies.
- Vendor's references
  - The vendor should provide three references that the organization may contact.
  - Required information includes name of the point of contact, business name, telephone number, e-mail address and a brief description of the services provided.

Proposal Evaluation

While pricing is important, it should not be the primary factor for selecting a vendor. The ability to demonstrate experience, commitment in providing services, and willingness to work with the organization in providing knowledge transfer should greatly influence the vendor selection process. The vendor evaluation process would also include the availability and cost associated with the tools used by the vendor to conduct the vulnerability scans that the organization could purchase on their own to conduct similar tests in the future. This would especially be important if the organization is required to conduct quarterly scans for PCI DSS.

FIGURE 18-4: Tips for Writing a Request for Proposal (RFP).

INTEGRATING THE RESULTS INTO YOUR PLAN

The results obtained from the evaluation process should be addressed in your security and/or risk management plan. The plan should prioritize tasks that need to be accomplished to reduce risks and bring the organization into compliance. Once documented in a plan, there should be a follow-up. The follow-ups usually ensure that recommendations have been implemented or compensating controls were applied. During a follow-up, a second wave of tests may be performed to validate that corrective actions have been actually taken by the system administrator and that the identified vulnerabilities no longer exist or have been addressed.

If for some reason a particular technical control that is specified in your policies cannot be implemented, then it should be documented as an exception, and you may choose not to list it in your risk management plan. This is a common problem with older applications and systems that were designed a long time ago before security and HIPAA were as important as they are today.

Also, there will be some "ongoing" tasks listed on your plan. For example, patch management, periodic vulnerability scans, and network penetration tests should be conducted to make sure that systems remain secure over time. For applications and systems that process and store credit card data, quarterly scans are required by the Payment Card Industry PCI Data Security Standard. The scans must be performed using an Approved Scanning Vendor (ASV) recognized by the PCI Security Standards Council. Scans also include the wireless network. Figure 18-5 lists the specific PCI DSS requirements for scanning and penetration tests as well as why it may be needed for HIPAA Security Rule compliance.

HIPAA Security Rule

There is nothing specific in the HIPAA Security Rule requiring network scanning. However, when the previous rounds of audit (2008–2009) were conducted by the OCR, they requested the following:

• Vulnerability scanning plans and the results from most recent vulnerability scan.

• Network penetration testing policy and procedure and the results from most recent network penetration test.

However, the HIPAA Audit Program Protocol (released in June 2012) did not include any audit test procedure addressing vulnerability scanning. www.hhs.gov/ocr/privacy/hipaa/enforcement/audit/index.html.

Payment Card Industry Data Security Standard (PCI DSS) requirements

PCI DSS has the following requirements for scanning:

11.1	Test for the presence of wireless access points and detect unauthorized wireless access points on a quarterly basis.
11.2	Run internal and external network vulnerability scans at least quarterly and after any significant change in the network (such as new system component installations, changes in network topology, firewall rule modifications, product upgrades).
11.2.2	Perform quarterly external vulnerability scans via an Approved Scanning Vendor (ASV), approved by the Payment Card Industry Security Standards Council (PCI SSC).
	Note: *Quarterly external vulnerability scans must be performed by an Approved Scanning Vendor (ASV), approved by the Payment Card Industry Security Standards Council (PCI SSC). Scans conducted after network changes may be performed by internal staff.*
11.3	Perform external and internal penetration testing at least once a year and after any significant infrastructure or application upgrade or modification (such as an operating system upgrade, a sub-network added to the environment, or a web server added to the environment).

FIGURE 18-5: Regulatory and Industry Requirements For Periodic Vulnerability Scans and Network Penetration Tests.

Vulnerability Management

A patch management program is one way to secure operating systems and application software against known vulnerabilities. Malicious code (worms, Trojans, etc.) and hackers target known vulnerabilities. That is why patch management of applications and systems should be part of your maintenance routine. Systems that are infrequently updated or patched run a higher risk of being exploited, which may result in downtime or worse, a breach of confidential information or a compromise of your enterprise security.

Patch management can be challenging, especially for smaller organizations. You should have a person or team for your department or organization assigned with the responsibility for staying updated on newly released patches and security fixes. These individuals should determine if or how a patch would affect the systems and applications deployed in your organization (Is it applicable?) and test the patch in a safe test environment. There may be operational or business reasons why applying a particular patch is not feasible. When that occurs, your system administrators should consider other compensating controls or safeguards to address the threat or document this as an exception. Unique to hospitals is the challenge of managing biomedical devices because of their rigorous review and approval process from the U.S. Food and Drug Administration (FDA); most vendors do not want their devices patched.

Keep in mind that unless the patch has been first evaluated and tested by the vendor, they may advise against applying patches to their systems. In some cases, the vendor may even stipulate that violation of their patch management rules voids any warranties or support-level agreements. Managing system security can be challenging. Figure 18-6 provides some tips.

CONCLUSION

Following is a brief summary of the key steps for testing your technical controls for applications and systems; most of them were covered in this chapter.

1. Scope of applications, systems and controls to be tested.
2. Determine project constraints (budgets and timelines), resources required (people and tools) and project deliverables.
3. Identify project steps.
4. Plan start dates.
5. Review documentation (policies, procedures, plans, previous evaluation reports, etc.).
6. Review control settings with the system administrator.
7. Run the vulnerability scans.
8. Conduct the penetration tests (if needed).
9. Analyze the data collected.
10. Document assessment findings.
11. Research and determine possible recommendations.
12. Prepare a Report of Findings and Recommendations.
13. Share the draft report and ask for feedback.
14. Update and finalize the report.
15. Schedule a meeting to discuss the report and determine remediation activities.
16. Create a risk management action plan.

When it comes to securely managing systems, start with the host system or server. Check for the following practices for securing systems which include:

- Removing the manufacturer's default passwords for the system.
- Uninstalling unneeded software or not installing it in the first place.
- Turning off or disabling unused services.
- Installing software patches or upgrades when appropriate.
- Documenting all system changes or upgrades.
- Securing remote access to the system.
- Limiting the use of the administrator (or supervisor User ID) account to a physical location or computer workstation.
- Quickly changing passwords when a system administrator leaves.
- Making system administrators use a separate user ID for their administrator activities from their general user access.
- Automatically reviewing audit logs (trails) for unusual activity.
- Creating "warning banners" that display at logon or connection stating that the system is for the exclusive use of authorized users and that their activity may be monitored.
- Verifying that logon banner does not reveal too much system information (i.e., operating system (OS), version, hardware, etc.).
- Creating audit logs to track certain types of activities and protecting the logs by transmitting them to a different system.
- Archiving audit logs.
- Monitoring access control lists for inactive accounts.
- Locking out user access after three to five unsuccessful logon attempts.
- Restricting access to directories or files that are critical to the system's operation.
- Conducting a risk analysis as part of every new design or project.
- Incorporating the concept of lifecycle planning into the design, development, testing, deployment, and maintenance of applications and systems.
- Using security vendors for conducting a periodic review of your technical controls.

FIGURE 18-6: Tips for Securely Managing Systems.

17. Conduct a follow-up to ensure vulnerabilities are being addressed.
18. Integrate prevention such as patch management and vulnerability scanning into your overall security risk management plan.

CHAPTER 19

Auditing Your Program

By Mary Anne S. Canant, MBA, CISA, CISSP, CHFP

This book provides guidance for security and other professionals responsible for oversight, development, maintenance, monitoring, assessment, and auditing an organization-wide information security program. The information security program should be reviewed and approved by management at a predetermined frequency. Review can be conducted formally by an internal auditor, an external auditor or consultant, and can be performed as a self-assessment/audit. One important benefit of using an internal or external auditor/consultant is the independence and objectivity they offer. Auditing a security program involves the evaluation/assessment/review of its components. One approach is to group and evaluate the administrative, physical, and technical safeguards defined by the HIPAA Security Rule.

Controls should be selected to address organizational mission or business needs and tolerance for risk, as well as compliance with the Security Rule and other regulations and industry requirements. All audits should take into consideration the organization's needs, constraints, and goals.

This chapter will describe requirements for audit evidence; outline audit protocols[1] for the HIPAA Security Rule standards involving administrative and physical safeguards; provide tips for reviewing and presenting improvement opportunities to management; explore emerging risks associated with employee-monitoring activities; include specific considerations for identifying potential opportunities for fraud; and suggestions for developing continuous assurance and fraud audit capabilities. While audit protocols for HIPAA Security Rule standards involving administrative and physical safeguards are outlined in this chapter, Chapter 18 of this book specifically addresses technical safeguards from the perspective of HIPAA Security Rule standard §164.308(a)(8) Evaluation.

GATHERING EVIDENCE

Audit procedures are the steps performed to meet an audit objective.[2] They include examining policies, standards and control procedures; interviewing employees; testing mechanisms and capabilities; and reviewing and analyzing records and supporting documentation. Audit procedures consist of a set of methods and objects including

TABLE 19-1: Audit Methods, Processes, Applicable Objects, and Examples.

Method	Process	Objects and Examples
Examine	Check, inspect, review, study, observe, analyze	Specification: policy, system requirement, plan, procedure, design, etc. Mechanism: hardware, software, and firmware functionality Activity: system operations, management, administrative exercise, etc.
Interview	Conduct discussions	Individual: CISO, CIO, system owner, etc. Groups: system administrators, network users, programmers, etc.
Test	Exercise an object under a condition	Mechanism: hardware, software, firmware Activity: system operations, management, and administration exercises

specifications, mechanisms, activities and individuals. Specifications are the document-based artifacts (e.g., policies, procedures, plans, system security requirements, functional specifications and architectural designs) associated with the security program and information systems. Mechanisms are the specific hardware, software or firmware safeguards and countermeasures employed within information systems to address threats. Activities are the specific protection-related actions supporting an information system and involving people (e.g., conducting system backup operations, monitoring network traffic and exercising a contingency plan). Individuals, or groups of individuals, are people applying those specifications, mechanisms or activities. Audit methods and related processes and objects are shown in Table 19-1.

Audit evidence includes the procedures performed; the results of procedures performed; source documents, records and coordinating information used to support the audit. Audit evidence also includes findings and results of the audit work and demonstrated work performed in compliance with applicable laws, regulations, and policies.[3] The interpretation of evidence is the basis of audit conclusions. Evidence meeting an audit objective must be sufficient, complete, relevant and reliable. When evaluating its reliability, consider the source, nature (e.g., written, oral, visual, electronic), and authenticity (e.g., digital and manual signatures, stamps), as well as the following indicators of reliable evidence:

- In written form, rather than oral expression.
- Obtained from independent sources.
- Obtained by the auditor rather than from the entity being audited.
- Certified by an independent party.
- Kept by an independent party.

Audit evidence is referenced in Tables 19-2 through 19-14 where audit protocols are outlined for each of the HIPAA Security Rule standards involving administrative and physical safeguards.

ADMINISTRATIVE SAFEGUARDS

Administrative safeguards form the foundation on which all other security standards depend. They include administrative actions and policies and procedures to manage the selection, development, implementation and maintenance of security measures to protect ePHI and to manage the conduct of the entity's workforce in relation to the protection of that information. Administrative safeguards address security management,

TABLE 19-2: Security Management Process—Audit Protocol.[1]

Activity: Acquire IT Systems and Services.	Y/N
Do formal or informal policies and procedures exist covering the specific features of the HIPAA Security Rule for information systems §164.306(a)1 and (b)2?	
Are formal or informal policies and procedures periodically updated and approved?	
Activity: Risk Analysis.	**Y/N**
Do formal or informal policies or practices exist for conducting an accurate assessment of potential risks and vulnerabilities to the confidentiality, integrity, and availability of ePHI?	
Is the risk analysis process or methodology updated to reflect changes in the entity's environment?	
Is a risk analysis conducted on a periodic basis?	
Have all systems that contain, process, or transmit ePHI been identified?	
Activity: Implement a Risk Management Program.	**Y/N**
Are current security measures sufficient to reduce risks and vulnerabilities to a reasonable and appropriate level to comply with § 164.306(a)?	
Is the security policy periodically updated and approved?	
Do security standards address data moved within the organization and data sent out of the organization?	
Activity: Develop and Deploy the Information System Activity Review Process.	**Y/N**
Has management developed and deployed formal or informal policy and procedures to review information system activities such as audit logs, access reports, and security incident tracking reports?	
Do formal or informal policies and procedures indicate an appropriate review process for information system activities?	
Does evidence show implementation of review practices?	
Does management periodically update and approve policies and procedures?	

Table 9-2 Footnotes

164.306(a) General requirements: Covered entities must do the following: (i.) Ensure the confidentiality, integrity, and availability of all electronic protected health information (ePHI) the covered entity creates, receives, maintains, or transmits; (ii.) protect against any reasonably anticipated threats or hazards to the security or integrity of such information; (iii.) protect against any reasonably anticipated uses or disclosures of such information that are not permitted or required under Subpart E of this part; and (iv.) ensure compliance with this subpart by its workforce.

(b) Flexibility of approach: (1.) Covered entities may use any security measures that allow the covered entity to reasonably and appropriately implement the standards and implementation specifications as specified in this subpart. (2.) In deciding which security measures to use, a covered entity must take into account the following factors: (i.) The size, complexity, and capabilities of the covered entity; (ii.) the covered entity's technical infrastructure, hardware, and software security capabilities; (iii.) the costs of security measures; and (iv.) the probability and criticality of potential risks to ePHI.

security responsibility, workforce security, information access management, security awareness and training, security incident procedures, contingency planning, evaluation and business associate contracts and other arrangements.

Security Management Process §164.308(a)(1)

The standard for security management process requires implementation of policies and procedures to prevent, detect, contain and correct security violations. Implementation involves the following activities:

- Acquiring information technology systems and services.
- Conducting risk analyses.

TABLE 19-3: Assigned Security Responsibility—Audit Protocol.

Activity: Select a Security Official To Be Assigned Responsibility for HIPAA Security.	Y/N
Has management assigned responsibility for HIPAA Security to a Security Official to oversee the development, implementation, monitoring, and communication of security policies and procedures?	
Have the responsibilities of the Security Official been clearly defined?	
Activity: Assign and Document the Individual's Responsibility.	**Y/N**
Did management clearly identify the roles and responsibilities of the Security Official in a job description?	
Did management communicate to the entire organization the roles and responsibilities of the Security Official?	

- Implementing a risk management program.
- Developing and deploying an information system activity review process.

Assigned Security Responsibility §164.308(a)(2)

The standard for assigned security responsibility requires identification of the security official who is responsible for the development and implementation of the policies and procedures required by the Security Rule. Implementation of this standard involves the following activities:

- Selecting a security official to be assigned responsibility for HIPAA Security.
- Assigning and documenting the individual's responsibilities.

Workforce Security §164.308(a)(3)

The standard for workforce security requires implementation of policies and procedures to ensure that all members of the workforce have appropriate access to ePHI and to prevent those workforce members who should not have access to ePHI from obtaining it. Implementation of this standard involves the following activities:

- Establishing clear job descriptions and responsibilities.
- Establishing criteria and procedures for hiring and assigning tasks.
- Implementing procedures for authorization and/or supervision.
- Establishing workforce clearance procedures.
- Establishing termination procedures.

Information Access Management §164.308(a)(4)

This standard requires implementation of policies and procedures for authorizing access to ePHI consistent with applicable requirements of the Security Rule. Implementation of this standard involves the following activities:

- Evaluating existing security measures related to access controls.
- Isolating healthcare clearinghouse functions.
- Implementing policies and procedures for authorizing access.
- Implementing policies and procedures for access establishment and modification.

Security Awareness and Training §164.308(a)(5)

The standard for security awareness and training requires implementation of a program for all members of the workforce (including management). Program implementation involves the following activities:

TABLE 19-4: Workforce Security—Audit Protocol.

Activity: Establish Clear Job Descriptions and Responsibilities.	Y/N
Has management formally documented levels of access to information systems that house ePHI?	
Are levels of access granted based on business need?	
Does evidence exist that the formal documentation establishing levels of access is appropriately approved and communicated?	
If this specification was not fully implemented, has the non-implemented component been identified and the rationale for its exclusion documented?	
Activity: Establish Criteria and Procedures for Hiring and Assigning Tasks.	Y/N
Do staff members have the necessary knowledge, skills, and abilities to fulfill assigned roles?	
Does management document its verification of the required experience/qualifications of the staff (per management policy)?	
If this specification was not fully implemented, has the non-implemented component been identified and the rationale for its exclusion documented?	
Activity: Implement Procedures for Authorization and/or Supervision.	Y/N
Has management established the level of authorization and/or supervision of workforce members who work with ePHI or in locations where it might be accessed?	
Does the entity's organization chart show chains of command and lines of authority?	
If this specification was not fully implemented, has the non-implemented component been identified and the rationale for its exclusion documented?	
Activity: Establish Workforce Clearance Procedures.	Y/N
Do procedures exist for granting access to ePHI?	
Does evidence of approval and verification of access to ePHI exist?	
If this specification was not fully implemented, has the non-implemented component been identified and the rationale for its exclusion documented?	
Activity: Establish Termination Procedures.	Y/N
Are there separate procedures for terminating access to ePHI when the employment of a workforce member ends, i.e., voluntary termination (retirement, promotion, transfer, change of employment) vs. involuntary termination (termination for cause, reduction in force, involuntary transfer)?	
Is a standard set of procedures in place to recover access control devices and deactivate computer access upon termination of employment?	
Does evidence of monitoring show that access to ePHI is promptly removed upon employee termination?	
If this specification was not fully implemented, has the non-implemented component been identified and the rationale for its exclusion documented?	

- Developing and approving a training strategy and a plan.
- Developing appropriate awareness and training content, materials and methods.
- Implementing the training.
- Monitoring and evaluating the training plan.
- Implementing security reminders.
- Providing protection from malicious software, monitoring log-ins and managing passwords.

TABLE 19-5: Information Access Management—Audit Protocol.

Activity: Evaluate Existing Security Measures Related to Access Controls.	Y/N
Do formal or informal policies and procedures exist relating to the security measures for access controls?	
Are these policies and procedures periodically updated and approved?	
If this specification was not fully implemented, has the non-implemented component been identified and the rationale for its exclusion documented?	
Activity: Isolate Healthcare Clearinghouse Functions.	Y/N
In the event a clearinghouse exists within the organization, are access controls consistent with the HIPAA Security Rule that protects ePHI from unauthorized access?	
Are policy and procedures for access consistent with the HIPAA Security Rule?	
Are these policies or practices periodically updated and approved?	
Activity: Implement Policies and Procedures for Authorizing Access.	Y/N
Are policies and procedures in place to grant access to ePHI (e.g., through access to a workstation, transaction, program, process, or other mechanism)?	
Are these policies and procedures periodically updated and approved?	
Does the entity's IT system have the capacity to set access controls?	
If this specification was not fully implemented, has the non-implemented component been identified and the rationale for its exclusion documented?	
Activity: Implement Policies and Procedures for Access Establishment and Modification.	Y/N
Do policies and standards exist to authorize, establish, document, review, and modify a user's right of access to a workstation, transaction, program, or process?	
Are these policies or standards periodically updated and approved?	
If this specification was not fully implemented, has the non-implemented component been identified and the rationale for its exclusion documented?	

Security Incident Procedures §164.308(a)(6)

The standard for security incident procedures requires the implementation of policies and procedures to address security incidents. Implementation of this standard involves the development of procedures for responding to and reporting security incidents.

Contingency Plan §164.308(a)(7)

The standard for contingency planning requires the establishment of policies and procedures for responding to an emergency or other occurrence (e.g., fire, vandalism, system failure and natural disaster) that damages systems containing ePHI. Implementation of the standard involves the following activities:

- Developing a contingency planning policy.
- Identifying preventive measures.
- Developing a data backup plan and a disaster recovery plan.
- Developing a recovery strategy.
- Developing and implementing an emergency-mode operation plan.
- Testing and revising procedures.

TABLE 19-6: Security Awareness and Training—Audit Protocol.

Activity: Develop and Approve a Training Strategy and a Plan.	Y/N
Do security awareness and training programs address specific requirements for HIPAA policies?	
Are specific HIPAA policies addressed in awareness and training courses?	
Are security awareness and training programs provided to the entire organization?	
Do security awareness and training programs outline the scope of the program?	
Have security awareness and training programs been reviewed and approved?	
If this specification was not fully implemented, has the non-implemented component been identified and the rationale for its exclusion documented?	
Activity: Develop Appropriate Awareness and Training Content, Materials, and Methods.	Y/N
Do training materials incorporate relevant and current IT security topics?	
Does a sample of training materials show they are updated with relevant and current information?	
Are training materials reviewed to ensure relevant and current information is included?	
If this specification was not fully implemented, has the non-implemented component been identified and the rationale for its exclusion documented?	
Activity: Implement the Training.	Y/N
Do employees receive all required training?	
Are required training courses designed to help employees fulfill their security responsibilities?	
Does evidence show that training courses are provided to employees to fulfill their security responsibilities?	
If this specification was not fully implemented, has the non-implemented component been identified and the rationale for its exclusion documented?	
Activity: Monitor and Evaluate the Training Plan.	Y/N
Is training conducted whenever there are changes in the technology and practices?	
Does evidence show that training materials are updated with new technology and practices?	
If this specification was not fully implemented, has the non-implemented component been identified and the rationale for its exclusion documented?	
Activity: Implement Security Reminders.	Y/N
Are security policies and procedures periodically updated?	
Does evidence show that policies and procedures are periodically updated?	
If this specification was not fully implemented, has the non-implemented component been identified and the rationale for its exclusion documented?	
Activity: Protection from Malicious Software; Log-in Monitoring; and Password Management.	Y/N
Do formal or informal policies and procedures exist to inform employees of the importance of protecting against malicious software and exploitation of vulnerabilities?	
Do formal or informal policies and procedures include guidance for guarding against, detecting, and reporting malicious software?	
Do formal or informal policies and procedures include guidance for creating, changing, and safeguarding passwords?	
Do formal or informal policies and procedures include guidance for monitoring log-in attempts and reporting discrepancies? (e.g., A user attempts to login and receives a message that the maximum login attempts were surpassed even though it was the user's first attempt. This condition could indicate that inappropriate attempts were made to access the user's account. The condition should be reported to the security officer or help desk.)	
Are formal or informal policies and procedures approved and updated as needed?	
If this specification was not fully implemented, has the non-implemented component been identified and the rationale for its exclusion documented?	

TABLE 19-7: Security Incident Procedures—Audit Protocol.

Activity: Develop and Implement Procedures to Respond to and Report Security Incidents.	Y/N
Are formal or informal policies and/or procedures in place for identifying, responding to, reporting, and mitigating security incidents?	
Are incident response procedures periodically updated based on changing organizational needs?	
Are incident response procedures communicated to appropriate entity personnel?	
Does formal or informal documentation show that post-incident analyses have been conducted?	
Do policies or procedures address identifying, documenting, and retaining a record of security incidents?	
Does management retain detailed evidence of security incidents?	
Are results of post-incident analysis documented and used to update and revise security policies or controls?	

TABLE 19-8: Contingency Plan—Audit Protocol.

Activity: Develop Contingency Planning Policy.	Y/N
Does a formal contingency plan exist with defined objectives?	
Is a process in place for identifying critical applications, data, operations, and manual and automated processes involving ePHI?	
Does the contingency plan define the overall objectives, framework, roles, and responsibilities of the organization?	
Is the contingency plan periodically updated and approved?	
Does the process used to identify critical applications, data, operations, and manual and automated processes involving ePHI incorporate the recommended performance criteria?	
Is the process periodically updated and approved?	
Activity: Identify Preventive Measures.	**Y/N**
How are preventive measures identified and deemed practical and feasible in the organization's given environment?	
Are preventive measures documented?	
Activity: Data Backup Plan and Disaster Recovery Plan.	**Y/N**
Do disaster recovery and data backup plans exist to restore lost data?	
Are disaster recovery and data backup plans periodically updated and approved?	
Do written procedures exist to create and maintain exact copies of ePHI?	
Are these procedures periodically updated and approved?	
Activity: Develop Recovery Strategy.	**Y/N**
Do procedures exist for recovering documents from emergency or disastrous events?	
Are these procedures periodically updated and approved?	
Activity: Develop and Implement an Emergency Mode Operation Plan.	**Y/N**
Are policies and procedures designed to enable the continuation of critical business processes that protect the security of ePHI while operating in emergency mode?	
Are these policies and procedures periodically updated and approved?	
Activity: Testing and Revision Procedure.	**Y/N**
Do policies and procedures exist for periodic testing and revision of contingency plans?	
Are these policies and procedures periodically approved and updated?	
If this specification was not fully implemented, has the non-implemented component been identified and the rationale for its exclusion documented?	

Table 19-9: Evaluation—Audit Protocol.

Activity: Determine Whether Internal or External Evaluation Is Most Appropriate.	Y/N
Are periodic technical and non-technical evaluations conducted by internal staff or external consultants to determine the extent to which the entity's policies and procedures meet the HIPAA Security Rule standards?	
For evaluations conducted by external consultants, does an agreement or contract exist and does it include verification of consultants' credentials and experience?	
For evaluations conducted by internal staff, does the documentation include all elements from the specified performance criteria?	
Activity: Develop Standards and Measurements for Reviewing All Standards and Implementation Specifications of the Security Rule.	Y/N
Do policies and procedures exist to ensure an evaluation considers all elements of the HIPAA Security Rule?	
Is the evaluation process periodically updated and approved?	
Activity: Conduct Evaluation.	Y/N
Do policies and procedures exist to ensure all necessary information needed to conduct an evaluation is obtained and documented in advance?	
Are these policies and procedures periodically approved and updated?	
Activity: Document Results.	Y/N
Do formal or informal policy and procedures require documentation of the evaluation's findings, remediation options, recommendations, and remediation decisions?	
Does evidence show that findings, remediation options, recommendations, and remediation decisions were documented?	
Are written reports of findings reviewed and approved by management?	
Activity: Repeat Evaluations Periodically.	Y/N
Do formal or informal security policies and procedures specify that evaluations will be repeated when environmental and operational changes are made that affect the security of ePHI?	
Are these policies and procedures periodically updated and approved?	

Evaluation §164.308(a)(8)

This standard requires a periodic technical and nontechnical evaluation based initially upon the HIPAA Security Rule standards and subsequently in response to environmental or operational changes affecting the security of ePHI. The evaluation should establish the extent to which the entity's security policies and procedures meet the HIPAA Security Rule standards. Implementation of the evaluation standard involves the following activities:

- Determining whether internal or external evaluation is most appropriate.
- Developing standards and measurements for reviewing all standards and implementation specification of the Security Rule.
- Conducting evaluations.
- Documenting results.
- Periodically repeating evaluations.

Business Associate Contracts and Other Arrangements §164.308(b)(1)

The standard for business associate contracts and other agreements allows a covered entity to permit a business associate to create, receive, maintain, or transmit ePHI on the covered entity's behalf only if the covered entity obtains satisfactory assurances that

TABLE 19-10: Business Associate Contracts and Other Arrangements—Audit Protocol.

Activity: Written Contract or Other Arrangement.	Y/N
Does a process exist to ensure contracts or agreements include security requirements to address confidentiality, integrity, and availability of ePHI?	
Are contracts or arrangements reviewed to ensure applicable requirements are addressed?	
Activity: Implement An Arrangement Other than a Business Associate Contract if Reasonable and Appropriate.	Y/N
Does a process exist to identify federal, state, or local government business associates?	

the business associate will appropriately safeguard the information. Assurance can be defined by a written contract or other arrangement. Implementation of the standard involves the following activities:

- Establishing contracts or other agreements.
- Implementing an arrangement other than a business associate contract.

PHYSICAL SAFEGUARDS

Physical safeguards are physical measures, policies and procedures to protect a covered entity's electronic information systems and related buildings and equipment from natural and environmental hazards, and unauthorized intrusion. Physical safeguards include facility access controls, workstation use, workstation security and device and media controls.

Facility Access Controls §164.310(a)(1)

Facility access controls require the implementation of policies and procedures to limit physical access to an entity's electronic information systems and the facility or facilities in when they are housed, while ensuring that properly authorized access is allowed. Implementation of facility access controls involves the following activities:

- Establishing facility access controls.
- Establishing contingency operations procedures.
- Conducting an analysis of existing physical security vulnerabilities.
- Developing a facility security plan.
- Maintaining maintenance records.

Workstation Use §164.310(b)

The workstation use standard requires implementation of policies and procedures that specify the proper functions to be performed, the manner in which those functions are to be performed and the physical attributes of the surroundings of a specific workstation that can access ePHI. Implementation of the standard involves the following activities:

- Identifying workstation types and functions or users.
- Identifying expected performance of each type of workstation.
- Analyzing physical surroundings for physical attributes.

TABLE 19-11: Facility Access Controls—Audit Protocol.

Activity: Establish Facility Access Controls.	Y/N
Do policies and procedures exist to limit physical access to electronic information systems and the facility or facilities in which they are housed, while ensuring that properly authorized access is allowed?	
Are these policies and procedures periodically updated and approved?	
Activity: Establish Contingency Operations Procedures.	Y/N
Do procedures exist for controlling facility access by staff, contractors, visitors, and probationary employees when restoring lost data in the event of an emergency and while acting under the Disaster Recovery Plan and Emergency Mode Operations Plan?	
Are these policies and procedures periodically updated and approved?	
If this specification was not fully implemented, has the non-implemented component been identified and the rationale for its exclusion documented?	
Activity: Develop a Facility Security Plan.	Y/N
Do formal or informal policies and procedures exist to safeguard the facility and equipment therein from unauthorized physical access, tampering, and theft?	
Are these policies and procedures periodically updated and approved?	
If this specification was not fully implemented, has the non-implemented component been identified and the rationale for its exclusion documented?	
Activity: Conduct an Analysis of Existing Physical Security Vulnerabilities.	Y/N
Do formal or informal policies and procedures exist regarding access to and use of facilities and equipment that house ePHI?	
Are these policies and procedures periodically updated and approved?	
If this specification was not fully implemented, has the non-implemented component been identified and the rationale for its exclusion documented?	
Activity: Maintain Maintenance Records.	Y/N
Do policies and procedures exist to document repairs and modifications to the physical components of a facility that are related to security (e.g., hardware, walls, doors, and locks)?	
Are these policies and procedures periodically updated and approved?	
If this specification was not fully implemented, has the non-implemented component been identified and the rationale for its exclusion documented?	

TABLE 19-12: Workstation Use—Audit Protocol.

Activity: Identify Workstation Types and Functions or Uses.	Y/N
Do processes exist for identifying workstations by type and location?	
Is each workstation classified based on the capabilities, connection, and allowable activities?	
Activity: Identify Expected Performance of Each Type of Workstation.	Y/N
Do formal or informal policies and procedures exist related to the proper use and performance of workstations?	
Does management periodically update and approve policies and procedures addressing the proper use and performance of workstations?	
Activity: Analyze Physical Surroundings for Physical Attributes.	Y/N
Do formal or informal policies and procedures exist to prevent or preclude unauthorized access to an unattended workstation, limit the ability of unauthorized persons to view sensitive information, and dispose of sensitive information as needed?	
Are these policies and procedures periodically updated and approved?	

TABLE 19-13: Workstation Security—Audit Protocol.

Activity: Identify and Implement Physical Safeguards for Workstations.	Y/N
Are physical security measures in place to prevent unauthorized access to restricted information?	
Are workstations located in secure areas?	
Are system time-outs used?	
Are workstations and laptops protected by password or some alternative authentication?	
How is the physical security policy communicated to employees?	
How does the user acknowledge understanding of the policy?	
Do doors have locks?	
Are cameras in place?	
Are security guards in place?	

TABLE 19-14: Device and Media Controls—Audit Protocol.

Activity: Implement Methods for Final Disposal of ePHI.	Y/N
How is the disposal of hardware, software, and ePHI data managed?	
Do formal policies and procedures address specified criteria regarding the disposal of hardware, software, and ePHI data?	
Do oversight policies and procedures address how management verifies the implementation of disposal policies?	
Is there evidence of management's verification that disposal procedures are implemented according to policy?	
Activity: Develop and Implement Procedures for Reuse of Electronic Media.	Y/N
Are processes established to remove ePHI before reusing electronic media and to identify who is responsible for overseeing those processes?	
Do policies and procedures include specified criteria for removing ePHI from electronic media before they are issued for reuse?	
Activity: Maintain Accountability for Hardware and Electronic Media.	Y/N
How is the location and movement of media and hardware containing ePHI tracked?	
Do policies and procedures address specified criteria regarding tracking the location of ePHI media and hardware?	
If this specification was not fully implemented, has the non-implemented component been identified and the rationale for its exclusion documented?	
Activity: Develop Data Backup and Storage Procedures.	Y/N
Are procedures established over the backup and restoration of ePHI data?	
Do formal or informal policies and procedures include specified criteria for the backup and restoration of ePHI data?	
Does documentation indicate where ePHI data are stored?	
If data are stored on site, is the facility's location secure and protected from the elements (e.g., the location is equipped with fire suppression system, fireproof safe, etc.)?	
If data are stored off site, are specified criteria documented to show that data are stored in a secure location (e.g., a contract with a service provider such as Iron Mountain, a SSSAE 16 report over the controls in place if the service is a third-party provider)? If the off site location is run by the entity, observations similar to the ones above may need to be made.	
For a selection of days, does evidence show that backups of ePHI data were performed successfully?	
Do policies or procedures include specified criteria to determine how often restoration tests are completed?	
If this specification was not fully implemented, has the non-implemented component been identified and the rationale for its exclusion documented?	

Workstation Security §164.310(c):

The workstation security standard addresses the identification and implementation of physical safeguards.

Device and Media Controls §164.310(d)(1)

The standard for device and media controls requires policies and procedures that govern the receipt and removal of hardware and electronic media (that contain ePHI) into and out of a facility, and the movement of these items within the facility. Implementation of the device and media controls standard involve the following activities:

- Implementing methods for final disposal of ePHI.
- Developing and implementing procedures for reuse of electronic media.
- Maintaining accountability for hardware and electronic media.
- Developing data backup and storage procedures.

REVIEW OF FINDINGS

If, based on completion of the audit protocols and unbiased, factual reporting, evidence indicates a control weakness, the auditor considers its current and potential materiality and the opportunity for improvement it presents. The auditor shares the improvement opportunity with management associated with the condition. Also shared is a description of the control weakness (and its effect or potential effect on the confidentiality, integrity and availability of data and systems or the exploitation that could occur as a result), criteria used in its determination and a recommendation. This information is discussed to ensure a clear understanding of the interpretation of the audit result and agreement on the improvement opportunity. Management is asked to draft an action plan for implementing the recommendation. The opportunity, the control criteria and its effect, the recommendation and management's action plan will be included in the draft report.

The draft report includes only those issues supported by clear evidence. Its content is discussed with appropriate personnel to confirm the accuracy of conditions cited and the viability of its recommendations. Audit results (i.e., opportunities, description of resulting potential for compromises to the information system or its environment of operation, and recommendations) are provided to information system owners and common control providers in the initial (draft) audit report. System owners may choose to implement security control improvements. If controls are modified, enhanced, or added during this process, they are reassessed by the auditor before the final report is published.

Compliance with Framework and Regulatory Requirements

Audits can be designed to assess compliance with specific frameworks and regulatory requirements. Security frameworks share common themes including risk—typically defined in terms of threat, vulnerability, likelihood of occurrence and impact—and controls. For a security audit, choices of frameworks include COBIT, the Health Information Trust Alliance (HITRUST), ISO 27002, NIST, and the Payment Card Industry Data Security Standard (PCI DSS). Standard setting bodies and professional organizations offer guidance including mapping tools for associating differing frameworks and regulations. NIST, for example, provides SP800-66 *An Introductory Resource Guide for Implementing Health Insurance Portability and Accountability Act* (HIPAA) *Security Rule*. And, NIST SP800-30 *Guide for Conducting Risk Assessments* can be used to help satisfy Meaningful Use requirement for a risk analysis.

Developed in collaboration with healthcare and information security professionals, the HITRUST Common Security Framework (CSF) was designed for the U.S. healthcare industry. With the inclusion of federal and state regulations, standards and frameworks including HIPAA, NIST, ISO, PCI DSS, and COBIT, the CSF is a comprehensive framework, yet it allows control requirements to be scaled and tailored for healthcare organizations of varying types and sizes.

PRESENTING THE FINDINGS TO SENIOR MANAGEMENT

Audit assists management by providing an independent and objective assessment of the design, implementation and operation of controls. The output and end result of the audit is a report, including opportunities for improvement discovered. The report should help management determine the effectiveness of the information system security controls, serve as an important factor in management's determination of risk, and help management understand business consequences and liabilities and make informed decisions.

Considering the intended uses of the audit report, it is important to communicate effectively. For senior executives, use business terms and translate information security issues into business risks and terms they can quickly understand (e.g., public confidence, patient relationships and survivability). Once management understands the issues, they can define acceptable risk and consequences. Reports to middle and line management should contain sufficient information to allow them to fully understand the improvement opportunities and implement action plans. Where appropriate, recommendations should include provisions for monitoring and follow-up.

Security Risk as a Business Risk

Business, senior, executive management, clinical staff, and IT professionals once viewed information security strictly as a technical matter. In many respects, however, security issues are linked to organizational and cultural factors rather than technologies. Today, effective security relies on the combined efforts of legal, managerial, operational, clinical, and technical staffs. Security is an enterprise concern—a business enabler/inhibiter, patient assurance/doubt, a legal asset/liability, and a technical answer/challenge.

ROLLING THE FINDINGS BACK INTO YOUR PROGRAM

Ultimately, the opportunities for improvement identified during the audit trigger updates to key security documents including the information security program, the security assessment report and the plan of action and milestones. Information system owners and providers of general IT controls (those applicable to all applications) should review the audit report and the updated risk assessment in cooperation with information systems management and the information security officer.

TABLE 19-15: Required Activities for Developing and Managing a Continuous Monitoring Activity.

Prioritize areas for coverage and select an appropriate continuous auditing approach.
Ensure the availability of key client personnel.
Select the appropriate analysis tool, e.g., in-house or vendor-provided software.
Develop continuous auditing routines to assess controls and identify deficiencies.
Determine the frequency of applying continuous auditing routines.
Define output requirements; develop a reporting process.
Establish relationships with relevant line and IT management.
Assess data integrity and prepare data.
Determine resource requirements, i.e., personnel, processing environment (the enterprise's IT facilities or IT audit facilities).
Understand the extent to which management performs its continuous monitoring role.

CONTINUOUS ASSURANCE AUDITING

Continuous monitoring is a management process used to maintain a systematic review of the effectiveness of policies, procedures and business processes. Continuous auditing is a methodology for identifying relevant events in near real-time. Continuous assurance is an automated, uninterrupted monitoring approach occurring at the confluence of management's continuous monitoring activities and audit's continuous auditing activities such that the auditor maintains oversight of management's monitoring. The auditor uses generalized audit software, test data generators, integrated test facilities and specialized audit and system software utilities. These types of tools allow management and auditor to monitor controls and risk continuously and gather selective evidence.[4]

Continuous assurance is used to provide timely reporting and lends itself to use in high-risk, high-volume, paperless environments. To provide continuous assurance, audit captures transactional and process data at the source and in the disaggregated and unfiltered form. Continuous assurance is intended to be an efficient and effective evaluation of the control environment, lead to increased audit coverage, and provide thorough and consistent analysis of data. Its purpose is to reduce risk. Successful implementation of continuous assurance auditing requires management buy-in and a phased approach initially addressing the most critical business systems. Table 19-15 includes activities that must be planned and managed when developing and maintaining a continuous auditing capability.

AUDITING FOR FRAUD

Consideration of fraud is a requirement of all audit planning exercises. Fraud can be committed by those inside and outside a company. Researchers find insider threats to be more damaging to a company's reputation and customer relations. Based on its 2011/2012 Fraud Survey, Kroll's senior managing director, Richard Plansky, reports that 60 percent of frauds are committed by insiders including senior managers, junior employees, third-party agents, or intermediaries.[5]

Use of Social Security numbers presents opportunities for ID theft. Sharp Healthcare, the San Diego-based integrated delivery system, took action after two former Sharp billing department employees pleaded guilty to felony ID theft.[6] The staff members used patient financial information, Social Security numbers, and names to impersonate patients and apply for credit cards to go on "shopping sprees," says CIO Bill Spooner. Using vendor software, "We now mask Social Security numbers on our display screens to prevent a dishonest employee from using that key identifier in the credit card application."

Two very common circumstances in patient financial service areas present opportunities for credit card fraud. The mail-in remit portion of a patient's bill typically includes space for credit card information. Those who submit payment by credit card are at risk for fraud as are those patients who make credit card payments by phone. It is important to establish appropriate procedures for those who intercept calls and remittances and to monitor these employees' activities.

Michael Gelles and Tara Mahoutchian of Deloitte Consulting advise management to maintain awareness of employees' incentives or pressures to commit fraud, the opportunity for fraud to occur, and rationalizations or attitudes that could influence individuals to commit fraud.[7] Consider potential indicators and possible precursors of insider threats including employees who repeatedly express discontent with their jobs or salary; express persistent worries about cash flow; have criminal records or unexplained access to financial resources; rarely take holidays or week-long vacations; and bully or harass their colleagues.

The information systems environment is at high risk for insider threats including fraud. Technically skilled, and often overworked, professionals with privileged accounts and access to massive stores of sensitive data—with street value—and to systems susceptible to fraud (e.g., payment systems and highly integrated applications) combined with a slow economy may prove tempting. Fraud factors in an information systems environment include weaknesses in access, inadequate segregation of duties and inadequate monitoring of privileged accounts and the accounts of high-risk users. An audit should include procedures identifying system-based overrides, testing for instances of inappropriate combinations of transactions, and examining workflow approvals and protections for sensitive files. SANS researchers recommend using separation of duties to manage fraud and conflicts of interest.

In its discussion paper on Fraud Detection Using Data Analytics in the Healthcare Industry, ACL, a business assurance technology company, identifies typical fraud schemes encountered in healthcare. Uses of data analysis for fraud detection and prevention are listed in Table 19-16.

Monitoring the Human Resource

Using new technologies and large data, employers are tracking employees' activities at work and after hours on social networks. Andrew Walls, vice president of research at Gartner Inc., recognizes an employer's surveillance of individuals as "an opportunity to mitigate and correct risk."[9] He recommends surveillance activities comply with ethical and legal standards. The U.S. Office of Special Counsel appears to agree. It released a memorandum[10] June 20, 2012, regarding agencies' monitoring of employee communi-

TABLE 19-16: Uses of Data Analysis to Detect and Prevent Fraud Schemes Encountered in Healthcare.[8]

Match OIG-excluded providers list with vendor and employee master files.
Find kickbacks paid in exchange for referring business.
Identify charges posted outside of proper GL period.
Highlight "upcoding" of procedures by identifying statistically outlying numbers.
Match vendor names, addresses, and tax IDs to employee payroll records.
Summarize large invoices without purchase orders, by amount, vendor, etc.
Compare list of enrolled employees to people receiving health insurance benefits.
Highlight billing for medically unnecessary tests.
Identify false, invalid, and duplicate Social Security numbers.
Highlight excessive use of high risk DRGs (diagnosis-related groups).
Identify excessive billing by a single physician.
Identify employee overtime abuses.
Report entries against authorization records for terminated employees.
Identify multiple payroll deposits to the same bank account.

cations and confidential whistleblower disclosures. Agencies are urged to review existing monitoring policies and practices for consistency with both the law and Congress's intent to provide a secure channel for protected disclosures.

Also in June 2012, the Transportation Security Administration (TSA) released a solicitation for a solution to guard against insider threats. The solution sought was to provide monitoring and logging capabilities—including keystrokes, e-mails, attachments, screen captures, file transfers, chats, network activities and website visits. Other requirements specify "end users must not be able to tell they are being monitored, and must not be able to kill the monitoring."[11]

"The TSA wants a solution for monitoring *and* surveillance," says Walls, and he describes the differences. Monitor refers to a technology used for collecting data from infrastructure. Surveillance refers to the overt and covert use of monitors to develop awareness of a person's or a group's activities within a given context. Monitoring is infrastructure/system event-centric. Surveillance targets specific people and the system events they generate. In his report, "Conduct Digital Surveillance Ethically and Legally," Walls identifies benefits and presents recommendations to avoid unethical and illegal circumstances. His recommendations are shown in Table 19-17.

Employee behavior. Because humans are human, human-related risk is inevitable. In an executive workshop at Dartmouth College for CISOs, Managing Director and Chief Information Risk Officer at Goldman Sachs, Philip Venables, advised colleagues to structure their organizations and processes so that no single individual could cause critical damage (e.g., one individual capable of completing an entire financial transaction, one individual capable of modifying a critical system in the production environment). "Situations where reliance is on one person doing something (or not doing something) are opportunities for improvement."[12] At Sachs, the emphasis of security

TABLE 19-17: Avoiding Unethical and Illegal Circumstances.

Prior to consideration of tools and methods, ensure surveillance and monitoring activities are supported in policy and relevant legal frameworks.
Where legally possible, inform affected individuals when and where monitoring may occur and how to report their concerns.
Identify approved tools and processes for surveillance and enforcing restrictions.
Establish procedures for using surveillance tools and collecting and managing information on user activities. Include signed authorization, notification processes, and processes for ending the surveillance, removing tools, and destroying unnecessary information.
Carefully select systems to be monitored; comply with ethical and legal guidelines.

improvement initiatives for employees has changed from awareness campaigns (featuring trinkets with security reminders) to an emphasis on improving process integration and design. Key insights from the Dartmouth workshop include:

- An organizational culture that values sound security practices is a more effective tool than are mandates.
- Generation-Y employees generally have more permissive, risk-enhancing behaviors involving information sharing, work schedules and locations and devices—behaviors that enhance risk.
- Manage the data, not the device. Apply the "Hotel California" strategy—allow data to check out, but never leave.
- Education and awareness are of limited value in large populations of users. Consumers need to take more personal responsibility and trade some privacy for security.
- Teach employees to think for themselves, trust their judgment and question what they perceive as risky practices. Executive CISOs viewed this as especially important for middle managers who often weigh security risks against potential business gains.
- Adherence to policies and procedures. Determining whether the workforce adheres requires an organization to measure the effectiveness of its formal guidance. Without monitoring, an organization is at risk of negligence. Management is responsible for systems of internal control including the formal documentation, communication, implementation, enforcement and ongoing monitoring of policies and procedures.

CONCLUSION

Information system security program audits are designed to assess the effectiveness of safeguards and controls. Because audit conclusions are based on the interpretation of evidence, it is important to select appropriate audit objectives, methods and objects. We used the HIPAA Audit Program Protocol as a framework for gathering evidence for subsequent assessment of its sufficiency, completeness, relevance and reliability. The HIPAA Audit Program Protocol is subject to change over time, so it is recommended that the reader periodically check for the latest version on the U.S. Department of Health & Human Services website.

Audit reporting requirements, compliance frameworks and management's requirements for incorporating audit results into the information security program and the overall risk management process were described. Tips for the review and presentation of the audit report were shared along with considerations for identifying security as a business risk. Continuous assurance auditing was introduced as a capability for reducing risk by monitoring the effectiveness of policies, procedures and business processes. Employee monitoring activities were explored from a different perspective than were more traditional security controls because these activities can increase an organization's risk if not managed appropriately. In closing, guidance was provided for establishing fraud audit capabilities.

REFERENCES

1. U.S. Department of Health & Human Services. HIPAA privacy & security audit program. Available at: www.hhs.gov/ocr/privacy/hipaa/enforcement/audit/index.html.

2. *Ibid.*

3. ISACA. IS auditing standard: S14 audit evidence. Available at: www.isaca.org/Knowledge-Center/Standards/Pages/Standard-for-IS-Auditing-S14-Audit-Evidence1.aspx.

4. ISACA. IS Auditing Guideline: G42 Continuous Assurance. Available at: www.isaca.org/Knowledge-Center/Standards/Pages/IS-Auditing-Guideline-G42-Continuous-Assurance1.aspx.

5. Plansky R. When fraud is an inside job: Five steps to consider. Kroll Global Fraud Report; 2012:19-20.

6. Lowers & Associates. ID theft: Steps for preventing fraud: Healthcare organizations lead charge with new controls. October 25, 2012. Available at: www.lowersrisk.com/news/news-listing/article/article/id-theft-steps-for-preventing-fraud/?tx_ttnews%5BbackPid%5D=1&cHash=cd2f113bc279629be68805fa5c584bf3.

7. Gelles M, Mahoutchian T. Mitigating the insider threat: Building a secure workforce. Deloitte Consulting LLP. March 2012. Available at: http://csrc.nist.gov/organizations/fissea/2012-conference/presentations/fissea-conference-2012_mahoutchian-and-gelles.pdf.

8. ACL Services Inc. Available at: www.acl.com.

9. Garter. Garter says monitoring employee behavior in digital environments is rising. [press release] May 29, 2012. Available at: www.gartner.com/it/page.jsp?id=2028215.

10. Lerner CN. Agency monitoring policies and confidential whistleblower disclosures to the Office of Special Counsel and to Inspector Generals. [memorandum] June 20, 2012. U.S. Office of Special Counsel. Available at: www.osc.gov/documents/press/2012/press/Agency%20Monitoring%20Policies%20and%20Confidential%20Whistleblower%20Disclosures%20to%20the%20Office%20of%20Special%20Counsel%20and%20Inspectors%20General.pdf.

11. Wait P. TSA wants to monitor employee computer activities. *Information Week*. June 25, 2012. Available at: www.informationweek.com/government/security/tsa-wants-to-monitor-employee-computer-a/240002665.

12. Tuck School of Business at Dartmouth, Glassmaeyer/McNamee Center for Digital Strategies. Human behavior and security culture: Managing information risk through a better understanding of human culture: An executive workshop for CISOs. July 19-20, 2011. Available at: http://digitalstrategies.tuck.dartmouth.edu/cds-uploads/publications/pdf/Human_BehaviorUS.pdf.

CHAPTER 20

Incident Handling

By Shelia T. Searson, CIPP, and Jennifer L. Cole, MSHI

This chapter focuses on the actual process of incident handling, taking into consideration all incidents involving patient information that could potentially result in a breach of patient information, without labeling them either a privacy or security incident. This chapter, a "how-to" guide, follows the information provided in Terrell Herzig's first book, *Information Security in Healthcare: Managing Risk*, within author Brian Evans' chapter on "The Importance of Incident Response."[1] This "prequel" delved into the details surrounding the response to a security incident and the many information security and forensic considerations. However, in some instances, an incident involving electronic information which will be reviewed through the security incident response plan may need to be examined concurrently through the privacy incident response plan for the purposes of determining if a breach of the patient's confidentiality occurred. This chapter provides that step-by-step process for managing all incidents, no matter what the medium.

Every organization, regardless of size, already has in place some sort of incident response plan, whether or not it is "official"—as in officially endorsed by administration. These unofficial incident response plans can range from, "Ignore it, and maybe it will go away," to "Oh, my gosh, we've had a breach! What do we do now?!" The goal of this chapter is to assist you in developing your organization's official—and appropriate—incident response plan for your unique environment.

Each organization must develop its own incident response plan, and the plan needs to be organization-wide so that responses can be consistent and so that information learned while responding to an incident can benefit the organization. Having one incident response plan allows the organization to appropriately train employees on how to respond if they suspect or learn of an incident that might threaten the privacy or security of patients' information or other sensitive data. One response plan provides the means to centralize the collection, management, and reporting of incident data, as well as making sure that all steps are consistently followed for each event. This issue becomes increasingly important because of federal and state regulatory requirements related to incident response. In the beginning, at the first report of an incident, many facts are unknown: How many patients are affected? How long have the data been exposed? Is there a potential for identity theft? Was this a theft or negligence? So many questions need answers. In addition, first responders often won't have the training and/ or experience to make the determination as to whether an incident is a breach, security incident or none of these. "One response plan" means that all questions are methodically asked, investigated and answered by persons who are trained to handle the incident response. Additionally, a single incident response plan provides a better avenue for communication if an incident must be escalated due to administrative, legal, financial or other risks.

One matter that must be central to an incident response plan and all the activities that occur while carrying out the plan is that of confidentiality. From the beginning when an incident is reported, according to the incident response plan there should be no discussion about the incident with anyone who is not part of the incident response team unless the issue must be escalated to administration for some reason. Discussing the incident with others outside the team could harm the investigation and/or the persons involved. This confidentiality rule carries through to the end of the investigation. Documented incident reports and the data collected during an investigation should be protected and afforded the same confidentiality and security as any other confidential information, such as employee records, patient medical records and Social Security numbers.

Information gathered while handling an incident can provide insight into how to better respond to future incidents and for precautions that can be taken to prevent similar incidents. These precautions can range in scope from additional training for workforce members to implementing a stronger security control. The key to one incident response plan is to benefit the entire organization and not just one unit or department.

Healthcare organizations are governed by multiple federal laws and regulations. Two sets of regulations that specifically address the issue of appropriate incident response are (1) the HIPAA Security Regulations[2] and (2) the federal final rule for Breach Notification for Unsecured Protected Health Information.[3]

The Health Insurance Portability and Accountability Act of 1996 (HIPAA) provides the framework for maintaining the confidentiality of patient health information through the guidance found in the HIPAA Privacy Rule. The HIPAA Security Regulations, with which most covered entities had to be compliant by April 20, 2005, present the guidelines to be followed to "ensure the confidentiality, integrity, and availability of all electronic protected health information the covered entity creates, receives, maintains, or transmits" (CFR §164.306(a)(1)).

The section of the HIPAA Security Regulations that apply for incident response is CFR §164.308(a)(6)(i), which states "Implement policies and procedures to address security incidents." CFR §164.308(a)(6)(ii) elaborates on that standard by specifying its implementation: "Response and Reporting (Required). Identify and respond to suspected or known security incidents; mitigate, to the extent practicable, harmful effects of security incidents that are known to the covered entity; and document security incidents and their outcomes."

The mandate is clear for electronic protected health information (PHI): Have policies and procedures in place to address security incident response and documentation in the most reasonable and appropriate ways for your covered entity.

The interim final rule for Breach Notification for Unsecured Protected Health Information (the Breach Notification Rule) went into effect for all HIPAA-covered entities and their business associates on September 23, 2009. This rule was born out of the American Recovery and Reinvestment Act or 2009's Health Information Technology for Economic and Clinical Health (HITECH) Act that was signed into law by President Barack Obama on February 17, 2009.[4] Section 13402 required the Secretary of the Department of Health & Human Services to issue the breach regulations within 180 days following the enactment of the law.

In addition, Section 13402 stated that the rule would begin applying to breaches "discovered on or after the date that is 30 days after the date of publication"—September 23, 2009. When the interim final rule of breach notification was published, comments regarding the contents of the rule were requested by October 23, 2009. On January 25, 2013, days before publication of this book, the final Breach Notification Rule was published. Edits were made to this chapter; however, time constraints did not allow for an in-depth analysis.

Although the breach notification rule was written to require HIPAA-covered entities to notify affected individuals of a breach of their unsecured PHI, it provides a rather detailed outline for covered entities to follow regarding documentation of the breach, procedure to determine the probability that PHI has been compromised, to the affected individuals, the involvement of business associates, and other appropriate notifications, depending on the unique circumstances of the breach. Each covered entity must develop its own process for meeting this federal requirement.

In addition to federal laws and regulations, state law impacting incident and incident response must be considered. Each organization must be informed and current with state requirements because some states are more conservative and impose tighter incident response guidelines than those expressed in federal law.

Before proceeding further with this chapter, it is important to establish consistent definitions of terms to prevent confusion. Be aware that this is an important practice within your organization as well. Not only should the workforce use the same terminology, but they should understand correct and consistent meanings for the terms used. For example, to "techies" a "breach" typically means an unauthorized access/penetration into the network or application and may or may not involve PHI. So the techies' definition of breach is different from that used in this discussion. For our purposes, when considering incident response in healthcare, the best definitions can be found in federal legislation.

Breach, from the Omnilous Rule, is defined as "the acquisition, access, use, or disclosure of protected health information in a manner not permitted under subpart E of this part which compromises the security or privacy of the protected health information."

Three exceptions to this breach definition are identified in the breach notification rule. Those exceptions will be discussed later. However, it is important to note that a breach could potentially compromise the privacy or security of the information. This is not just an information security issue. Examples of a breach include discussing a patient's PHI with someone who does not have a need to know the information, a misdirected fax, the loss of a paper medical record or the theft of an unencrypted thumb drive that contains data on patients.

Security incident. From the HIPAA Security Regulations, CFR §164.304, comes the definition for security incident: "The attempted or successful unauthorized access, use, disclosure, modification, or destruction of information or interference with system operations in an information system."

Security incidents result from breakdowns in information security and/or technology or human error. Examples of security incidents include the sharing of logons and passwords, a misdirected e-mail containing confidential information, a successful hacker, an unplanned downtime of a system or application and a violation of a security policy or procedure. A security incident can be a breach if it involves the unauthorized use or disclosure of PHI. Incident response specifically for security incidents is discussed in a separate section later in this chapter.

For the purposes of this chapter discussion, the term *incident* will be used to describe a potential breach or security incident. Incident will be the reference used for the event while it is reported and investigated, before it is determined whether or not it is a breach or security incident.

Each incident, whether a breach of patient information or a security incident, is unique. Therefore, the incident response has the potential of being unique and needing to be carefully altered depending on the details of the incident. However, even though each incident is unique, a certain set of building blocks should be in place and ready for action when a potential incident is reported.

One key building block of every incident response plan is the establishment of the incident response team. Communication is vitally important for incident response, so this team is composed of persons who have the authority to manage the multiple possible activities needed to appropriately follow up on a breach or security incident. The size and make-up of the team are governed by the size and type of the organization; in the case of larger, complex organizations, the incident response team may be tiered according to responsibility in follow-up from the incident. Let's begin with the larger group. Persons in the following positions should be considered for inclusion on the incident response team:

- Chief Information Officer
- Privacy Officer
- Information Security Officer
- Legal Counsel
- Director of Risk Management
- Director of Information Technology
- Director of Public/Community Relations
- Director of Human Resources
- Director of Compliance
- Director of Research or Institutional Review Board (if research data involved)

In addition, this group can decide if or when to escalate the incident to senior management. However, to ensure appropriate timing and consistency of the message, the assignment of reporting an incident to the president, chief executive officer, or other executive should be given to one individual with one other person named as the backup.

In like manner, a decision must be made as to who will handle the tasks of providing required announcements to the news media or requests for information about any incident from the news media or other outside organizations. Most usually this will be the Director of Public/Community Relations—the reason for the Director's inclusion on the incident response team. However, make sure that everyone understands who is managing this important task and to whom they should direct all questions or requests from outside the organization.

A subset of the incident response team provides the perfect group to oversee the responsibilities of documenting, reporting and determining the the compromise results for all incidents. Every incident is not a breach or security incident. But often that determination cannot be made until the incident is investigated and the details of that investigation considered. The smaller group, consisting of three to five persons, can provide this leadership for the organization. Consider utilizing the talents of the following:

- Chief Information Officer
- Privacy Officer
- Security Officer
- Legal Counsel
- Director of Risk Management (for this working group)

Then, the larger group can be called upon when the incident warrants. However, the team reviewing the incidents with regard to the compromise standard must be persons who can be objective about each situation and able to make the right decisions, even if some of those decisions require the organization to admit guilt or carelessness.

Now that the teams have been created, the next building block to put into place is a set of resources necessary for the various follow-up activities. As you recall, each incident is unique, but having all resources ready to use if needed saves time and anxiety when time could be at a premium and anxiety is running high. The following is a list of resources to consider for your organization:

- Incident report form.
- Risk assessment for determining if PHI was compromised.
- Template for breach notification letter.
- Plan and template for releasing breach information to the media.
- Plan for posting information on organization's website.
- Plan for accommodating phone calls.
- Agreement with credit protection/monitoring services.
- Arrangements with vendor(s) to manage incident response and follow-up.

The single most important tool for incident response is the Incident Report Form. This document needs to carefully and thoughtfully incorporate each issue that might need to be recorded about an incident. Consider especially the information required by the federal HIPAA/HITECH Breach Notification Rule and by any state regulations that your organization must follow. Do not depend on a document with large spaces to "summarize" the incident or the findings of an investigation. Ask for specific information. One example is in relation to dates. Spaces should be provided to record the following:

- Date of the incident.
- Date of discovery.
- Date the Privacy Office (or whatever office manages the incident response investigation) was notified.
- Date the investigation was completed.
- Date risk assessment was completed, if appropriate.
- Dates when all follow-up activities were completed.
- Date the disciplinary action is to be carried out.

Name persons in the report: who reported the incident, to whom was the incident initially reported, who investigated, and so on. Be sure to include the type of information involved such as:

- Was it hard copy, such as a paper record or printout?
- Was it electronic, such as an e-mail or a spreadsheet on a laptop?
- Was it a facsimile?
- Was the incident the result of a discussion with an unauthorized person or a phone message left on an answering machine?

Again, include everything that would be needed for any investigation. It is better to have a form that addresses every possible detail and not need to respond to certain items than to have to go back days, weeks or months later to determine the missing facts. The contents of this document become invaluable when an incident must be revisited, as in response to a complaint or audit. Be sure to include all items which must be reported to the U.S. Department of Health & Human Services (see Table 20-1) in the event of a reportable HIPAA breach.

The Breach Notification Rule presumes that a breach is reportable unless it can be demonstrated by a risk assessment that there is a low probability that the PHI has been compromised. To make the appropriate determination, certain factors must be included in the risk assessment: (1) nature and extent of PHI involved (types of information, identifiers included, likelihood of identifying individuals or using the information in a manner harmful to the individuals); (2) the unauthorized persons who used the PHI or to whom a disclosure was made in error; (3) whether or not PHI was actually acquired or viewed; and (4) the extent to which the risk to the PHI has been mitigated. The importance of this document, and completing it thoroughly and thoughtfully, cannot be stressed enough.

The former list of tools includes several templates and plans to be developed and in place in case they are needed. Hopefully, they will grow cobwebs in your incident response arsenal, but have them there nonetheless. Develop a template for a general breach notification letter that meets all the criteria found in the Breach Notification Rule, as well as any additional requirements of notification letters found in state or local regulations. Obtain approval of this letter template from administration, legal, risk management, public relations and other appropriate interested parties. Having this agreement now will make the task of developing a specific notification letter go more smoothly.

Under certain circumstances, especially if a breach involves more than 500 individuals, healthcare organizations have additional responsibilities to communicate that the breach occurred: notify the media and post the details of the breach on the

TABLE 20-1: Additional Breach Information for HHS Reporting.

Breach Information			
Date(s) of breach		Date(s) of discovery	
Approximate number of individuals affected: _____			
Type of breach:	❏ Theft ❏ Loss ❏ Improper Disposal ❏ Unauthorized Access ❏ Hacking/IT Incident ❏ Other - ❏ Unknown		
Indicate the location of the information at the time of the breach:	❏ Laptop ❏ Desktop Computer ❏ Network Server ❏ E-mail ❏ Other Portable Electronic Device ❏ Electronic Medical Record ❏ Paper ❏ Other -		
Indicate the type of protected health information involved in the breach:	❏ Demographic Information ❏ Financial Information ❏ Clinical Information ❏ Other -		
Safeguards in place prior to the breach:	❏ Firewalls ❏ Packet Filtering (router-based) ❏ Secure Browser Sessions ❏ Strong Authentication ❏ Encrypted Wireless ❏ Physical Security ❏ Logical Access Control ❏ Antivirus Software ❏ Intrusion Detection ❏ Biometrics		
Notice of Breach and Actions Taken			
Date(s) individual notices were provided:		Was a substitute notice required? ❏ Yes ❏ No	❏ Yes ❏ No
Indicate the actions taken to respond to the breach:	Security and/or Privacy Safeguards Mitigation Sanctions Policies and Procedures Other -		

Reprinted by permission of Tom Walsh Consulting, LLC

TABLE 20-2: Additional Risk Factors to Consider in a Risk Assessment.

Risk Factors
To be used as guidelines for conducting a risk assessment.
Was the information that was disclosed truly considered PHI?
• If the health information was solely employment records held by the covered entity in its role as an employer, this is not PHI and not subject to the breach notification. (Reference: 45 CFR 160.103)
• However, while the information may not be considered PHI, it may be classified as Personally Identifiable Information (PII) and fall under State law for breach notification.
Was the data encrypted or stored in a proprietary format?
• Perhaps the data encryption does not meet FIPS 140-2 standards, but would it still pose a significant challenge to the recipient to decipher the information?
Who had access to the information?
• Was the access intentional or outside of their scope or authority?
• Was the user or the recipient subject to HIPAA Privacy and Security Rules?
What type and amount of information was disclosed?
• Was there a limited amount of data that was exposed?
• Could the type of information disclosed pose a greater risk for identity theft? (Example: Name, date of birth, and Social Security number)
How was access to the information obtained?
• Was the access unintentional or done in good faith?
What is the likelihood that the person who had access to the information would retain the information?
Was there an opportunity to immediately mitigate the impermissible use or disclosure?
• Was there some type of assurance obtained from the recipient that the information would not be further disclosed or would be securely destroyed?
Was the media containing the unsecured PHI returned prior to being accessed?
• Does forensic analysis prove that the recovered media containing unsecured PHI was not opened, altered, transferred, or otherwise compromised? For example, a lost laptop is returned without being accessed.

Reprinted by permission of Tom Walsh Consulting, LLC

organization's website. Having in place both the plan and template for notifying the media, as well as the plan for how to quickly post the information on the organization's website, reduces the confusion when needed.

If a breach of protected health information calls for notification, then a phone number must be given in case the affected individual(s) wants more information. Most departments, units or organizations cover the extra calls if the breach is small. However, if the breach involves hundreds or thousands of persons—and we have heard of those in the past—then having a plan for accommodating large numbers of phone calls is helpful.

On occasion, the breach or security incident necessitates offering credit protection or credit monitoring services to the affected individuals. Because you cannot predict when you will need these services or for how many persons, it is best to be prepared and have in place an agreement with a company that provides credit protection/monitoring services. Doing this before it is needed allows the healthcare organization to negotiate for the best services at the best costs. Remember: If you release any patient information to the vendor, you must include a Business Associate Agreement (BAA) to the contract of services.

Healthcare organizations now have an option available for managing the details of an incident response, as well as all follow-up activities. Many vendors have emerged that offer these varying combinations of services. If your organization is interested in this service, be certain to ensure that all federal and state requirements for incident response are met by the vendor and that documentation of the incident from discovery to closure is complete. Again, be sure to include a business associate agreement to the contract of services.

Now that all the teams and resources are in place, the next building block is development of the actual incident response plan. An incident response plan for security incidents is required by the original HIPAA Security Regulations; therefore, most healthcare organizations will already have their plans in place. However, a brief review of this topic is in order—which may reveal that some healthcare organizations need to update their current policies, procedures and/or plans. As you are building the incident response plan for your organization, keep in mind that the plan should include escalation procedures that may need to be activated at any time while responding to an incident. Initially, maybe only one or two core members of the incident response team are involved. However, depending on the investigation, the incident may warrant escalation and may require involvement from others, including outside agencies or services (e.g., forensic experts, legal, etc.).

When developing any plan for implementation across the entire organization, each healthcare organization must take into consideration its unique environment: its size, its type of facility, the best means to communicate with the entire workforce, and so on. But the one activity that is paramount to the success of a security incident response plan is the successful completion of a risk analysis. Do not confuse a risk analysis with a risk gap analysis or some other instrument to determine basic risks. A risk analysis, which is required by the HIPAA Security Regulations and other regulatory bodies, is a comprehensive study to determine risks, analyze them, develop a plan to prioritize and manage them, and establish a procedure to regularly update the risk analysis to keep the organization's risk profile current. A risk analysis does not have to be complicated, but it must be thorough. The best practices for a risk analysis are contained in publications from the National Institute of Standards and Technology (NIST) or the U.S. Department of Commerce. The two publications are NIST SP 800-30 *Risk Management Guide for Information Technology Systems*[5] and NIST SP 800-39 *Managing Information Security Risk Organization, Mission, and Information System View.*[6]

A security incident response plan primarily focuses on the responsibilities that reside in the information technology departments of the organization. Again, the National Institute of Standards and Technology (NIST) has a recently updated publication that provides clear and concise activities to include in the incident response plan, as well as information on policy development. This document is NIST SP 800-61 Revision 2 *Computer Security Incident Handling Guide.*[7]

If it is found that a security incident involves protected health information (PHI), then it is also a breach which must be reported and investigated according to the organization-wide incident response plan. When an incident involving PHI is suspected, the workforce members must be trained on how to respond. Provide education which tells them of the importance of their efforts to protect patients' confidentiality and the confidential information that is maintained throughout the organization. Help them to see that they are part of a team and to be alert to breakdowns in policy and procedure related to privacy and security issues. Provide them with the information they need to contact the appropriate person(s) if they are aware of a potential incident. This information should include contact names and phone numbers and/or e-mail addresses. The obvious contacts are supervisors, privacy and security officers, compliance representatives and information technology help desks. If possible, provide a hotline to receive these calls. Always remind the workforce that you want their assistance. It is much better to respond to a call and discover that no breach or security incident occurred than to let things go and discover two or three weeks later that PHI was erroneously disclosed or lost. Therefore, regularly disseminate the organization's plan of action for reporting an incident.

Once the contacts for the initial report are determined, the plan's next step is to get these reports from various locations across the organization to one central location from which the incident response is managed. Many organizations look to the privacy office, but compliance or risk management or even legal counsel offices are possibilities. Determine the best clearinghouse for your environment. For the purposes of this chapter, the privacy office is deemed responsible.

When the potential incident is reported, the privacy office records the basic information and sets into motion the activities to gather the information for the incident reporting form: who, what, when, where and how. For many organizations, especially larger ones, maintaining a log of incidents is a valuable tool for incident response. A log or spreadsheet will help ensure that no incident falls off the radar before it is completely investigated, managed and closed. It will assist with the preparation of reports, most notably the annual report of reportable privacy breaches that must be made to the U.S. Department of Health & Human Services, as required by the Breach Notification Rule.

Gathering the information for the incident form can be a team effort. Although the incident response process is managed through a particular office such as the privacy office, often one office is not staffed well enough or does not have the appropriate relationship with the workforce in the area in which the incident occurred to be effective in gathering the details required to complete the incident response form. Therefore, to assist with the investigation, it is a good practice to have persons within the healthcare organization's departments or units who have the assigned responsibility to assist the privacy office. These individuals can be named "coordinators" or "leaders" for all issues related to privacy and security—communicating changes in policy or procedure, sending awareness e-mails to remind workforce members of privacy and security compliance issues, and so on—not just for the purpose of incident response. Using individuals in the departments in this way broadens the organization's culture and environment for privacy and security. In effect, this practice enlarges your privacy and information security teams.

Investigating an incident may take several days or weeks. However, always be mindful that a deadline is imposed on healthcare organizations if the incident results in a breach of patient information that may be reportable. The Breach Notification Rule mandates that if it is determined that a breach of PHI occurred then the covered entity must notify the affected individual (or next of kin) as soon as possible but not later than 60 days from discovering the breach or from when the breach should have been known by "exercising reasonable diligence."

Even though there is a 60-day window, which can tick by quickly when investigating the intricacies of some incidents, do not rush the investigation process. The main focus is to get all the facts:

- How was the incident discovered?
- What information is at risk?
- What PHI was involved?
- What was the format of the information?
- Is this a loss or theft or a case of carelessness or malicious intent?
- How many individuals were affected?
- Where did the incident happen?
- Has the information been recovered?

Another issue to address is to determine if something can be done to immediately correct or stop the loss of data while the incident is being investigated. In the case of a security incident, be certain to take appropriate action for the technology involved and note whether or not the data were encrypted. The facts need to be documented in an objective fashion. The report must be filled with facts and evidence, not thoughts and feelings. Bottom line: get the complete set of facts so that the incident can be correctly and objectively evaluated.

The incident report should specify the safeguards in place at the time of the incident. These include administrative, physical and technical safeguards. Consider developing a checklist of safeguards on the incident report form for which the appropriate ones can be checked. This will save time and provide consistency in reporting and allow for including appropriate safeguards for your organization's environment. This list could include things like firewall, physical security, policy and so on.

When the investigation is complete and the facts are being assessed, if the incident involved the use, or disclosure of PHI, consider the three exceptions for which notification is not required. These exceptions are outlined in the Breach Notification Rule: (1) Unintentional/good faith acquisition, access, or use of PHI by employee or business associate; (2) Inadvertent disclosure by an authorized individual to another within the same entity if PHI is not further used or disclosed; (3) Disclosure in which an unauthorized person could not reasonably retain the information. This evaluation is a good item to include in the incident reporting form.

As mentioned earlier when discussing the incident report form, a risk assessment must be completed to demonstrate low probability that the PHI was compromised. No risk assessment is necessary if the organization knows the breach did occur and plans to notify affected individuals. Develop a risk-scoring process for this purpose, and ensure that it is used consistently for each breach. The goal is to assess if there is a low probability that the PHI was compromised. The Breach Notification Rule provides certain factors which must be included in the risk assessment to help determine whether or not the data was compromised: (1) nature and extent of PHI involved (types of information, identifiers included, likelihood of identifying individuals or using the information in a manner harmful to the individuals); (2) the unauthorized persons who used the PHI or to whom a disclosure was made in error; (3) whether or not PHI was actually acquired or viewed; and (4) the extent to which the risk to the PHI has been mitigated. The smaller group from the incident response team can review and finalize the decision. The outcome of the assessment should be briefly but thoroughly documented with the risk of harm being noted as being low, medium, or high. Following this assessment is an opportune time to consider whether or not an incident rises to the level that should be communicated to senior management. If it is determined that senior management needs to be informed, then follow your internal notification plan by having the designated individual make that phone call or send that e-mail.

If the incident is a breach of PHI, then the Breach Notification Rule is explicit about the process to notify affected individuals, as well as other federal and/or local agencies. Following is information related to the federal rule for breach notification. However, some healthcare organizations will need to consider state laws or regulations related to assessment of risks and breach notification in addition to the federal rule. Additional reporting may be required.

Individuals affected by a breach, as required by federal law, must be notified of the breach by means of a letter of notification which is sent by way of first class mail. One exception to this requirement can be made. The notification can be sent by way of e-mail if patient has previously agreed to receive e-mail communications. However, due to the possible sensitivity of the information contained in the notification, consider encrypting the e-mail rather than transmitting it unprotected across the Internet.

If it is known that any person affected by the breach is deceased, then the notification can be sent to the individual's next of kin or personal representative, if that address is available.

Any notification letter must include the following five elements:
1. A brief description of what happened, the date of the breach, and the date of discovery.
2. The types of unsecured PHI involved in the breach.
3. Steps the individual should take to protect from potential harm such as identity theft or fraud (could involve offering credit protection or monitoring services).
4. A brief description of what the covered entity is doing to investigate the breach and to prevent future breaches.
5. Contact information, such as a toll-free number, an e-mail address, a website, or a mailing address, that the affected individual(s) can use if they want more information or need to ask questions.

The notification letter is provided for the patients. Therefore, it is important that the letter be clearly written using easy-to-understand language and include appropriate dates. In addition, ensure that the persons taking the calls are well-informed about the incident, so that the patients calling in receive prompt, accurate information. If the circumstances of the breach involve offering credit protection or monitoring services, enclose with the letter clear and thorough instructions on how to access the service.

A well-written, complete letter of notification will boost the patients' feelings that the organization is taking the incident and their safety seriously. Maintain a copy of the notification letter for your incident response records along with the date that the letter was mailed.

The Breach Notification Rule requires that each covered entity maintain a breach log that is submitted annually to the U.S. Department of Health & Human Services. The contents of this log will be posted on the department's website. However, if a breach affects more than 500 persons, additional requirements are in place to comply with the federal breach notification rule. This is the point at which the organization will utilize plans and templates developed earlier to efficiently fulfill these required tasks. The covered entity must take the following actions:

- Immediately notify the U.S. Department of Health & Human Services of the breach. The purpose of this notification is to provide the department with the details they need to post the breach on their public website, appropriately nicknamed "The Wall of Shame."
- Contact major media outlets in the organization's demographic area so that details of the breach can be communicated. Work your plan that identifies individual responsibilities for accomplishing this task, and utilize the already available template for releasing breach information to the media.
- Post details of the breach on the organization's website home page for a minimum of 90 days. Again, promptly execute your established plan for completing this task. Provide the persons responsible for completing this task with the breach details necessary for the posting. Because of your planning for this possibility, they know their role.

Because of diligent planning for breach notification, when not in a time of crisis, fulfilling these tasks becomes manageable.

There is one other step that might be required. After mailing the notification letters to the affected persons, some letters may be returned because of incorrect addresses. If there are fewer than ten letters returned, then the covered entity should attempt to contact the persons by telephone or other means of communication. However, if ten or more letters are returned because of bad addresses, then the organization must provide a substitute notice. The organization should make every possible attempt to reduce the number of undeliverable mailings. Providing the substitute notice can be embarrassing to the organization and will likely not reach the individuals anyway. Use online white pages or other services to try to find new addresses for the individuals. The substitute notice must be supplied in one of two ways: (1) a prominent posting on the organization's web home page, or (2) a conspicuous notice in a newspaper or on radio or television. If the second way is selected, then the media utilized must be in the geographic areas where the individuals needing to be contacted most likely reside. The substitute notice must also include a toll-free telephone number that persons may call to learn whether or not their health information was involved in the breach. This toll-free number must remain active for a minimum of 90 days. Also note that the breach notification rule allows for contacting affected individuals by telephone or another means if the circumstances of the breach require the urgent measure.

Each time the incident response plan is set into motion, be consistent in following the prescribed steps while, at the same time, being aware of ways to improve the process. Always be prepared to learn from these incidents.

CONCLUSION

Incident response is a time- and resource-consuming activity. However, it is also required. Therefore, healthcare organizations need to realize some value from this hard work rather than just fulfilling a regulatory mandate. One way that the organization can benefit from the incident response activities is to review the incidents—both those that are reportable and those that prove a low probability that the PHI was compromised —to learn the causes of the incidents. The security management process of the HIPAA Security Rule requires organizations to "implement procedures to regularly review records of information system activities" and cites "security incident tracking reports" as an example. [§164.308(a)(1)(ii)(D)] This review offers insight into the reasons, and possible trends, for these privacy and security incidents. In most healthcare organizations, incident trends do emerge—trends that can often be addressed through awareness activities and/or additional training of the workforce.[8]

If, upon review of the incident log, it is determined that a high number of incidents were directly related to members of the workforce looking at patient information without a work-related need to know, then include reminders about appropriate access to PHI in newsletters, e-mails and staff meetings. Include a section about work-related need-to-know access in your organization's annual compliance training. Use any communication means at your disposal to highlight this activity as inappropriate. Remember, the more times the message is delivered, the better the message is retained. Preventing inappropriate behavior is much more beneficial to an organization than an occurrence that must be investigated according to the organization's incident response plan.

Another positive outcome from the review of incidents is evidence that could lead the organization to better clarify or even change its policies and procedures related to patient privacy and/or information security. When incidents frequently occur around a particular cause, re-examine the policies and procedures surrounding that activity. Additional information for clarification purposes may need to be added to that policy/ procedure. After close examination, it might be determined that the policy/procedure may need to be changed—or tweaked—to better address the activities in question. Policies and procedures were never meant to remain stagnant. Data from incidents could be valuable in keeping the organization's privacy and information security policies and procedures current and valid.

Breach notification regulations have given rise to a number of resources that some healthcare organizations may wish to consider. First, breach insurance is available for purchase. Breach insurance would help with the financial costs related to the incident response which could include, but are not limited to, the costs of preparing and mailing notification letters, providing credit protection or monitoring, and fines. The organization's risk management department may be interested in pursuing this resource. Be certain to consider the cost, the specific coverage and other features of breach insurance to determine if it is appropriate for your organization.

Another business development in the incident response world is the proliferation of companies that offer incident response applications and tools. These tools provide healthcare facilities with solutions to manage the many tasks associated with investigating, documenting and providing notification of incidents. Products are available to aid organizations of all sizes, as well as handle incidents of all sizes. The authors are not recommending any such application or tool, but making the readers aware that these tools are available. As in every situation related to business continuity in healthcare, weigh the cost and the benefits to your organization.

For HIPAA-covered entities, the HIPAA Privacy Rule stipulates a mechanism for securing third-party vendors, suppliers or individuals to provide services to the covered entity when the situation would involve the third party having access to the covered entity's PHI. So that this exchange of PHI can occur, the covered entity enters into a Business Associate Agreement (BAA) with the third party, also known as a business associate. A BAA is a legal document which binds a third-party individual or vendor (business associate), who uses or discloses PHI, to the HIPAA Regulations when performing services on a covered entity's behalf.

The covered entity/business associate relationship was further impacted by the Health Information Technology for Economic and Clinical Health (HITECH) Act that was part of the American Recovery and Reinvestment Act of 2009. The HITECH Act applies the same HIPAA privacy and security provisions and penalties to business associates as are applied to covered entities. Business associates may only use and disclose PHI as permitted by the HIPAA Privacy Rule. Business associates must implement administrative, physical and technical safeguards that reasonably and appropriately protect the confidentiality, integrity and availability of any electronic PHI that it creates, receives, maintains or transmits on behalf of the covered entity. Finally, the business associate is involved with incident response and breach notification if the business associate becomes aware of a breach or security incident involving the PHI of a covered entity to whom it supplies services.

Covered entities should clearly state in their BAA the incident response process. Specify the time frame within which the covered entity must be notified of the incident. Indicate the process for reporting the incident, especially include whom to contact. Keep in mind when defining these terms within your agreements that it is the covered entity's responsibility to notify the affected person(s) if a breach occurs even if the business associate or one of its subcontractors was the cause of the breach. Ensure that the number of days within which the business associate must notify the covered entity of an incident is limited so that there will be sufficient time to investigate the incident, determine if it is a breach, and still report the breach to affected individuals, if required, within the allotted 60 days (the number of days could be fewer due to some state laws). Another consideration for the BAA is the inclusion of a statement which would involve the business associate in paying the direct and indirect costs associated with the breach notification requirements as outlined in the breach notification rule if the business associate or one of its subcontractors is responsible for the breach.

Once an incident is determined to be a breach that involves the personal health information of patients, the organization becomes immediately aware that there are many risks and consequences associated with breaches. Some risks, most likely, quickly come to mind while others may not be as evident at first glance. The risks from a breach fall into four main categories within healthcare organizations: (1) risks to the individuals whose PHI is compromised, (2) risks to the organization, (3) risks to research or other studies, and (4) risks to employees or investigators. The risks to affected individuals include, but are not limited to, embarrassment or humiliation, hurt or physical harm, misuse of their personal data, victims of fraud or scams and identify theft. The risks to an organization resulting from a breach include many losses:

- Loss of information and/or equipment.
- Loss of trust of its constituencies.
- Harm to the organization's reputation or brand.
- Loss of future grant or research awards.

The organization could be the focus of negative publicity, litigation and penalties and fines. The HIPAA fines alone could reach up to $1.5 million per violation. The institution's research or clinical study activities can also be affected by a breach if data are lost or if the integrity of the data is compromised. In addition, the funding for the research project could be placed in jeopardy should a breach occur. Lastly, a breach can affect employees and investigators. The risks to these persons include the loss of data, time, funding and reputation; embarrassment; disciplinary action, up to and including termination of employment; and fines and penalties. If the breach is one involving PHI, the fines and penalties could include both monetary fines (up to $1.5 million per violation) and prosecution with incarceration (up to 10 years in prison). With the risks being so high, in addition to implementing privacy and information security plans to prevent incidents from occurring, the organization must be realistic and develop and execute an incident response plan that is thorough, flexible and doable by both the leaders on the incident response teams and the general workforce.

To that end, a valuable activity for the healthcare organization to consider is a test or practice drill of the newly documented incident response plan. Though not required, it is a good idea. This exercise could help expose some gaps that need attention during the more relaxed planning stage rather than the stressful time of investigating a real incident.

Providing excellent healthcare while keeping patient information confidential and secure is the primary focus of every healthcare organization. However, incidents do occur, and some incidents could result in breaches of patients' PHI. Therefore each organization must be prepared with an incident response plan to best manage the multiple activities required when responding to incidents.

REFERENCES

1.   Herzig TW. *Information Security in Healthcare: Managing Risk*. Chicago: HIMSS; 2010.

2.   The Health Insurance Portability and Accountability Act of 1996 (HIPAA) Privacy Rule, Final Rule, Parts 160 & 164, December 2000.

3.   Breach Notification for Unsecured Protected Health Information, Interim Final Rule, Parts 160 & 164, August 2009.

4.   American Reinvestment and Recovery Act of 2009 (ARRA) Electronic Health Record Incentive Program: Final Rule, Parts 412, 413, 422, July 2010.

5. Stoneburner G, Goguen A, Feringa A. *Risk Management Guide for Information Technology Systems.* NIST Special Publication 800-30. July 2002.

6. Scarfone K, Grance T, Masone K. *Managing Information Security Risk: Organization, Mission, and Information System View.* NIST Special Publication 800-39, March 2011.

7. Cichonski P, Millar T, Grance T, Scarfone K, et el. *Computer Security Incident Handling Guide.* NIST Special Publication 800-61; Rev 2, August 2012.

8. The Health Insurance Portability and Accountability Act of 1996 (HIPAA) Security Rule, Final Rule, Parts 160, 162, & 164, February 2003.

9. Modifications to the HIPAA Privacy, Security, Enforcement, and Breach Notification Rules Under the HITECH Act and the Genetic Information Nondiscrimination Act; Other Modifications to the HIPAA Rules, 45 CFR Parts 160 & 164, January 2013.

CHAPTER 21

Information Systems Implementation

By Linda Wilson, MSHI, RHIA

Electronic health record (EHR) systems are benchmark technology in medicine and an efficient way to track and facilitate safe, accurate treatment. EHRs are patient-focused, productive and better for patient safety than the alternative paper records. Providers worldwide are turning to electronic media to provide quicker, accurate and more reliable treatment for their patients. Acquiring the best system for the facility is the ultimate goal for all information system administrators, and outsourcing some IT operations can free up needed resources.

In 1999, the Institute of Medicine (IOM) published *To Err is Human*, which revealed that as many as 98,000 individuals die each year due to medical errors.[1] There was a strong push after this fact was made known to correct such errors in the healthcare field which lead the industry to where we are today. Duplicate medicines given, misread written prescriptions, wrong site or wrong procedures performed on unknowing sedated patients were among the faults made by care providers.

The federal government has indicated that it confidently believes in the benefits of the EHR by introducing incentives to help healthcare providers afford their purchase and implementation. They are encouraging widespread implementation for every physician, whether in single or group practice or a facility. Medicare has been authorized to make incentive payments to clinicians who implement a certified EHR. In the HITECH Act, these federal Meaningful Use incentives are planned with the goal of increasing acceptance so that every American will have a secure EHR.[2] Implementing a certified EHR and meeting the Meaningful Use criteria will mean that they now qualify for promised monetary incentives and can avoid the sanctions that will be imposed if the criteria are not met by 2015. This certainly is a solution for small practices that need to convert to the EHR or simply need the space such an implementation would free up.

Former President George W. Bush established the Office of the National Coordinator for Health Information Technology in 2004 to develop, maintain, and direct the implementation of a strategic plan. The idea was to use interoperable health information technology to reduce errors, improve quality and produce greater value in both public and private healthcare environments.[3] The Federal Health IT Strategic Plan had two goals: (1) patient-focused healthcare; and (2) population health, with four objectives under each goal. The themes of privacy and security, interoperability, IT adoption and collaboration governance recur across the goals.

Private practices all the way up to larger facilities knew they had to do something to prevent the statistics announced by the IOM report from steadily increasing. The electronic health record promised to correct most misread errors and bring increased accuracy into scenarios involving administration of duplicate medication or the wrong medication. However, most physicians were not able to afford this priceless tool, the EHR. Therefore, the hybrid record was created to transition to the full EHR. This meant scanning paper records into a system while preparing digital records as well. Scanning is crucial to the lifespan of a medical record, whether it is to preserve it forever or to add it to an Enterprise Document Management System (EDMS).

GETTING STARTED

The decision to go from paper to electronic is easy, but knowing how to get there is sometimes complex. There are myriad ways to create an electronic health record. The most common records in use at this time are the hybrid health records, with the scanning of records helping to bridge the gap between paper and the electronic world. Transition centers worldwide hold paper in bulk while facilities scan the entire record room, a portion of records or scan on demand. Paper storage is steadily becoming a thing of the past. Paper storage is expensive and has a greater risk of unintentional destruction than media storage. Paper records are kept until the record is needed, then it is scanned into the system and digitally delivered to the user. Providers support the implementation of the EHR to provide quality healthcare. They can provide safer medication use and greater efficiency while using this new electronic tool.

Scanning and Archiving

Multimedia health records can consist of many different types of records such as text files and radiology or document images. EDMSs are document-imaging systems that can manage many types of data while maintaining record integrity with use of bar codes, indexing, automated templates and optical readers. EDMSs help the organization achieve a paperless environment. Placing bar codes on the records ensures easy identity and indexing to keep the documents in appropriate categories. Documents are also placed in chronological order or sequence. The EDMS reads the bar codes, which can be queried by document type or content. If users need a certain document such as a discharge summary for a final diagnosis, they simply query the discharge summary. The system identifies and pulls the document by the designated bar code.

Picture archiving and communications systems (PACS) is a feature that organizations may acquire to store images such as those in radiology. Computer output to laser disk (COLD) is also used to provide images for use in healthcare environments. Providers capture the images and then upload them or transfer them to disk to be able to view them on computer monitors. Placing scanned documents, diagrams, lab reports, checklists, templates and tables into a computerized patient-based record (CPR) were the first efforts toward an EHR. (See Figure 21-1.)

With implementation, real estate used for storing paper records can be transformed into clinical areas or paper may be stored in a transition center. More patient care can

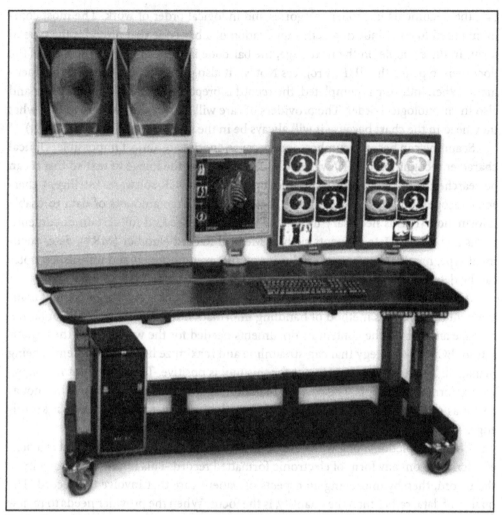

FIGURE 21-1: Computerized Patient-Based Record.

be provided in the newly vacated record storage areas. A little renovation and the previously standard record room becomes a state-of-the-art clinical work area. Clearly, the world of healthcare is currently in a cycle of non-stop change.

Scanning can eliminate backlogs and overflows. The method of scanning and delivery must be considered before purchase of the equipment is made. The desired outcome should be well thought-out beforehand because this cannot be easily changed once it has begun. The volume of documents/images must be measured. The condition of the records must be deliberated. If the documents are not in a pristine state, the images will not be readable. Scanning audits must be performed with each record as it is prepared, scanned and indexed into the system. Scanning audits are done by technicians during or after the scanning is complete. Each record must be validated and verified before the paper can be sent to rest or destroyed. We have to ensure quality by monitoring data integrity.

Document indexing is done after the validation and verification stages. It enhances retrieval of scanned or electronically fed documents. Indexing is the process of putting the documents in proper categories and in logical order of work. The most commonly used form of indexing is the application of a bar code that provides the type of form. In the example on the next page, the bar code indicates the identification of the document type for the EHR (Progress Notes). It also gives the sort order of the document. When indexing is completed, the record is prepared in universal chart order and also in chronological order. The providers of care will always know where to find what they need in the chart because it will always be in the same place. (See Figure 21-2.)

Scanning can become cumbersome because queries are almost impossible. Optical character recognition (OCR) was developed to convert the image to text so that it can be searched and edited. Most equipment comes with OCR software. Intelligent character recognition (ICR) is also in use for converting large amounts of data to usable information. This is necessary to be able to search the record for certain documents, terms and values. Data elements such as Medical Record Number (MR#), date, document type, naming convention, preliminary, and even unsigned and unfinished notes can be detected.

Another common tool essential for record management is enterprise content management (ECM). This method of handling information helps to strategically organize, manage and deliver the content or documents needed for the workflow of the organization. ECM is a strategy that can streamline and maximize how your content is being managed. The return on investment for this tool is positive. The cost of not managing your information is high. The cost for maintaining the content is expensive but not as costly as unstructured information, improper data management or even lost knowledge. This could also drive down the cost of doing business.

Chart completion along with ease of coding and more efficient treatment is a benefit derived from any form of electronic formatted record. This improves the quality of the record, thereby improving all aspects of patient care that involve the record. The quality of data, rather than the quantity, is the focus. When the provider needs to review the history of the patient, to check previous medications used or compare ranges of lab results, the quality of the medical record is essential. The end product is necessary to the continuity of the treatment and to the longevity of the organization. Administrative action should be considered if the records are not kept legible. Quality is essential. A quality record is required to be accurate, timely, comprehensive, relevant and precise. Decisions are also important regarding the timely capture of information.

Ancillary integration is a prime factor in the design. The EHR is not about automating the record, it is about enhancing its utility. Cost control, compliance and efficiency are the main goals in integration, but the main objective is continuity of care for the patient. Complete and consistent records must be kept for each patient. The goals of the EHR implementation are to capture data at the point of care, provide decision support and integrate data from multiple sources.

We know that security is usually about technology, but it is *always* about people. Training development and creation of training manuals are another key component to EHR implementation and keeping the information secure. Policies and procedures should be developed according to the use of the application. Step-by-step instructions

PROGRESS NOTES

PRO0170

		ABBREVIATIONS	
		USE	DO NOT USE
		Daily or Every Other day	qd or qod
		UNITS	IU OR Iu
		UNIT	U
		10 mg	10.0 mg
		0.2 mg	.2 mg
		Morphine Sulfate	MS, MSO4
		Magnesium Sulfate	MgSO4

| 784-568000 | Rev. 9/07 | ST. VINCENT'S BIRMINGHAM ~ BIRMINGHAM, ALABAMA |

FIGURE 21-2: Process Order. *From St. Vincent's Birmingham, used with permission.*

to navigate through the features and functions of the EHR should be shared with each user. Training is essential to the EHR implementation success.

Outsourcing IT Operations and Remote Hosting

Outsourcing IT operations may involve consultants at first, but the ultimate goal is to evolve to include the appropriate IT solutions in a more permanent state. With staff and IT budgets already stretched, employing an IT vendor outside the company is sometimes the most sensible way to stay focused on what matters most. The organization must also adapt or procure the most suitable software to fit their daily functions. There are steps to take to acquire these necessary ventures. A functional needs assessment must be performed before reviewing any products or making the decision to purchase an application. Every department should be surveyed to determine the needs of the users. The information security personnel should help to secure the most relevant EHR tool for the care of the patient volume. Each organization must define its own requirements, and an assessment of the overall need is the first step. All stakeholders must be involved; each department should be surveyed for their contribution of needs for the EHR. A strategy to select the most appropriate vendor and product will be underway. Request for proposals (RFP) can be submitted to various vendors. This could take months to process, but it will narrow down the playing field considerably. The RFP should include everything from size and specifications, functions and features, cost and time to implement. There should also be discussion of support. When the equipment is installed, there should be IT support from the vendor to help minimize problems on daily operation and any bugs that may be uncovered. After successful implementation, there will be a period when extra outside IT staff are still needed to work through any changes that may arise. Also, frequent maintenance issues need to be addressed such as updates, backups and downtime.

The organization must perform its due diligence of investigating the remaining products, once the list is narrowed to a few select vendors. Site visits can be made to arrange demonstrations. Administrators or users at other organizations can be interviewed to determine if the product does what it says it will do. Certification is also a way to guarantee the EHR will function as advertised. There are organizations that have been approved by the U.S. Department of Health & Human Services to certify EHRs. This does not mean that it is the best for your facility; it just means the EHR has been tested and certified to meet federal government requirements.

The process of determining the best solution will involve an acquisition strategy and looking at best of fit, best of breed, or best of suite.[4] This is useful when deciding if you want the EHR from the vendor with whom you have already contracted or if you want whatever is the best product that is on the market. *Best of fit* is all applications from one vendor. *Best of breed* is looking at all products from many vendors. Some organizations go with the best clinical application or the best financial components. It all depends on what the organization's senior leadership feels is the most important to the organization.

There are different rollout strategies from phased-in to "big bang." Some providers prefer the phased-in strategy because they can gradually learn the application. Some want to go from paper to electronic and not have to document on two different clinical systems. Eventually the electronic version will win out with its efficiency and higher quality productivity. Getting to the total electronic record is a challenge. You have to decide how the old information will be converted. The organization can abstract records as the patient presents for admission or can scan documents from previous visits for each new patient in the EHR. Data conversion between old and new systems is challenging and should only be done when it is essential.

IT resources play a big part in the overall structure of the organization. There may be a need to outsource the entire IT department or just contract consultants during the labor-intensive implementation period. Some vendors may offer functionality to remotely host and fulfill their support obligation. This will help reduce costs because later you will need them only sporadically during the upgrades and maintenance. You can selectively outsource IT functions and maintain functionality of the organization while following the strategic plan. The IT structure will be impaired, however, and security and compliance will need to be addressed. Help Desk support and maintenance are an easy contract venture to procure through an external service provider or third-party vendor.

Purchasing Cloud Services

Purchasing cloud services is another complex encounter with vendors. Some vendors only provide cloud services for e-mail. Other third-party companies offer services for data warehousing. Cloud computing can be offered as hardware and software needs delivered over an Internet network. Tiered warehousing is the ultimate goal for storage. Applications run faster, are more manageable and more rapid access is achieved. This allows the more active data to be tiered in the first level and to be more accessible. The inactive information will be kept in a more stable permanent storage source.

Cloud storage is a concept that has been around for years but only recently has become more relevant to users. The term "cloud" came from the network of services being offered under the global function of the Internet. (See Figure 21-3.)

Lifecycle management and document archiving are usually not built into the solution when the applications are first brought to the table. Consideration of the data will determine the levels and capacity of the storage. Depending on the level of need for the data, it will be retrievable in tiers of storage. Some information must be retained

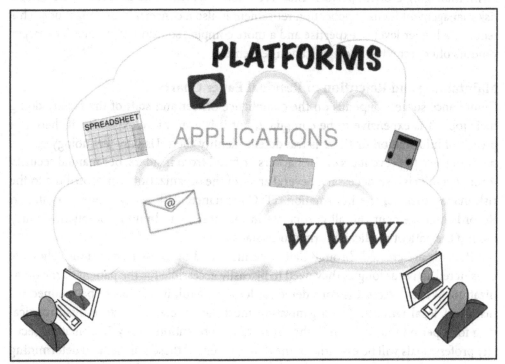

FIGURE 21-3: Cloud Storage.

according to the federal, state or facility retention plan even if it is not used in the daily patient management. Some data are used routinely but not often and should also be kept. The active facts, figures, documents and files that are used on a daily basis to treat patients or operate the organization are tiered to the most active level. This simple act of deciding where the data will live could help the productivity of your system and improve process efficiency of the organization. Simply adding more storage is not necessarily the solution. Cloud storage may be the answer for many entities that see compounding data growth.

Procuring such a service will be an endeavor that should be studied before resources are engaged. The fact that data grow at exponential rates is evident and means that more space should be acquired. Information storage has a key role in information management. You must understand the lifecycle of the data. All data have a retention period and all data should be kept according to the guidelines. It is inevitable that the information that you store should be subsequently retrievable. The business should have access to all vital documents.

It is estimated that databases are growing at a rate of 60 percent year after year. It's no wonder that many organizations have increasing costs when storing all of that data–along with the impaired performance of their applications.[5] Archiving continues to be the primary source for managing storage growth and also the performance of the application. Archiving and application retirement is seen in larger production databases.

Database archiving technologies are evolving, and their role is becoming more evident in compliance, application management and e-discovery. Capacity management is usually given to the information technology department as their responsibility, but information governance is ever becoming the responsibility of the Compliance department. Managing growth, performance, retention, reporting and eDiscovery now has a risk management focus. Application retirement is also a concern in organizations. This requires a higher level of expertise and a more complex solution of storage. The larger vendors offer archiving and application retirement.

Maintaining and Retention of Residual Paper Charts

Compliance success depends on the compliance officer and staff of the facility doing their jobs. It is expensive to be compliant, but it is even more expensive if there is a breach of information or there is fraudulent identity theft. Usually technology can be put into place to prevent access by hackers or fraud from insiders, but manual security through audits is also necessary. Several areas of the organization can contribute to the risk management of the information. IT, Compliance, Risk Management, Legal, and Records Management can all participate in the strategy to build a compliance policy around the patient medical information database.

Records are created through daily treatment and business transactions. They are considered active as long as they need to be easily accessible for the patient or the organization. When a record is considered no longer useful, it still has to be retained for historical, legal reasons. The organization must have a means to store this historical data for a period that is given in the organization's retention policy. Information security professionals will be essential in the development of these policies and determining retention periods. Most healthcare organizations keep medical records at least seven years per federal law. Some facilities that routinely store records beyond the seven-year minimum, however. Keeping a record forever is not cost-effective but some entities choose to keep them past their useful life and past their legal retention period. Some documents have historical value and are permanently preserved. The legal value of a record is given within the statues and regulations of the law. The lifecycle of a document or record is dictated in the retention guidelines from the federal, state or facility policies.

Maintaining records in an electronic format has obvious benefits, but it can also create challenges. Questions to consider include: where will they be stored; who has access, can they be deleted or manipulated; how they will be preserved; will they be stored on several devices? These are a few things to consider when creating policies for archiving records and developing retention schedules as well. Regardless of the format of the records, facilities must keep years of information according to their state jurisdiction and federal law.

Disaster recovery is a hot topic in health information management. To those still using paper, disaster recovery is questionable in such an environment. Paper records become almost impossible to retrieve after damaged from water or fire. They can swell to double their size, making them unidentifiable and unrecoverable. But, if documents are saved electronically, it is not such a risk. A good business continuity plan can save your records if you are faced with a disaster. A bad plan or one that does not exist can mean ruin for your records. Disaster recovery is a necessary tool when dealing with any type of information, especially medical records. Scanning is one method to plan ahead for disaster recovery. The scanned documents can be kept and accessed by many users for treatment, daily operations or maintained for the primary purpose of recovery.

CONCLUSION

Organizations are faced with the task of securing an electronic health record. This may require outsourcing staff, purchasing costly equipment and devoting time and labor to secure the ultimate goal of better treatment for the patients. All EHRs are not the same. Due diligence must be given to procure the correct application for the facility. Requests for proposals, research, demonstrations, negotiations, design, testing and training must be performed before the implementation. All stakeholders, including clerical users, clinical providers, executives and even patients, should be queried and surveyed to make sure their desires are heard and met. Much work on the front end will promise much greater success on the outcome.

Training manuals including new policies and procedures must be developed. Each department workflow must be analyzed and re-developed to make sure it is changed to include the new electronic tool. All employees that have an impact on patient care will need to be trained in the new application. Time should be allowed for lengthy research, design, testing and training. The training is one of the most valuable pieces. If the users are not trained adequately, the system cannot function to its potential.

Compliance and retention of the records are of importance and should not be overlooked. All medical records are protected by federal law. The HIPAA guidelines require that the facilities provide private and secure means to keep the patient information confidential. Understanding how long to keep a record is also part of federal law and can help the facility to minimize threat of information loss if the records are destroyed in a timely legal manner. Keeping the patient information safe is the ultimate goal of the Chief Information Security Officer. Business continuity plans will help the facility from becoming jeopardized if a disaster occurs.

REFERENCES

1. Kohn LT, Corrigan J, Donaldson MS. eds. *To Err is Human: Building a Safer Health System.* Washington, DC: Committee on Quality of Healthcare in America, Institute of Medicine, 1999.

2. American Recovery and Reinvestment Act of 2009. Title XIII Health Information Technology for Economic and Clinical Health, February 17, 2009.

3. Bush, President George W. Executive Order #13335, April 27, 2004.

4. AHIMA. Electronic Health Records, A Practical Guide for Professionals and Organizations.

5. www-01.ibm.com/software/info/rte/bdig/dlg-1-post.html. Accessed August 8, 2012.

Appendix A

By Susan Gatehouse

Table A-1: Potential Impact (Confidentiality, Integrity, Availability)

POTENTIAL IMPACT			
Summarizes the potential impact definitions for each security objective—confidentiality, integrity, and availability			
Security Objective	**LOW**	**MODERATE**	**HIGH**
Confidentiality Preserving authorized restrictions on information access and disclosure, including means for protecting personal privacy and proprietary information. [44 U.S.C., SEC. 3542]	The unauthorized disclosure of information could be expected to have a **limited** adverse effect on organizational operations, organizational assets, or individuals.	The unauthorized disclosure of information could be expected to have a **serious** adverse effect on organizational operations, organizational assets, or individuals.	The unauthorized disclosure of information could be expected to have a **severe or catastrophic** adverse effect on organizational operations, organizational assets, or individuals.
Integrity Guarding against improper information modification or destruction, and includes ensuring information non-repudiation and authenticity. [44 U.S.C., SEC. 3542]	The unauthorized modification or destruction of information could be expected to have a **limited** adverse effect on organizational operations, organizational assets, or individuals.	The unauthorized modification or destruction of information could be expected to have a **serious** adverse effect on organizational operations, organizational assets, or individuals.	The unauthorized modification or destruction of information could be expected to have a **severe or catastrophic** adverse effect on organizational operations, organizational assets, or individuals.
Availability Ensuring timely and reliable access to and use of information. [44 U.S.C., SEC. 3542]	The disruption of access to or use of information or an information system could be expected to have a **limited** adverse effect on organizational operations, organizational assets, or individuals.	The disruption of access to or use of information or an information system could be expected to have a **serious** adverse effect on organizational operations, organizational assets, or individuals.	The disruption of access to or use of information or an information system could be expected to have a **severe or catastrophic** adverse effect on organizational operations, organizational assets, or individuals.

TABLE A-2: Technical Security Features by Regulatory Body.

TECHNICAL SECURITY FEATURES	Applicable? Yes (-) or No ( )			
REGULATORY OR SECURITY BODY	FISMA	HIPAA	PCI DSS	ISO 27000
FIPS Compliance	-	-		
Categorization of System (FIPS)	-	-		
Identification of System Risks	-	-	-	-
Establish Security Policies	-	-	-	-
Identification of Security Controls	-	-	-	-
Network Security Reference	-	-	-	-
Configuration Specifications	-	-	-	-
User Data Privacy Provisions		-		-
Security Considerations in the System Development Lifecycle	-	-		-
Cell Phone and Personal Digital Assistant (PDA) Security	-		-	
General Server Security	-	-	-	-
Protection of Confidentiality of Personally Identifiable Information (PII)	-	-	-	-
Bluetooth Security	-			
Extensible Authentication Protocol (EAP) Methods Used in Wireless Network Access Authentication	-		-	-
Use of Personal Identity Verification (PIV) Credentials in Physical Access Control Systems	-	-	-	
Information Security Testing and Assessment	-	-	-	
Securing External Devices for Tele-work and Remote Access	-			
Secure Sockets Layer (SSL) in Virtual Private Networks (VPN)	-	-	-	-
Storage Encryption Technologies for End User Devices	-	-	-	-
Key Derivation Using Pseudorandom Functions	-			
Applications Using Approved Hash Algorithms	-		-	-
Randomized Hashing for Digital Signatures	-		-	-
PIV Visual Card Topography	-			
Cell Phone Forensics	-			
Security of Radio Frequency Identification (RFID) Systems	-		-	
Wireless Robust Security Networks IEEE 802.11i	-		-	-
PIV Card to Reader Interoperability	-			
Secure Web Services	-	-		-
Intrusion Detection and Prevention Systems (IDPS)	-	-		-
Computer Security Log Management	-	-		-
Random Number Generation Using Deterministic Random Bit Generators	-			
Assurances for Digital Signature Applications	-		-	
Media Sanitization		-		

TECHNICAL SECURITY FEATURES	Applicable? Yes (-) or No ( )			
REGULATORY OR SECURITY BODY	FISMA	HIPAA	PCI DSS	ISO 27000
Integration of Forensic Techniques into Incident Response	-			
PIV Data Model Test Guidelines	-			
PIV Card Application and Middleware Interface Test Guidelines	-			
Test, Training, and Exercise Programs for IT Plans and Capabilities	-	-		
Malware Incident Prevention and Handling	-	-		-
Secure Domain Name System (DNS) Deployment	-	-	-	
Integration of Forensic Techniques into Incident Response	-		-	
PIV Data Model Test Guidelines	-			
PIV Card Application and Middleware Interface Test Guidelines	-			
Test, Training, and Exercise Programs for IT Plans and Capabilities	-	-	-	
Malware Incident Prevention and Handling	-			-
Secure Domain Name System (DNS) Deployment	-			

Source: *Information Security Journal: A Global Perspective A General Comparison of FISMA, HIPAA, ISO, 27000, PCI DSS Standards, Taylor & Francis Group, LLC.*

TABLE A-3: Common Technical Security Features.

EXAMPLE: Health Information Management Department	Cumulative Score High Water H=High M=Moderate L=Low				
Common Technical Security Features for ISO, PCI, HITECH, HIPAA, FISMA	93	93	93	279	93
Feature	Confidentiality	Integrity	Availability	Weight	**RISK
1. Identification of System Risks	H	H	H	9	M
2. Establish Security Policies	H	H	H	9	H
3. Identification of Security Controls	H	H	H	9	M
4. Network Security Reference	H	M	H	8	L
5. Configuration Specifications	H	H	L	7	L
6. User Data Privacy Provisions	H	H	H	9	M
7. General Server Security	H	H	H	9	L
8. Protection of Confidentiality of Personally Identifiable Information (PII)	H	H	H	9	H
9. Use of PIV Credentials in Physical Access Control Systems	H	M	L	6	H
10. Information Security Testing and Assessment	H	M	L	6	L
11. SSL in VPNs	H	M	L	6	H
12. Storage Encryption Technologies for End User Devices	H	H	H	9	L
13. Secure Web Services	H	M	L	6	L
14. Intrusion Detection and Prevention Systems (IDPS)	H	H	H	9	L
15. Computer Security Log Management	H	H	L	7	M
16. Test, Training, and Exercise Programs for IT Plans and Capabilities	H	M	L	6	M
17. Malware Incident Prevention and Handling	H	M	H	8	H
18. Biometric Data Specification for Personal Identity Verification	H	H	L	7	L
19. Security Configuration Checklists Program for IT Products: Guidance for Checklist Users and Developer	H	H	H	9	M
20. Mapping Types of Information and Information Systems to Security Categories	H	M	L	6	L
21. Building an Information Technology Security Awareness and Training Program	H	H	H	9	M
22. Guidelines on Electronic Mail Security	H	M	L	6	M
23. Securing Public Web Servers	H	H	L	7	L
24. Firewalls and Firewall Policy	H	H	L	7	L
25. Patch and Vulnerability Management Program	H	H	L	7	L
26. Management of Risk from Information Systems	H	M	L	6	M
27. Security Certification and Accreditation	H	H	L	7	M
28. Information Technology Security Services	H	H	H	9	L

EXAMPLE: Health Information Management Department	Cumulative Score High Water H=High M=Moderate L=Low				
Common Technical Security Features for ISO, PCI, HITECH, HIPAA, FISMA	93	93	93	279	93
Feature	Confidentiality	Integrity	Availability	Weight	**RISK
29. Contingency Planning for Information Technology Systems	H	H	H	9	M
30. Public Key Technology and the Federal PKI Infrastructure	H	M	L	6	L
31. Information Security Training Requirements	H	M	L	6	L
Total Weighted Value	93	81	59	233	52
Security Categorization Applied to Information Types	100%	87%	63%	84%	56%

Source: Information Security Journal: A Global Perspective
A General Comparison of FISMA, HIPAA, ISO 27000, PCI DSS Standards, Taylor & Francis Group, LLC.

Table A-4: Sample Risk Rating Chart

The following are common technical security features for FISMA/NIST, ISO 27000, PCI DSS and HIPAA:

1. Identification of System Risks
2. Establish Security Policies
3. Identification of Security Controls
4. Network Security Reference
5. Configuration Specifications
6. User Data Privacy Provisions
7. General Server Security
8. Protection of Confidentiality of Personally Identifiable Information (PII)
9. Use of PIV Credentials in Physical Access Control Systems
10. Information Security Testing and Assessment
11. SSL in VPNs
12. Storage Encryption Technologies for End User Devices
13. Secure Web Services
14. Intrusion Detection and Prevention Systems (IDPS)
15. Computer Security Log Management
16. Test, Training, and Exercise Programs for IT Plans and Capabilities
17. Malware Incident Prevention and Handling
18. Biometric Data Specification for Personal Identity Verification
19. Security Configuration Checklists Program for IT Products: Guidance for Checklist Users and Developer
20. Mapping Types of Information and Information Systems to Security Categories
21. Building an Information Technology Security Awareness and Training Program
22. Guidelines on Electronic Mail Security
23. Securing Public Web Servers
24. Firewalls and Firewall Policy
25. Patch and Vulnerability Management Program
26. Management of Risk from Information Systems
27. Security Certification and Accreditation
28. Information Technology Security Services
29. Contingency Planning for Information Technology Systems
30. Public Key Technology and the Federal PKI Infrastructure
31. Information Security Training Requirements

The table represents the overlap of: Legislative acts and private sector standards that contain many of the same technical features. It provides a good starting point based on government and private sector discipline for understanding how "security" may impact users segment of the business model. Keep in mind that each of the technical features provide opportunity for security review and each can impact business operations. The review process documents how the severity of impacts by "risk" and probability with Confidentiality, Integrity, and Availability included as parameters for each element and how to balance "cost" to effect. Example: Enforcing existing policy or spending big dollars on automated processes. An immediate breach with HIM confidentiality would be very costly and could be avoided.

APPENDIX B

Most Common Vulnerabilities

SANS Top 25 Programming Errors	OWASP Top 10 Web Programming Errors
Variables not neutralizing SQL commands	Injection
Variables not neutralizing OS commands	Cross site scripting
Variables without size limit checks	Broken authentication and session management
Web variables not neutralizing variables during page generation	Insecure direct object references
Missing authentication for critical functions	Cross site request forgery
Missing authorization	Security misconfiguration
Hard coded credentials	Insecure cryptographic storage
Unrestricted upload of files (with dangerous type)	Unrestricted URL access
Reliance on untrusted inputs in security decisions	Insufficient transport layer protection (cryptography)
Execution with unnecessary privileges	Un-validated redirects or forwards
Cross-site request forgery	
Improper limitations of a path name to a restricted directory	
Incorrect authorization	
Inclusion of functionality from an untrusted control sphere	
Incorrect permission assignment for a critical resource	
Incorrect calculation of buffer size	
Improper restriction of excessive authentication attempts	
URL redirection to untrusted site	
Uncontrolled format string	
Integer overflow or wraparound	
Use of potentially dangerous function	
Download of code without integrity check	
Missing encryption of sensitive data	
Use a one-way hash without a salt	
Use of a broken or risky cryptographic algorithm	

Index

"*f*" next to page number denotes a Figure
"*t*" next to page number denotes a Table

O

P

Printed in the United States
by Baker & Taylor Publisher Services